Nelson Spelling

Teacher's Book 2
for Books 3, 4, 5 & 6

CONTENTS

How Nelson Spelling works	2
The National Curriculum in England	6
The Curriculum in Scotland	14
The Curriculum in Wales	15
The Curriculum in Northern Ireland	17
Teaching spelling	19
Key spelling rules	23
Word frequency tables	24
Book 3	26
Book 4	58
Book 5	90
Book 6	124
Revision Book answers	156
Glossary	160

OXFORD
UNIVERSITY PRESS

How Nelson Spelling works

YEAR	PUPIL BOOK	WORKBOOKS	RESOURCES & ASSESSMENT	TEACHING SUPPORT
RECEPTION / P1		Workbook Starter A, Workbook Starter B		
YEAR 1 / P2	Pupil Book 1A, Pupil Book 1B	Workbook 1A, Workbook 1B	Resources and Assessment Book	Teacher's Book 1
YEAR 2 / P3	Pupil Book 2	Workbook 2A, Workbook 2B		
YEAR 3 / P4	Pupil Book 3		Resources and Assessment Book For Books 3 & 4	
YEAR 4 / P5	Pupil Book 4			Teacher's Book 2
YEAR 5 / P6	Pupil Book 5		Resources and Assessment Book For Books 5 & 6	
YEAR 6 / P7	Pupil Book 6	Revision Book		

Nelson Spelling is a structured, comprehensive, yet flexible programme for spelling, designed for use with children aged 5–11. It can also be used with older pupils who may be experiencing some problems. It has been devised to support within the classroom a twin-track approach to spelling – developing both memory skills and understanding. Visual and aural memory skills are combined with a thorough understanding of the most significant language structures.

Nelson Spelling comprises 7 levels. The Starter Level comprises two workbooks covering the main grapheme-phoneme correspondences, designed to be used alongside a synthetic phonics teaching programme. Levels 1 to 6 are each made up of 28 units of work. Each unit has a Teacher's Book page, a Pupil Book double-page spread, and a Focus and Extension Resource sheet. Levels 1 and 2 are further supported by workbook pages. More detail about each of the components is given below.

The Pupil Book provides the core spelling curriculum for the year, differentiated to ensure children can progress through the key spelling patterns, at their own pace.

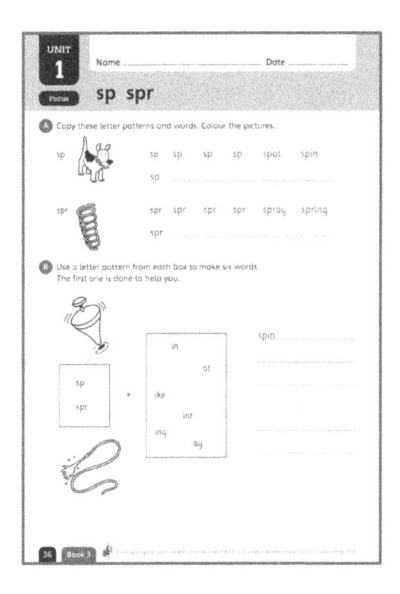

The *Focus Resource* sheet is designed for the less able pupil who needs further practice in the essential teaching point.

The *Extension Resource* sheet provides for the child who can cope with more demanding work arising from, or linked to, the unit teaching points.

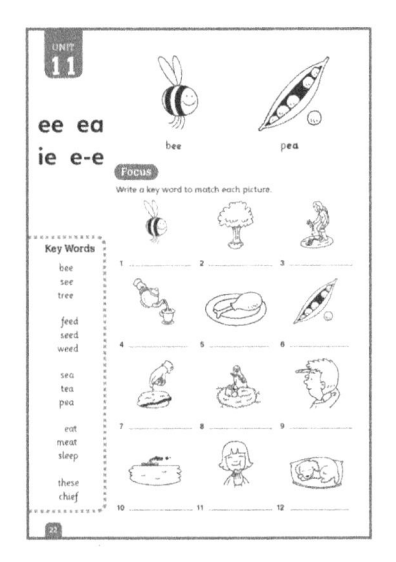

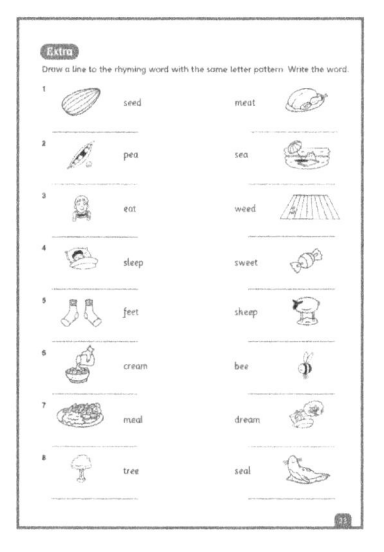

The Workbooks for Starter Level practise common phonemes and graphemes. For Books 1 and 2 they offer Focus and Extension practice.

The Revision Book for Year 6 recaps all of the spelling knowledge that children have accumulated throughout the course.

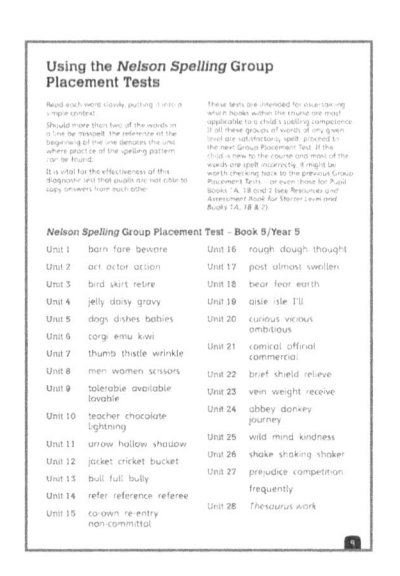

Group and individual tests are provided in the Resources and Assessment books to indicate suitable placement of a child that is new to the scheme, and to monitor progress through the scheme.

The Teacher's Book has a support page providing an easy reference spread from the Pupil Book, answers, a helpful resource list of words for further work, and notes and suggestions relating to the unit.

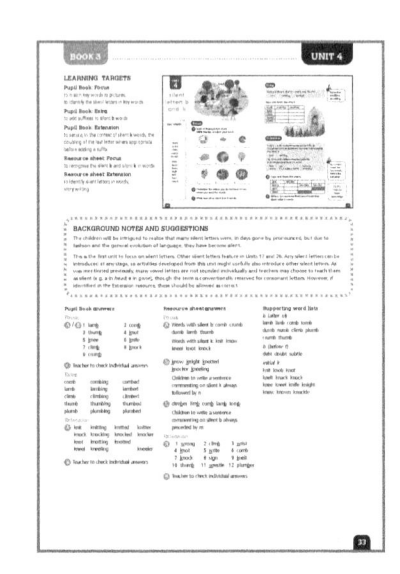

Word lists

Several word lists are provided during the course:

- **Key Words** appear on each Pupil Book page and are the main exemplars of the spellings for that unit.
- **Tricky Words** appear on some Pupil Book pages and give the common exception words from the Appendix to the National Curriculum in England (except where those words have already been covered).
- **Words to Learn** appear in the Resources and Assessment Books and are a full set of words children need to learn. At KS1 they cover the 100 high-frequency words from Letters and Sounds as well as the National Curriculum.
- **Supporting word lists** appear in the Teacher's Books for each unit, and give a further bank of words for teachers to use for games etc. for further practice. The asterisk denotes important, but irregular, words that can/should be covered within these units.
- **National Curriculum (England) required words** appear in *Resources and Assessment Book for Books 3 & 4* and *Resources and Assessment Book for Books 5 & 6*, and give all of the statutory words that are to be learned. These lists, as well as the others, might be used to provide appropriate work for short dictation activities, checking on the progress of pupils as the programme develops.

Teaching approaches

Nelson Spelling is organised so it is possible to lead structured lessons but with children working more or less at their own pace. In reality there are usually advantages to keeping groups of children working at the same pace, so additional related activities can be worked on by several pupils together – the children often get added motivation by supporting each other when learning spellings. *Nelson Spelling* has been designed to offer a range of classroom management options to be considered in relation to any whole-school spelling policy.

Working as a whole class

The whole class works on the same unit, with some children being restricted to the *Focus* activities, others progressing to the *Extra* and some going on to the *Extension* exercises. Additional differentiation is provided by the two related Resource sheets (*Focus* and *Extension*) and, for Pupil Books 1A, 1B and 2, the accompanying Workbooks. Used in this way, many teachers might choose to allocate a regular timetabled session, which can be supported by the use of the spelling lists as take-home work.

Group work

If the class becomes more spread, it might be sensible to have the children grouped, with each group working on a particular unit. This is more likely to be effective if the amount of time allocated to 'formalised' spelling activities varies between the children, depending on need. It is still feasible to work this way within a regular timetabled slot given the constant structure of the Pupil Books throughout the course.

Individual work

You may prefer children to use the Pupil Books and Resource sheets individually or in pairs. If you do so, you will need to take great care to record the work done. The photocopiable record sheets in the Resources and Assessment books may be useful. This approach will be most appropriate if you decide to let each child work at his or her own pace, or if you use the course to support children who have individual spelling needs.

Assessment

Placement tests

The placement tests are designed to help you decide at which level pupils should start the course.

- The **Nelson Spelling Scheme Placement Test** gives general guidance on the spelling achievement of a pupil or group of pupils. It comprises a selection of typical key words and spelling patterns encountered in the teaching units of the pupil textbooks.
- The **Individual Placement Tests** should be taken after the Scheme Placement Test to give more guidance.
- The **Group Placement Tests** are more detailed and level-specific tests, to be used for pupils who are thought to be ready to move up a level.

The Placement tests, and further details about how to administer them, are found in the Resources and Assessment Books.

Formative assessment: Check-ups

There are frequent Check-ups throughout the *Nelson Spelling* course. These short assessments cover the skills which have been taught in the preceding units. Check-ups are found in the Pupil Books and the answers are found in the Teacher's Books.

Assessment tests

These tests are not designed to indicate a specific curriculum attainment level, although the programme has been devised to ensure that children progressing satisfactorily from level to level will be achieving what is required by the new curriculum in England and other curriculum bodies.

The National Curriculum in England

Nelson Spelling provides a carefully structured course for teaching spelling to children in Years 1–6. The course is designed to build children's competence and confidence as they progress. Children are taught spelling strategies including understanding morphology and etymology, as well as adding to their store of tricky words, homophones, and frequently misspelt words. The Scope and Sequence charts of each book give a detailed breakdown of the spelling concepts covered in each unit.

Programme of Study	Book 1A	Book 1B	Book 2	Book 3	Book 4	Book 5	Book 6
YEAR 1							
Pupils should be taught to:							
Spell							
words containing each of the 40+ phonemes already taught	All units	All units					
Common exception words	Unit 1, 3, 10, 11, 12, 13, 14	Unit 16, 18, 19, 20, 23 and 26	Unit 1–6, 9, 11, 12, 18, 20, 22, 27	Unit 2, 4, 7, 12, 13, 21	Unit 8	Unit 20, 21	Unit 4, 8, 12, 20, 23, 25, 27
the days of the week		Unit 24					
Name the letters of the alphabet							
Name the letters of the alphabet in order	Unit 1	Unit 28					
using letter names to distinguish alternative spellings with same sound	Unit 10, 11, 12, 13, 14	Unit 17, 18, 19, 20, 21, 22	Unit 1, 2, 11, 12, 27 (homophones), 3, 4, 5, 7, 8, 9, 10, 13, 18, 20	Unit 2, 5, 10, 16, 18	Unit 10, 12, 20, 22, 25	Unit 9, 13, 19, 20, 21	Unit 18, 19, 23
add prefixes and suffixes							
using the spelling rule for adding –s or –es as the plural marker for nouns and the third person singular marker for verbs	Unit 6, 9		Unit 19, 20	Unit 7	Unit 19, 2, 21	Unit 5	Unit 1, 2
using the prefix un–		Unit 27	Unit 5	Unit 21	Unit 6, 27		Unit 3
using –ing, –ed, –er and –est where no change is needed in the spelling of root words	Unit 7, 8, 9, 11, 12	Unit 17	Unit 11	Unit 4, 9, 14	Unit 27	Unit 1, 2	
apply simple spelling rules and guidance, as listed in English Appendix 1							
write from memory simple sentences dictated by the teacher that include words using the GPCs and common exception words taught so far.							
APPENDIX							
The sounds /f/, /l/, /s/, /z/ and /k/ spelt ff, ll, ss, zz and ck	Unit 4, 9						
The /ŋ/ sound spelt n before k	Unit 4						
Division of words into syllables		Unit 25			Unit 23, 26	Unit 11, 12	Unit 11, 15, 22, 24, 25
'tch' sound	Unit 5						

The National Curriculum in England (cont.)

Programme of Study	Book 1A	Book 1B	Book 2	Book 3	Book 4	Book 5	Book 6
The /v/ sound at the end of words	Unit 12				Unit 24		
Adding s and es to words (plural of nouns and the third person singular of verbs)	Unit 6, 9		Unit 19, 20	Unit 7	Unit 2, 19, 21	Unit 5	Unit 1, 2
Adding the endings –ing, –ed and –er to verbs where no change is needed to the root word	Unit 7, 9 11, 12	Unit 17	Unit 11	Unit 4, 9, 14	Unit 27		
Adding –er and –est to adjectives where no change is needed to the root word	Unit 8				Unit 27		
ai, oi	Unit 10 (a-e, ai, ay)	Unit 17 (oi, oy)	Unit 1 (a-e, ai, ay) Unit 7 (oi, oy)				
ay, oy	Unit 10 (a-e, ai, ay)	Unit 17 (oi, oy)	Unit 1 (a-e, ai, ay) Unit 7 (oi, oy)				
a-e	Unit 10 (a-e, ai, ay)		Unit 1 (a-e, ai, ay)				
e-e	Unit 11 (ee, ea, ie, e-e)		Unit 2 (ee, ea, e-e)				
i-e	Unit 12 (i-e, ie, igh, y)		Unit 3 (i-e, igh, y)				
o-e	Unit 13 (oa, o-e, oe, ow)		Unit 4 (o-e, oa, ow)				
u-e	Unit 14 (oo, u-e, ue, ew)		Unit 5 (u-e, oo, ew)				
ar		Unit 16	Unit 6 (ar)			Unit 1	Unit 18 (schwa)
ee	Unit 11 (ee, ea ,ie, e-e)		Unit 2 (ee, ea, e-e)				
ea (sea, dream)	Unit 11 (ee, ea, ie, e-e)		Unit 2 (ee, ea, e-e)				
ea (head, bread)		Unit 18 (ear, ea)	Unit 8 (ear, ea)		Unit 1		
er (her, term)		Unit 19 (er, ir, ur)	Unit 9 (er, ir, ur)				
er (schwa – better, under)		Unit 19 (er, ir, ur)	Unit 9 (er, ir, ur)		Unit 3		Unit 18
ir		Unit 19 (er, ir, ur)	Unit 9 (er, ir, ur)			Unit 3	
ur		Unit 19 (er, ir, ur)	Unit 9 (er, ir, ur)		Unit 3		
oo (food, pool)	Unit 14 (oo, u-e, ue, ew)		Unit 5 (u-e, oo, ew)				
oo (book, took)		Unit 23 (oo)	Unit 5 (u-e, oo, ew)				

The National Curriculum in England (cont.)

Programme of Study	Book 1A	Book 1B	Book 2	Book 3	Book 4	Book 5	Book 6
oa (boat, coat)	Unit 13 (oa, o-e, oe, ow)		Unit 4 (o-e, oa, ow)				
oe (toe, goes)	Unit 13 (oa, o-e, oe, ow)						Unit 2
ou (out, mouth)		Unit 20 (ou, ow)	Unit 10 (ou, ow)				
ow (now, how)		Unit 20 (ou, ow)	Unit 10 (ou, ow)				
ow (blow, slow)	Unit 13 (oa, o-e, oe, ow)		Unit 4 (o-e, oa, ow)			Unit 11	
ue (blue, clue)	Unit 14 (oo, u-e, ue, ew)		Unit 5 (oo, u-e, ew)				
ew (new, few)	Unit 14 (oo, u-e, ue, ew)		Unit 5 (u-e, oo, ew)				
ie (lie, tie)	Unit 12 (i-e, ie, igh, y)					Unit 18	Unit 23
ie (chief, field)	Unit 11 (ee, ea, ie, e-e)					Unit 18, 22	Unit 23
igh (high, night)	Unit 12 (i-e, ie, igh, y)		Unit 3 (i-e, igh, y)		Unit 17	Unit 18	
or (for, short)		Unit 21 (or, ore, aw, au)	Unit 11 (or, ore, aw, au)				
ore (more, score)		Unit 21 (or, ore, aw, au)	Unit 11 (or, ore, aw, au)				
aw (saw, draw)		Unit 21 (or, ore, aw, au)	Unit 11 (or, ore, aw, au)				
au (author, August)		Unit 21 (or, ore, aw, au)	Unit 11 (or, ore, aw, au)				
air (air, fair)		Unit 22 (air, ear, are)	Unit 12 (air, ear, are)				
ear (dear, hear)		Unit 18 (ear, ea)	Unit 8 (ear, ea)			Unit 18	
ear (bear, pear, wear)		Unit 22 (air, ear, are)	Unit 12 (air, ear, are)			Unit 18	
are (bare, dare)		Unit 22 (air, ear, are)	Unit 12 (air, ear, are)			Unit 1	
Words ending –y (/iː/ or /ɪ/ depending on accent)		Unit 15	Unit 20	Unit 6		Unit 4	Unit 5
New consonant spellings ph and wh		Unit 26		Unit 24			Unit 7
Using k for the /k/ sound	Unit 4 (Teacher's Book)						
Adding the prefix –un		Unit 27	Unit 15	Unit 21	Unit 6, 27	Unit 2	Unit 3

8

The National Curriculum in England (cont.)

Programme of Study	Book 1A	Book 1B	Book 2	Book 3	Book 4	Book 5	Book 6
Compound words		Unit 25	Unit 1, 12	Unit 25		Unit 15	Unit 16
Common exception words	Unit 1, 3, 10, 11, 12, 13, 14	Units 16, 18, 19, 20, 23 and 26	Unit 1–6, 9, 11, 12, 18, 20, 22, 27	Unit 2, 4, 7, 12, 13, 21	Unit 8	Unit 20, 21	Unit 4, 8, 12, 20, 23, 25, 27
YEAR 2							
Pupils should be taught to:							
Spell by							
Segmenting spoken words into phonemes and representing these by graphemes, spelling many correctly							
Learning new ways of spelling phonemes for which one or more spellings are already known, and learn some words with each spelling, including a few common homophones							
Learning to spell common exception words	Unit 1, 3, 10–14	Unit 16, 18, 19, 20, 23, 26	Unit 1–6, 9, 11, 12, 18, 20, 22, 27	Unit 2, 4, 7, 12, 13, 21	Unit 8	Unit 20, 21	Unit 4, 8, 12, 20, 23, 25, 27
Learning to spell more words with contracted forms			Unit 25	Unit 15		Unit 15	Unit 27
Learning the possessive apostrophe (singular)			Unit 19	Unit 11	Unit 21		
distinguishing between homophones and near-homophones			Unit 1, 2, 11, 12, 27	Unit 16, 18	Unit 22	Unit 19	Unit 17
Add suffixes to spell longer words, including ment, ness, ful, less, ly			Unit 13, 24	Unit 14 (full, ness, ment, less) Unit 22 (ly)	Unit 8 (ly) Unit 15 (less, ness, ment, ly)	Unit 1, 2, 13, 26	Unit 4, 5, 14
Apply spelling rules and guidance, as listed in English Appendix 1							
write from memory simple sentences dictated by the teacher that include words using the GPCs, common exception words and punctuation taught so far.							
APPENDIX							
The /dʒ/ sound spelt as ge and dge at the end of words, and sometimes spelt as g elsewhere in words before e, i and y			Unit 7	Unit 10		Unit 27	Unit 25
The /s/ sound spelt c before e, i and y			Unit 6	Unit 3			Unit 15, 25
The /n/ sound spelt kn and (less often) gn at the beginning of words			Unit 2	Unit 4		Unit 7	Unit 15
The /ɹ/ sound spelt wr at the beginning of words			Unit 22	Unit 26		Unit 7	Unit 15
The /l/ or /əl/ sound spelt –le at the end of words			Unit 18	Unit 5			
The /l/ or /əl/ sound spelt –el at the end of words			Unit 18	Unit 5			

The National Curriculum in England (cont.)

Programme of Study	Book 1A	Book 1B	Book 2	Book 3	Book 4	Book 5	Book 6
The /l/ or /əl/ sound spelt –al at the end of words			Unit 18	Unit 5			
Words ending –il			Unit 18	Unit 5			
The /aɪ/ sound spelt –y at the end of words	Unit 12		Unit 20				
Adding –es to nouns and verbs ending in consonant-letter–y			Unit 20	Unit 7		Unit 4, 5	Unit 1
Adding –ed, –ing, –er and –est to a root word ending in –y with a consonant before it	Unit 12	Unit 17	Unit 28 Unit 21 (Resource Book)	Unit 8 (er, est) Unit 9 (ing)		Unit 1	Unit 5
Adding the endings –ing, –ed, –er, –est and –y to words ending in –e with a consonant before it			Unit 21	Unit 5, 9, 14 (ing, ed), Unit 6 (y)	Unit 27	Unit 1	Unit 4
Adding –ing, –ed, –er, –est and –y to words of one syllable ending in a single consonant letter after a single vowel letter	Unit 7, 8	Unit 17	Unit 21	Unit 4, 9 (ing, ed)	Unit 2, 19, 27	Unit 1, 2	
The /ɔː/ sound spelt a before l and ll, e.g. ball			Unit 13	Unit 2	Unit 18	Unit 17	Unit 5
The /ʌ/ sound spelt o, e.g. mother			Unit 14				
The /iː/ sound spelt –ey, e.g. donkey			Unit 20			Unit 24	Unit 1
The /ɒ/ sound spelt a after w and qu			Unit 23	Unit 11			
The /ɜː/ sound spelt or after w			Unit 11	Unit 11			
The /ɔː/ sound spelt ar after w			Unit 6, 23	Unit 11			
The /ʒ/ sound spelt s			Unit 26	Unit 23, 13	Unit 9, 12		
The suffixes –ment, –ness, –ful, –less and –ly			Unit 24	Unit 14	Unit 8 (ly), Unit 15 (less, ness, ment, ly)	Unit 1, 2, 13, 26	Unit 4, 5
Contractions			Unit 25	Unit 15		Unit 15	Unit 27
The possessive apostrophe (singular nouns)			Unit 19	Unit 11	Unit 21		
Words ending in –tion			Unit 26	Unit 12	Unit 11, 24		
Homophones and near-homophones			Unit 1, 2, 11, 12, 27	Unit 16, 18	Unit 22	Unit 10, 16, 19	Unit 17, 11
Common exception words	Unit 1, 3, 10–14	Unit 16, 18–20, 23, 26	Unit 1–6, 9, 11, 12, 18, 20, 22, 27	Unit 2, 4, 7, 12, 13, 21	Unit 8	Unit 20, 21	Unit 4, 8, 12, 20, 23, 25, 27

The National Curriculum in England (cont.)

Programme of Study	Book 1A	Book 1B	Book 2	Book 3	Book 4	Book 5	Book 6
YEAR 3 AND YEAR 4							
Pupils should be taught to:							
use further prefixes and suffixes and understand how to add them (Appendix 1)	Unit 4, 6, 7, 8	Unit 17	Unit 13, 15, 21, 24, 26, 28	Unit 12, 13, 19, 20, 21, 23	Unit 1, 6, 7, 10, 13–15, 17, 18, 24, 25, 27	Unit 1, 2, 9, 14, 15, 20, 21, 26	Unit 3, 4, 5, 20, 21
spell further homophones			Unit 1, 2, 11, 12, 27	Unit 16, 18	Unit 1, 22	Unit 10, 16, 19	Unit 17, 11
spell words that are often misspelt (Appendix 1)	Unit 1, 3, 10, 11, 12, 13, 14	Unit 16, 18–20, 23, 26	Unit 1–6, 9, 11, 12, 18, 20, 22, 27	Unit 2, 4, 7, 13, 21	All units	All units (Unit 13)	All units (Unit 13)
place the possessive apostrophe accurately in words with regular plurals [for example, girls', boys'] and in words with irregular plurals [for example, children's]					Unit 21		
use the first two or three letters of a word to check its spelling in a dictionary			Unit 1, 2, 9, 22, 27	Unit 28	Unit 5, 28		Unit 3, 18, 28 (and throughout)
write from memory simple sentences, dictated by the teacher, that include words and punctuation taught so far.							
APPENDIX							
Adding suffixes beginning with vowel letters to words of more than one syllable		Unit 17	Unit 13, 28	Unit 5, 8	Unit 10, 19, 24, 25, 27	Unit 9, 14, 20	Unit 4
The /ɪ/ sound spelt y elsewhere than at the end of words				Unit 18			
The /ʌ/ sound spelt ou, e.g. trouble				Unit 17	Unit 5		
More prefixes, e.g. In–, sub–, super–		Unit 27	Unit 13, 15	Unit 20, 21	Unit 6, 7, 13, 14, 18, 27	Unit 1, 2, 9, 14, 15, 20, 21, 26	Unit 3–5, 20, 21
Suffix –ation			Unit 26 (tion)	Unit 12	Unit 11		Unit 4
Suffix –ly			Unit 24	Unit 22	Unit 8	Unit 13	Unit 5
Words with endings sounding like /ʒə/ or /tʃə/, e.g. treasure			Unit 26	Unit 23	Unit 3, 9		
Endings which sound like /ʒən/, e.g. confusion				Unit 13	Unit 12, 24		
The suffix -ous, e.g. poisonous				Unit 19	Unit 10	Unit 20	Unit 5, 20
Endings which sound like /ʃən/, spelt –tion, –sion, –ssion, –cian, e.g. musician			Unit 26 (tion)	Unit 12 (tion), Unit 13 (sion)	Unit 11, 12		Unit 20
Words with the /k/ sound spelt ch (Greek in origin), e.g. chemist				Unit 17	Unit 5		

The National Curriculum in England (cont.)

Programme of Study	Book 1A	Book 1B	Book 2	Book 3	Book 4	Book 5	Book 6
Words with the /ʃ/ sound spelt ch (mostly French in origin), e.g chef				Unit 18	Unit 16		
Words ending with the /g/ sound spelt –gue and the /k/ sound spelt –que (French in origin), e.g. antique					Unit 16		Unit 10
Words with the /s/ sound spelt sc (Latin in origin), e.g. science				Unit 17	Unit 5	Unit 7	Unit 10
Words with the /eɪ/ sound spelt ei, eigh, or ey, e.g. eight				Unit 18		Unit 23	Unit 23
Possessive apostrophe with plural words					Unit 21		
Homophones and near-homophones			Unit 1, 2, 11, 12, 27	Unit 16, 18	Unit 1, 22	Unit 10, 16, 19	Unit 17, 11
YEAR 5 AND YEAR 6							
Pupils should be taught to:							
use further prefixes and suffixes and understand the guidance for adding them	Unit 4, 6–8	Unit 17	Unit 13, 15, 21, 24, 26, 28	Unit 12, 13, 19, 20, 21, 23	Unit 1, 6, 7, 10, 13-15, 17, 18, 24, 25, 27	Unit 1, 2, 9, 14, 15, 20, 21, 26	Unit 3, 4, 5, 20, 21
spell some words with 'silent' letters, e.g. knight, psalm, solemn			Unit 22	Unit 4, 17	Unit 5	Unit 7	Unit 8, 15 (silent letters) Unit 11, 24, 25, 27 (unstressed letters)
continue to distinguish between homophones and other words which are often confused				Unit 16, 18	Unit 22	Unit 19	Unit 17
use knowledge of morphology and etymology in spelling and understand that the spelling of some words needs to be learnt specifically, as listed in Appendix 1						Throughout	Throughout
use dictionaries to check the spelling and meaning of words			Unit 1, 2, 9, 22, 27	Unit 2, 12, 17, 18, 20, 21, 28	Unit 5–7, 9, 11, 13, 14, 16–19, 24, 26, 28	Unit 2, 3, 6–8, 14–17, 19, 23, 27	Unit 28 and throughout
use the first three or four letters of a word to check spelling, meaning or both of these in a dictionary				Unit 28	Unit 5, 28	Unit 7, 14 and throughout	Unit 3, 18, 28 and throughout
use a thesaurus						Unit 28	

The National Curriculum in England (cont.)

Programme of Study	Book 1A	Book 1B	Book 2	Book 3	Book 4	Book 5	Book 6
APPENDIX							
Endings which sound like /ʃəs/ spelt –cious or –tious, e.g. gracious				Unit 19 (cious)		Unit 20	
Endings which sound like /ʃəl/						Unit 21	Unit 14
Words ending in –ant, –ancel–ancy, –ent, –encel–ency					Unit 25	Unit 9	
Words ending in –able and –ible						Unit 9	
Words ending in -ably and -ibly						Unit 14	
Adding suffixes beginning with vowel letters to words ending in –fer							
Use of the hyphen						Unit 15	Unit 3
Words with the /i:/ sound spelt ei after c						Unit 23	Unit 23
Words containing the letter-string ough						Unit 16	Unit 12
Words with 'silent' letters (i.e. letters whose presence cannot be predicted from the pronunciation of the word)				Unit 4 (b and k) Unit 17 (o, h and c)	Unit 5	Unit 7	Unit 8, 11, 15, 24, 25, 27
Homophones and other words that are often confused, e.g. aloud / allowed, serial / cereal, compliment / compliment, affect / effect, draft / draught			Unit 1, 2, 11, 12, 27	Unit 16, 18	Unit 1, 22	Unit 16, 10, 19	Unit 17, 11

Scotland: Curriculum for Excellence

Nelson Spelling provides a carefully structured course for teaching spelling to children in Primary 1–7. The course is designed to build children's competence and confidence as they progress. Children are taught spelling strategies including understanding morphology and etymology, as well as adding to their store of tricky words, homophones, and frequently misspelt words. The Scope and Sequence charts of each book give a detailed breakdown of the spelling concepts covered in each unit.

Year group	Primary 1	Primary 2	Primary 3	Primary 4	Primary 5	Primary 6	Primary 7
Nelson Spelling resources	Workbook Starter A Workbook Starter B	Pupil Book 1A Pupil Book 1B Workbook 1A Workbook 1B	Pupil Book 2 Workbook 2A Workbook 2B	Pupil Book 3	Pupil Book 4	Pupil Book 5	Pupil Book 6 Revision Book
	Teacher's Book 1 for Starter Level and Books 1A, 1B & 2				Teacher's Book 2 for Books 3, 4, 5 & 6		
	Resources and Assessment Book for Starter Level and Books 1A, 1B & 2			Resources and Assessment Book for Books 3 & 4		Resources and Assessment Book for Books 5 & 6	
Scotland Curriculum for Excellence levels Note: this level guidance is approximate	**First** **Writing – Tools for writing** • using knowledge of technical aspects to help my writing communicate effectively within and beyond my place of learning *I can spell the most commonly-used words, using my knowledge of letter patterns and spelling rules and use resources to help me spell tricky or unfamiliar words.* **LIT 1–21a**				**Second** **Writing – Tools for writing** • using knowledge of technical aspects to help my writing communicate effectively within and beyond my place of learning *I can spell most of the words I need to communicate, using spelling rules, specialist vocabulary, self-correction techniques and a range of resources.* **LIT 2–21a** *(Continuing to Third: I can use a range of strategies and resources and spell most of the words I need to use, including specialist vocabulary, and ensure that my spelling is accurate.* **LIT 3–21a**)		

14

Wales: Foundation Phase Language, Literacy and Communication Skills Area of Learning and Key Stage 2 English Programme of Study

Nelson Spelling provides a carefully structured course for teaching spelling to children in Years R–6. The course is designed to build children's competence and confidence as they progress. Children are taught spelling strategies including understanding morphology and etymology, as well as adding to their store of tricky words, homophones, and frequently misspelt words. The Scope and Sequence charts of each book give a detailed breakdown of the spelling concepts covered in each unit.

Year group	Reception	Year 1	Year 2	Year 3	Year 4	Year 5	Year 6
	Workbook Starter A Workbook Starter B	Pupil Book 1A Pupil Book 1B Workbook 1A Workbook 1B	Pupil Book 2 Workbook 2A Workbook 2B	Pupil Book 3	Pupil Book 4	Pupil Book 5	Pupil Book 6 Revision Book
Nelson Spelling resources	Teacher's Book 1 for Starter Level and Books 1A, 1B & 2			Teacher's Book 2 for Books 3, 4, 5 & 6			
	Resources and Assessment Book for Starter Level and Books 1A, 1B & 2			Resources and Assessment Book for Books 3 & 4		Resources and Assessment Book for Books 5 & 6	
Writing accurately Handwriting, Grammar, Punctuation and Spelling	Learners are able to: • discriminate between letters • distinguish between upper- and lower-case letters and show an awareness of full stops • use correct initial consonant by beginning to apply phonic knowledge • begin to use spelling strategies such as sound symbol correspondence and oral segmentation with support such as clapping sounds in vowel-consonant and vowel-consonant-vowel-consonant words • use spelling support such as phonic mats, flashcards and other resources • use familiar and high frequency words in writing	Learners are able to: • spell some words conventionally, including consonant-vowel-consonant and common digraphs, e.g. *th, ck* • use spelling strategies such as sound–symbol correspondence and segmenting • use spelling support such as picture dictionaries, spelling mats and other resources • spell high-frequency words correctly	Learners are able to: • use spelling strategies such as segmenting, simple roots and suffixes, e.g. *-ing, -ed* • use knowledge of syllables to spell polysyllabic words • use a dictionary • spell high-frequency words correctly	Learners are able to: • spell plural forms, e.g. *-s, -es, -ies* • use past tense of verbs consistently, e.g. *consonant doubling before -ed* • use strategies including knowledge of word families, roots, morphology and graphic knowledge to spell words, e.g. *most common polysyllabic words* • spell all high frequency words correctly	Learners are able to: • use punctuation [...] apostrophes for omission, e.g. *it's (it is)* • use strategies including knowledge of word families, roots, morphology, derivations and graphic knowledge to spell words, e.g. *words with more complex patterns*	Learners are able to: • use the full range of punctuation to guide the reader in complex sentences, e.g. [...] apostrophes for possession • use a variety of strategies to spell words with complex regular patterns, e.g. *exercise, competition*	Learners are able to: • use strategies to spell correctly polysyllabic, complex and irregular words

Wales: Foundation Phase Framework for Children's Learning for 3 to 7-year-olds in Wales and English in the National Curriculum for Wales

Year group	Reception	Year 1	Year 2	Year 3	Year 4	Year 5	Year 6
Nelson Spelling resources	Workbook Starter A Workbook Starter B	Pupil Book 1A Pupil Book 1B Workbook 1A Workbook 1B	Pupil Book 2 Workbook 2A Workbook 2B	Pupil Book 3	Pupil Book 4	Pupil Book 5	Pupil Book 6 Revision Book
	Teacher's Book 1 for Starter Level and Books 1A, 1B & 2			Teacher's Book 2 for Books 3, 4, 5 & 6			
	Resources and Assessment Book for Starter Level and Books 1A, 1B & 2			Resources and Assessment Book for Books 3 & 4		Resources and Assessment Book for Books 5 & 6	
	Foundation Phase Framework for Children's Learning for 3 to 7-year-olds in Wales **Writing: Skills** The Foundation Phase should enable children to enjoy experimenting with written communication and to make progress in their ability to: • develop their ability to spell common and familiar words in a recognisable way. **Foundation Phase Outcome 5** Simple words are usually spelled correctly, and where there are inaccuracies, the alternative is phonically plausible. **Foundation Phase Outcome 6** Spelling is usually accurate.			**Key Stages 2–4** **English in the National Curriculum for Wales** Broad lines of progression in the level descriptions for writing **Use of skills in writing:** Important early understanding of spelling relates to letter strings and sound-symbol relationships (Level 1). Pupils then build on this understanding to spell increasingly complex words (Levels 2 to 5). Independence in spelling is seen in pupils' ability to spell unfamiliar words (Level 6 to Exceptional Performance), and to check what they write. **Writing: Skills (6.)** Pupils should be given opportunities to communicate in writing and to: • develop and use a variety of strategies to enable them to spell correctly **Attainment target 3: Writing (Level 2)** Simple, monosyllabic words are usually spelled correctly, and where there are inaccuracies the alternative is phonetically plausible. **Attainment target 3: Writing (Level 3)** Spelling is usually accurate, including that of common, polysyllabic words. **Attainment target 3: Writing (Level 4)** Spelling conforms to regular patterns and is generally accurate. **Attainment target 3: Writing (Level 5)** Words with complex regular patterns are usually spelled correctly. **Attainment target 3: Writing (Level 6)** Spelling is generally accurate, including that of irregular words.			

Northern Ireland: Levels of progression in Communication across the curriculum: Primary (Levels 1–5)

Nelson Spelling provides a carefully structured course for teaching spelling to children in Primary 1–7. The course is designed to build children's competence and confidence as they progress. Children are taught spelling strategies including understanding morphology and etymology, as well as adding to their store of tricky words, homophones, and frequently misspelt words. The Scope and Sequence charts of each book give a detailed breakdown of the spelling concepts covered in each unit.

Year group	Primary 1	Primary 2	Primary 3	Primary 4	Primary 5	Primary 6	Primary 7
Nelson Spelling resources	Workbook Starter A Workbook Starter B	Pupil Book 1A Pupil Book 1B Workbook 1A Workbook 1B	Pupil Book 2 Workbook 2A Workbook 2B	Pupil Book 3	Pupil Book 4	Pupil Book 5	Pupil Book 6 Revision Book
	Teacher's Book 1 for Starter Level and Books 1A, 1B & 2			Teacher's Book 2 for Books 3, 4, 5 & 6			
	Resources and Assessment Book for Starter Level and Books 1A, 1B & 2			Resources and Assessment Book for Books 3 & 4		Resources and Assessment Book for Books 5 & 6	
Framework for Literacy Development	Foundation Stage		Key Stage 1 Pupils are expected to reach Level 2 by the end of Key Stage 1. There is also an expectation that they will progress by at least one level between each Key Stage.		Key Stage 2 Pupils are expected to reach Level 4 by the end of Key Stage 2. There is also an expectation that they will progress by at least one level between each Key Stage.		
Levels of progression in Communication across the curriculum: Primary (Levels 1–5) • talk about, plan and edit work • write with increasing accuracy and proficiency.	By the end of Y1	Progressing towards KS1	Level 1/2	Level 2	Level 3	Level 4	Level 4/5
	Most children should: begin to problem-solve how to write words through beginning to apply sound-symbol correspondence, using familiar words to make new words or finding words in the environment	Most children should: show increased independence when writing words by applying sound-symbol correspondence, making analogies and accessing words from a range of sources	Pupils can: (Level 1) write words using sound-symbol correspondence (Level 1) write personal and familiar words In a limited and specified range of forms, pupils can: (Level 2) spell and write common and familiar words recognisably	In a range of forms, for different audiences and purposes, pupils can: (Level 2) spell and write common and familiar words recognisably	In a range of specified forms and for specified audiences and purposes, pupils can: (Level 3) make improvements to their writing (Level 3) spell and write frequently used and topic words correctly	In a range of forms, for different audiences and purposes, pupils can: (Level 4) check writing to make improvements in accuracy and meaning (Level 4) use accurate grammar and spelling on most occasions	In a range of forms, for different audiences and purposes, including in formal situations, pupils can: (Level 5) redraft to improve accuracy and meaning (Level 5) use accurate grammar and spelling

Northern Ireland: Key Stages 1 And 2 Areas of Learning – Language and Literacy

Year groups	Primary 1	Primary 2	Primary 3	Primary 4	Primary 5	Primary 6	Primary 7
Nelson Spelling resources	Workbook Starter A Workbook Starter B	Pupil Book 1A Pupil Book 1B Workbook 1A Workbook 1B	Pupil Book 2 Workbook 2A Workbook 2B	Pupil Book 3	Pupil Book 4	Pupil Book 5	Pupil Book 6 Revision Book
	Teacher's Book 1 for Starter Level and Books 1A, 1B & 2			Teacher's Book 2 for Books 3, 4, 5 & 6			
	Resources and Assessment Book for Starter Level and Books 1A, 1B & 2			Resources and Assessment Book for Books 3 & 4		Resources and Assessment Book for Books 5 & 6	
Language and Literacy	**Foundation Stage** **Writing** Children should be enabled to: • begin to problem-solve how to write using sound-symbol correspondence as the first strategy		**Key Stage 1** Pupils are expected to reach Level 2 by the end of Key Stage 1. There is also an expectation that they will progress by at least one level between each Key Stage. **Writing** Children should be enabled to: • use a variety of skills to spell words in their writing • spell correctly a range of familiar, important and regularly occurring words			**Key Stage 2** Pupils are expected to reach Level 4 by the end of Key Stage 2. There is also an expectation that they will progress by at least one level between each Key Stage. **Writing** Children should be enabled to: • use a variety of skills to spell words correctly	

TEACHING SPELLING

Do we need to teach spelling?

One of the most vigorous debates in education has been, as Dr Margaret Peters once famously put it, whether spelling is 'caught or taught'. Can children learn to spell just by being exposed to words in print, or should they be taught to spell in a discrete and structured way? Some children develop spelling skills through reading, but research has shown that even 'careful' readers need some structured input in order to gain full mastery of spelling.

Is there one correct way, or 'best' way to teach spelling, and do we need to teach spelling pro-actively at all? If so, what are the main aspects of language that a teacher who wants to create a balanced spelling programme should take into account and encourage? The following pages seek to answer these questions.

A whole-school policy

A whole-school policy will give clarity and consistency for staff and children and it is important that it is discussed, agreed and 'signed-up to' by all the staff. Such an agreed policy document should address:

- the agreed spelling philosophy and strategy
- the use of structured course materials
- other spelling support materials in each classroom and work area
- the role of parents
- supporting children with particular spelling needs, including intensive spelling recovery programmes.

The place of memory

Memory

- visual memory
- auditory memory
- devices to stimulate and train memory

Visual memory

Serial probability

Most adults can hold large numbers of visual patterns in their memory. Despite the huge number of possible variations, most of us are able to recognise when a particular string of letters doesn't 'look right'. This is known as 'serial probability' and is an important component in learning to spell. It is developed more quickly if children are systematically taught the common phonemically regular patterns, to which they can add, in an organised way, the less frequent or irregular occurrences.

We can help children develop their memory by organising and categorising information. This is especially important for young children who do not have significant experience of the printed word.

Auditory memory

Sound discrimination

Researchers such as Westward have shown that for many children, visual memory alone is not enough. He has shown that, for many children, the ability to discriminate through hearing is equally as important as visual discrimination.

Working on sound/symbol relationships in a phonic programme to underpin early reading can have the spin-off benefit of helping with visual and auditory memory. Both *Letters and Sounds: Principles and Practice of High Quality Phonics* and the National Curriculum in England (2014) recognise this.

Poor visual and aural memory

For some children, visual and auditory memory develops slowly. For these children, grouping words with similar letter strings and sounds can be especially useful. Teachers will have their own ways of helping children with poor memories, but the key is probably not to demand too much and risk discouraging them. Most children will achieve greater success if the memorising is little and often.

Devices to stimulate and train memory

The handwriting/spelling link

As long ago as the 1940s, the spelling guru Professor Fred Schonell stressed that the 'visual, auditory and articulatory elements must be firmly cemented in writing'. This was supported by Margaret Peters in her research, and has been confirmed by many teachers since. Not only can the use of handwriting help to reinforce the spelling of groups of words with similar letter strings, but the handwriting practice offered is, in itself, also a valuable and useful activity. Spelling and handwriting are excellent bedfellows.

'Handwriting' does not have to mean a smooth joined style, although the sooner children can join the better, as it will help them hold patterns of letter strings in their mind. At the very beginning, when working with single letters and sounds, making letters in the air as well as on paper can be a useful method of memory stimulation and 'programming'. Equipment such as plastic letters and sandpaper letter shapes can be useful too.

Look, Say, Cover, Write, Check

A well-tried and effective device to help children memorise individual and groups of words is 'Look, Say, Cover, Write, Check'. Each of the *Nelson Spelling* Pupil Books has a flap on the front cover. Children should use the flap to cover the word list (though they should realise that it is far more effective to try to learn just a few of the words at a time, not the whole list). Once children are familiar with the 'Look, Say, Cover, Write, Check' technique, they can use it for the early, frequently-used but irregular words, such as *was*, *said* and *they*.

Mnemonics

The use of handwriting and 'Look, Say, Cover, Write, Check' are the main approaches to aid the development of memory, but others, such as the use of mnemonics can be used too. Mnemonics can have useful, if limited, applications especially with those one-off problem words – remembering the cess pit in the middle, means you'll never again misspell 'ne*cess*ary'!

The place of understanding

Structural understanding

- phonographical awareness
- word morphology
- etymology
- syllabification
- semantics and syntax

Phonographical awareness

44 phonemes but 26 graphemes!

English has 44 sounds (phonemes) variously represented by 26 letters (graphemes). Most English words are spelled as they sound, so learning the grapheme-phoneme correspondences gives a solid foundation on which to build. There is a growing body of evidence that children progress faster in reading and other language skills if they follow a structured phonics programme from the earliest stages.

Rhyme and analogy

Reading (decoding) and spelling (encoding) are best planned in parallel. Research by Goswami and Bryant on rhyme and alliteration, found that whilst reading and spelling seem to develop independently in the first two years, thereafter a change occurs and the two processes definitely seem to facilitate one another. As they note:

It is probably a short intellectual step from knowing that 'light', 'fight', 'sight' and 'tight' all end in the same sound, to understanding that that is why they all share a common spelling pattern.

Equally fascinating and significant is what Bryant found when working with Bradley. They clearly established that sensitivity to rhyme and alliteration in 4 and 5-year-old non-readers correlates closely with spelling ability three or more years later. A well-planned and carefully structured phonics programme will benefit not only younger children but older ones too. Older children who need additional support with reading often benefit from a structured and organised phonemic emphasis on spelling.

Word morphology

Roots and affixes

Morphology is concerned with the parts of the word that carry meaning, most commonly roots or stems, and their relevant suffixes and prefixes. Understanding how the 'bits fit together' improves children's chances of spelling a word correctly. The word *unnecessary* is notoriously difficult to remember, but realising that it is composed of the root *necessary* and the prefix **un** will help clear the first hurdle.

When children are learning the rules of English spelling, it will help them to understand the morphology of the words in question. For example, to understand how to spell the adverb *happily*, it helps to know that it comprises the frequently used suffix **ly** and the root *happy*, in which the **y** has followed the rule and been changed to an **i**.

An understanding of morphology can also help with spelling compound words and contractions. Many words used by young writers are compound (e.g. *sometimes, something, outside, football* and *birthday*) or contractions (e.g. *don't* and *didn't*). Once children are clear about how these words are constructed from their 'base' words, then problems of remembering where to put the apostrophe and which letters are omitted begin to melt away.

Etymology

A living language

A long history of language influxes since the Anglo-Saxon era has led English to develop into the form we speak and write today. Latin (together with its own Greek influences) had been introduced with the Romans and subsequently many other language 'importations' have come to contribute to our modern English words and spelling. Not only is this fascinating for children to discover, but a recognition of the impact of the specific letter strings on our spelling, such as **phy** from Greek, can also be helpful.

Syllabification

Useful chunks

Morphology and syllabification are different from one another. Whilst morphology relates to meaning, syllabification relates to the speech 'impulses' of a word. The two should not be confused, for they can be, and very often are, quite different. A good example is the word *development*. Morphologically the word comprises the root *develop* and the suffix **ment**. However, when split into speech impulses, or syllables, it might be split *de/vel/op/ment*.

Both morphology and syllabification play an important part in *Nelson Spelling*, but it helps to be aware of the important distinction between them. Syllables often comprise useful 'chunks' of words that children can recall more easily than strings of individual letters.

Semantics and syntax

Significance of meaning

An awareness of semantics and syntax (word meaning) becomes significant in such contexts as deciding between old favourites such as the homophones *their* and *there*, and later in whether or when to spell *practice* with a **c** or an **s**.

Some other issues

As many teachers know, most children enjoy working in an environment where spelling is supported and taught, but it is important to strike a sensible balance to make best use of pupils' and teachers' time. A school spelling policy needs to take account of a spelling scheme, the supporting resources, and the clear recognition by the children of when accurate spelling matters and when it is less important.

Working through the carefully graded sequence of units in *Nelson Spelling* will provide a sound foundation, but it is also important to sensitively correct errors in children's work, and take the opportunity they present for diagnosis and further teaching. You will also want to have spontaneous spelling lessons, for example picking up on a particular letter string, or words connected to a theme or subject.

The role of the teacher

In a busy classroom, it is impossible to supply every child with 'spellings' at the moment of need. Children therefore need to see their teacher as a support and 'partner'.

Correcting errors and public presentation

When you look at children's draft pieces of work, you should acknowledge positively any reasonable attempts at spelling. This is the time to correct any errors, because you also need to make it clear that quality control matters when writing for public presentation. The definition of 'going public' needs to be understood by everyone, and will certainly include work for display, and in any books which will potentially have an audience, such as other pupils, parents, other teachers, inspectors and school governors. You will need to encourage children to take pride in well-presented work.

Looking for patterns of difficulty

It is important to be constantly alert to patterns of spelling difficulty. If a type of error recurs, you might want to give children the appropriate unit in *Nelson Spelling*, even if this happens to be out of sequence. Alternatively, you might prefer to provide a list of similar words with the same letter pattern for the child to learn and practise. For most patterns, these lists can be found in the Supporting word lists given in each unit in this Teacher's Book.

Frequently occurring difficulties are regularly highlighted as a result of the end of key stage assessments which, for example, have noted:

At KS1 (age 7) children need to:

- distinguish between long and short vowels in single syllable words
- identify separate phonemes in words of different length
- apply knowledge of visual patterns as well as phonics to attempt unfamiliar words
- understand how adding endings to words can affect the spelling of the word stem, e.g. **ing, ed, er**
- learn to spell common words where there are different ways of representing the vowel digraphs, e.g. *brake, break*
- learn how to analyse words of more than one syllable using knowledge of morphemic structure.

At KS2 (age 11) it was noted that children should:

- use their knowledge of word roots to ensure the correct spelling of unstressed vowels, e.g. *vanish/vaneshing; injure/injered*
- learn ways to check their accuracy when using prefixes and suffixes, e.g. check pronunciation of *swimming/swiming, regardless/regardles*.

Supporting independent spelling

Wall displays

We should constantly be seeking to help children achieve independence in spelling. 'Spelling support' should be a permanent feature of every writing area in every classroom or work area. Especially for younger age groups, it is useful to provide word lists, probably on the wall, of difficult words which have a high frequency. Lists of such words are given on pages 26–27 of this book. Word lists from other subjects across the curriculum can also be posted on the wall. The wall display might also feature one or more of the letter patterns which have been the focus of *Nelson Spelling* units recently studied.

Dictionaries and thesauruses

Dictionaries, word books and thesauruses will be useful for many children, but they will only be effective if children are confident and competent in using them. *Nelson Spelling* gives some opportunities for basic dictionary skills, but there is no substitute for constant practice, especially when a child or group has a few minutes to spare.

Using computers

If children are using a computer programme that has a spell-checking facility, they must use it to check the spellings. Not all errors will have been remedied, but most will - and children will have picked up the right attitude to spelling accurately. Word processing can also be used as an extension to other spelling reference resources.

Home-school links

As with reading, spelling is one of the areas where home support can enhance the effectiveness and speed of learning. Great care is needed when briefing parents: one-to-one support can be invaluable, but too much pressure of the wrong sort can become counter-productive.

Taking spellings home

Each unit in *Nelson Spelling* has a Words to Learn list, which relates closely to the pupil book pages. We recommend that children take copies of the words home to learn and that they should be tested regularly so that a pattern and purpose can become established. Without this checking and testing, the drive to learn the spellings will lose its momentum.

Some schools allow children to take home the pupil books, each unit of work potentially providing a self-contained 'homework' package. Again this should only be done if properly explained beforehand, and then monitored.

On-going support

Other ways in which parent support can be helpful in an on-going way include:

- calling attention to other words that have a similar letter string to those recently practiced – especially in environmental print contexts
- always being available to write down words needed in the course of written work at home – then testing it using the 'Look, Say, Cover, Write, Check' method
- praising good effort in spelling, especially if the error is a phonemically 'reasonable' attempt, before correcting any error
- playing spelling games, such as finding small words within longer words and collecting as many words as possible with a given letter string.

KEY SPELLING RULES

The majority of spelling rules can most immediately be understood from an appreciation of morphology (roots, suffixes and prefixes, contractions, compound words, plural constructions) and etymology (origins, meanings, foreign words). These are progressively introduced, developed and revised alongside the teaching of the regular patterns sound/letter correspondences.

The following list, whilst not exclusive, represents for the benefit of the teacher the main useful rules. It is suggested that these might be introduced in particular circumstances with individual children, though on occasions it may be appropriate to build a class or group lesson around a particular rule.

The only sure rule is that nearly every spelling rule has its exceptions! Nevertheless, as a knowledge of rules can improve the odds of spelling a word correctly, they certainly have their place.

General rules

1. **q** is never written without **u** (queen).
2. No English words end with **v** and very few end with **i** or **j**.
3. 'ee' or 'i' sounds at the end of a word are usually represented by **y**.
4. The /k/ sound after a short vowel is written **ck** (except multisyllable words ending in **ic**).
5. **i** comes before **e** (when the sound is 'ee') (piece), except after **c** (receive; ceiling; receipt) or when the sound is not 'ee' (eight; reign; heir).
6. If nouns and verbs are formed from the same root the noun usually ends in **ce** and the verb in **se** (e.g. practice/practise; advice/advise; licence/license).

Making plurals

1. To make the plural form of most nouns, we just add **s** (goat/goats; shop/shops).
2. To make a plural if the noun ends with **s, x, sh** or **ch** we add **es** (bus/buses; bush/bushes).
3. To make the plural if the noun ends in a consonant + **y**, we change **y** to **i** and add **es** (baby/babies).
4. To make the plural of a noun that ends in a vowel + **y**, we just add **s** (day/days).
5. To make the plural of a noun that ends in **f** or **fe**, we normally change the **f** or **fe** to **v** and add **es** (wolf/wolves; wife/wives).
6. To make the plural of a noun that ends in **o**, we normally add **es** (hero/heroes; volcano/volcanoes), unless it ends in **oo**, or is a music word, or is a shortened form (cuckoo/cuckoos; cello/cellos; photo/photos).

Using suffixes

1. To add a suffix when a word ends with **e**: drop the **e** if the suffix begins with a vowel or is **y** (ice/icing/icy) keep the **e** if the suffix begins with a consonant (wake/wakeful). Some exceptions: true/truly; argue/argument; due/duly.
2. To add a suffix **able** or **ous** to a word that ends in **ce** or **ge**, retain the **e** to keep the **c** or **g** soft (notice/noticeable; manage/manageable; outrage/outrageous).
3. To add a suffix to a short word, or a word where the last syllable is stressed, look at the letter before the last:
   - if it's a single vowel we normally double the last letter before adding the suffix (hop/hopping/hopped; transmit/transmitter).
   - if it's not a single vowel we normally just add the suffix (sing/singing; read/reading; profit/profited).

Note: **w, x** and **y** are never doubled.

4. To add a suffix when a word ends with **y** (that sounds 'ee'), change the **y** to an **i** before adding the suffix (ugly/ugliness).
5. **ul** or **il** at the end of a word only have one **l** (spoonful; until).
6. **able** is a five-times more frequent suffix than **ible**, especially if the antonym (opposite) begins with **un** (reliable/unreliable; resistible/irresistible).

Using prefixes

1. To add a prefix – just do it! (un+sure/unsure; mis+spelt/misspelt; im+moral/immoral). Don't adjust for double letters!
2. **al** at the beginning of a word only has one **l** (also; always).

WORD FREQUENCY TABLES

Several tables indicating the frequency of words used by children have been researched, but a certain amount of care needs to be given to their application in the context of writing and spelling.

The more useful lists in the current context are those that have been specifically derived from the words children write or speak, such as those produced by Dee Reid and Bridie Raban. Not surprisingly there is a fair degree of correlation between such lists as these and the lists based on the words children read, such as that produced by Masterson, Stuart, Dixon and Lovejoy (Children's Printed Word Database, 2003), the 'Key Words' of McNally and Murray and the 'Basic Word List' of Dolch, subsequently revised and updated. However, there are also some differences, so for obvious reasons this course has been more alert to the words children use in their writing than in their reading. Nevertheless, the influences of all these lists will be seen in the selections made. The divergences between the lists tend to be more pronounced in the later stages. As is demonstrated in the following charts, the early stages lists of words required for reading and writing are reasonably similar.

The selection of words is also driven in part by the words required for schools in England to teach, as listed in the National Curriculum for English (2014).

12 words represent 25% of all words read by early readers

Eleven of these twelve words are also to be found in the top 20 words used in writing, with only *that* falling outside.

The numerals denote the position in the *Word for Word* writing frequency tables below.

'Regular'		'Irregular'	
and	1	a	3
in	10	he	8
is	19	I	4
it	7	of	16
that	34	the	2
		to	5
		was	6

The next 20 words represent approximately a further 10% of all words read.

Note: The majority fall within the top 50 required for writing.

'Regular'	'Irregular'
as 79	all 42
at 43	be 72
but 27	are 49
had 18	for 30
him 51	have 38
his 37	one 26
not 46	said 17
on 15	so 24
	they 13
	we 9
	you 23

These two charts demonstrate that teaching by focusing on these words, in terms both of reading and spelling, will have been time very well spent.

There are other useful lists, devised with a didactic purpose. Two notable examples which have helped inform the selection of words used in *Nelson Spelling* are those based on the work of Schonell, and subsequently revised, and the Morris-Montessori Word List, created from the linguistically-based *Phonics 44* system devised by Dr Morris.

Nelson Spelling is linguistically structured and developmental, and the course has been so arranged to ensure that most of the early words required in writing are covered in the first units, especially at Levels 1 and 2. Inevitably, though, there are some words that need to be addressed slightly earlier than they would naturally appear in the sequence of spelling patterns and spelling word families in the course.

The 50 words most frequently written by 7/8-year-olds:

and	was	went	of	she	one	with	go	saw	not
the	it	my	said	when	but	day	his	all	like
a	he	they	had	you	me	out	have	at	very
I	we	then	is	so	up	that	came	her	are
to	in	on	got	there	for	some	were	home	get

The next 200 words most frequently written by 7/8-year-olds:

him	do	tree	long	another	ear	cave	suddenly
down	after	over	looked	heard	things	trees	wind
back	what	again	too	king	witch	woke	dinner
mum	as	yes	thought	more	something	never	find
them	dog	from	by	playing	know	tried	sad
because	off	us	walk	fire	think	best	run
put	see	boy	cat	white	give	bit	turned
into	people	away	upon	garden	story	dark	clothes
will	two	this	who	nice	walked	end	football
did	come	old	way	friends	castle	always	top
man	our	found	dragon	don't	didn't	baby	wanted
little	school	lived	red	oh	food	boat	why
time	once	play	round	take	opened	lot	sunflower
big	if	girl	mummy	hair	park	wood	around
house	door	told	well	three	giant	daddy	bird
called	ran	fell	where	help	gone	green	head
would	no	morning	gave	here	room	it's	sea
dad	next	started	lots	how	sister	lady	thing
their	took	other	want	played	asked	soon	gold
has	good	water	friend	eyes	blue	fair	hole
can	an	your	children	shop	or	its	walking
be	about	am	make	balloon	outside	men	ever
could	night	first	tea	black	bad	Mr	let
going	name	just	through	Christmas	brother	only	lost
bed	made	now	car	look	sleep	snowman	mother

If, in addition to working through the units in Levels 1 and 2, the following groups of words are taught, the pupils will systematically have covered all the 250 most frequently used words by 7/8-year-olds by the end of Level 1.

1	2	3	4	5	6	7
story	mummy	eyes	who	asked	castle	tried
baby	daddy	clothes	where	after	giant	opened
lady	little		were	never	people	
only	dinner				because	8
	suddenly					snowman
						sunflower

25

Book 3 Scope and Sequence

Unit	Pupil Book Focus	Pupil Book Extra	Pupil Book Extension	Resource Book Focus	Resource Book Extension
1	**sp, spr** finding target words	wordsearch puzzle	adding vowel letters in the correct place within given sentences	word building	identifying synonyms; using a dictionary to write definitions
2	**all, al** using the *al* prefix	using *al* suffixes	identifying prefix meanings	word building	using *l/ll*; adding the *ly* suffix
3	**soft c** finding target words	matching *ice* words with definitions	identifying *ce, ci, cy* patterns	identifying ice/ace patterns	alphabetical ordering
4	**silent letters b and k** finding target words	completing a table with *b + ing/ed*	doubling last letter before suffix	sorting silent letters	using silent letters
5	**le, el, al, il endings** finding target words	completing a table with *le + ing/ed*	*nnel* pattern quiz	completing endings puzzle	cloze activity; writing definitions
6	**some y endings** cloze activity	doubling last letter before *y* ending	dropping *e* before suffix	word building	making and writing adjectives
7	**making plurals** making simple plurals	making *es* plurals	changing *y* to *i* plurals	identifying and using *s/es*	using *ies/ys*
8	**y+er, y+est** finding target words	making comparatives	making superlatives	word building	using *y+er/y+est*
9	**ing, ed** selecting target words	adding *ing/ed*	dropping *e* before suffix	adding *ing*; writing sentences	doubling final letter and dropping the *e*
10	**soft g, ge, dge** sorting by word family	dropping *e* before suffix	making *nge* words and definitions	word building; writing funny sentences	matching definitions; writing sentences
11	**wa, qua** finding target words	target word quiz	making singular possessive sentences	finding target words; completing wordsearch	solving quiz with clues
12	**tion, ation** finding target words	cloze activity	identifying *shion/tion*; making *tion* family words	adding *tion* to build words	using *ation/ition/otion* in sentences
13	**sion** finding target words	identifying *sion* rhyming words	matching words to definitions	adding *sion* to build words	using *ession/ission/ossion* in sentences
14	**adding suffixes** applying suffixes	changing *y* to *i* before suffix	making word families	adding *ness/ment*; making sentences	identifying syllables
15	**contractions** deconstructing contractions	identifying when to use *you're / your*	making contractions	deconstructing and making contractions	making contractions; writing sentences

The darker cells introduce statutory material for this year group in the National Curriculum for England.
The paler cells denote revision of a topic covered in previous years.

Unit	Pupil Book Focus	Pupil Book Extra	Pupil Book Extension	Resource Book Focus	Resource Book Extension
16	homophones finding target words	choosing homophones	identifying and writing mnemonics	word-matching; writing sentences	cloze activity; using target words in sentences
17	silent letters o, h, and c finding target words	finding *ch* words in wordsearch	using a dictionary to find definitions	identifying letter patterns	identifying silent letters; correcting spelling test
18	ei, y and other tricky words finding target words	target word quiz	identifying homophones	identifying *le* letter patterns; writing sentences	target letter quiz; writing definitions; rhyming clues
19	ous cloze activity	matching adjectives with nouns	identifying *ious/eous* words	building *ous* words	identifying letter patterns; writing sentences with target words
20	dis, mis, in, im, il, ir finding target words	understanding prefix meanings	using a dictionary to find related words	target letter patterns; picture clues	completing wordsearch; writing sentences
21	un, de, re, pre, non finding target words	understanding prefix meanings	using a dictionary to find related words	building words using target prefixes	completing wordsearch; writing sentences
22	ly ending finding target words	adding *ly* to root words	changing *y* to *i* before suffix	word building	writing sentences with target words; identifying *ly* words
23	sure, ture finding target words	target word quiz	identifying *ture/cher* words	word building	identifying letter patterns; writing sentences
24	wh, ph cloze activity	finding small words within words	target word quiz	word building	cloze activity; *wh* words quiz
25	compound words making compound words from word sums	making compound words	identifying compound words	building compound words	making compound words; using target words in sentences
26	silent w finding target words	making word webs	completing wordsearch	word building; writing sentences	cloze activity; correcting incorrect spelling in prose
27	words in words finding small words within short words	finding small words within longer words	identifying small words as spelling support	finding words within words	finding words within longer words; using a dictionary to find words containing three small words
28	dictionary work vowels and consonants	alphabetical ordering	finding and writing dictionary definitions	alphabetical ordering	putting homophones in alphabetical order

BOOK 3 — UNIT 1

LEARNING TARGETS

Pupil Book: Focus
to identify and copy key words from a picture

Pupil Book: Extra
to find target words in a wordsearch puzzle

Pupil Book: Extension
to consider what percentage of the letters used in English words are vowels

Resource sheet: Focus
to practise target letter patterns and complete word sums

Resource sheet: Extension
to find synonyms;
to use target letter patterns in the context of definitions

BACKGROUND NOTES AND SUGGESTIONS

For spelling, **sp** is an important consonant letter pairing. It has occurred in previous units and is returned to here, together with the triple sequence of **spr**.

Children can be extended by being encouraged to think about other frequent initial triple-letter patterns, notably the onomatopoeic **spl** words.

Pupil Book answers

Focus
spin spot spill spark speak

Extra

A speak spring spill sprout spark spell sprint spin(s) spray

B Teacher to check individual sentences

Extension
1 The cat jumped over the fox.
2 He got cross and ran after the cat.
3 The cat ran up the tree.
4 "You will have to come down one day," said the fox.

Resource sheet answers

Focus

A Children should copy the patterns

B spin spot spike sprint spring spray

Extension
1 spark
2 sparse
3 specific
4 spice
5 speculate
6 specimen
7 speck
8 speckle
9 spectacles
10 spouse

B Teacher to check individual answers

Supporting word lists

span spat space spade Spain
spark spawn
spell spend spent speck speak
speed speech
spin spit spill spilt spike
spot spoon spook sport spout
spun
spy
sprang sprain spray
sprint spring
sprung

BOOK 3 — UNIT 2

LEARNING TARGETS

Pupil Book: Focus
to secure the use of **al** as a prefix

Pupil Book: Extra
to make adjectives by adding **al**, and nouns by removing **al**

Pupil Book: Extension
to add **al**, **ad** and **a** as a prefix

Resource sheet: Focus
to complete word sums incorporating the target letter patterns

Resource sheet: Extension
to identify misspelt words;
to add the **ly** suffix to words ending in **al**

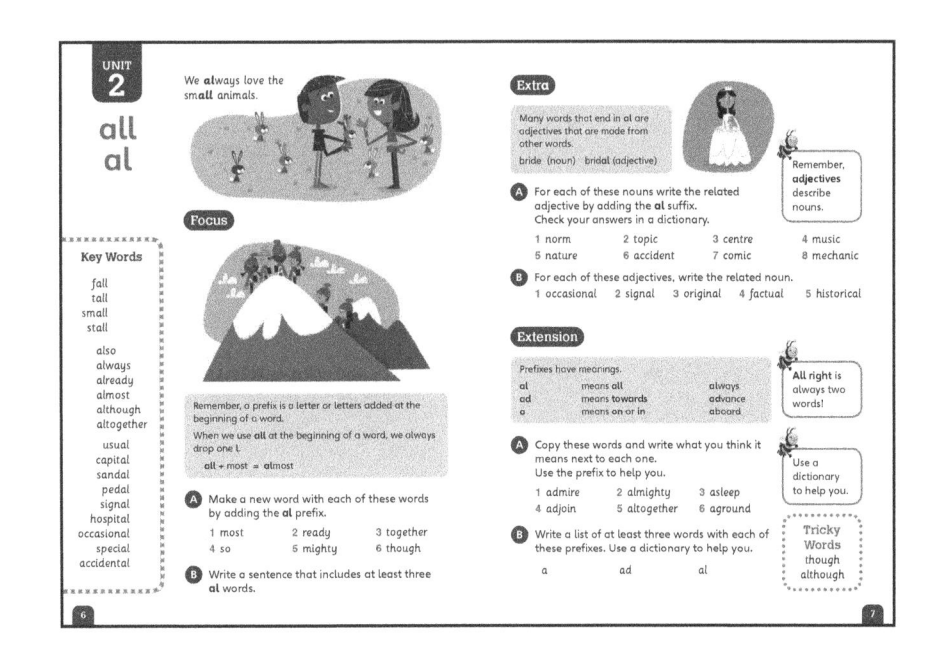

BACKGROUND NOTES AND SUGGESTIONS

The vowel sound in *ball* is represented by the vowel digraph **al**, not, as is often assumed, **all**. This is important in helping to clarify the letters representing the vowel in words such as *talk* and *walk*. It also helps to explain why, when **al** forms a prefix (e.g. *always*), it has a single **l**. However, to make things confusing for the child, the prefix **al** does actually mean *all*!

There are no rules to determine whether a word should end in **al** rather than **le** or **el**. The only limited support available is to remember that when added as a suffix to a word ending in **ic** or **on**, it will be **al** (e.g. *musical, national*).

Pupil Book answers

Focus
A
1 almost   2 already
3 altogether   4 also
5 almighty   6 although

B Teacher to check individual answers

Extra
A
1 normal   2 topical
3 central   4 musical
5 natural   6 accidental
7 comical   8 mechanical

B
1 occasion   2 sign
3 origin   4 fact
5 history

Extension
A Teacher to check individual answers

B Teacher to check individual answers

Resource sheet answers

Focus
A Children should copy the patterns

B fall tall always almost small stall signal sandal occasional accidental

C fall sandal accidental stall

Extension
A
1 also   2 careful
3 spoonful   4 faithful
5 always   6 altogether
7 wonderful   8 although
9 sorrowful   10 thoughtful
11 skillful   12 fulfill

The last two words have a single **l** and a double **ll**.

B
1 actually   2 eventually
3 gradually   4 usually
5 originally   6 really

C Teacher to check individual answers

Supporting word lists

all
all ball call fall hall tall wall small stall *shall

+ing
calling falling talking walking stalking

+est
tallest smallest baldest

prefix al
already always altogether also although almighty almost

medial al
talk walk stalk
bald scald
halt malt salt

final/suffix al

initial vowel a
actual sandal vandal capital natural national factual radical casual cathedral

initial vowel e
medal metal pedal petal dental medical central mechanical special general equal

initial vowel i
signal clinical historical accidental bridal final spiral

initial vowel o
coral comical topical tropical hospital horizontal moral original occasional total postal local

initial vowel u
usual musical

other
normal royal loyal crystal

BOOK 3
UNIT 3

LEARNING TARGETS

Pupil Book: Focus
to identify and copy key words in a picture;
to differentiate hard and soft **c** phonemes

Pupil Book: Extra
to answer clues which focus on **ice** words

Pupil Book: Extension
to recognise soft **c** phonemes and sort them into lists accordingly

Resource sheet: Focus
to trace and copy letter patterns and complete word sums

Resource sheet: Extension
to secure alphabetical ordering

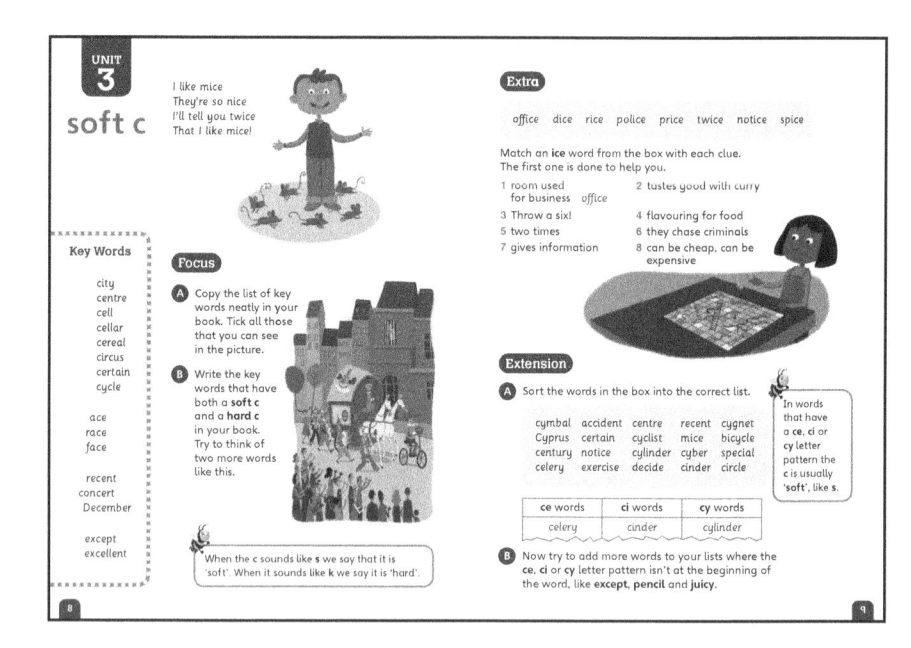

BACKGROUND NOTES AND SUGGESTIONS

A useful way to introduce this unit is to arrange for the class or group to collect words which include the **ca, ce, ci, cy, co** and **cu** letter patterns, and from these to draw out that **ce, ce** and **cy** usually have the effect of 'softening' the **c**. *Celt* and *Celtic* are sometimes exceptions to this.

Notice also what happens to words with the **cc** pattern, e.g. *succeed*.

Pupil Book answers

Focus
A city centre cell circus cycle face cereal

B circus cycle concert
Teacher to check individual answers

Extra
1 office 2 rice 3 dice 4 spice
5 twice 6 police 7 notice 8 price

Extension
A ce: centre recent certain mice century notice celery
ci: accident special exercise decide cinder circle
cy: cymbal cygnet Cyprus cyclist bicycle cylinder cyber

B Teacher to check individual answers

Resource answers

Focus
A Children should copy the patterns

B spice rice price lice trace race place lace space (trice)

Extension
A 1 o q 2 m n o p 3 u v w x
4 n o p 5 i k 6 f g h

B Teacher to check individual answers

C 1 face lace pace race
2 ice nice rice spice
3 pace palace peace place
4 ceiling cell cement cereal

Supporting word lists

initial ce
cell cent cease cedar cellar cement
centre central ceiling certain centaur
celery cereal century certify celebrate
centipede cemetery centurion
ceremony certificate

medial ce
recent accept excel except cancel
excess exceed process proceed
success succeed grocer concert
December excellent innocent

final ce
ace face lace pace race
ice dice mice nice rice slice price spice
twice splice notice office police service
truce spruce peace

initial ci
city civic civil cigar
cinder circus circuit circle citrus
cinema circular citizen

medial ci
acid pencil icing decide
accident ferocity electricity simplicity

initial cy
cycle cyclone Cyclops cymbal cygnet
cynic cylinder

final cy
icy lacy fancy juicy spicy agency
currency frequency conspiracy

final nce
dance lance glance prance trance chance
advance distance entrance
fence offence pence sentence defence
absence commence
mince since wince prince convince ounce
announce bounce pounce

30

BOOK 3

UNIT 4

LEARNING TARGETS

Pupil Book: Focus
to match key words to pictures;
to identify the silent letters in key words

Pupil Book: Extra
to add suffixes to silent **b** words

Pupil Book: Extension
to secure, in the context of silent **k** words, the doubling of the last letter where appropriate before adding a suffix

Resource sheet: Focus
to recognise the silent **b** and silent **k** in words

Resource sheet: Extension
to identify silent letters in words;
story writing

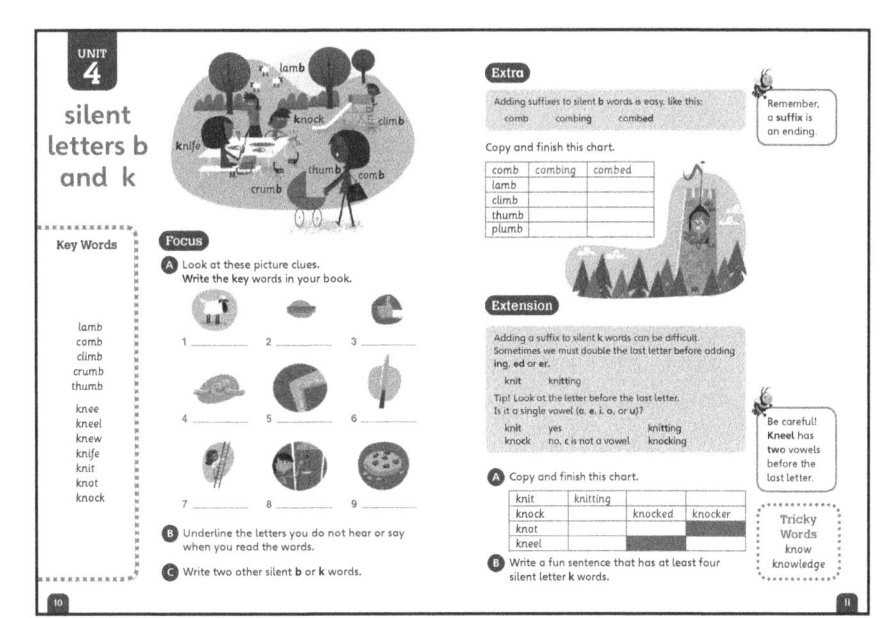

BACKGROUND NOTES AND SUGGESTIONS

The children will be intrigued to realise that many silent letters were, in days gone by, pronounced, but due to fashion and the general evolution of language, they have become silent.

This is the first unit to focus on silent letters. Other silent letters feature in Units 17 and 26. Any silent letters can be introduced at any stage, so activities developed from this unit might usefully also introduce other silent letters. As was mentioned previously, many vowel letters are not sounded individually and teachers may choose to teach them as silent (e.g. **a** in *head*; **e** in *gone*), though the term is conventionally reserved for consonant letters. However, if identified in the Extension resource, these should be allowed as correct.

Pupil Book answers

Focus

A / B
1 lamb
2 comb
3 thumb
4 knot
5 knee
6 knife
7 climb
8 knock
9 crumb

C Teacher to check individual answers

Extra

comb	combing	combed
lamb	lambing	lambed
climb	climbing	climbed
thumb	thumbing	thumbed
plumb	plumbing	plumbed

Extension

A
knit	knitting	knitted	knitter
knock	knocking	knocked	knocker
knot	knotting	knotted	
kneel	kneeling		kneeler

B Teacher to check individual answers

Resource sheet answers

Focus

A Words with silent **b**: comb crumb dumb lamb thumb

Words with silent **k**: knit know kneel knot knock

B know knight knotted knocker kneeling

Children to write a sentence commenting on silent **k** always followed by **n**

C climber limb comb lamb tomb

Children to write a sentence commenting on silent **b** always preceded by **m**

Extension

A
1 wrong
2 climb
3 wrist
4 knot
5 write
6 comb
7 knock
8 sign
9 knelt
10 thumb
11 wrestle
12 plumber

B Teacher to check individual answers

Supporting word lists

b (after m)
lamb limb comb tomb
dumb numb climb plumb
crumb thumb

b (before t)
debt doubt subtle

initial k
knit knob knot
knelt knack knock
knee kneel knife knight
knew known knuckle

31

BOOK 3 — UNIT 5

LEARNING TARGETS

Pupil Book: Focus
to identify and write key words

Pupil Book: Extra
to practise adding inflectional endings
to words ending in **le**

Pupil Book: Extension
to find **nnel** words in a quiz

Resource sheet: Focus
to match target words to clues and pictures

Resource sheet: Extension
to complete a cloze activity using target words;
to complete words with target endings

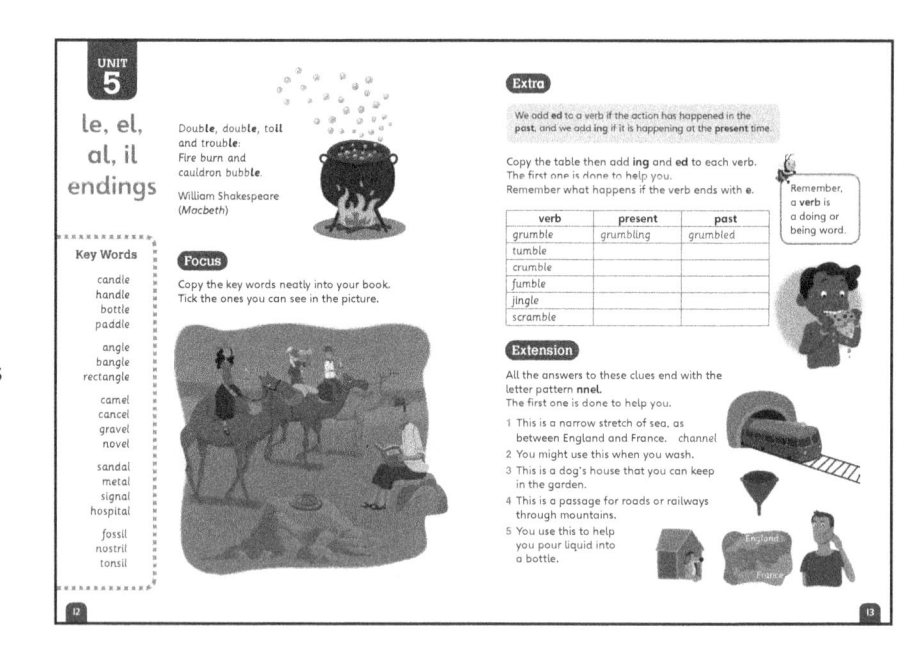

BACKGROUND NOTES AND SUGGESTIONS

There are very many words ending in **le**. The sets of words listed below are 'regular', thus enabling the child to focus without confusion on the final **le**. It is usually advantageous to work on groups of words with similar spelling patterns before mixing them.

There are no rules to determine whether a word should end in **al** rather than **le** or **el**. The only limited support available is to remember that when added as a suffix to a word ending in **ic** or **on** it will be **al** (e.g. *musical*, *national*).

From the *Supporting word lists* it can be seen that many of the **el** words have medial double letters, and others have rhyming patterns. Select groups for individuals to learn as appropriate.

Pupil Book answers

Focus
candle bottle bangle camel novel sandal fossil

Extra
grumble	grumbling	grumbled
tumble	tumbling	tumbled
crumble	crumbling	crumbled
fumble	fumbling	fumbled
jingle	jingling	jingled
scramble	scrambling	scrambled

Extension
1 channel 2 flannel 3 kennel
4 tunnel 5 funnel

Resource sheet answers

Focus

A
1 camel 2 gravel 3 hostel
4 chisel 5 cockerel 6 jewel
7 travel 8 kennel

B cockerel camel jewel chisel

C Teacher to check individual answers

Extension

A
1 paddle jungle
2 middle tropical
3 cancel hostel
4 medical
5 hospital
6 middle
7 angle metal
8 travel camel grumble

B
1 mechanical
2 bangle
3 cancel
4 horizontal
Children to write a definition for each word.

Supporting word lists

initial vowel a
actual sandal vandal capital natural
national factual radical casual cathedral
initial vowel e
medal metal pedal petal dental medical
central mechanical special general equal
initial vowel i
signal clinical historical accidental bridal
final spiral
initial vowel o
coral comical topical tropical hospital
horizontal moral original occasional total
postal local
initial vowel u
usual musical
other
normal royal loyal crystal

gamble ramble bramble scramble
bumble fumble humble jumble mumble
rumble crumble grumble stumble
dimple pimple simple
rumple crumple
candle handle
kindle spindle dwindle swindle

bundle trundle
angle bangle dangle jangle tangle
spangle strangle rectangle
jingle mingle single tingle
bungle jungle
tinkle winkle crinkle twinkle
sprinkle nestle trestle
bristle gristle thistle
bustle hustle rustle
jostle

initial vowel a
camel panel barrel pastel channel flannel
gravel travel cancel label
chapel parallel
channel chapel satchel
caramel mackerel
initial vowel e
kennel vessel kestrel level
initial vowel i
tinsel swivel minstrel shrivel chisel
initial vowel o
hovel novel grovel shovel model mongrel
hostel cockerel
initial vowel u
duffel funnel tunnel mussel fuel cruel
other
parcel vowel towel scoundrel
pencil fossil nostril

BOOK 3

UNIT 6

LEARNING TARGETS

Pupil Book: Focus
to complete a cloze activity using key words and rhyming words

Pupil Book: Extra
to consider changes that are sometimes needed when **y** is added to a short word

Pupil Book: Extension
to consider changes that are sometimes needed when **y** is added to a word ending in **e**

Resource sheet: Focus
to complete a word fan and match target words to pictures

Resource sheet: Extension
to make adjectives by adding **y**

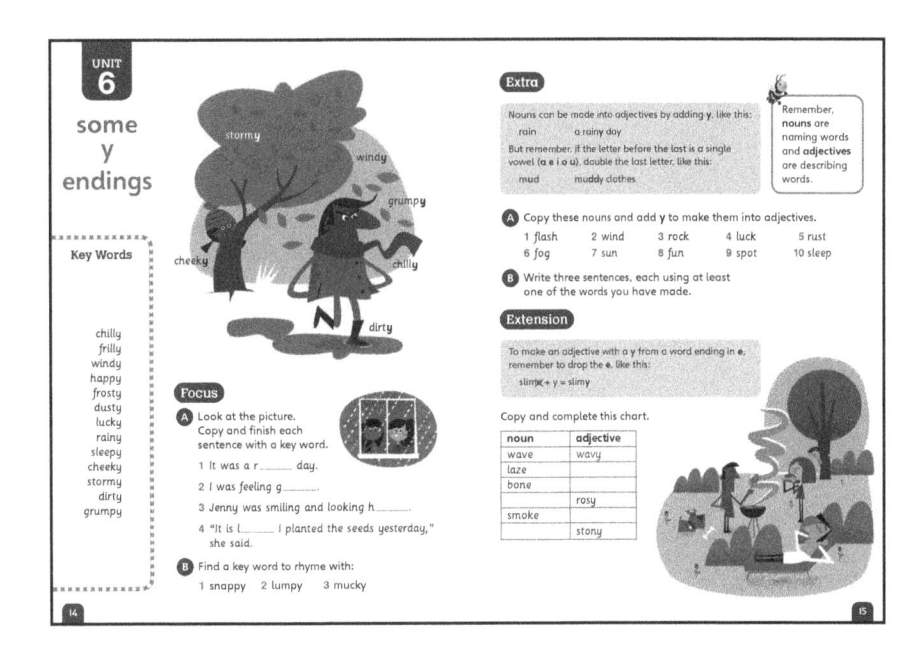

BACKGROUND NOTES AND SUGGESTIONS

This unit is a good opportunity to work on these related rules:

- nouns can be made into adjectives by adding **y**
- if the letter before the last is a single vowel then double the last letter (m**u**d, mu**dd**y)
- if the word ends in **e**, drop the **e** before adding the **y** (slim**e**, slim**y**).

The **y** (sounding ee) nouns (and adjectives) offer an opportunity to practise some of the other letter patterns learnt earlier in the course. The *Supporting word lists* are arranged in groups to help facilitate this possibility.

By selecting words from the Key Words list, the effect of double consonants 'shortening' the preceding vowel can be demonstrated (e.g. b*a*by, h*a*ppy)

Pupil Book answers

Focus

A 1 rainy 2 grumpy
3 happy 4 lucky

B 1 happy 2 grumpy
3 lucky

Extra

A 1 flashy 2 windy 3 rocky
4 lucky 5 rusty 6 foggy
7 sunny 8 funny 9 spotty
10 sleepy

B Teacher to check individual answers

Extension

wave	wavy
laze	lazy
bone	bony
rose	rosy
smoke	smoky
stone	stony

Resource sheet answers

Focus

A noisy crazy sunny bossy lazy
mighty brainy chilly creamy

B brainy sunny chilly noisy
Teacher to check individual answers

Extension

A 1 foggy 2 rainy 3 funny
4 stony 5 greasy 6 easy
7 marshy 8 nutty

B 1 milk 2 chat 3 salt 4 noise
5 haze 6 luck 7 soot 8 dot

C Teacher to check individual answers

Supporting word lists

cranky flashy scratchy messy smelly
rocky frosty lucky dusty rusty rainy
brainy milky risky frilly windy chilly fussy
sleepy cheeky leafy creaky creamy
mighty croaky moody sooty salty stormy
hardy marshy dirty cloudy

dotty bossy foggy spotty chatty muddy
tubby runny funny sunny nutty furry

lazy hazy crazy wavy easy icy slimy
bony rosy smoky stony noisy greasy

nouns
daddy nanny nappy tabby granny
jelly jetty penny teddy berry cherry
dolly holly hobby lorry poppy
buggy dummy gully mummy
puppy tummy
baby lady gravy
story

other word classes
flashy scratchy lazy crazy
messy smelly pretty
silly chilly
dotty bossy foggy rocky spotty
fussy muddy funny sunny
lucky mucky dusty rusty
rainy brainy
easy leafy creaky creamy
sleepy cheeky

33

BOOK 3 UNIT 7

LEARNING TARGETS

Pupil Book: Focus
to write the plural of words by adding **s**

Pupil Book: Extra
to write the plural of words by adding **es**

Pupil Book: Extension
to write the plural of words that end in **y**;
to recognise that an alternative word is sometimes required to form the plural

Resource sheet: Focus
to make the plural of nouns that end with **s**, **x**, **sh** or **ch**

Resource sheet: Extension
to make the plural form of nouns that end with **s**, **x**, **sh**, **ch** or **y**

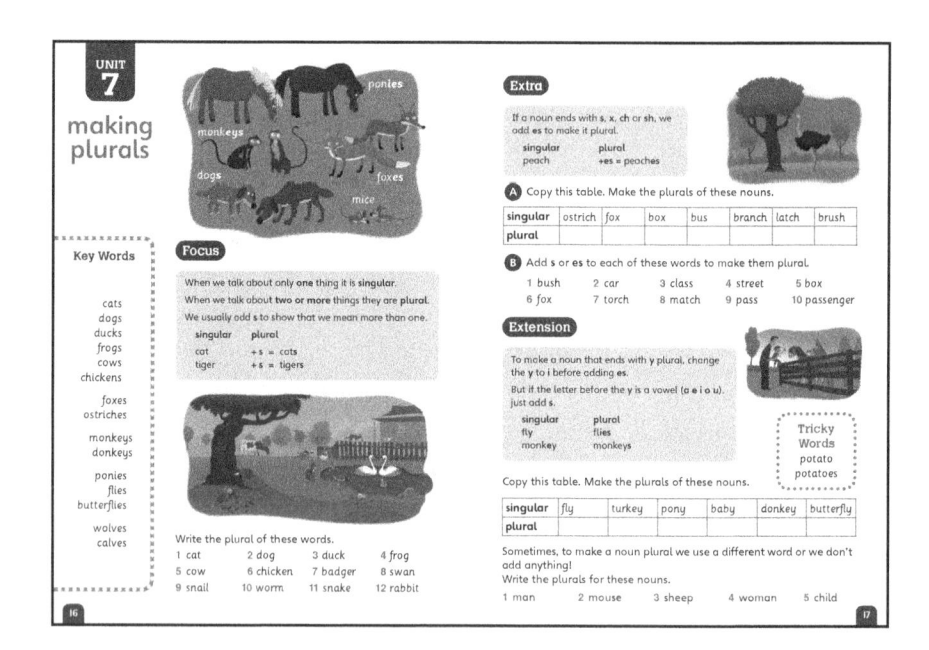

BACKGROUND NOTES AND SUGGESTIONS

The correct formulation of plurals is an important skill for spelling. Fortunately the vast majority of words conform to a few basic rules and 'sub-rules'. These are introduced here and in later units and then revised throughout the rest of the course as opportunities lend themselves.

In this unit, the rules addressed are:
- most nouns, including those that end in **e**, simply add **s**
- for words that end with **s**, **x**, **ch** or **sh** we add **es**
- words ending in **y** add **s** if the final letter is preceded by a vowel letter, but if not, change the **y** to **i** and add **es**.

In this unit, attention is given to forming the plural of a noun if the letter before the **y** is a vowel, when we just add **s**.

Pupil Book answers

Focus

A
1 cats 2 dogs 3 ducks
4 frogs 5 cows 6 chickens
7 badgers 8 swans 9 snails
10 worms 11 snakes 12 rabbits

Extra

A ostriches foxes boxes buses
branches latches brushes

B
1 bushes 2 cars 3 classes
4 streets 5 boxes 6 foxes
7 torches 8 matches 9 passes
10 passengers

Extension

A flies turkeys ponies babies
donkeys butterflies

B 1 men 2 mice 3 sheep
4 women 5 children

Resource sheet answers

Focus

A
1 goats 2 buses 3 snakes
4 lunches 5 cats 6 boxes
7 mills 8 bushes 9 snacks
10 dresses 11 bees 12 watches
13 jumpers 14 combs 15 gates
16 atlases 17 ships 18 wishes
19 streams 20 circles

Extension

butterflies boxes boys trolleys berries bushes ponies flies lorries dresses shoes ducks boats foxes lunches

Supporting word lists

Words that take s
There are a great number, including:
game table pen cup pond book school teacher

Some words that take es
ash bush glass inch watch brush dish kiss tax box grass pass bus gas sandwich fox class

Some words ending in consonant + y
army berry jelly party city penny baby fly puppy nappy cherry lorry daisy posy story fairy

Some words ending in vowel + y
donkey monkey key day display toy delay ray boy valley trolley chimney turkey journey abbey alley jockey

34

BOOK 3 — UNIT 8

LEARNING TARGETS

Pupil Book: Focus
to match key adjectives to pictures and associated activity

Pupil Book: Extra
to form comparative adjectives from words ending with **y**

Pupil Book: Extension
to form superlative adjectives from words ending with **y**

Resource sheet: Focus
to complete word fans adding the suffixes **er** and **est**

Resource sheet: Extension
to secure the spelling of words ending with **y** to which the suffixes **er** and **est** are added

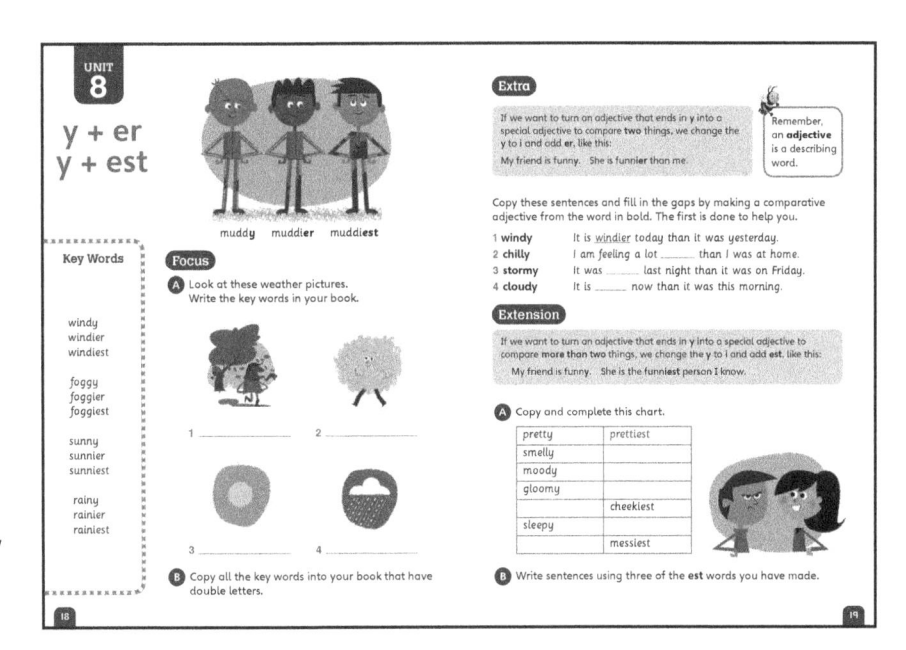

BACKGROUND NOTES AND SUGGESTIONS

For most words, when forming the comparative (**er**) or superlative (**est**) we just add the suffix (*quicker*, *quickest*). However, for most words ending in **e** we drop the **e** before adding the suffix (e.g. *later*, *latest*). For most short words containing a single short vowel before the final consonant, we double the final consonant (e.g. *bigger*, *biggest*). For words ending in **y**, we change **y** to **i** before adding the suffix (e.g. *chillier*, *chilliest*).

It will be possible to extend this work with some children by considering that there are many important exceptions when forming these comparing adjectives e.g. *good, better, best*; *far, farther, farthest*.

Also, consider what happens to such base words as *curious, sensible, intelligent* i.e. we use *more* and *most*.

Pupil Book answers

Focus
A 1 windy 2 foggy
3 sunny 4 rainy

B foggy foggier foggiest
sunny sunnier sunniest

Extra
1 windier 2 chillier
3 stormier 4 cloudier

Extension
A pretty — prettiest
smelly — smelliest
moody — moodiest
gloomy — gloomiest
cheeky — cheekiest
sleepy — sleepiest
messy — messiest

B Teacher to check individual answers

Resource sheet answers

Focus
A Children should copy the pattern
shorter
slower
taller
deeper
higher

B Children should copy the pattern
shortest
slowest
tallest
deepest
highest

Extension

small	smaller	smallest
large	larger	largest
deep	deeper	deepest
hot	hotter	hottest
clever	cleverer	cleverest
heavy	heavier	heaviest
smelly	smellier	smelliest
sleepy	sleepier	sleepiest
cloudy	cloudier	cloudiest
sunny	sunnier	sunniest
muddy	muddier	muddiest
smart	smarter	smartest
icy	icier	iciest
foggy	foggier	foggiest
tiny	tinier	tiniest
lazy	lazier	laziest

Supporting word lists
happy cranky hilly milky frilly chilly
floppy spotty fussy dusty lazy crazy rainy
sleepy easy greasy icy mighty
bony smoky stormy noisy

BOOK 3 — UNIT 9

LEARNING TARGETS

Pupil Book: Focus
to match key words with the **ing** prefix to pictures and associated activity

Pupil Book: Extra
to secure the spelling rules for adding inflectional endings to words not ending in **e**

Pupil Book: Extension
to secure the spelling rules for adding inflectional endings to words ending in **e**

Resource sheet: Focus
to double the final consonant of short words before adding **ing**

Resource sheet: Extension
to secure adding **ing** rules, particularly dropping the final **e**

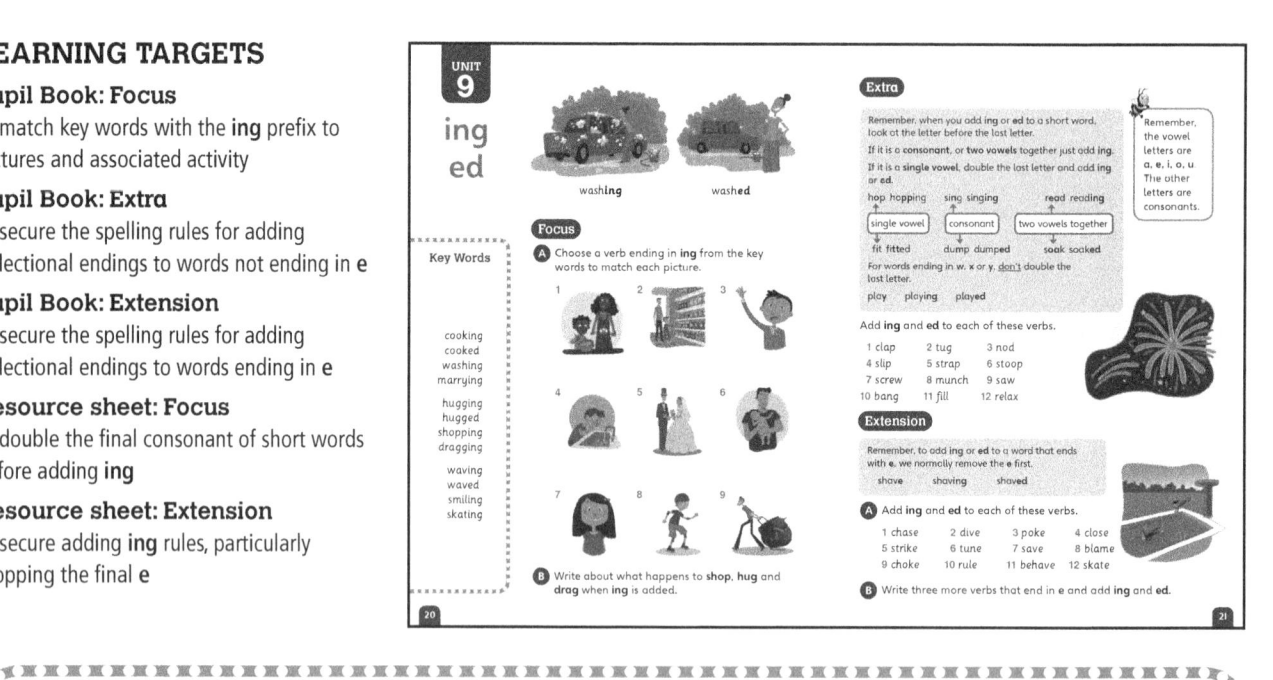

BACKGROUND NOTES AND SUGGESTIONS

Much work in the course has already been devoted to the addition of inflectional endings. This unit seeks to revise and secure these important spelling patterns and their related rules.

Remind the children of the importance of these suffixes in indicating the time or tense of a sentence. It also helps children in identifying the word class of 'verb' to realise that verbs are the words to which **ing** and **ed** can be added.

Use the opportunity whilst undertaking the work in this unit to consider verbs for which the conventional tense endings do not apply, possibly making collections in groups, e.g. **ow-ew**, **ing-ang**, **ind-ound**, **ell-old**.

Pupil Book answers

Focus

A 1 cooking 2 shopping 3 waving
4 washing 5 marrying 6 hugging
7 smiling 8 skating 9 dragging

B The final letter is doubled before **ing** is added

Extra

1 clapping clapped
2 tugging tugged
3 nodding nodded
4 slipping slipped
5 strapping strapped
6 stooping stooped
7 screwing screwed
8 munching munched
9 sawing sawed
10 banging banged
11 filling filled
12 relaxing relaxed

Extension

A 1 chasing chased
2 diving dived
3 poking poked
4 closing closed
5 striking striked
6 tuning tuned
7 saving saved
8 blaming blamed
9 choking choked
10 ruling ruled

11 behaving behaved
12 skating skated

B Teacher to check individual answers

Resource sheet answers

Focus

A 1 jumping 2 dusting
3 splashing 4 falling

Teacher to check individual answers

B 1 chopping 2 mopping
3 dripping 4 dropping
5 running 6 hopping
7 clapping 8 swimming
9 slipping 10 shopping
11 skidding 12 hugging

Extension

A 1 sitting 2 bathing
3 sleeping 4 boxing
5 selling 6 jumping
7 cutting 8 shopping
9 blowing 10 shooting
11 banging 12 singing
13 slipping 14 pressing
15 trying

B 1 waving 2 walking
3 raking 4 bouncing
5 sleeping 6 saving
7 stopping 8 skating
9 grazing 10 blaming
11 diving 12 hiking
13 sliding 14 packing
15 winning

Supporting word lists

Some words to which ing/ed can be added without modification
act acting pant panting camp camping
land landing stand standing
help helping melt melting bend bending
mend mending send sending
milk milking film filming lift lifting
limp limping list listing
sulk sulking hunt hunting
bump bumping dump dumping
jump jumping dust dusting rust rusting
grunt grunting

Some words to which ing/ed can be added after doubling the final consonant
bat batting fan fanning pat patting
tap tapping wag wagging clap clapping
flap flapping plan planning slap slapping
grab grabbing get getting let letting
peg pegging set setting wed wedding
dig digging fit fitting hit hitting
rip ripping sip sipping sit sitting
tip tipping win winning clip clipping
flip flipping slip slipping drip dripping
grin grinning trim trimming trip tripping
swim swimming hop hopping
jog jogging mop mopping nod nodding
rob robbing sob sobbing blot blotting
lop flopping plot plotting slot slotting
drop dropping trot trotting but butting
cut cutting hug hugging rub rubbing
run running plug plugging
drum drumming

BOOK 3 — UNIT 10

LEARNING TARGETS

Pupil Book: Focus
to identify and copy target 'soft' **g** words from a picture;
to complete a simple puzzle using target key words

Pupil Book: Extra
to secure the rule for adding inflectional endings to words ending with **e**

Pupil Book: Extension
to teach about word definitions in the context of words with the **nge** letter pattern

Resource sheet: Focus
to complete a **dge** word words fan and match words to picture clues

Resource sheet: Extension
to complete words and definitions based on target rhymes

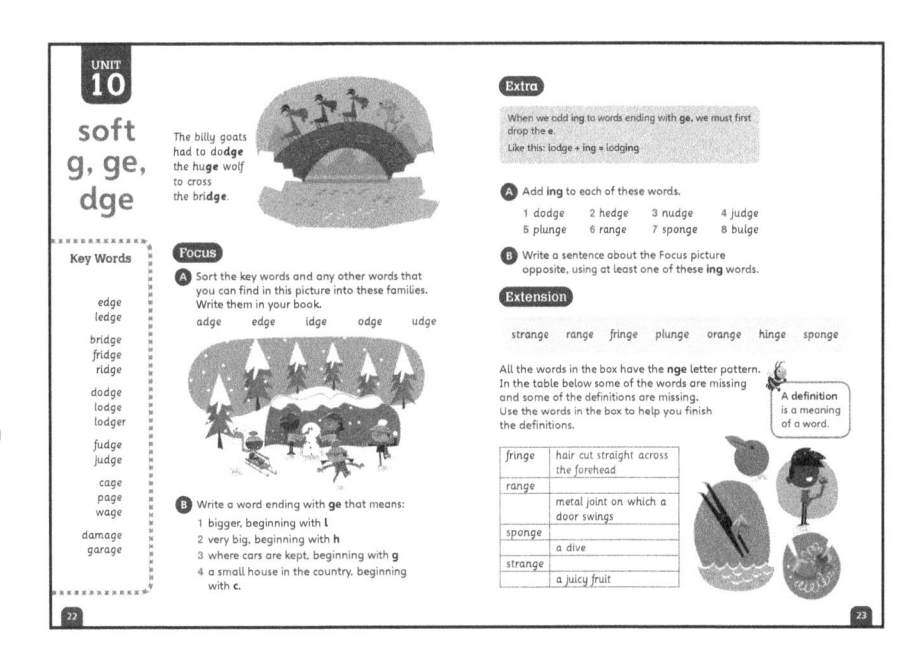

UNIT 10 — soft g, ge, dge

The billy goats had to do**dge** the hu**ge** wolf to cross the bri**dge**.

Key Words
edge
ledge
bridge
fridge
ridge
dodge
lodge
lodger
fudge
judge
cage
page
wage
damage
garage

Focus

A. Sort the key words and any other words that you can find in this picture into these families. Write them in your book.
adge   edge   idge   odge   udge

B. Write a word ending with **ge** that means:
1 bigger, beginning with **l**
2 very big, beginning with **h**
3 where cars are kept, beginning with **g**
4 a small house in the country, beginning with **c**.

Extra

When we add **ing** to words ending with **ge**, we must first drop the **e**.
Like this: lodge + ing = lodging

A. Add **ing** to each of these words.
1 dodge   2 hedge   3 nudge   4 judge
5 plunge   6 range   7 sponge   8 bulge

B. Write a sentence about the Focus picture opposite, using at least one of these **ing** words.

Extension

strange   range   fringe   plunge   orange   hinge   sponge

All the words in the box have the **nge** letter pattern. In the table below some of the words are missing and some of the definitions are missing. Use the words in the box to help you finish the definitions.

A definition is a meaning of a word.

fringe	hair cut straight across the forehead
range	
	metal joint on which a door swings
sponge	
	a dive
strange	
	a juicy fruit

BACKGROUND NOTES AND SUGGESTIONS

The letter **j** is never used at the end of English words – the sound is represented by **dge** or **ge**.

Although not usually classed as such, it can be helpful for children to think of the **d** in **dge** pattern words as 'silent'. Thus revision of true silent-letter words can usefully be carried out as an extension of this unit.

Elsewhere in words, the /j/ sound is usually spelt as **g** when it comes before **e**, **i** or **y** e.g. *gem, giant, energy*.

It is helpful to share with the children the parallels when considering 'soft' **g** words, the 'soft' **c** words. (See Pupil Book 3, Unit 3)

Pupil Book answers

Focus

A. edge   hedge   ridge   dodge   sledge

B. 1 larger   2 huge
   3 garage   4 cottage

Extra

A. 1 dodging   2 hedging   3 nudging
   4 judging   5 plunging   6 ranging
   7 sponging   8 bulging

B. Teacher to check individual answers

Extension

fringe
range
hinge
sponge
plunge
strange
orange

Teacher to check individual answers for definitions

Resource sheet answers

Focus

A. fudge   hedge   fridge   bridge   sludge
   sledge   dodge   judge   edge

B. judge   fudge   hedge   bridge

C. Teacher to check individual answers

Extension

A.
misjudge	judge wrongly
ridge	a long hill or mountain
villagers	people who live in a village
dislodged	removed from a fixed position
edge	rim or border
garage	a building where cars are kept or repaired
manager	a person in charge of others
bridge	structure allowing access over an obstacle
voyage	a long journey by ship
dodge	jump aside quickly

B. 1 hedge   2 rage
   3 lodge   4 fudge
   5 sledge   6 acknowledge

Teacher to check individual sentences

Supporting word lists

badge badger cadge cadger gadget
edge edger hedge ledge ledger wedge
midge midget bridge porridge
dodge lodge lodger
fudge judge nudge grudge trudge budget

final ge (without silent d)
age cage page rage sage wage
cabbage damage garage garbage
package advantage
huge bulge

BOOK 3 — UNIT 11

LEARNING TARGETS

Pupil Book: Focus
to identify **wa** and **qua** key words from a picture;
to introduce the **swa** letter pattern

Pupil Book: Extra
to use rhyming words to secure the **wa** phoneme/grapheme relationship

Pupil Book: Extension
to secure singular possessive forms in the context of **wa** words

Resource sheet: Focus
to match words to picture clues;
to find key words in a wordsearch

Resource sheet: Extension
to complete words with the **wa** and **swa** word patterns;
to answer and make clues with **wa** and **swa** words

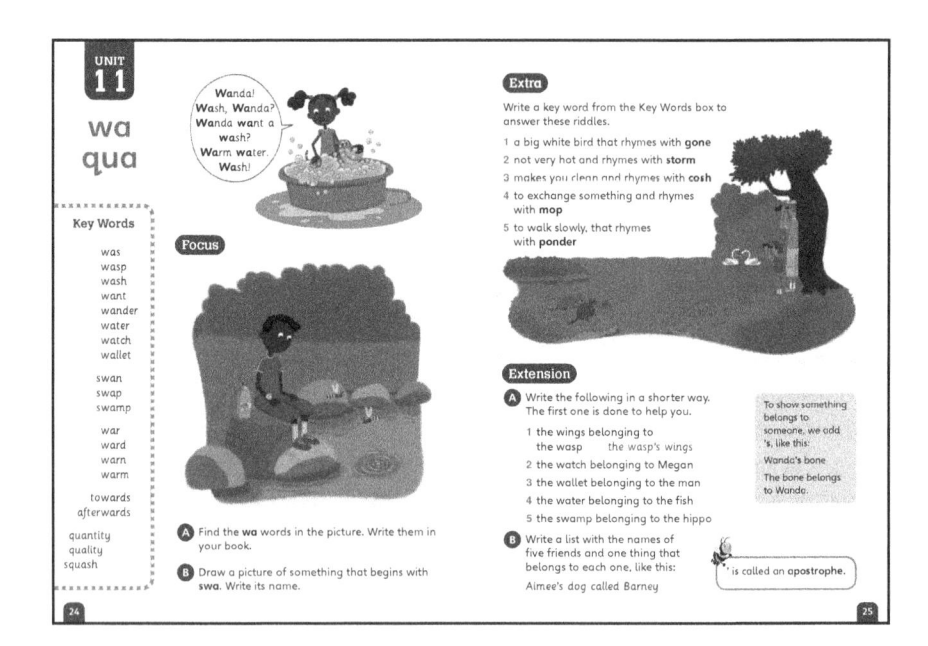

BACKGROUND NOTES AND SUGGESTIONS

Four very high frequency words (*was, wasn't, want, water*) make this one of the more significant 'irregular' letter patterns.

The singular possessive apostrophe is introduced in the Pupil Book Extension section.

Pupil Book answers

Focus

A wasp water watch

B Teacher to check individual answers

Extra
1 swan
2 warm
3 wash
4 swap
5 wander

Extension

A 1 the wasp's wings
2 Megan's watch
3 the man's wallet
4 the fish's water
5 the hippo's swamp

B Teacher to check individual answers

Resource sheet answers

Focus

A 1 swan   2 water   3 swamp
4 wasp   5 warm   6 wallet
7 wash   8 watch

B water warm swap swamp swan wander

Extension

A swamp watch watch wash towards warm swan wasp swap was afterwards warn wander wallet

B 1 swamp   2 wander   3 afterwards
4 wallet   5 wash   6 warm

C Teacher to check individual answers

Supporting word lists

was wasn't wasp wallet wand want
wash watch water
war ward warden warm warn
swan swap swamp swab swat
quantity quality qualify quarter squash

BOOK 3 — UNIT 12

LEARNING TARGETS

Pupil Book: Focus
to match key words to pictures

Pupil Book: Extra
to complete a cloze activity using **tion** words

Pupil Book: Extension
to find **tion** family words

Resource sheet: Focus
to complete a word fan and match target words to pictures

Resource sheet: Extension
to complete words with given letter patterns and use words in sentences

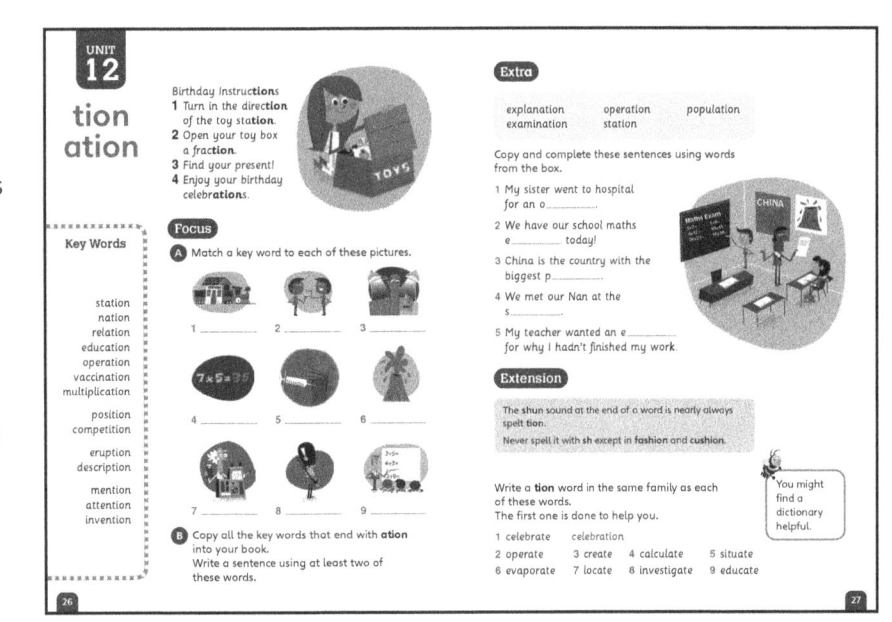

BACKGROUND NOTES AND SUGGESTIONS

As with the **sion** pattern words (Unit 13), many of these can be difficult to learn, but working on the words in groups as shown in the Supporting word lists can ease some difficulties. It is helpful that there are several significant spelling pattern 'sub-families' in the **tion** family.

Note that **tion** words tend to be more common than **sion** words and are most commonly preceded by an **a**.

Pupil Book answers

Focus

A
1 station
2 relation
3 operation
4 multiplication
5 vaccination
6 eruption
7 invention
8 attention
9 education

B station nation relation education operation vaccination multiplication
Teacher to check individual answers

Extra
1 operation
2 examination
3 population
4 station
5 explanation

Extension
1 celebration
2 operation
3 creation
4 calculation
5 situation
6 evaporation
7 location
8 investigation
9 education

Resource sheet answers

Focus

A Children to trace and copy the pattern.

B station eruption position invention description relation education attention vaccination

C eruption relation education vaccination

Extension

A relation   position   potion
occupation   addition   motion
multiplication   condition   promotion

B relation potion occupation motion

C Teacher to check individual answers

Supporting word lists

ation
nation station ration
location relation vacation
celebration conservation
conversation education explanation
occupation operation population
situation vaccination examination
investigation multiplication

ition
ambition condition edition ignition
position addition tuition
ammunition competition recognition
repetition expedition

otion
lotion potion devotion
motion emotion
promotion commotion

etion
completion deletion discretion

ption
eruption disruption deception
reception caption option
description

ction
action faction fraction traction
attraction extraction subtraction
section connection direction
election infection objection
selection fiction friction distinction
suction instruction
function junction

ntion
mention attention detention
intention invention

BOOK 3 — UNIT 13

LEARNING TARGETS

Pupil Book: Focus
to match key words to pictures

Pupil Book: Extra
to find rhyming target words and to use them in contexts

Pupil Book: Extension
to match words and definitions

Resource sheet: Focus
to complete a word fan and match target words to pictures

Resource sheet: Extension
to complete words with given letter patterns and use words in sentences

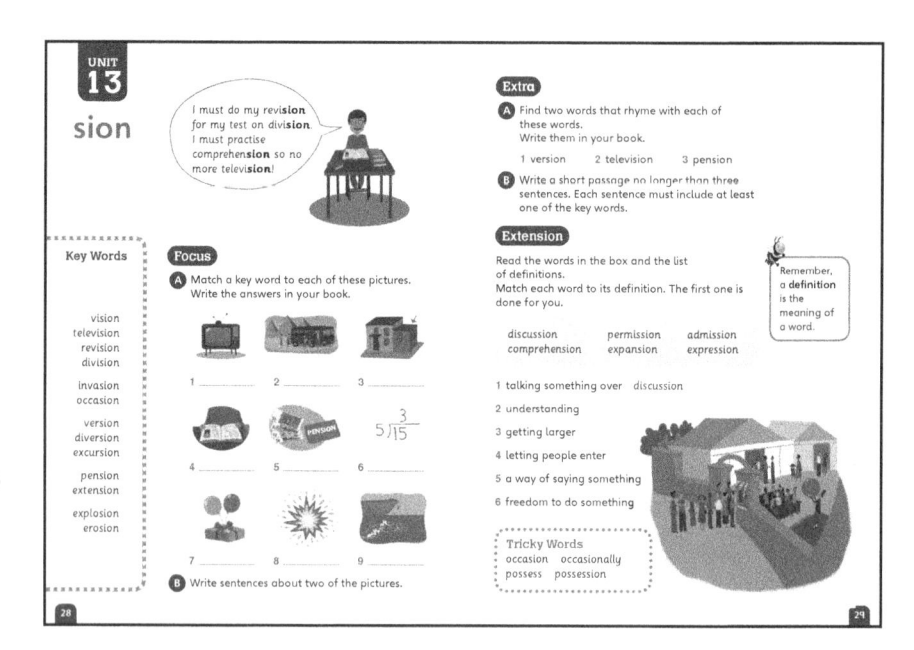

BACKGROUND NOTES AND SUGGESTIONS

As with the **tion** in the previous unit, many of these words can prove difficult to learn for some children, but working on the words in groups as shown in the *Supporting word lists* can ease some difficulties.

Note that **tion** words (see Unit 12) tend to be more common than **sion** words, which are often formed from verbs ending in **d** or **de**, e.g. *collide/collision, divide/division*.

Pupil Book answers

Focus

A 1 television   2 excursion
   3 extension   4 revision
   5 pension   6 division
   7 occasion   8 explosion
   9 erosion

B Teacher to check individual answers

Extra

A/B Teacher to check individual answers

Extension
1 discussion   2 comprehension
3 expansion   4 admission
5 expression   6 permission

Resource sheet answers

Focus

A Children to copy the pattern

B television explosion invasion division
   revision vision extension occasion
   erosion

C division television extension vision

Extension

A session   mission   concussion
   expression admission   discussion
   procession permission percussion

B percussion admission
   procession discussion

C Teacher to check individual answers

Supporting word lists

usion
fusion transfusion confusion
conclusion exclusion inclusion
delusion illusion disillusion

ision
vision television provision
supervision revision division
decision incision precision collision

asion
invasion occasion persuasion

osion
explosion erosion corrosion

ersion
version conversion diversion
immersion

ension
pension suspension tension
extension dimension
comprehension

ansion
mansion expansion

ession
session aggression compression
depression impression progression
expression oppression suppression
obsession possession
recession concession succession
procession profession confession

ission
mission admission commission
omission permission submission
transmission intermission

ussion
concussion discussion percussion

assion
passion compassion

BOOK 3 — UNIT 14

LEARNING TARGETS

Pupil Book: Focus
to match key words to pictures;
to add the suffixes **ful**, **ness** and **ment** as appropriate

Pupil Book: Extra
to secure the rule to change **y** to **i** before adding suffixes to certain words

Pupil Book: Extension
to introduce a selection of other suffixes

Resource sheet: Focus
to make and use new words by adding target suffixes

Resource sheet: Extension
to practise syllabification of words

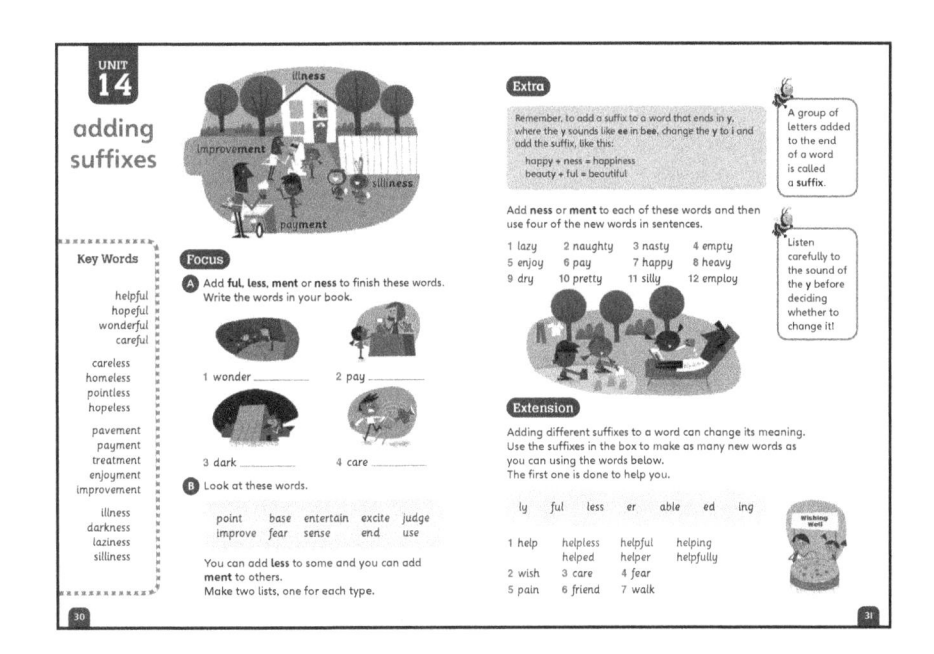

BACKGROUND NOTES AND SUGGESTIONS

Developing an awareness and understanding of the meaning of suffixes can be a significant aid to good spelling:
- **ful** means 'full of'
- **less** means 'without'
- **ment** means 'condition of'
- **ness** means 'state of'.

Although these might sound sophisticated, children can enjoy getting to grips with these ideas when comparing the root word with the word after the suffix is added.

All the suffixes that are practised in this unit are common and frequently used in the writing of children of this age. The work might be introduced by writing words on the board from the same family, each containing one of the suffixes, e.g. *careless, careful*.

It is important to teach that these particular suffixes are 'consonant' suffixes (i.e. the first letter of each is a consonant) and thus follow the rule that whilst they can be added to most words without adaptation, if the root word ends in **y** (and sounds like **ee**), it must be changed to **i**.

Note that **ly** is often, though by no means always, used in conjunction with **ful**.

Also note that if the word ends in **n**, add **ness** not **ess**, and if the word has a modifier ('magic') **e**, don't drop it before adding the suffix (e.g. improv**e**ment).

Pupil Book answers

Focus
A
1 wonderful   2 payment
3 darkness   4 careless

B
pointless   excitement
useless   entertainment
endless   basement
senseless   improvement
fearless   judgement

Extra
1 laziness   2 naughtiness
3 nastiness   4 emptiness
5 enjoyment   6 payment
7 happiness   8 heaviness
9 dryness   10 prettiness
11 silliness   12 employment

Teacher to check individual sentences

Extension
1 helpless   helpful   helping
   helped   helpfully
2 wishful   wished   wishing
   wishfully
3 careless   careful   carer
   cared   caring   carefully
4 fearful   fearless   feared
   fearing
5 painful   painless   pained
   painfully
6 friendly   friendless
7 walker   walked   walking

BOOK 3

Resource sheet answers

Focus

A
illness	payment
darkness	agreement
fitness	enjoyment
weakness	treatment
likeness	punishment

B treatment
illness
agreement

C Teacher to check individual answers

Extension

A 1 fi<u>t</u>ness   2 ugli<u>n</u>ess
3 de<u>p</u>artment   4 ca<u>r</u>eful
5 ma<u>n</u>agement   6 la<u>z</u>iness
7 a<u>ss</u>ignment   8 a<u>rr</u>angement

B 1 gov/ern/ment   2 a/muse/ment
3 ex/cite/ment   4 es/tab/lish/ment
5 nast/i/ness   6 hea/vi/ness
7 hap/pi/ness   8 dis/cour/age/ment
9 won/der/ful   10 pur/pose/ful
11 par/lia/ment   12 en/ter/tain/ment
13 mon/u/ment   14 mon/u/men/tal

Supporting word lists

careful dreadful faithful grateful
helpful thoughtful sorrowful wonderful
plentiful beautiful dutiful
fanciful merciful

helpless hopeless pointless senseless
useless careless thoughtless
homeless lifeless fearless jobless thankless
headless speechless
endless merciless

darkness illness weakness greyness
greenness meanness likeness soreness
laziness ugliness nastiness happiness
emptiness heaviness business dryness

attachment agreement payment enjoyment
entertainment treatment
improvement statement basement
pavement involvement excitement
encouragement advertisement judgement
arrangement replacement argument

Some other ment words
fragment cement implement monument
department ornament parliament

Check-Up 1

Focus

1 spots	2 bridge	3 cage	4 cellar
5 lamb	6 knot	7 candle	8 camel
9 cows	10 foxes	11 monkeys	12 hospital
13 watch	14 swan	15 station	16 television

Extension

A 1 windy   2 lucky   3 sunny   4 foggy   5 wavy   6 smoky

B 1 cows   2 chickens   3 badgers   4 swans
5 boxes   6 classes   7 torches   8 brushes
9 ponies   10 babies   11 monkeys   12 donkeys

C 1 warmer warmest   2 cloudier cloudiest   3 foggier foggiest   4 mistier mistiest

D 1 excitement   2 senseless   3 wonderful   4 darkness

E 1 laziness   2 happiness   3 silliness   4 naughtiness

42

BOOK 3 UNIT 15

LEARNING TARGETS

Pupil Book: Focus
to explore simple contractions

Pupil Book: Extra
to introduce the problem of homophones associated with abbreviations

Pupil Book: Extension
to use contractions in sentences

Resource sheet: Focus
to make simple contractions;
to 'explode' simple contractions

Resource sheet: Extension
to make and use contractions

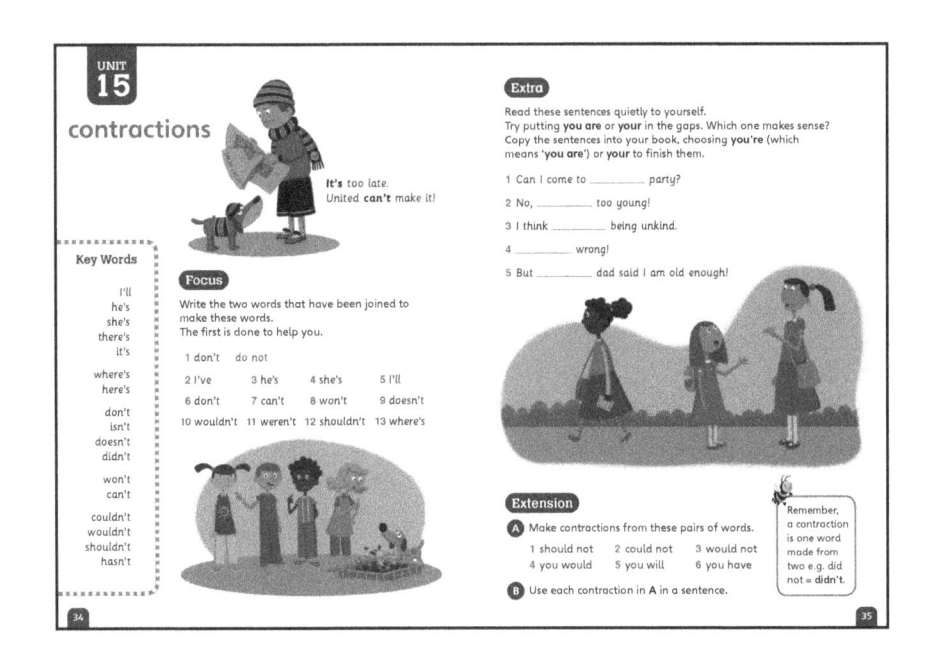

BACKGROUND NOTES AND SUGGESTIONS

The most important point for children to appreciate is that when writing abbreviations, the apostrophe should be placed exactly where the letter or letters have been omitted. There are a few circumstances where this is not quite straightforward (e.g. *shan't*, where letters have been omitted in more than one position i.e. *shall not*).

Another point to teach is that our language has evolved to create a few contraction spellings that are at variance with the words apparently contracted (e.g. *won't*, the contraction of *will not*).

In the context of the Pupil Book Extra activity, draw the children's attention to the homophone issue in other words (*its/it's*, and *theirs/there's*).

Pupil Book answers

Focus
1. do not
2. I have
3. he is
4. she is
5. I will
6. do not
7. cannot*
8. will not
9. does not
10. would not
11. were not
12. should not
13. where is

*'cannot' is a special case as it is a compound word. This may need further explanation.

Extra
1. your
2. you're
3. you're
4. You're
5. your

Extension
A
1. shouldn't
2. couldn't
3. wouldn't
4. you'd
5. you'll
6. you've

B Teacher to check individual answers

Resource sheet answers

Focus
A
1. I'll
2. won't
3. they've
4. I've
5. she's
6. there's
7. couldn't
8. he'll

B
1. I <u>won't</u> see you tomorrow. will not
2. <u>We've</u> got to leave early. We have
3. It is a shame I <u>couldn't</u> come. could not
4. <u>There's</u> a chance we might be back early. There is

Extension
A
1. she'll
2. they've
3. won't
4. that's
5. could've
6. there's
7. wouldn't
8. I'll

B Teacher to check individual answers

C Teacher to check individual answers

Supporting word lists

I'm I'll I've I'd
he's she's it's there's that's
you're we're they're
you've we've they've
you'd he'd she'd we'd they'd
don't can't isn't doesn't won't aren't
shan't
haven't couldn't wouldn't shouldn't
wasn't weren't
o'clock pick 'n' mix ma'am

BOOK 3 — UNIT 16

LEARNING TARGETS

Pupil Book: Focus
to match words to picture clues

Pupil Book: Extra
to use some less frequent homophones

Pupil Book: Extension
to suggest how mnemonics can be used to support decisions on homophone use

Resource sheet: Focus
to match appropriate homophones to pictures

Resource sheet: Extension
to select and use correct homophones

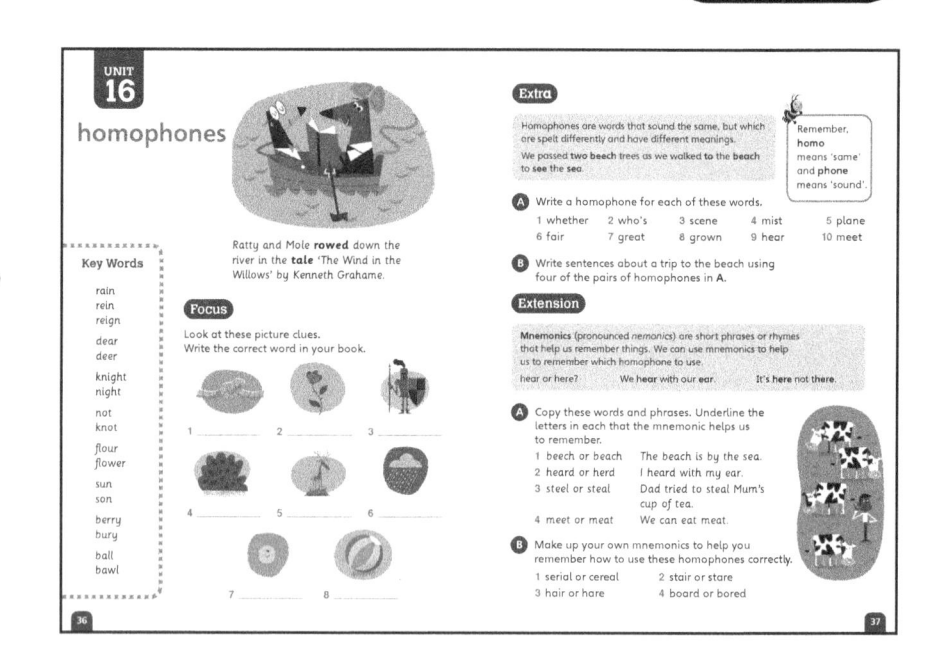

BACKGROUND NOTES AND SUGGESTIONS

Homophones are words with the same (*homo*) sound (*phone*) but different spelling and meanings whereas homonyms have the same sound and spelling but different meanings.

In this unit we develop and extend earlier work on homophones, moving on from words which are high-frequency in children's writing to those which are less often used but still cause problems from time to time. Reports on children's performance have suggested that children should learn to spell words where there are different ways of representing vowel diagraphs, such as *brake* and *break*, which covers most homophones.

Pupil Book answers

Focus
1 knot 2 flower 3 knight
4 berry 5 deer 6 rain
7 sun 8 ball

Extra
A
1 weather 2 whose 3 seen
4 missed 5 plain 6 fare
7 grate 8 groan 9 here
10 meat

B Teacher to check individual answers

Extension
A 1 b<u>e</u>ach 2 <u>heard</u> 3 <u>steal</u> 4 m<u>eat</u>

B Teacher to check individual answers

Resource sheet answers

Focus
A berry knot ball flower tail beach

B Teacher to check individual answers

Extension
A
1 cheap 2 brake 3 flour
4 great 5 herd 6 knight
7 would 8 plane 9 peace
10 mane

B Teacher to check individual answers

Supporting word lists

Some of these are not strictly homophones, but are 'near homophones' and are being included because in some regions they can sound very similar and cause confusion.

were we're
where wear
there their they're
you yew ewe
to two too
be bee
new knew
right write
through threw
hole whole
are our
see sea
no know
morning mourning
great grate
I eye
in inn
heard herd
might mite
place plaice
eyes ice
for four
of off

BOOK 3 — UNIT 17

LEARNING TARGETS

Pupil Book: Focus
to match key words to pictures

Pupil Book: Extra
to introduce the idea that some words with silent letters are derived from other languages

Pupil Book: Extension
to secure the concept of word definitions, in the context of silent letters

Resource sheet: Focus
to be aware that silent letters are often accompanied by the same letters

Resource sheet: Extension
to identify and correct misspellings involving silent letters

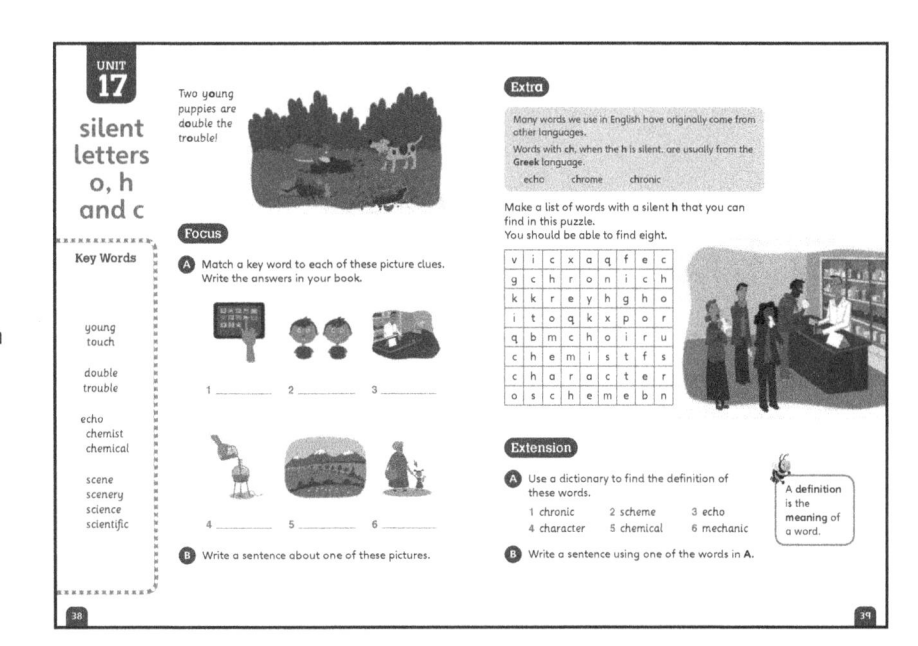

BACKGROUND NOTES AND SUGGESTIONS

The children will be intrigued to realise that many silent letters were, in days gone by, pronounced, but due to fashion and the general evolution of language, they have become silent.

This unit follows from Book 2, Unit 22 to focus on **o**, **h** and **c**. Other silent letters will be dealt with later as they are a persistent and ever-present difficulty for children learning to spell accurately. But any silent letters can be introduced at any stage, so activities developed from this unit might usefully also introduce other silent letters.

As has been suggested previously, many vowel letters are not sounded individually and teachers may choose to teach them as silent (e.g. **a** in *head*; **e** in *gone*), though the term is conventionally reserved for consonant letters. However, if identified in the Pupil Book Extension resource, these should be allowed as correct.

Related to silent letters are the unstressed letters, especially vowels, and these are covered in depth as the course progresses.
There are some specific patterns to explore with the children in this unit, including:
- silent **h** is often preceded by **c**
- silent **c** is often associated with an **s**.

It is interesting to ask the children to spot other silent letter associations (e.g. **wh mb gn mn st**)

Pupil Book answers

Focus

A 1 touch 2 double 3 chemist
   4 science 5 scenery 6 young

B Teacher to check individual answers

Extra
chronic chrome echo chemist character chorus choir scheme

Extension

A / **B** Teacher to check individual answers

Resource sheet answers

Focus

A echo   scene
   character   science
   chemist   scenery
   chemical   scent
   chaos   scientific

B s_c_ene s_c_ience s_c_enery
   s_c_ientific s_c_ent

Children to write a sentence commenting on silent **c** always preceded by **s**

C e_ch_o _ch_aos _ch_aracter
   _ch_emist _ch_emical

Children to write a sentence commenting on silent **h** always preceded by **c**

Extension

A 1 write   2 double   3 science
   4 echo   5 knife   6 knock
   7 crumb   8 touch   9 scene
   10 trouble 11 wrist   12 climber
   13 young   14 knight 15 wrap
   16 rhino

B honestly science thumbnail wriggle – need to be written correctly

C 1 ex_h_ibition 2 num_b_
   3 you_n_ger 4 s_c_enery

Teacher to check individual answers

Supporting word lists

abscess ascend
conscience conscious crescent
descend disciple
fascinate
muscle scene scent scissors

double trouble colonel

ache anchor architect
chaos character chemical choir
chord chorus
echo
loch
mechanic monarch
orchestra orchid
scheme school stomach
technical

45

BOOK 3 — UNIT 18

LEARNING TARGETS

Pupil Book: Focus
to match key words to pictures;
to practise further homophones

Pupil Book: Extra
to find key words as answers to a quiz

Pupil Book: Extension
to encourage the use of dictionaries and
secure the concept of word definitions

Resource sheet: Focus
to match key words to pictures;
to write key words in sentences

Resource sheet: Extension
to become more familiar with target words
through a number of different exercises

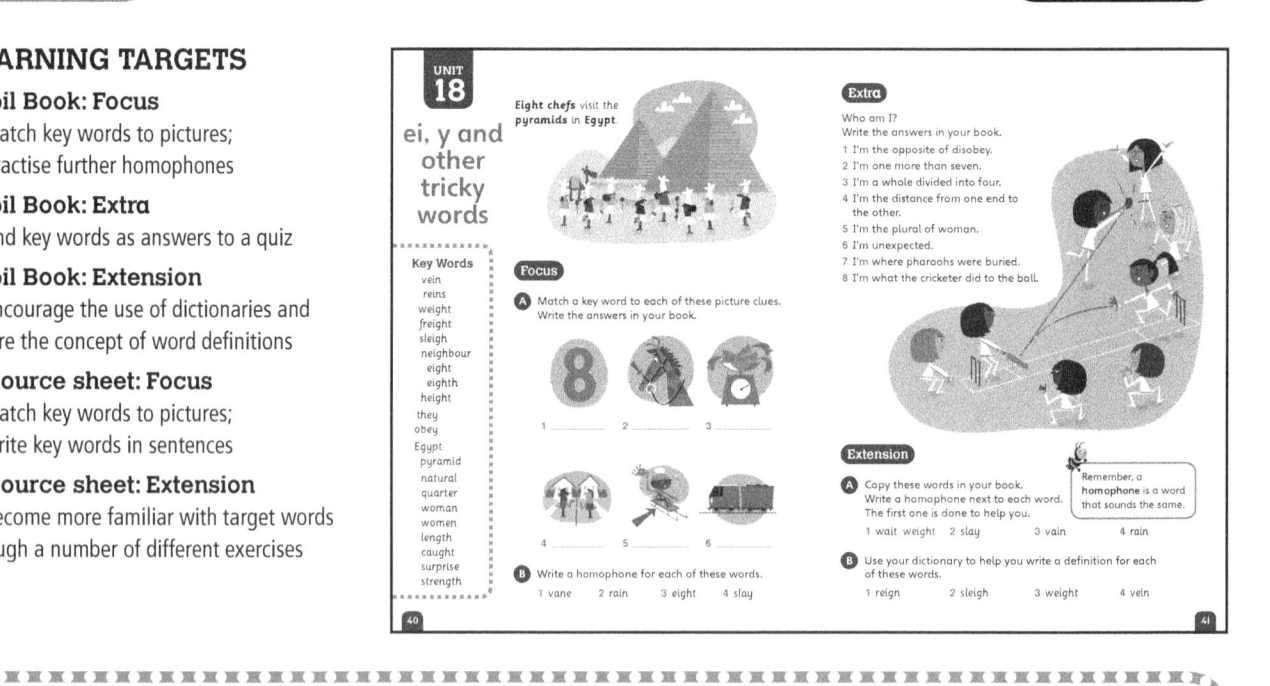

BACKGROUND NOTES AND SUGGESTIONS

From time to time throughout the course, units will be devoted to 'tricky' words. Whilst most difficult words have been integrated into the core units, some are better dealt with separately and these are grouped in units such as this.

This will be a sensible time to encourage the use of reference tools such as spell checkers or dictionaries. However, entering a few letters might lead to being offered the wrong words. Discuss how more than one attempt is often required and that the child shouldn't, uncritically, simply use the first word suggested.

Pupil Book answers

Focus
A
1 eight   2 reins   3 weight
4 neighbour   5 sleigh   6 freight

B
1 vain   2 rein
3 ate   4 sleigh

Extra
1 obey   2 eight   3 quarter
4 length   5 women   6 surprise
7 pyramid   8 caught

Extension
A
1 weight   2 sleigh
3 vein   4 reign

B Teacher to check individual answers

Resource sheet answers

Focus
A
1 surprise   2 caught   3 strength
4 woman   5 Egypt   6 eighth
7 quarter   8 obey

B Teacher to check individual answers

Extension
A
1 address   2 finish   3 koala
4 chimney   5 calendar   6 friend

B Teacher to check individual answers

C Teacher to check individual answers

Supporting word lists

ie

as in bee
niece piece siege
brief grief frieze
shield chief thief shriek
belief believe relief relieve yield
handkerchief mischief medieval obedient
glacier

as in hen
friend patient ancient

as in high
lie die pie tie
fiery quiet science

as in ear
pierce fierce pier

as in few
view review interview

ei

as in tree (cei words)
receive receipt deceive ceiling
perceive conceit

as in cape
rein veil vein feint
reign beige
neigh weigh eight weight
sleigh freight
eighty eighteen eightieth
neighbour sovereign foreign

as in kite
height
either neither
eiderdown

others
their leisure weird protein heir
sovereign foreign

BOOK 3

UNIT 19

LEARNING TARGETS

Pupil Book: Focus
to complete a cloze activity using the target words

Pupil Book: Extra
to match nouns and adjectives with a common root

Pupil Book: Extension
to recognise and practise words in which the **ous** suffix is preceded by either **i** or **e**

Resource sheet: Focus
to complete a word fan;
to match target words to pictures

Resource sheet: Extension
to complete words with given letter patterns;
to use words in sentences

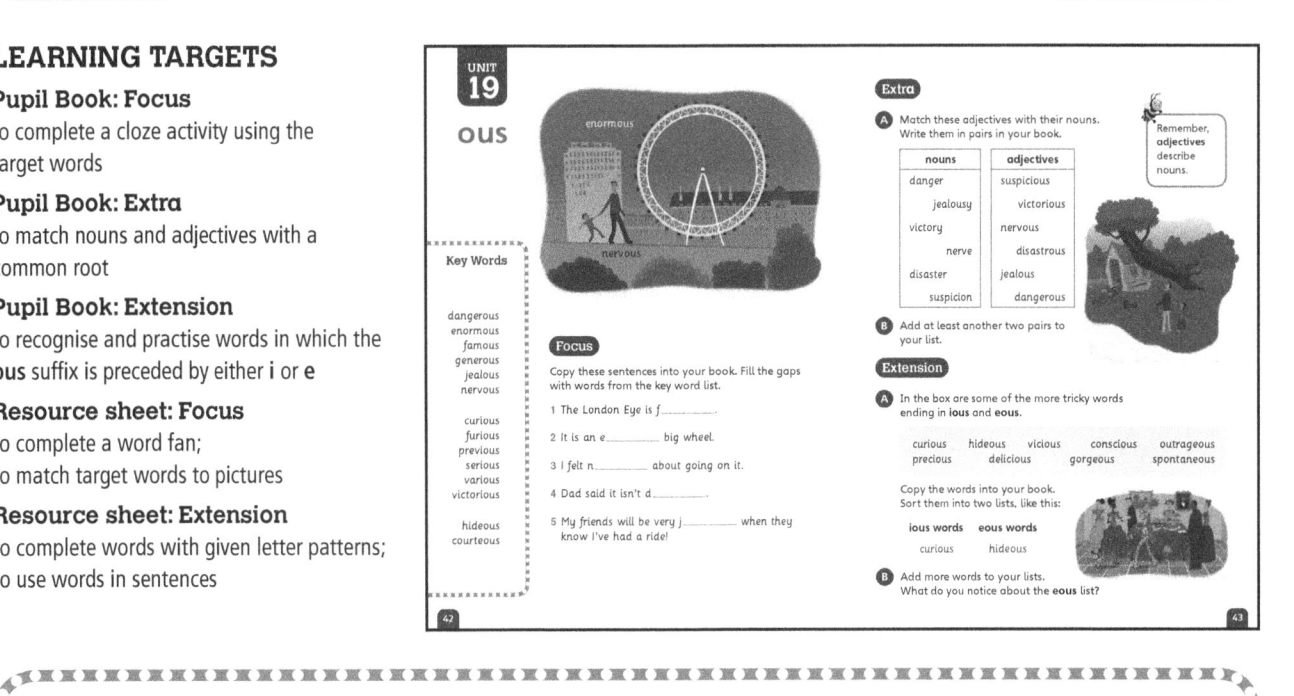

BACKGROUND NOTES AND SUGGESTIONS

The key to this spelling pattern is knowing when to include the **i** and when to omit it. The grouping in the *Supporting word lists* may help. Sometimes it is sounded - if so include it (e.g. *various*); but there are other important words where it is silent and these need to be learnt, though in some cases it helps to think whether related words would have an **i** (e.g. *anxious, anxiety*), and it should always be used between a **c** and **ous** (e.g. *gracious, precious*).

Remember also that the medial **e** in *outrageous* and *courageous* is necessary for the central **age** phoneme.

Pupil Book answers

Focus
1 famous 2 enormous 3 nervous
4 dangerous 5 jealous

Extra
A
danger	dangerous
jealousy	jealous
victory	victorious
nerve	nervous
disaster	disaterous
suspicion	suspicious

B Teacher to check individual answers

Extension
A ious: curious vicious conscious
precious delicious
eous: hideous outrageous gorgeous
spontaneous

B Teacher to check individual answers

Resource sheet answers

Focus
A Children should copy the pattern

B famous dangerous nervous
various hideous generous jealous
courteous victorious

C nervous generous
dangerous victorious

Extension
A famous various outrageous
generous serious courageous
marvellous suspicious hideous

B famous marvellous suspicious
courageous serious

C Teacher to check individual answers

Supporting word lists

famous nervous jealous enormous
generous dangerous prosperous
marvellous ridiculous glamorous
numerous tremendous

outrageous courageous

various curious furious previous serious
victorious glorious suspicious
anxious cautious gracious
malicious precious

BOOK 3 — UNIT 20

LEARNING TARGETS

Pupil Book: Focus
to match key words to pictures

Pupil Book: Extra
to reinforce the rule that prefixes are added without amending the root word, even if this results in double letters

Pupil Book: Extension
to use a dictionary to find other words with the target prefixes

Resource sheet: Focus
to add the prefix to words

Resource sheet: Extension
to identify words that begin with each of the prefixes **mis**, **dis**, **in** and **im** in a wordsearch

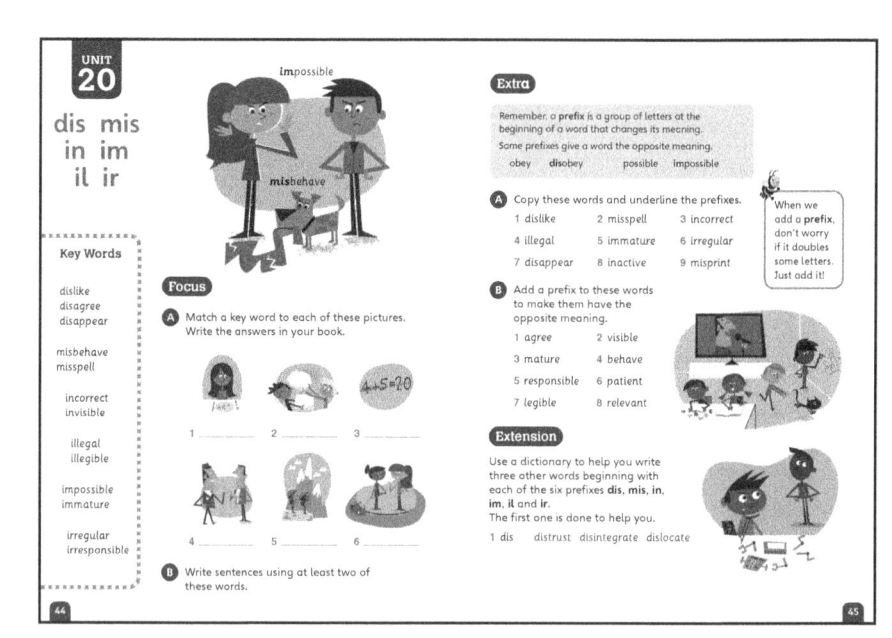

BACKGROUND NOTES AND SUGGESTIONS

This unit revisits the use of prefixes introduced in Book 2 Unit 15.

The general rule with prefixes is that they are added without the need for any adjustment to the spelling.

Prefixes are used to amend or change the meaning of a word and are important components in building words and ensuring good spelling. This particular group of prefixes form the antonym of root words to which they are attached.

Suffixes are developed further in several later units of the course.

Pupil Book answers

Focus
A
1. dislike
2. misbehave
3. incorrect
4. illegal
5. impossible
6. irresponsible

B Teacher to check individual answers

Extra
A
1. <u>dis</u>like
2. <u>mis</u>spell
3. <u>in</u>correct
4. <u>il</u>legal
5. <u>im</u>mature
6. <u>ir</u>regular
7. <u>dis</u>appear
8. <u>in</u>active
9. <u>mis</u>print

B
1. disagree
2. invisible
3. immature
4. misbehave
5. irresponsible
6. impatient
7. illegible
8. irrelevant

Extension
Teacher to check individual answers

Resource sheet answers

Focus
A Children should copy the patterns

B misplace misbehave
misjudge misread

C misplace misread misbehave

Extension
A
misbehave   disagree
misspell   dislike
misread   disobey
misplace   disbelieve
inability   imperfect
incomplete   important
inactive   impossible
invisible   impolite

B Teacher to check individual answers

Supporting word lists

negative prefix forms

disable disadvantage disagree disappear
disapprove discharge discolour disconnect
discourage dishonest dislike dislodge
disloyal disobey displease disprove
disqualify disregard distrust

negative 'sense'

discriminate disaster disease dismal
distress disturb disgust dismiss

inconvenient incomplete independent
inequality infrequent invalid insufficient
insensitive incorrect inadequate
incapable inoffensive

impossible improbable imperfect
impassable
impertinent impatient immature

illegible illiterate illegal

irrelevant irrational irregular irreplaceable

misbehave miscalculate miscall
mischance misclassify misconceive
misconduct
misdirect misfit misfortune misfunction
misguided
misjudge mislead mismatch misplace
misprint
misquote misspell mistrust

BOOK 3 UNIT 21

LEARNING TARGETS

Pupil Book: Focus
to match key words to pictures

Pupil Book: Extra
to reinforce the rule that prefixes are added without amending the root word, even if this results in double letters

Pupil Book: Extension
to use a dictionary to find other words with the target prefixes

Resource sheet: Focus
to add the prefix **un** to words

Resource sheet: Extension
to find target words in a wordsearch puzzle

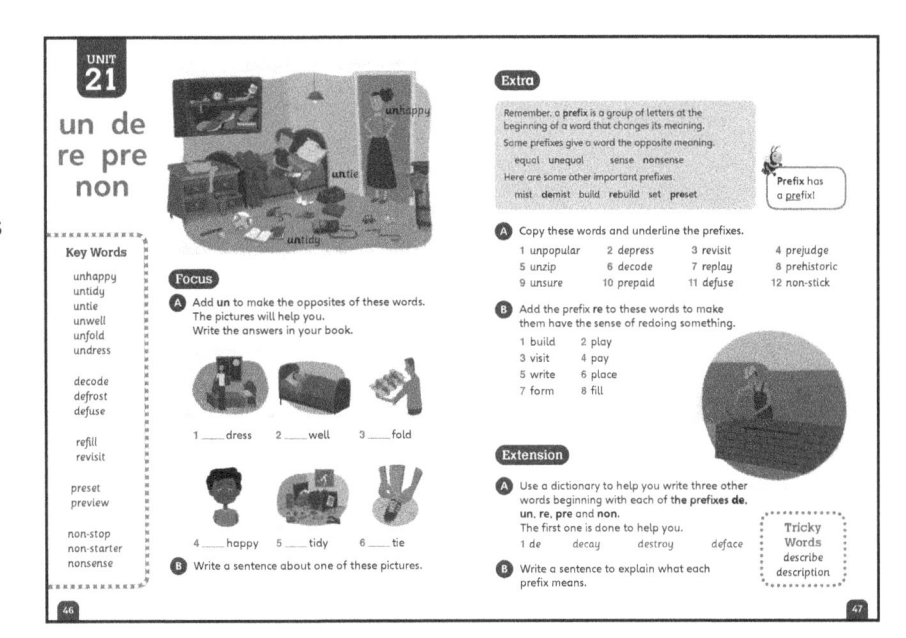

BACKGROUND NOTES AND SUGGESTIONS

This unit revisits the use of prefixes introduced in Book 2 Unit 15 and the previous unit in this book.

The general rule with prefixes is that they are added without the need for any adjustment to the spelling, and this is secured here.

Prefixes are used to amend or change the meaning of a word and are important components in building words and ensuring good spelling. This group of prefixes form the antonym of root words to which they are attached or provide a sense of redoing something.

Suffixes are developed further in several later units of the course.

Pupil Book answers

Focus
A 1 undress 2 unwell 3 unfold
  4 unhappy 5 untidy 6 untie

B Teacher to check individual answers

Extra
A 1 <u>un</u>popular 2 <u>de</u>press
  3 <u>re</u>visit 4 <u>pre</u>judge
  5 <u>un</u>zip 6 <u>de</u>code
  7 <u>re</u>play 8 <u>pre</u>historic
  9 <u>un</u>sure 10 <u>pre</u>paid
  11 <u>de</u>fuse 12 <u>non</u>-stick

B 1 rebuild 2 replay 3 revisit
  4 repay 5 rewrite 6 replace
  7 reform 8 refill

Extension
A / **B** Teacher to check individual answers

Resource sheet answers

Focus
A Children should trace and copy the pattern

B unwell untie unkind untidy

C untidy untie unwell unkind

Extension
A unaided unaware uncomfortable unconscious uneasy unexpected unfortunate ungrateful unload undone undo unsure unable unused unsteady unbutton unwind unscrew untidy undid

B Teacher to check individual answers

Supporting word lists

unable unaided unarmed unaware unbearable unclean uncover undo undress uneven unfair unfit unfold unlikely unload unlock unlucky unpack untie unhappy untidy unpopular unpick unseen unusual unzip unofficial

negative prefix forms
descend depress decline defrost defuse deface decompose detour deform degrade defraud

negative 'sense'
decay deceive derive deduce defend defy destroy desperate despair desolate

rebound rebuild recycle recall refill reform retreat recede return replace revisit replay rewrite repay

precaution predict previous premature preface prefix prenatal prepare premonition preserve presume prevent

non-attender non-basic non-breakable non-combative
non-conformist non-connection
non-dependent
non-detachable
non-exclusive
non-explosive non-fiction non-issue
nonsense non-smoking non-tidal
non-working

BOOK 3 UNIT 22

LEARNING TARGETS

Pupil Book: Focus
to match target words and pictures and a related activity

Pupil Book: Extra
to add **ly** to selected root words

Pupil Book: Extension
to secure the rule for adding **ly** to roots ending in **y**

Resource sheet: Focus
to complete a word fan and match words to pictures

Resource sheet: Extension
to revise rules when adding the suffix **ly**

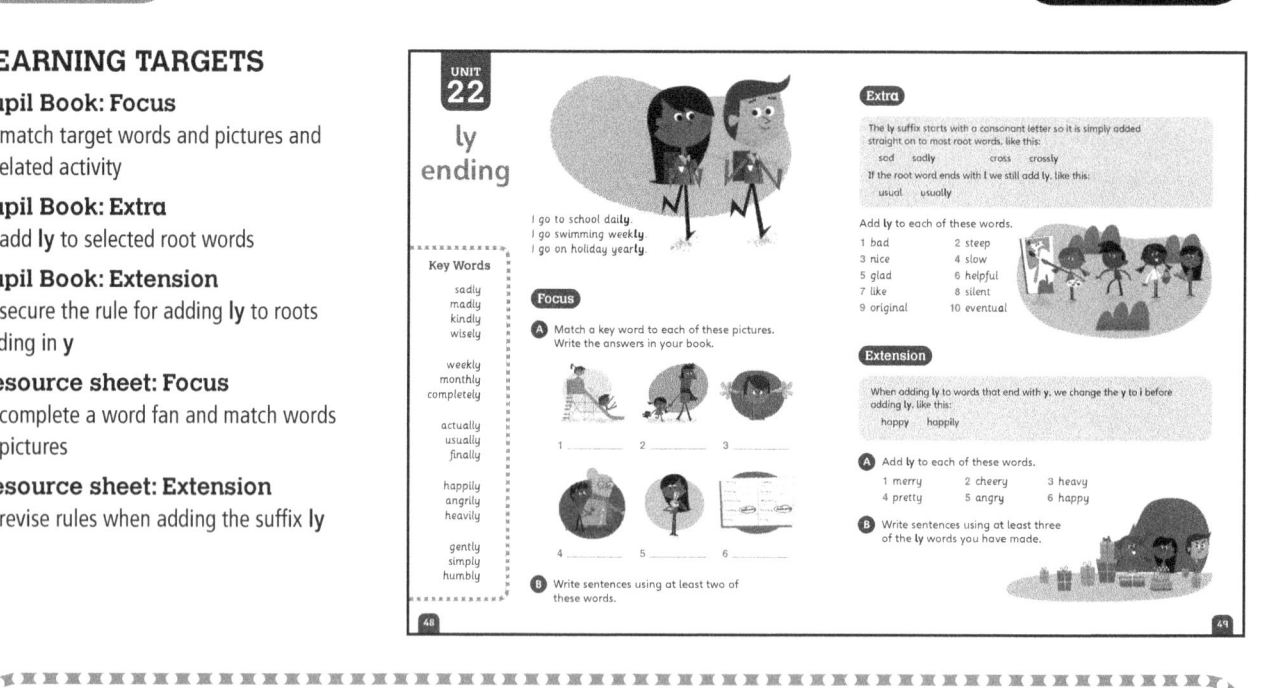

BACKGROUND NOTES AND SUGGESTIONS

Suffixes are normally added to form a related word from a different word class, or part of speech. Some children might be ready to begin to consider this. For example, by adding **ly** we are usually changing adjectives (e.g. *quick, wise*) to adverbs (*quickly, wisely*) i.e. *The quick brown fox ran quickly.*

When the suffix **fully** (as in *carefully*) is being used it is in fact an amalgam of two suffixes, **ful** and **ly**.

In the Pupil Book Extension section the rule is secured for changing the final **y** to **i** before adding **ly**. This will continue to challenge some children and so will be returned to frequently elsewhere in the course.

Pupil Book answers

Focus
A 1 happily 2 sadly 3 angrily
   4 kindly 5 gently 6 weekly

B Teacher to check individual answers

Extra
1 badly 2 steeply 3 nicely
4 slowly 5 gladly 6 helpfully
7 likely 8 silently 9 originally
10 eventually

Extension
A 1 merrily 2 cheerily 3 heavily
   4 prettily 5 angrily 6 happily

B Teacher to check individual answers

Resource sheet answers

Focus
A Children should copy the pattern

B lovely slowly wisely monthly finally happily simply humbly heavily

C slowly finally monthly happily

Extension
A 1 wisely 2 angrily
   3 urgently 4 merrily
   5 thoughtfully

Teacher to check individual sentences

B Teacher to check individual answers

Supporting word lists

madly badly gladly slowly quickly
seriously nicely steeply crossly wisely
bluntly cleverly urgently violently
silently completely furiously

heavily merrily prettily happily

careful dreadful faithful grateful helpful
thoughtful sorrowful wonderful
plentiful beautiful dutiful fanciful merciful

Some words to which ly can be added without modification
glad sad bad thankful high low quick slow
sudden definitely secondly brisk perfect
prompt certain love sharp rough smooth
short proud

Some words to which end in y to which ly can be added with modification
angry day happy easy heavy merry ready
quirky queasy scary shaky speedy

BOOK 3 UNIT 23

LEARNING TARGETS

Pupil Book: Focus
to match key words to pictures

Pupil Book: Extra
to match target words to clues in a puzzle

Pupil Book: Extension
to distinguish between the word endings **ture** and **cher**

Resource sheet: Focus
to complete a word fan;
to match words to pictures

Resource sheet: Extension
to link words to the correct letter pattern;
to use key words to complete sentences

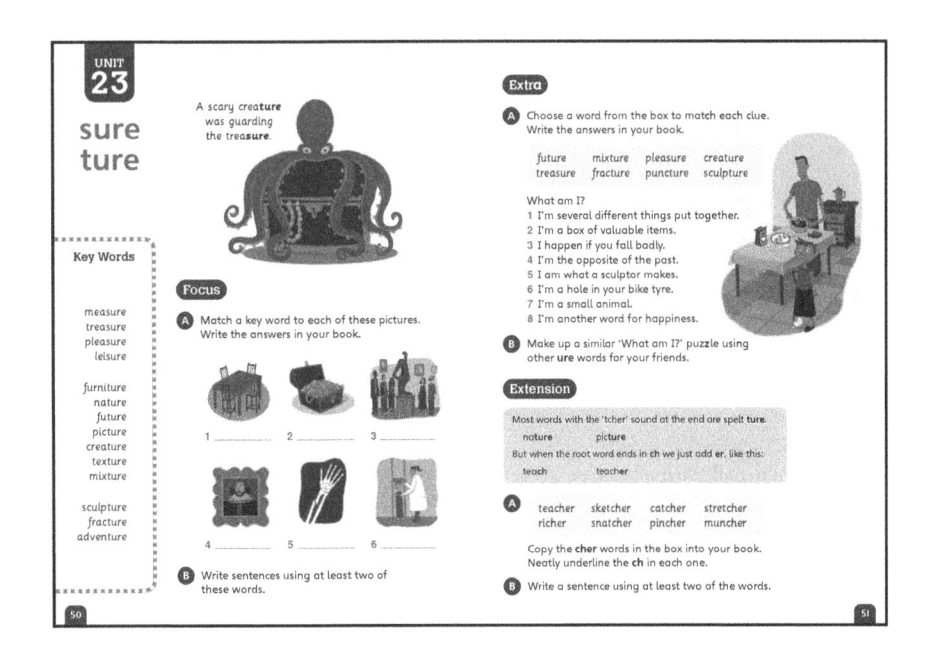

BACKGROUND NOTES AND SUGGESTIONS

This is an important group of words and the work and activities in this introductory unit will be developed and expanded later in the course (see Book 4 Unit 9).

Most of words in this unit are those in which the letter pattern is an integral part of the stem of the word (*future, measure*) as opposed to those in which the **ure** component is a direct suffix (e.g. *depart, departure*). The latter will be introduced later, though can be brought into the work now for children who need to be extended.

Pupil Book answers

Focus
A
1 furniture 2 treasure
3 sculpture 4 picture
5 fracture 6 measure

B Teacher to check individual answers

Extra
A
1 mixture 2 treasure
3 fracture 4 future
5 sculpture 6 puncture
7 creature 8 pleasure

B Teacher to check individual answers

Extension
A tea**ch**er sket**ch**er cat**ch**er stret**ch**er
ri**ch**er snat**ch**er pin**ch**er mun**ch**er

B Teacher to check individual answers

Resource sheet answers

Focus
A Children should copy the pattern

B nature picture texture mixture
fracture capture creature adventure
signature

C creature picture fracture signature

Extension
A
sure	ture
enclosure	nature
exposure	denture
measure	sculpture
closure	structure
treasure	future
composure	fracture
	mixture
	adventure

B
1 sculpture 2 treasure 3 future
4 enclosure 5 closure 6 fixture

C Teacher to check individual answers

Supporting word lists

nature future
lecture picture puncture
texture fixture mixture
sculpture scripture
structure fracture manufacture
denture venture adventure
departure signature
furniture architecture agriculture
moisture creature

measure treasure pleasure displeasure
composure exposure
closure disclosure enclosure
leisure pressure

BOOK 3 — UNIT 24

LEARNING TARGETS

Pupil Book: Focus
to select key words to complete a cloze activity

Pupil Book: Extra
to find words within words

Pupil Book: Extension
to complete a target word quiz

Resource sheet: Focus
to complete a word fan and match words to pictures

Resource sheet: Extension
to use target words to complete a cloze activity; to complete a **wh** quiz

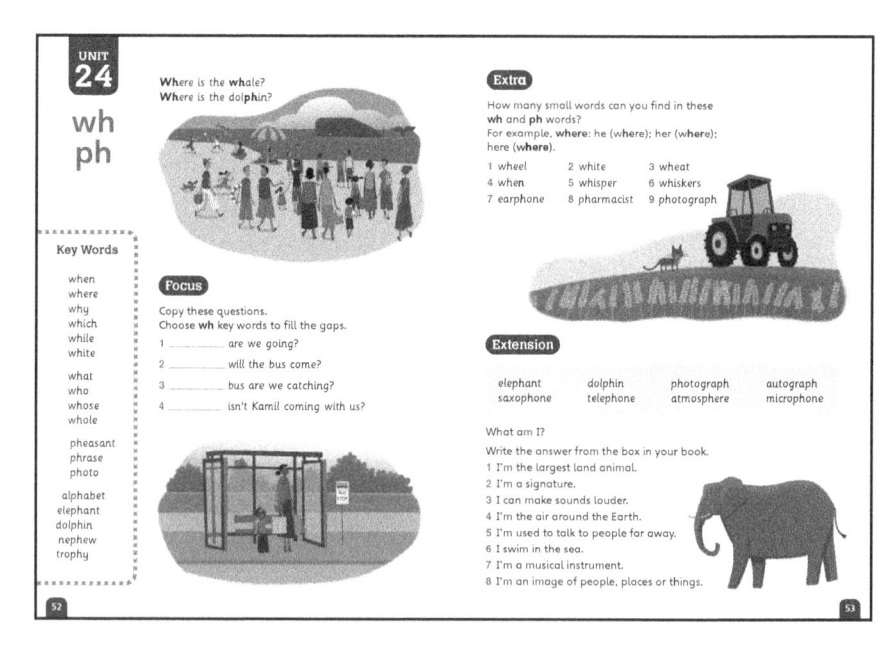

BACKGROUND NOTES AND SUGGESTIONS

Of the consonant digraphs **wh** and **ph**, **wh** is the far more significant at this stage. The question words are the most important **wh** words at the early stages, and can provide a useful focus for a lesson, as can *where* in compound words (*nowhere, anywhere, everywhere, somewhere*).

Unfortunately several **wh** words include irregular characteristics for the weaker spellers, so this is an opportunity for those children to practise the words using the 'Look, Say, Cover, Write, Check' technique.

Most words with the **ph** digraph are of Greek origin and most are quite sophisticated. A selection of the rather more frequently used and accessible words are found in the *Supporting words list* below. The /f/ sound is not usually spelt 'ph' in short, everyday English words.

Pupil Book answers

Focus
1 Where
2 When
3 Which
4 Why

Extra
1 heel eel he
2 hit I it
3 he heat at a eat
4 he hen
5 his is I whisp
6 his is I whisk
7 ear phone on one
8 harm arm I is
9 photo hot to tog graph rag

Extension
1 elephant
2 autograph
3 microphone
4 atmoshere
5 telephone
6 dolphin
7 saxophone
8 photograph

Resource sheet answers

Focus
Ⓐ Children should copy the pattern

Ⓑ when where wheel wheat which whip while white why

Ⓒ where wheel wheat what

Extension
Ⓐ "<u>Whose</u> football boots are these?" asked Mr Lindman.

"<u>What</u> colour are they?" asked Ashok.

"<u>Who</u> can tell! They are so muddy," replied his teacher.

"<u>What</u> shall I do with them?" said Ashok.

"Take them to the office to see if they know <u>who</u> has lost their boots," said Mr Lindman.

"<u>What</u> shall we do if they don't know <u>whose</u> they are?" asked the boy.

"I don't care <u>what</u> you do with them – just please get the muddy boots out of my clean classroom," said Mr Lindman crossly.

Ⓑ 1 white 2 whisper
3 wheels 4 whale
5 what/why/who/where/when
6 whiskers 7 whistle

Supporting word lists

whack
when
whip which whiz whisk whisky
whisker whistle whisper
whale
wheel wheat
while whine white
why
whirl

Irregular wh words
as in hare:
where wherever
as in moo:
who whom whose whoever
as in rose:
whole wholly
as in dog:
what

pharaoh phone phonics
photo photograph phrase physical
apostrophe nephew orphan
triumph trophy typhoon geography

BOOK 3　　　　　　　　　　　　　　　　　　　UNIT 25

LEARNING TARGETS

Pupil Book: Focus
to make compound words from picture clues

Pupil Book: Extra
to make a selection of compound words from single nouns

Pupil Book: Extension
to identify compound words in continuous prose

Resource sheet: Focus
to complete word fans for some frequent compound words

Resource sheet: Extension
to make and apply a selection of compound words

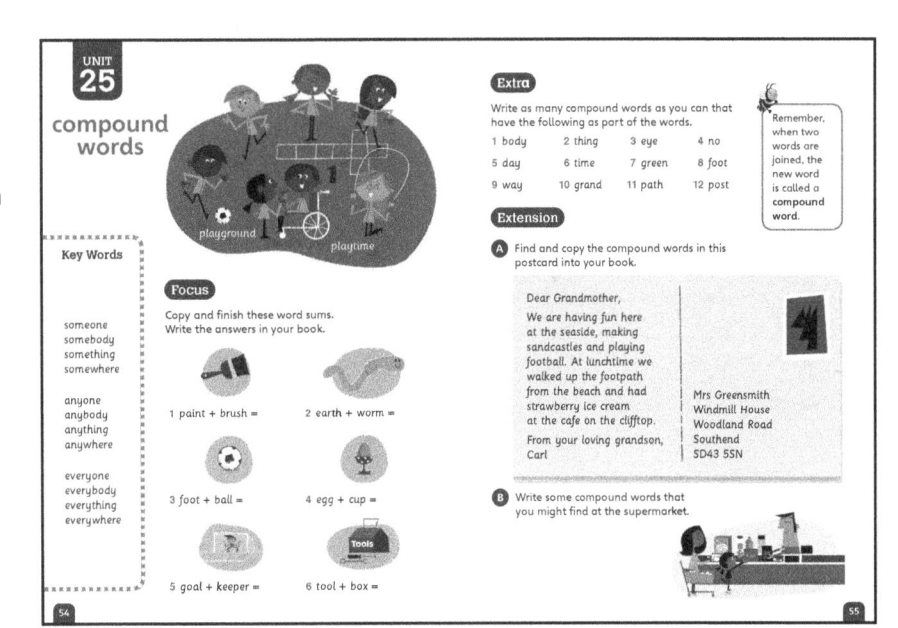

BACKGROUND NOTES AND SUGGESTIONS

This unit secures and develops the concept of compound words. As was noted when they were introduced earlier, compound words are normally words constructed by joining two other words, usually nouns e.g. *paint + brush = paintbrush.*

However, many compound words are made from word classes other than nouns e.g. *every + one = everyone*, and not all compound words are strictly single words. For example, some can be hyphenated, as in *make-up*, and these are often, though not always, adjectives (e.g. *high-flying, self-service*). Others can be two separate words used together effectively as a single noun (e.g. *car park, tape recorder*).

At this stage in the course we are concentrating on the conventional compound words, but for those wishing to extend the teaching to the other forms, examples are offered below in the *Supporting word lists*.

Pupil Book answers

Focus
1. paintbrush
2. earthworm
3. football
4. eggcup
5. goalkeeper
6. toolbox

Extra
suggested answers:
1. somebody everybody nobody busybody anybody
2. something nothing everything anything
3. eyeball eyebrow eyelash eyelid eyesight eyesore eyewitness (eye-opener)
4. nobody nothing nowhere
5. today yesterday someday heyday midday *days of the week*
6. lunchtime teatime bedtime breaktime lifetime (half-time)
7. greengrocer greenhouse (green fingers, village green, putting green)
8. football footlights footnote footprint footstep
9. passageway driveway carriageway roadway pathway runway subway
10. grandparent grandfather grandmother grandchild granddaughter grandson grandstand
11. pathway footpath
12. postbox postman postwoman postcard postmark (post office)

Extension
1. Grandmother seaside sandcastles football lunchtime footpath strawberry clifftop grandson Greensmith Windmill Woodland Southend
2. Teacher to check individual answers

Resource sheet answers

Focus

Ⓐ Children should copy the word.
　　someone　　something　　somewhere

Ⓑ Children should trace and copy the word.
　　anyone　　anything　　anywhere

Ⓒ Children should trace and copy the word.
　　everyone　　everything　　everywhere

Extension

Ⓐ bedroom lampshade spotlight matchbox lipstick homework fingerprint earthquake crossword tablecloth matchstick lamplight

Ⓑ Teacher to check individual answers

Supporting word lists

Two words joined together
bedroom fireman knitwear playground
crossword flashlight lampshade
schoolmaster dartboard football
lighthouse
skateboard earthquake greengrocer
lipstick spotlight farmhouse homework
manhole tablecloth fingerprint housewife
matchbox upstairs downstairs
bricklayer weekend earthworm playground
sideboard breakfast deadline gunpowder
windmill dustbin clockwise grandparent
grandchild chambermaid foghorn
showjumping

Two words joined with a hyphen
by-product high-class know-all
man-made dry-clean high-flying
long-range self-service flat-footed
hitch-hike low-lying skin-tight
hard-hearted hot-blooded
make-up spin-off

Two separate words used together as a noun
crash barrier living room swimming bath
cricket bat ground floor tape measure
skimmed milk tape recorder football pitch

BOOK 3 — UNIT 26

LEARNING TARGETS

Pupil Book: Focus
to match key words and pictures

Pupil Book: Extra
to make a word web of root words with silent letters

Pupil Book: Extension
to find and copy silent **w** words from a wordsearch puzzle;
to answer a puzzle using the target words

Resource sheet: Focus
to complete a word fan and match target words to pictures

Resource sheet: Extension
to identify silent letters and complete a cloze activity;
to complete a correction activity

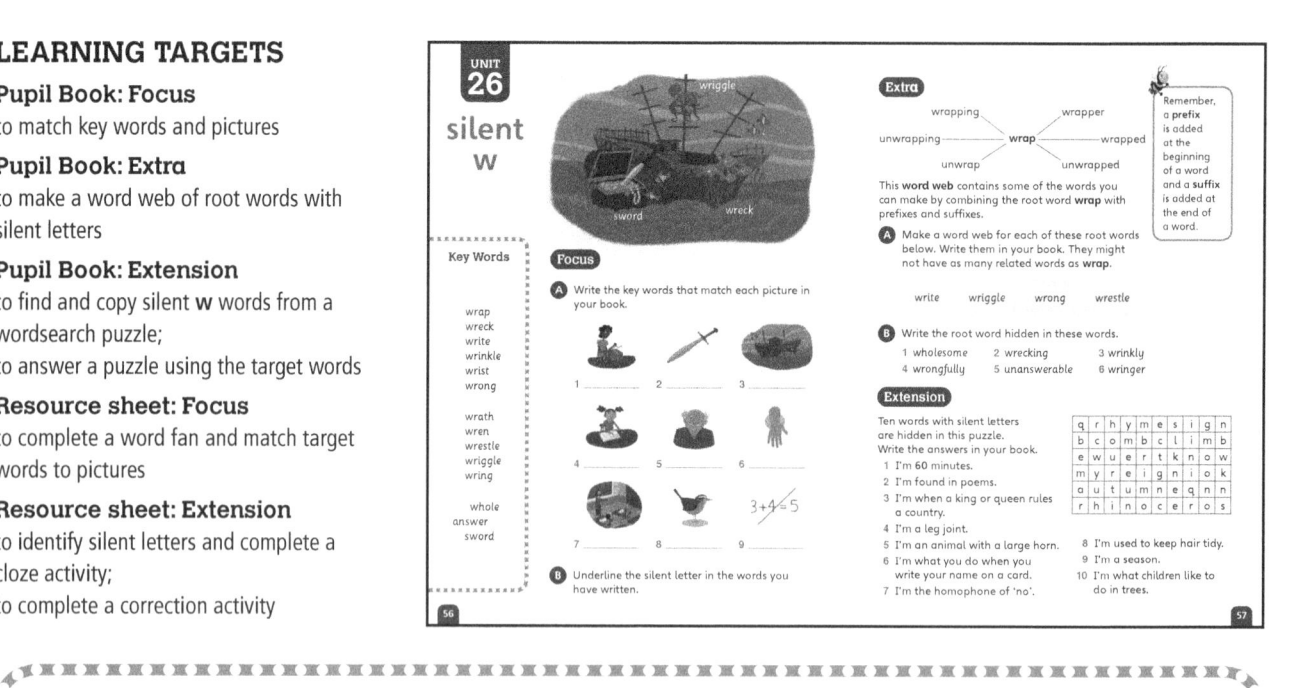

BACKGROUND NOTES AND SUGGESTIONS

The silent **w** is normally associated with an **r**, though there are exceptions to this.

Similarly, it is interesting to ask the children to think of other silent letter associations (e.g. **wh mb gn mn st**).

Other units teaching silent letters in this book are Units 4 and 17, as well as Unit 22 in Book 2.

Pupil Book answers

Focus

A/B
1 wrap
2 sword
3 wreck
4 write
5 wrinkle
6 wrist
7 answer
8 wren
9 wrong

Extra

A
1 write written writer writing
2 wriggle wriggler wriggled wriggling
3 wrong wronged wrongful wrongfully
4 wrestle wrestling wrestled wrestler

B
1 whole   2 wreck   3 wrinkle
4 wrong   5 answer   6 wring

Extension
1 hour   2 rhyme
3 reign   4 knee
5 rhinoceros   6 sign
7 know   8 comb
9 autumn   10 climb

Resource sheet answers

Focus

A wrap write wreck wrist wrong
wrestle wring wriggle

B wreck write wriggle wrist

C Teacher to check individual answers

Extension

A guide wrote rhinoceros touching wrinkled wriggly know climbing writing exhibits signed

(Note: The child might legitimately circle other letters, such as a final e, or one of a pair of double consonants.)

B
1 wrote guide
2 exhibits rhinoceros
3 touching wrinkled wriggly
4 know climbing
5 writing signed

C We all liked our trip to your sanctuary. Thank you for being such a good guide. The whole class knows the trouble you have taken showing us all the different exhibits. On the way back the bus driver took a wrong turn which made us two hours late.

Supporting word lists

wrap wrapper wrapped wrapping
wriggle wriggled wriggler wriggling
wrinkle wrinkled wrinkly
write written wrote
wreck wrecker wrecked wreckage
wringer wretched wrangle wrist
whole wholemeal wholesome wholly
sword swordfish
answer answered answering

BOOK 3 — UNIT 27

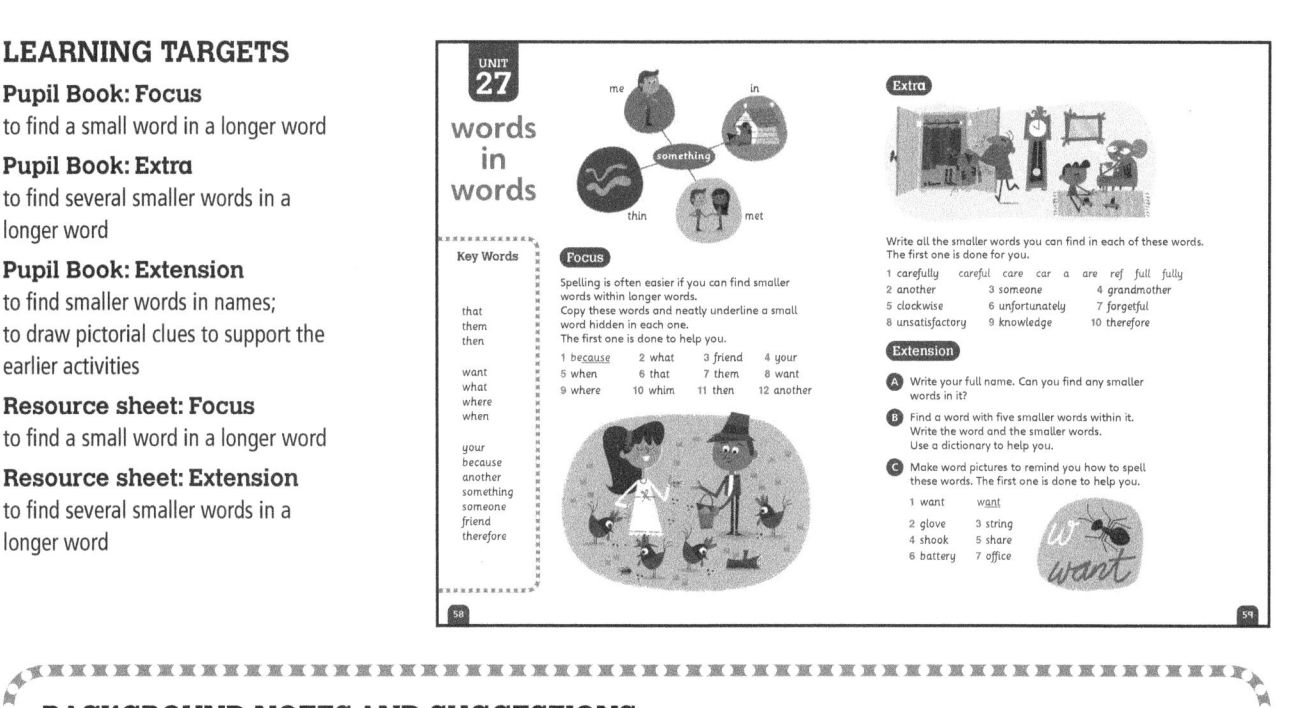

LEARNING TARGETS

Pupil Book: Focus
to find a small word in a longer word

Pupil Book: Extra
to find several smaller words in a longer word

Pupil Book: Extension
to find smaller words in names;
to draw pictorial clues to support the earlier activities

Resource sheet: Focus
to find a small word in a longer word

Resource sheet: Extension
to find several smaller words in a longer word

BACKGROUND NOTES AND SUGGESTIONS

One of the props that some children find helpful to support their spelling is to find smaller words within longer words. These smaller words act as visual clues on which they can base their attempt and, rather similar to the way mnemonics can be used, the smaller embedded word can help to ensure that the 'core' of the word is correct – around which the other letters can be built. It is thus important that the smaller words have their letters appearing consecutively.

The children will note that some of the words they find retain their original meaning, particularly in the case of root/base words and compound words (e.g. *swimming* and *grandson*).

Pupil Book answers

Focus

1 be**cause** be**cause** be**cause** be**cause**
2 **what** what
3 fri**end**
4 **your** your
5 **when** when
6 **that** that
7 **them** them them
8 w**ant**
9 w**here** w**here** w**here**
10 wh**im**
11 **then** then then
12 an**other** an**other** an**other** an**other** an**other** an**other**

Extra

1 carefully — car a are care ref full fully
2 another — a an not other the he her no
3 someone — so some me on one
4 grandmother — gran grand an and mother moth the he her a ran
5 clockwise — clock lock wise is
6 unfortunately — unfortunate fortunate(ly) for fort or ate at tuna
7 forgetful — for forget or get forge
8 unsatisfactory — sat at is fact factor satisfactory factory act or actor
9 knowledge — know no now led ledge edge owl
10 therefore — the there he her here ref for fore or ore

Extension

Ⓐ Teacher to check individual answers
Ⓑ Teacher to check individual answers
Ⓒ Teacher to check individual answers

Resource sheet answers

Focus

Ⓐ 1 car 2 lean
   3 bee/bee 4 tea/ear

Ⓑ 1 car/are 2 no/now
   3 twin/in/win 4 all/tall
   5 some/one/me/on

Extension

Ⓐ 1 hesitate: he sit I it at a ate
   2 hereafter: he here a aft after her
   3 homework: home me mew work or
   4 horizontally: horizon horizontal or I on tall tally a all ally
   5 hospitable: spit I it tab table a able
   6 hostage: host stag stage tag a age
   7 hovercraft: hover over craft raft a aft
   8 hundredweight: hundred red we weigh weight eight I

Ⓑ Teacher to check individual answers

BOOK 3 — UNIT 28

LEARNING TARGETS

Pupil Book: Focus
to secure the terms vowel and consonant;
to practise ordering skills

Pupil Book: Extra
to revise and secure alphabetical ordering by
second and third letter

Pupil Book: Extension
to use a dictionary for checking definitions

Resource sheet: Focus
to secure alphabetical ordering by first
and second letter

Resource sheet: Extension
to secure alphabetical ordering by first,
second and third letter

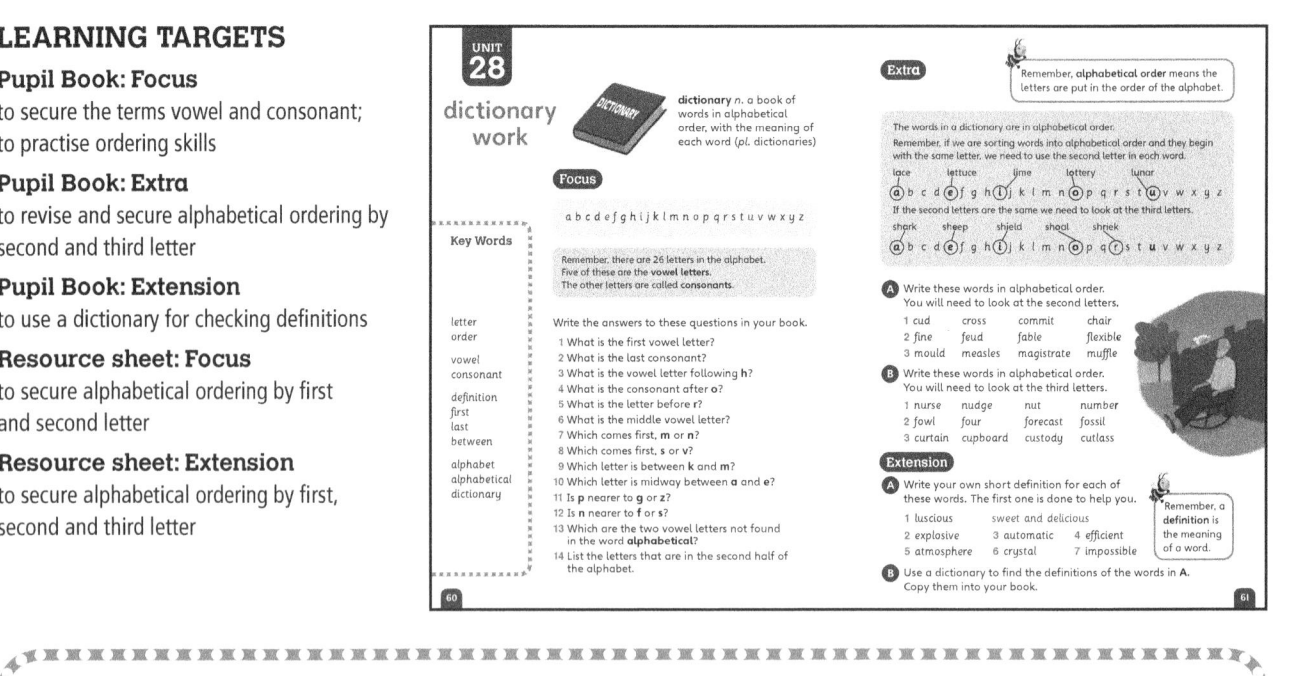

BACKGROUND NOTES AND SUGGESTIONS

This unit provides an opportunity to secure alphabetical ordering skills and to begin to become comfortable with using a dictionary for checking definitions of words.

Pupil Book answers

Focus

1 a	2 z	3 i	4 p
5 q	6 i	7 m	8 s
9 l	10 c	11 g	12 s
13 o u	14 n o p q r s t u v w x y z		

Extra

A 1 chair commit cross cud
2 fable feud fine flexible
3 magistrate measles mould muffle

B 1 nudge number nurse nut
2 forecast fossil four fowl
3 cupboard curtain custody cutlass

Extension

A Teacher to check individual answers

B Teacher to check individual answers

Resource sheet answers

Focus

A
1 bell	2 sell	3 tell
1 bike	2 hike	3 like

B
1 scorn	2 shorn	3 sworn
1 saw	2 shawl	3 straw
1 score	2 snore	3 store
1 scare	2 share	3 snare

Extension

A 1 above 2 glove 3 shove

B 1 sneak 2 speak 3 steal

C 1 carefully 2 cleverly 3 completely

D 1 picture 2 pleasure 3 puncture

E 1 rain reign rein
2 ewe yew you
3 knead kneed need
4 cent scent sent
5 road rode rowed
6 seas sees seize

BOOK 3

Check-Up 2

Focus

1 spring   2 fridge   3 page   4 swan
5 thumb   6 knitting   7 handle   8 hospital
9 station   10 television   11 chef   12 eight
13 furniture   14 treasure   15 wheel   16 toothbrush
17 wrist   18 sword   19 football   20 elephant

Extra

A 1 bells   2 buses   3 matches   4 dresses
5 boxes   6 dishes   7 mysteries   8 factories
9 plays   10 libraries   11 monkeys   12 flies

B 1 walking   2 crying   3 slipping
4 loving   5 grumbled   6 helpful
7 cried   8 happily   9 merciless
10 pleasure   11 slowest   12 merrier
13 smoky   14 heaviest   15 shaky

C 1 irresponsible   2 immature   3 impatient
4 unsure   5 illegible   6 disagree
7 invisible   8 irrelevant   9 misspell

D 1 nonsense   2 defrost   3 refill
4 revisit   5 preview   6 nonstick

E 1 he's   2 isn't   3 he'll   4 there's
5 I'm   6 she'd   7 don't   8 couldn't
9 doesn't   10 wouldn't   11 shouldn't   12 I'd

Extension

A Teacher to check individual answers

B 1 calf chase cluck costume
2 ship slippery smoke strong sudden
3 damp destroy disappoint donkey dull
4 absent adventure agree altogether another apple

C 1 comb   2 climb   3 wrong   4 written   5 knife
6 knock   7 double   8 chemist   9 scenery   10 echo
11 school   12 character

D 1 weather   2 seen   3 missed   4 hear
5 reins   6 flour

E 1 dangerous   2 nervous   3 suspicious   4 victorious

Book 4 Scope and Sequence

Unit	Pupil Book Focus	Pupil Book Extra	Pupil Book Extension	Resource Book Focus	Resource Book Extension
1	*ea* finding rhyming words	wordsearch quiz	making target word webs; homophones	letter patterns; picture matching	target word quiz; writing sentences
2	*ask ast ass* checking word patterns; target word quiz	making *s, es* plurals	adding suffixes	letter patterns; identifying rhyming words	using *s/es* plurals; alphabetical ordering
3	*ur ure* finding target words	identifying 'double' sounds	wordsearch quiz; letter patterns; writing sentences	letter patterns; word building	word building; wordsearch
4	double consonants finding target words	matching words to definitions	making a double consonant alphabet	word sorting; word building	identifying correct spellings
5	silent letters o, h and c target word quiz	alphabetical ordering	identifying *cess* words	word sorting; identifying silent letters	using a dictionary to correct silent letter words; sentence writing
6	*dis mis in im il ir un* finding target words	target word quiz	indentifying prefix rules	matching words to definitions; using prefixes	using and sorting prefixes; sentence writing
7	*de re pre non* adding target prefixes	wordsearch quiz; matching definitions	finding dictionary definitions	letter patterns; adding prefixes; sentence writing	writing definitions
8	*ly* ending wordsearch quiz; writing sentences	applying *ly* suffix	identifying *ly* suffix rules	identifying *il/ily/cally* words; cloze activity	finding root words; cloze activity
9	*sure ture* cloze activity	matching related words	using *ure* words	letter patterns; word building	solving clues; completing a wordsearch
10	*ous ious eous* cloze activity	identifying *ious/eous*	adding *ous/ious* to target words	*ous/ious* letter patterns; writing sentences	dropping final *e*; sorting adjectives
11	*tion ation* finding target words	identifying *tion* families	making abstract nouns	picture matching; writing sentences	identifying verbs; completing verb/noun table
12	*sion ssion cian* wordsearch quiz	matching words to definitions	identifying rules for target suffixes	word building; completing a wordsearch	word building; completing verb/noun table
13	*auto circ anti* finding target words	finding definitions	understanding phrases with target prefixes	letter patterns; word building	using a dictionary to write phrases and sentences
14	*trans tele bi sub super* finding target words	identifying meanings of target prefixes	introducing more prefixes	letter patterns; using prefixes in sentences	using a dictionary to complete prefix table

The darker cells introduce statutory material for this year group in the National Curriculum for England.
The paler cells denote revision of a topic covered in previous years.

Unit	Pupil Book Focus	Pupil Book Extra	Pupil Book Extension	Resource Book Focus	Resource Book Extension
15	**ship hood** adding target suffixes	understanding word roots	using multiple suffixes	picture matching; writing sentences	using the *ic* suffix; writing sentences
16	**words from French ch que gue** building target words	matching definitions	writing definitions	picture matching; writing sentences	matching words to definitions; writing definitions and sentences
17	**igh** finding target words	building word families	dictionary practice	identifying spelling patterns; cloze activity	word sorting; writing sentences
18	**a al ad af** correctly using *al* prefix	understanding target prefix meanings	applying prefixes in written language	dictionary work; writing sentences	word sorting; story writing
19	**f ff fe ves** writing plural forms	writing plurals for *f/fe* words	adding suffixes	writing *ves* plurals	identifying spelling rules
20	**en on** building target words	completing key words	identifying nouns and adjectives	word building; writing sentences	cloze activity; using a dictionary to write definitions
21	**using apostrophes** identifying plural possessives	making simple plural possessive	understanding irregular plural possessives	identifying and writing the possessive apostrophe	using the plural possessive
22	**homophones** finding homophones	identifying double and triple homophones	using homophones in sentences	picture matching; writing sentences	identifying correct homophones; using a dictionary to write sentences
23	**syllables** identifying word beats	dividing words by syllables	identifying syllables and double consonants	identifying syllables; dividing words into syllables	identifying syllables; joining syllables
24	**ive** finding target words	finding *ive/ion* family words	using *ive* words; writing definitions	word building; sentence writing	using suffixes
25	**able ible** cloze activity	identifying *able/ible* rules	using *able/ible* following *e*	letter patterns; word building	using *ably/ibly*; writing sentences
26	**unstressed vowels** wordsearch quiz	identifying unstressed vowels	understanding unstressed vowels and syllables	finding unstressed vowels; writing sentences	identifying unstressed letters and syllables
27	**word roots** finding word roots	word building	identifying Latin and Greek roots	adding suffixes to build words	making a word web; completing prefix/suffix chart
28	**dictionary work** alphabet quiz	alphabetical ordering	writing definitions using a dictionary	alphabetical ordering	using guide words

BOOK 4   UNIT 1

LEARNING TARGETS

Pupil Book: Focus
to write rhyming word answers to clues

Pupil Book: Extra
to find and copy target words in a wordsearch puzzle

Pupil Book: Extension
to introduce **ea** as **a** in *break*

Resource sheet: Focus
to match target words to pictures

Resource sheet: Extension
to complete target word puzzle;
to use target words in sentences

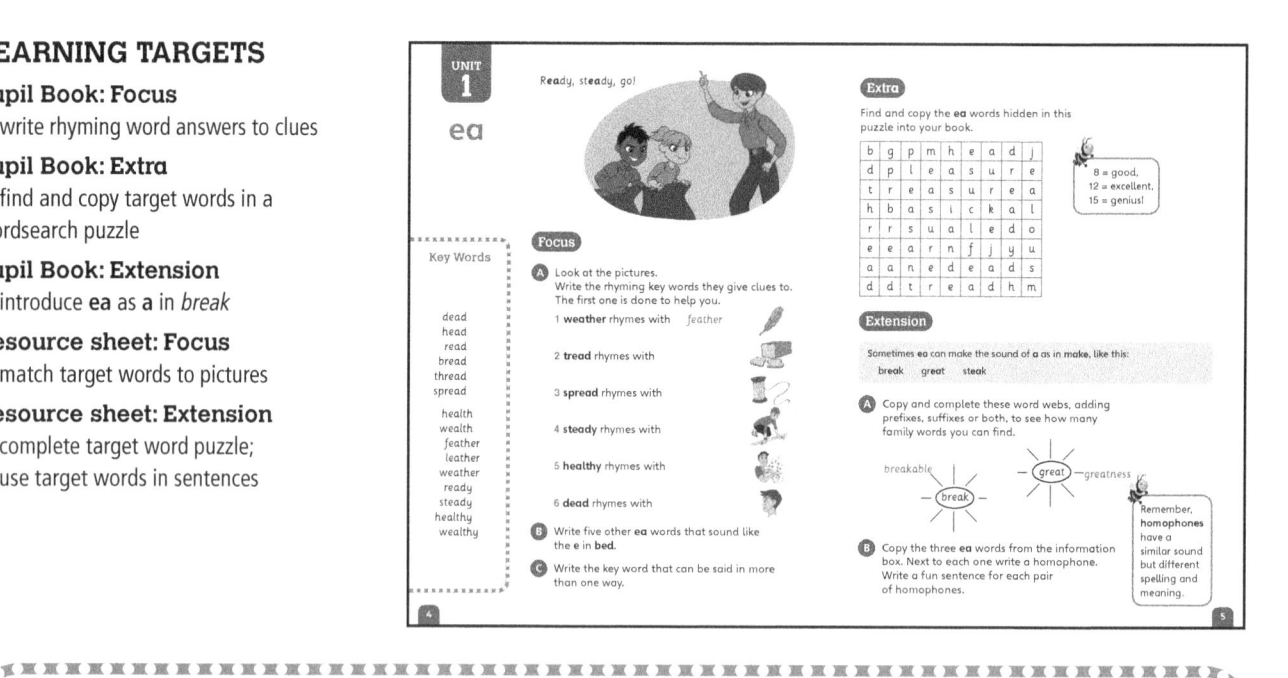

BACKGROUND NOTES AND SUGGESTIONS

There are a number of irregular **ea** words, which have been introduced previously in the course. This unit focuses particularly on the 'irregular' short **ea** (as in *head*) words, but also includes within the Pupil Book Extension section, **ea** as a long **a** sound, as in *break*.

It might be helpful to revisit the **ea** sounds, both 'regular' and 'irregular', as an introduction to the unit (see *Supporting words list*).

Pupil Book answers

Focus

A   1 feather   2 bread   3 thread
     4 ready   5 wealthy   6 head

B Teacher to check individual answers

C read

Extra

bread dead tread read dread head
thread ready measure(r) pleasure treasure
pleasant jealous earn ear

Extension

A Teacher to check individual answers

B break – brake
     great – grate
     steak – stake
     Teacher to check individual sentences

Resource sheet answers

Focus

A Children should copy the patterns

B dread spread weather feather

C weather meadow bread head
    heavy thread

Extension

A   1 head   2 steady
    3 wealth   4 feathers
    5 meadow   6 thread
    7 heather   8 deafening
    9 breath   10 weapons
    11 dead   12 heavy

B Teacher to check individual answers

Supporting word lists

dead head lead read
bread dread tread stead
thread spread
breadth instead bedspread
deaf dealt meant realm
sweat breast dreamt threat

ear dear fear gear hear near
rear tear year
clear smear spear beard
death health wealth stealth breath breadth
spread instead bedspread
feather heather leather weather
heavy ready deadly deathly wealthy
already deafen heaven weapon
sweater threaten
meadow jealous jealousy

peasant pleasant pheasant
measure pleasure treasure dreadful
break great steak
breaker breakable breaker
break-up breakfast
great greatest greatly greatness
beam seam team gleam cream dream
steam scream stream
deal heal meal peal seal veal steal
beak leak teak freak speak sneak
tweak streak
bead lead read plead
heap leap reap cheap
each beach peach reach teach
bleach preach
east beast feast least yeast
heave leave weave

BOOK 4 **UNIT 2**

LEARNING TARGETS

Pupil Book: Focus
to identify target letter patterns and exceptions;
to identify key words in a puzzle

Pupil Book: Extra
to secure plural spelling rules as related to the target words

Pupil Book: Extension
to secure spelling rules for adding inflectional endings as related to the target words

Resource sheet: Focus
to practise and use **ask ast ass** patterns

Resource sheet: Extension
to use **es** to form plurals;
to practise alphabetical ordering

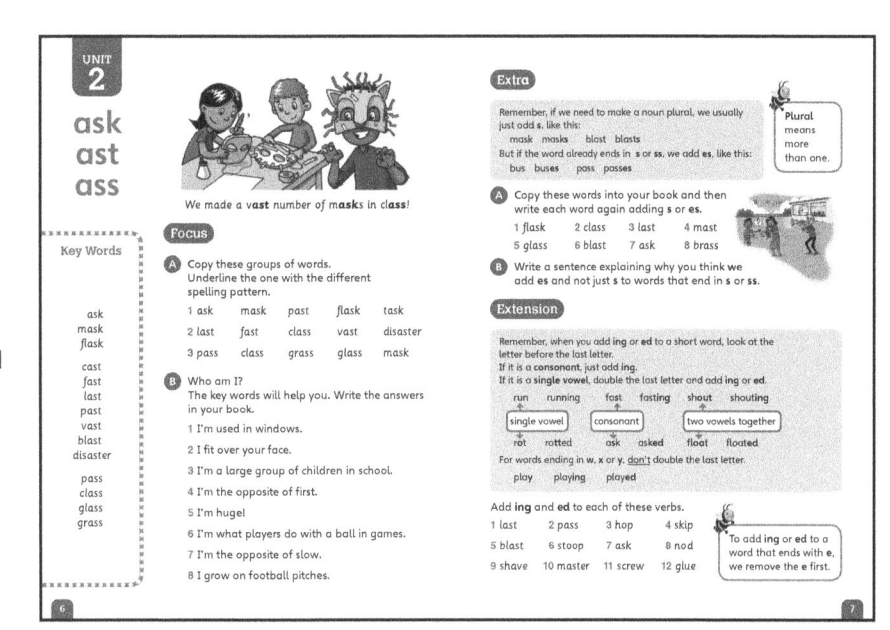

BACKGROUND NOTES AND SUGGESTIONS

Of all the spelling patterns, this is probably more subject to regional variation of pronunciation, most notably in areas of the north of England where colloquially many of the words would be said with a short **a**. This, of course, does not invalidate the unit – it simply makes it easier and more straightforward for children in such areas.

Pupil Book answers

Focus

A 1 ask mask <u>past</u> flask task
   2 last fast <u>class</u> vast disaster
   3 pass class grass glass <u>mask</u>

B 1 glass   2 mask
   3 class   4 last
   5 vast   6 pass
   7 fast   8 grass

Extra

A 1 flasks   2 classes
   3 lasts   4 masts
   5 glasses   6 blasts
   7 asks   8 brasses

B Teacher to check individual answers

Extension

1 lasting lasted
2 passing passed
3 hopping hopped
4 skipping skipped
5 blasting blasted
6 stooping stooped
7 asking asked
8 nodding nodded
9 shaving shaved
10 mastering mastered
11 screwing screwed
12 gluing glued

Resource sheet answers

Focus

A Children should copy the letter patterns

B flask mast class grass

C mask last pass fast

Extension

A 1 masts   2 glasses
   3 classes   4 passes
   5 bunches   6 torches
   7 stars   8 foxes
   9 mothers   10 brushes
   11 crosses   12 dresses
   13 sacks   14 boxes
   15 wishes   16 watches
   17 punches   18 matches
   19 peaches   20 lashes

B 1 bunches classes glasses masts
     passes torches
   2 lashes matches peaches punches
     watches wishes

Supporting word lists

lf	calf half
lm	calm palm qualm
ft	craft draft shaft after
nt	plant slant grant chant
nd	demand
sk	ask bask cask mask task flask
sp	gasp rasp clasp grasp
st	cast fast last mast past vast blast master
ff	staff
ss	class glass brass grass
th	bath path lather rather
nce	dance prance chance
nch	branch

61

BOOK 4 — UNIT 3

LEARNING TARGETS

Pupil Book: Focus
to identify key words in a picture and associated activity

Pupil Book: Extra
to identify **ur**, **ir** and **er** phonemes in the same word

Pupil Book: Extension
to find target words in a wordsearch puzzle and add inflectional endings to them

Resource sheet: Focus
to complete word sums incorporating the target letter patterns

Resource sheet: Extension
to distinguish between **ire**, **ure** and **ere** spellings

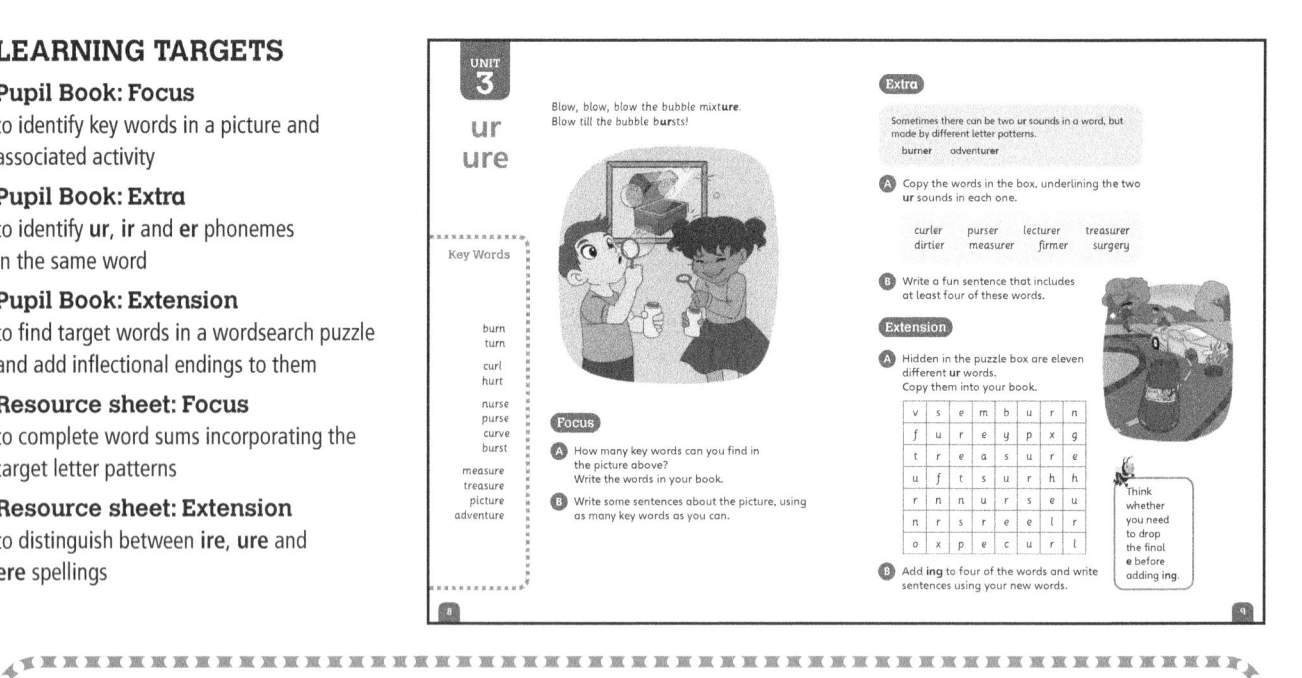

BACKGROUND NOTES AND SUGGESTIONS

The **ur** vowel digraph occurs quite often, but in spelling acquisition its most significant context is in the suffixes **sure** and **ture** (see Unit 9).

Pupil Book answers

Focus

A curl burst treasure picture

B Teacher to check individual answers

Extra

A c<u>ur</u>ler p<u>ur</u>ser lect<u>ur</u>er treas<u>ur</u>er
d<u>ir</u>t<u>ie</u>r meas<u>ur</u>er f<u>ir</u>m<u>er</u> s<u>ur</u>g<u>er</u>y

B Teacher to check individual answers

Extension

A treasure purse sure surf fur
measure nurse turn burn
curl hurl

B Teacher to check individual answers

Resource sheets answers

Focus

A Children should copy the patterns

B turn   burn
curl   hurl
nurse   purse

C nurse purse curl turn

Extension

A
1 cure   2 fire
3 here   4 future
5 sure   6 hire
7 furniture   8 wire
9 pure

B lurch   pure
nurse   measure
curved   surely
turn   future
curl   sure
pleasure
picture
treasure

Supporting word lists

urn burn turn churn
fur
curl hurl
hurt
surf turf
urge surge
nurse purse
curve
burnt
burst
nature future
picture puncture
texture mixture
sculpture scripture
structure fracture
denture adventure
furniture
measure treasure pleasure

BOOK 4 .... UNIT 4

LEARNING TARGETS

Pupil Book: Focus
to select key words to match pictures and associated activity

Pupil Book: Extra
to secure the spelling rules for vowel letters before double consonants

Pupil Book: Extension
to secure the spelling rule for making double consonant words

Resource sheet: Focus
to determine missing letters and sort accordingly

Resource sheet: Extension
to select and check correct spellings

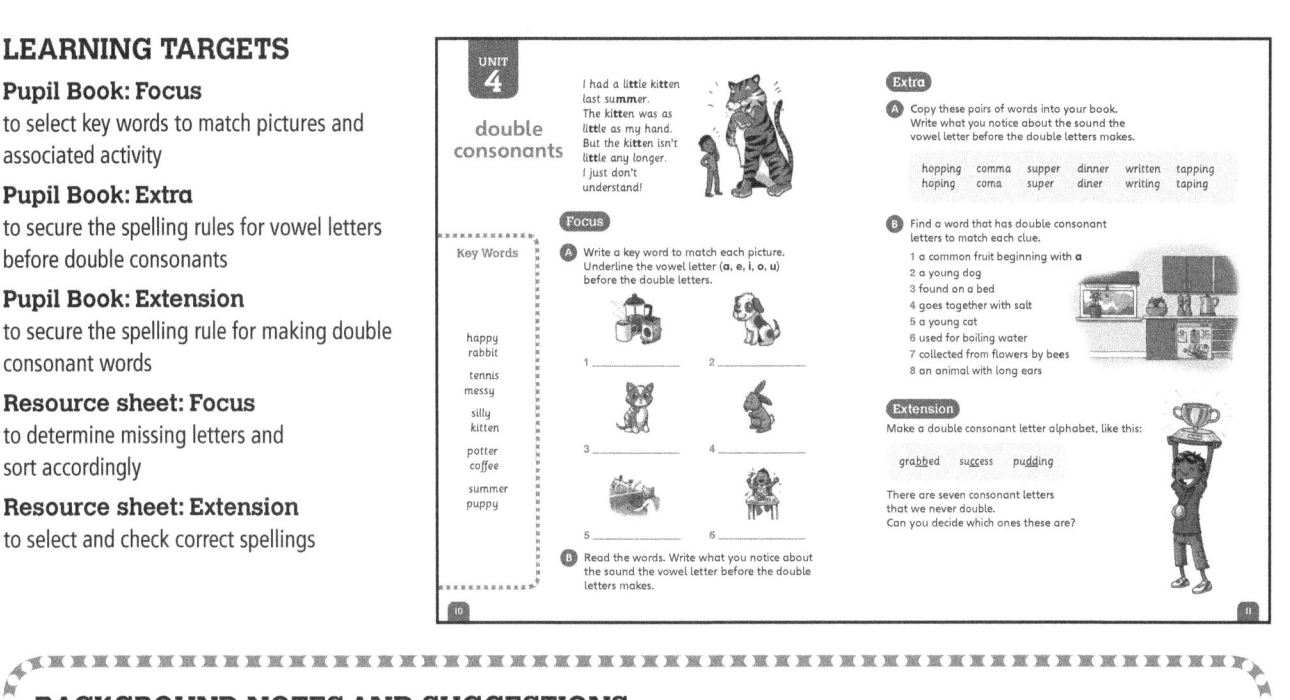

BACKGROUND NOTES AND SUGGESTIONS

Much work has already been devoted in the course to the addition of inflectional endings. This unit seeks to revise and secure these important spelling patterns and their related rules.

Remind the children of the importance of these suffixes in indicating the time or tense of a sentence. It also helps children with identifying the word class of the 'verb' by recognising that 'being' verbs are the words to which **ing** and **ed** can be added.

Use the opportunity, whilst undertaking the work in this unit, to consider verbs for which the conventional tense endings do not apply, possibly making collections in groups, e.g. **ow-ew, ing-ang, ind-ound, ell-old**.

Pupil Book answers

Focus
A 1 coffee   2 puppy   3 kitten
   4 rabbit   5 tennis   6 messy

B Teacher to check individual answers, noting that the vowel letter before the double consonants is short.

Extra
A Teacher to check individual answers, noting that the letter following a long vowel is a single consonant, whereas the letters following the short vowel sound is a double consonant.

B 1 apple   2 puppy   3 pillow
   4 pepper   5 kitten   6 kettle
   7 pollen   8 rabbit

Extension
Teacher to check individual answers
h, j, k, q, v, w, x can not be doubled

Resource sheet answers

Focus
A
ss words	ll words	ff words	tt words
pressing	frill	off	bottle
dress	tell	puff	battle
cross	well	baffle	little
fuss	filling		
puss	pull		
	still		
	full		

B 1 smell   2 dress
   3 little   4 well
   5 off   6 cross

Extension
1 across   2 balloon
3 between   4 disappear
5 difficult   6 swimming
7 address   8 necessary
9 opposite   10 addition
11 different   12 quarrel
13 follow   14 innocent
15 stopped   16 suddenly
17 business

Supporting word lists

There are many verbs with which to practise these rules. Here are a few:

Just add inflectional ending
shock bash cash dash gash lash mash
fish wish rush
clash flash slash crash smash splash swish
blush brush crush

Double the final letter before adding the inflectional ending
flag flap flip flog flop
plan plod plop plot plug
slam slap slim slip slit slot slug
blob blot
clap clip clog cram crop
drag drip drop drum
grab grin grip
trap trim trot

Drop the e before adding the inflectional ending
take rave save wave shave tame shame
bake blame blaze flake graze laze save
skate tape wave shake shave
hike like dive file smile pine wipe
hope slope poke smoke choke close probe
prune rule use glue

63

BOOK 4

UNIT 5

LEARNING TARGETS

Pupil Book: Focus
to practise silent letters by finding answers to a quiz

Pupil Book: Extra
to secure second-letter alphabetical ordering using silent-letter words

Pupil Book: Extension
to find smaller words in longer words as a support for difficult spellings

Resource sheet: Focus
to identify silent letters in words

Resource sheet: Extension
to identify and correct misspellings involving silent letters

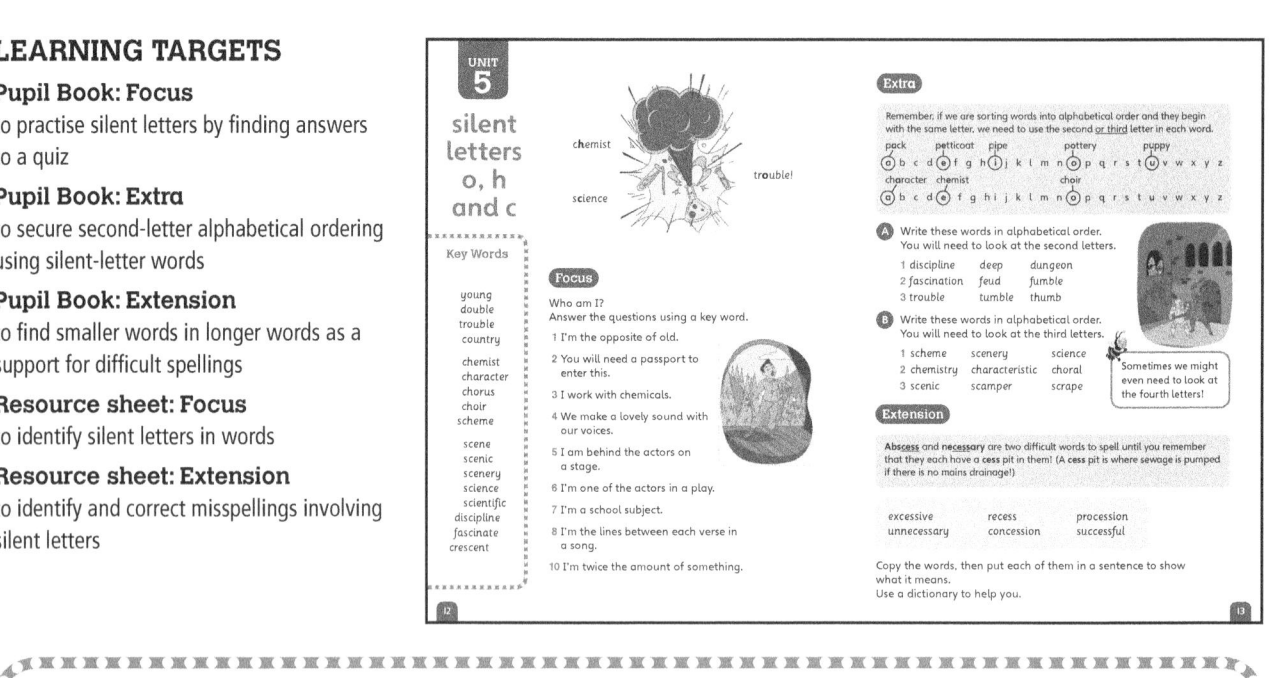

BACKGROUND NOTES AND SUGGESTIONS

The children will be intrigued to realise that many silent letters were, in days gone by, pronounced, but due to fashion and the general evolution of language they have become silent.

This unit follows from Unit 17 in Book 3 to focus on **o**, **h** and **c**. Silent letters are a persistent and ever-present difficulty for children learning to spell accurately. But any silent letters can be introduced at any stage, so activities developed from this unit might usefully also introduce other silent letters.

As has been suggested previously, many vowel letters are not sounded individually and teachers may choose to teach them as silent (e.g. **a** in *head*; **e** in *gone*), though the term is conventionally reserved for consonant letters.

Related to silent letters are the unstressed letters, especially vowels, and these are covered in depth as the course progresses.

There are some specific patterns to explore with the children in this unit, including:

- silent **h** is often preceded by **c**
- silent **c** is often associated with an **s**.

It is interesting to ask the children to spot other silent letter associations (e.g. **wh mb gn mn st**).

Pupil Book answers

Focus
A 1 young 2 country 3 chemist
4 choir 5 scenery 6 character
7 science 8 chorus 9 double

Extra
A 1 deep discipline dungeon
2 fascination feud fumble
3 thumb trouble tumble

B 1 scenery scheme science
2 characteristic chemistry choral
3 scamper scenic scrape

Extension
Teacher to check individual answers

Resource sheet answers

Focus
A young   chemist   scenery
trouble   choir   science
country   scheme   discipline
double   character scissors

B chemist scene young character
crescent scientific trouble fascinate
country choir discipline scheme
double scenic chorus

Extension
A 1 tongue   2 thistle
3 wreck   4 honest
5 climb   6 answer
7 column   8 gnaw
9 whisper   10 whole
11 ghost   12 listen
13 rhubarb 14 castle
15 rheumatism 16 thumb

B 1 designer
2 gnat
3 whisper
4 tomb
5 plumbing
6 wrath
7 rhinoceros
8 island

Teacher to check individual sentences

Supporting word lists
abscess ascend
conscience conscious crescent
descend disciple
fascinate
muscle scene scent scissors
double trouble colonel
ache anchor architect
chaos character chemical choir
chord chorus
echo

BOOK 4　　　　　　　　　　　　　　　　　　UNIT 6

LEARNING TARGETS

Pupil Book: Focus
to match key words to pictures and an associated activity

Pupil Book: Extra
-to find the roots of a selection of words with the target prefixes

Pupil Book: Extension
to reinforce the rule that prefixes are added regardless of whether this causes a doubling of letters

Resource sheet: Focus
to match target words to clues and pictures

Resource sheet: Extension
to identify meanings of selected prefixes and find words that incorporate the prefixes

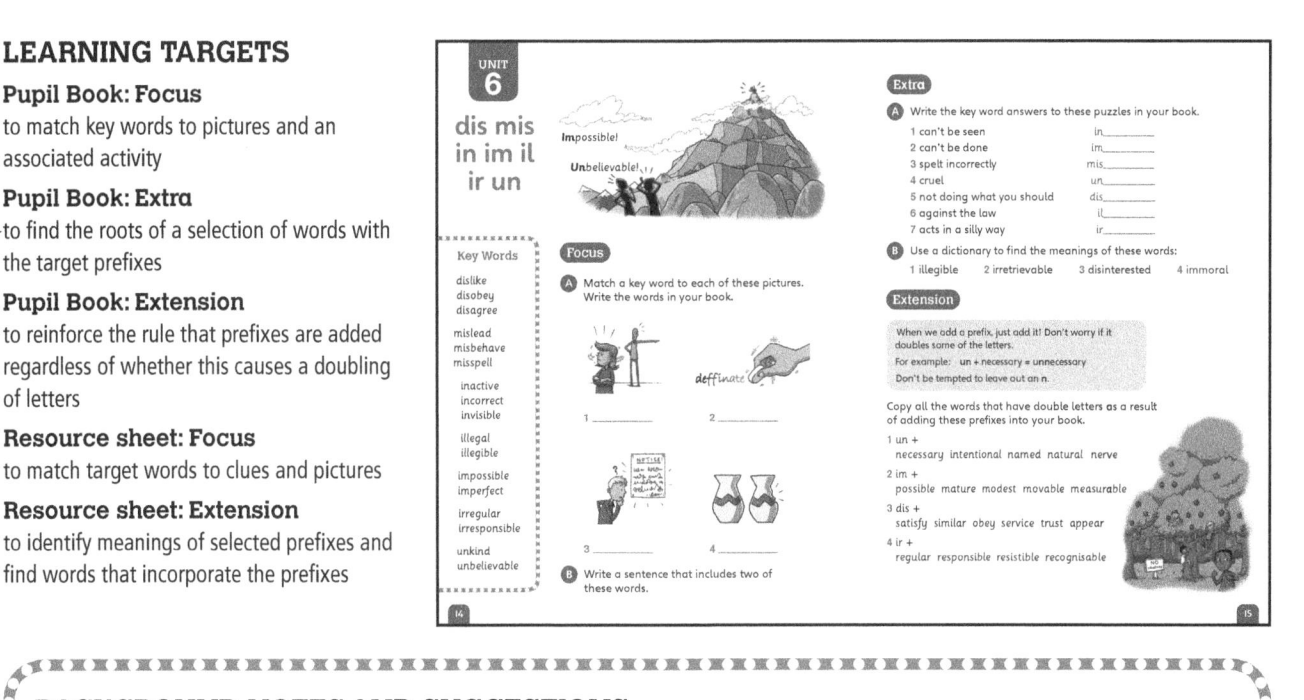

BACKGROUND NOTES AND SUGGESTIONS

This unit revisits the prefixes introduced in Book 3 Unit 20.

The general rule with prefixes is that they are added without the need for any adjustment to the spelling.

Prefixes are used to amend or change the meaning of a word and are important components in building words and ensuring good spelling. This particular group of prefixes form the antonym of root words to which they are attached.

Suffixes are developed further in several later units of the course.

Pupil Book answers

Focus

A 1 disobey　　2 misspell
　　3 illegible　　4 imperfect

B Teacher to check individual answers

Extra

1 invisible　2 impossible　3 misspelt
4 unkind　5 disobedient　6 illegal
7 irresponsible

B Teacher to check individual answers

Extension

1 unnecessary unnamed unnatural unnerve
2 immature immodest immovable immeasurable
3 dissatisfy dissimilar disservice
4 irregular irresponsible irresistible irretrievable

Resource sheet answers

Focus

A 1 impossible
　　2 misbehave
　　3 inaccurate
　　4 imperfect
　　5 disappoint
　　6 untidy
　　7 unhappy
　　8 incorrect

B misbehave incorrect
　　disappoint unhappy

Extension

A 1 (able)
　　2 un(able)
　　3 en(able)
　　4 dis(able)
　　5 in(ability)

Teacher to check children's individual sentences

B Teacher to check individual answers

C Teacher to check individual answers

Supporting word lists

negative prefix forms

disable disadvantage disagree disappear
disapprove discharge discolour
disconnect
discourage dishonest dislike dislodge
disloyal disobey displease disprove
disqualify disregard distrust

negative 'sense'

discriminate disaster disease dismal
distress disturb dismal disgust dismiss
inconvenient incomplete independent
inequality infrequent invalid insufficient
insensitive incorrect inadequate
incapable
inoffensive

impossible improbable imperfect
impassable
impertinent impatient immature

illegible illiterate illegal

irrelevant irrational irregular
irreplaceable

misbehave miscalculate miscall
miscarriage
mischance misclassify misconceive
misconduct
misdirect misfit misfortune misfunction
misguided
misjudge
mislead
mismatch
misplace misprint
misquote misspell mistrust

BOOK 4 — UNIT 7

LEARNING TARGETS

Pupil Book: Focus
to complete word sums involving prefixes

Pupil Book: Extra
to find words with target prefixes in a wordsearch puzzle;
to relate these words to definitions

Pupil Book: Extension
to use a dictionary to write definitions of target words

Resource sheet: Focus
to add appropriate target prefixes to root words

Resource sheet: Extension
to complete a prefix table

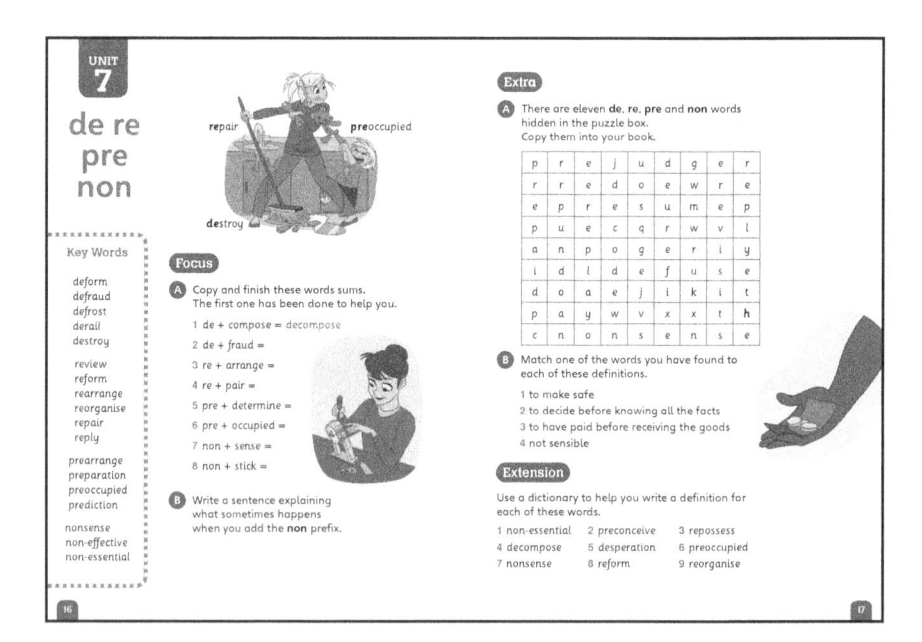

BACKGROUND NOTES AND SUGGESTIONS

This unit revisits the prefixes introduced in Book 3 Unit 21.

The general rule with prefixes is that they are added without the need for any adjustment to the spelling.

Prefixes are used to amend or change the meaning of a word and are important components in building words and ensuring good spelling. This particular group of prefixes form the antonym of root words to which they are attached.

Suffixes are developed further in several later units of the course.

Pupil Book answers

Focus
A
1 decompose 2 defraud
3 rearrange 4 repair
5 predetermine 6 preoccupied
7 nonsense 8 nonstick

B Teacher to check individual answers

Extra
A presume replay decode revisit defuse prejudge redo prepaid nonsense reply refix

B
1 defuse 2 prejudge
3 prepaid 4 nonsense

Extension
Teacher to check individual answers

Resource sheet answers

Focus
A Children should copy and trace the patterns.

B
1 reorganise 2 preoccupied
3 defraud 4 rearrange
5 nondrip 6 prehistoric
7 reform 8 nonessential

C Teacher to check individual answers

Extension
defrost rearrange prearrange nonsense
derail recapture prehistoric non-starter
deform redraw prejudge non-smoker
devalue reintroduce precaution non-stick

Teacher to check individual definitions

Supporting word lists

unable unaided unarmed unaware
unbearable unclean uncover undo
undress uneven unfair unfit unfold
unlikely unload unlock unlucky unpack
untie unhappy untidy unpopular unpick
unseen unusual unzip unofficial

negative prefix forms
descend depress decline defrost defuse
deface decompose detour deform
degrade defraud

negative 'sense'
decay deceive derive deduce defend
defy destroy desperate despair desolate

rebound rebuild recycle recall
refill reform
retreat recede return replace
revisit replay rewrite repay

precaution predict previous premature
preface prefix prenatal prepare
premonition preserve presume prevent

non-attender non-basic non-breakable
non-combative
non-conformist non-connection
non-dependent
non-detachable non-drinker non-exclusive
non-explosive non-fiction non-issue
nonsense non-smoking non-tidal
non-working

BOOK 4 — UNIT 8

LEARNING TARGETS

Pupil Book: Focus
to find **ly** words in a wordsearch box and associated activity

Pupil Book: Extra
to secure the main rules for adding **ly** to root words

Pupil Book: Extension
to consider the exceptions to rules adding **ly**; to complete cloze activity

Resource sheet: Focus
to sort and use words with **ly** endings

Resource sheet: Extension
to recognise word roots and reinforce spelling rules for **ly** endings

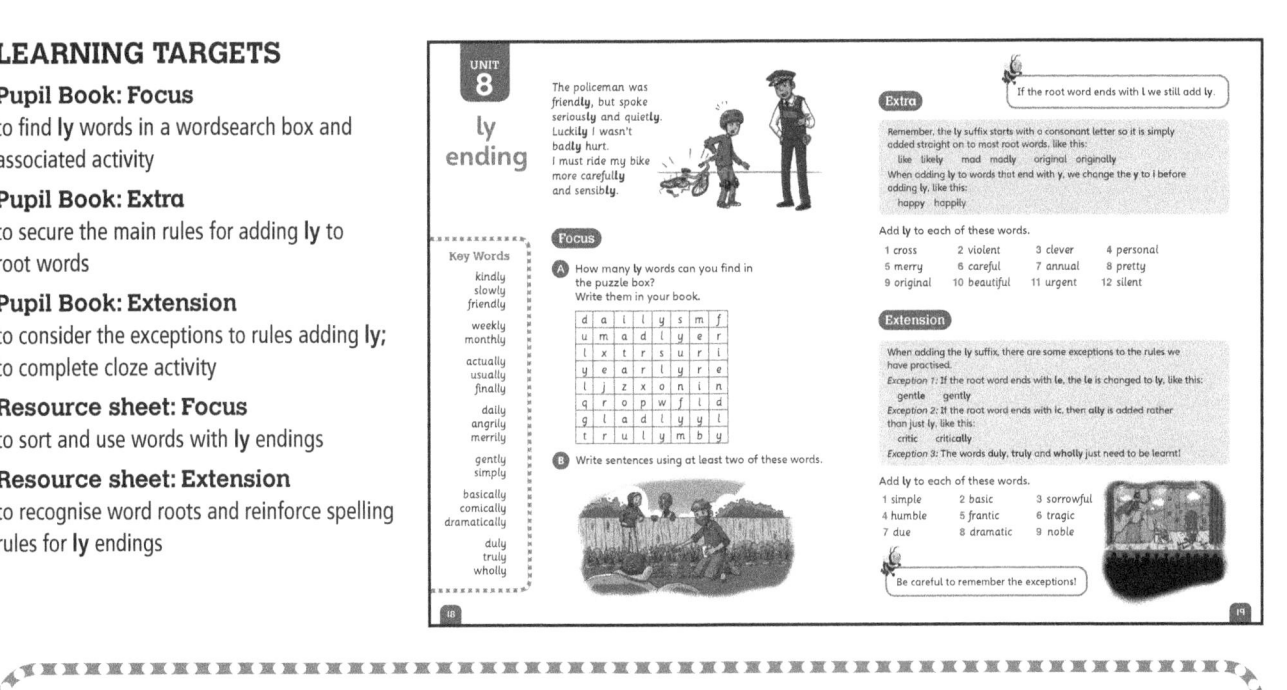

BACKGROUND NOTES AND SUGGESTIONS

Suffixes are normally added to form a related word from a different word class, or part of speech. For example, by adding **ly** we are usually changing adjectives (e.g. *quick, wise*) to adverbs (*quickly, wisely*) i.e. *The quick brown fox ran quickly.*

When the suffix **fully** (as in *carefully*) is being used it is in fact an amalgam of two suffixes, **ful** and **ly**.

In the Pupil Book Extension section the exceptions to rules adding **ly** are described and practised.

Pupil Book answers

Focus
A daily duly yearly slowly truly gladly merrily friendly madly

B Teacher to check individual answers

Extra
1. crossly
2. violently
3. cleverly
4. personally
5. merrily
6. carefully
7. annually
8. prettily
9. originally
10. beautifully
11. urgently
12. silently

Extension
1. simply
2. basically
3. sorrowfully
4. humbly
5. frantically
6. tragically
7. duly
8. dramatically
9. nobly

Resource sheet answers

Focus
A
kindly	easily	critically
monthly	hungrily	historically
friendly	merrily	drastically
slowly	lazily	heroically

B Teacher to check individual answers

C
1. slowly
2. friendly
3. monthly
4. kindly
5. hungrily
6. easily

Extension
A
1. familiar
2. love
3. stupid
4. usual
5. lazy
6. basic
7. critic
8. hungry
9. tear
10. thought
11. tragic
12. busy
13. extreme
14. joke
15. rhythm
16. ordinary

B The **ly** suffix starts with a <u>consonant</u> letter so it is simply added straight onto most root words. However, when adding **ly** to words that end in <u>y</u>, we change the <u>y</u> to an i before adding **ly**.

There are some exceptions to the rules. If the root word ends in **le**, the <u>le</u> is changed to <u>ly</u>. If the root word ends with **ic**, then <u>ally</u> is added rather than just **ly**.

Supporting word lists

madly badly gladly slowly quickly
seriously nicely steeply crossly wisely
bluntly cleverly urgently violently
silently completely furiously

heavily merrily prettily happily

careful dreadful faithful grateful
helpful thoughtful sorrowful wonderful
plentiful beautiful dutiful
fanciful merciful

Some words to which ly can be added without modification
glad sad bad thankful high
low quick slow sudden
definitely secondly brisk
perfect prompt certain love sharp
rough smooth short proud

Some words to which end in y to which ly can be added with modification
angry day happy easy heavy
merry ready quirky queasy scary
shaky speedy

BOOK 4 — UNIT 9

LEARNING TARGETS

Pupil Book: Focus
to complete a cloze activity using target words

Pupil Book: Extra
to match **ure** words with their roots

Pupil Book: Extension
to find and write related **ure** words

Resource sheet: Focus
to complete a word fan and match pictures to words

Resource sheet: Extension
to find answers to clues in a wordsearch puzzle

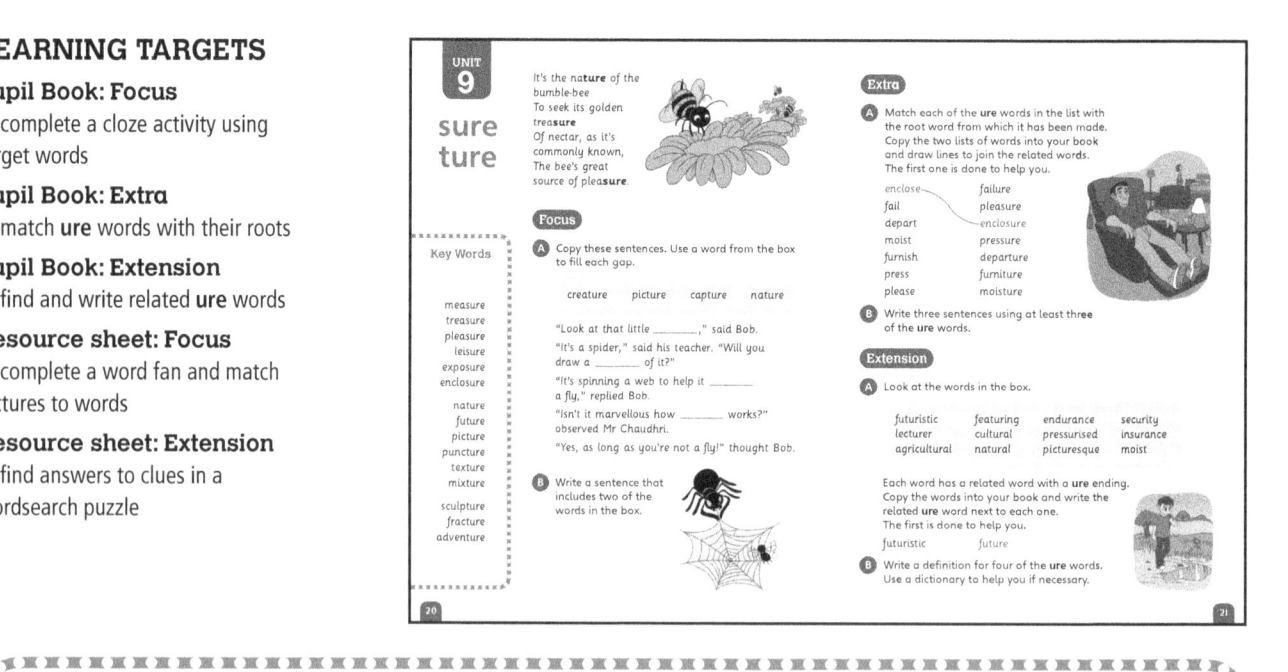

BACKGROUND NOTES AND SUGGESTIONS

This is an important group of words and the work and activities in this unit develop and expand work from Book 3 Unit 23.

The words in this unit are a mixture of those in which the letter pattern is an integral part of the stem of the word (e.g. *future*, *measure*) and those in which the **ure** component is a direct suffix (e.g. *depart*, *departure*).

Pupil Book answers

Focus

A creature picture capture nature

B Teacher to check individual answers

Extra

A *Children should draw lines to connect the following:*
enclose ——— enclosure
fail ——— failure
depart ——— departure
moist ——— moisture
furnish ——— furniture
press ——— pressure
please ——— pleasure

B Teacher to check individual answers

Extension

A 1 futuristic future
2 featuring feature
3 endurance endure
4 security secure
5 lecturer lecture
6 cultural culture
7 pressurised pressure
8 insurance insure
9 agricultural agriculture
10 natural nature
11 picturesque picture
12 moist moisture

B Teacher to check individual answers

Resource sheet answers

Focus

A Children should copy the pattern

B enclosure leisure measure exposure
pleasure pressure closure treasure

C leisure closure treasure measure

Extension

1 measure
2 treasure
3 leisure
4 exposure
5 nature
6 posture
7 picture
8 texture
9 mixture
10 mature
11 future
12 sure

Supporting word lists

nature future
lecture picture puncture
texture fixture mixture
sculpture scripture
structure fracture manufacture
denture venture adventure
departure signature
furniture architecture agriculture
moisture creature

measure treasure pleasure displeasure
composure exposure
closure disclosure enclosure
leisure pressure

BOOK 4 — UNIT 10

LEARNING TARGETS

Pupil Book: Focus
to complete a cloze activity using target words

Pupil Book: Extra
to lead towards awareness of **i** and **e** often preceding **ous**

Pupil Book: Extension
to teach the rule for amending the root before adding **ous**

Resource sheet: Focus
to make and use new words by adding target suffixes

Resource sheet: Extension
to secure words ending with **ous**, **ious**, **eous** and **orous**

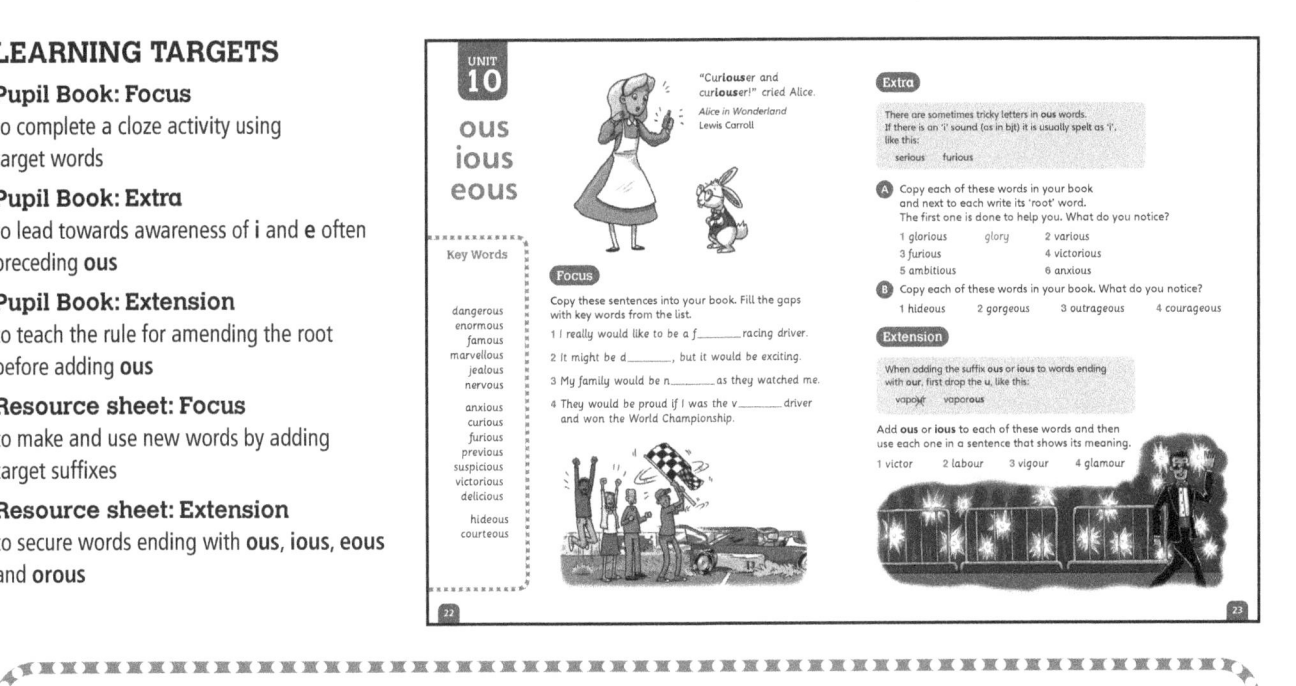

BACKGROUND NOTES AND SUGGESTIONS

The key to this spelling pattern is knowing when to include the **i** and when to omit it. The grouping in the *Supporting word lists* may help. Sometimes it is sounded – if so include it (e.g. *various*); but there are other important words where it is silent and these need to be learnt, though in some cases it helps to think whether related words would have an **i** (e.g. *anxious – anxiety*), and it should always be used between a **c** and **ous** (e.g. *gracious, precious*).

Remember also that the medial **e** in *outrageous* and *courageous* is necessary for the central **age** phoneme.

Pupil Book answers

Focus
1 famous 2 dangerous
3 nervous 4 victorious

Extra
A 1 glorious glory
   2 various vary
   3 furious fury
   4 victorious victory
   5 ambitious ambition
   6 anxious anxiety

B Teacher to check individual answers, with child noting the **eous** suffixes.

Extension
1 victorious 2 laborious
3 vigorous 4 glamorous

Teacher to check individual answers

Resource sheet answers

Focus
A
famous	various
nervous	curious
jealous	furious
enormous	previous
dangerous	serious

B famous nervous dangerous curious

C Teacher to check individual answers

Extension
A 1 fam<u>e</u> 2 nerv<u>e</u>
   3 grac<u>e</u> 4 ridicul<u>e</u>
   5 outrag<u>e</u> 6 courag<u>e</u>

Teacher to check individual answers

B enormous generous marvellous famous dangerous

furious curious anxious suspicious precious various

courageous gorgeous outrageous

glamorous humorous vigorous

Supporting word lists

famous nervous jealous enormous
generous dangerous prosperous
marvellous ridiculous glamorous
numerous tremendous

outrageous courageous

various curious furious previous serious
victorious glorious suspicious
anxious cautious
gracious malicious precious

BOOK 4 — UNIT 11

LEARNING TARGETS

Pupil Book: Focus
to match key words to pictures and associated activity

Pupil Book: Extra
to practise words from the **ction** sub-family

Pupil Book: Extension
to introduce the concept of abstract nouns and **ion** suffixes

Resource sheet: Focus
to match words to pictures and use in sentences

Resource sheet: Extension
to make nouns from given words with the addition of the **ion** suffix;
to complete verb/noun table

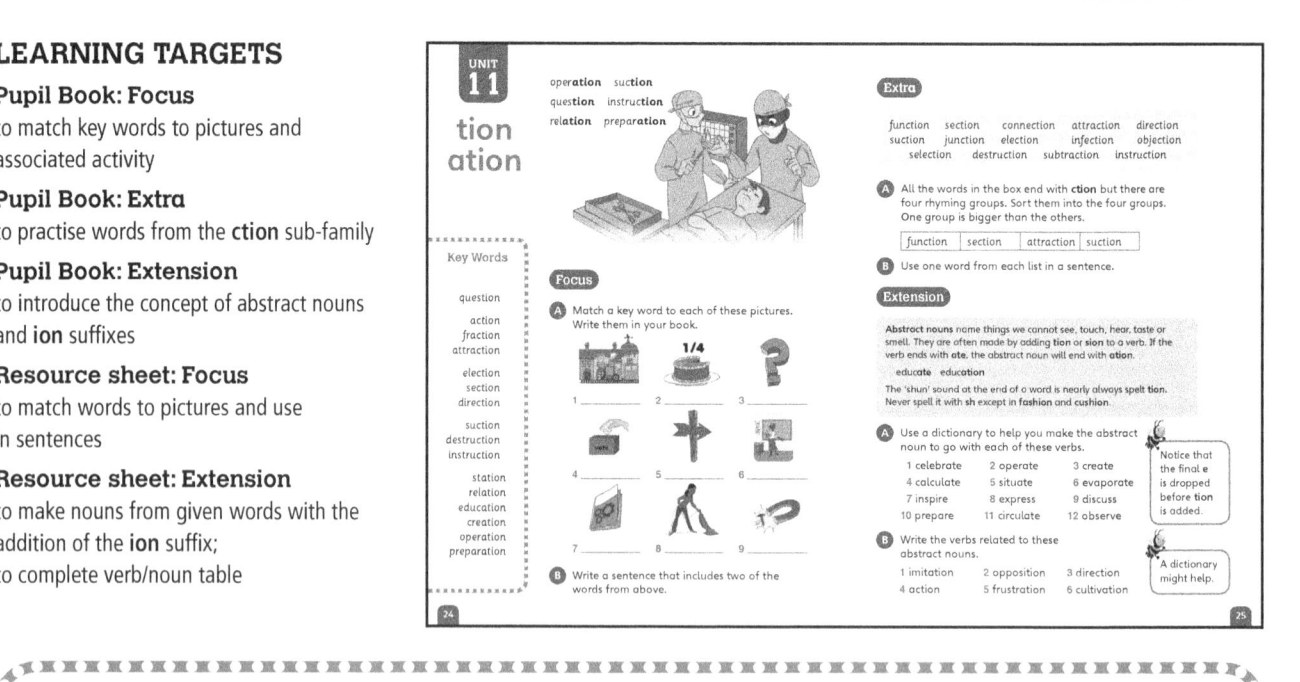

BACKGROUND NOTES AND SUGGESTIONS

As with the **sion** pattern words (Book 4 Unit 12), many of these can be difficult to learn, but working on the words in groups as shown in the *Supporting word lists* can ease some difficulties. It is helpful to realise that there are several significant spelling pattern 'sub-families' in the **tion** family.

Note that **tion** words tend to be more common than **sion** words and are most commonly preceded by an **a**.

Pupil Book answers

Focus

A
1 station   2 fraction
3 question   4 election
5 direction   6 education
7 instruction   8 suction
9 attraction

B Teacher to check individual answers

Extra

function   attraction   suction
junction   subtraction instruction
destruction

section
connection
direction
election
infection
objection
selection

B Teacher to check individual answers

Extension

A
1 celebration   2 operation
3 creation   4 calculation
5 situation   6 evaporation
7 inspiration   8 expression
9 discussion   10 preparation
11 circulation   12 observation

B
1 imitate   2 oppose
3 direct   4 act
5 frustrate 6 cultivate

Resource sheet answers

Focus

relation   education
celebration   direction
action   operation

Teacher to check individual answers.

Extension

A
1 creation   2 situation
3 operation   4 relation
5 toleration   6 dictation
7 rotation   8 dedication

B
1 observation   2 reservation
3 imagination   4 combination
5 invitation   6 occupation
7 determination 8 sensation

C
navigate navigation
accelerate acceleration
cultivate cultivation
combine combination
imitate imitation
consider consideration
celebrate celebration
connect connection

Supporting word lists

ation
nation station ration
location relation vacation
celebration conservation
conversation education explanation
occupation operation population
situation vaccination examination
investigation multiplication

ition
ambition condition edition ignition
position addition tuition
ammunition competition recognition
repetition expedition

otion
lotion potion devotion
motion emotion
promotion commotion

etion
completion deletion discretion

ption
eruption disruption
deception reception caption
option description

ction
action faction fraction traction
attraction extraction subtraction
section connection direction
election infection objection
selection fiction friction distinction
suction instruction
function junction

ntion
mention attention detention
intention invention

BOOK 4 · UNIT 12

LEARNING TARGETS

Pupil Book: Focus
to identify and copy key words from a wordsearch puzzle

Pupil Book: Extra
to match target words and definitions

Pupil Book: Extension
to examine some of the exceptions to the normal **sion** pattern

Resource sheet: Focus
to complete and find target words using given letter patterns;
to find target words in a wordsearch

Resource sheet: Extension
to make nouns from given words with the addition of the **ion** suffix

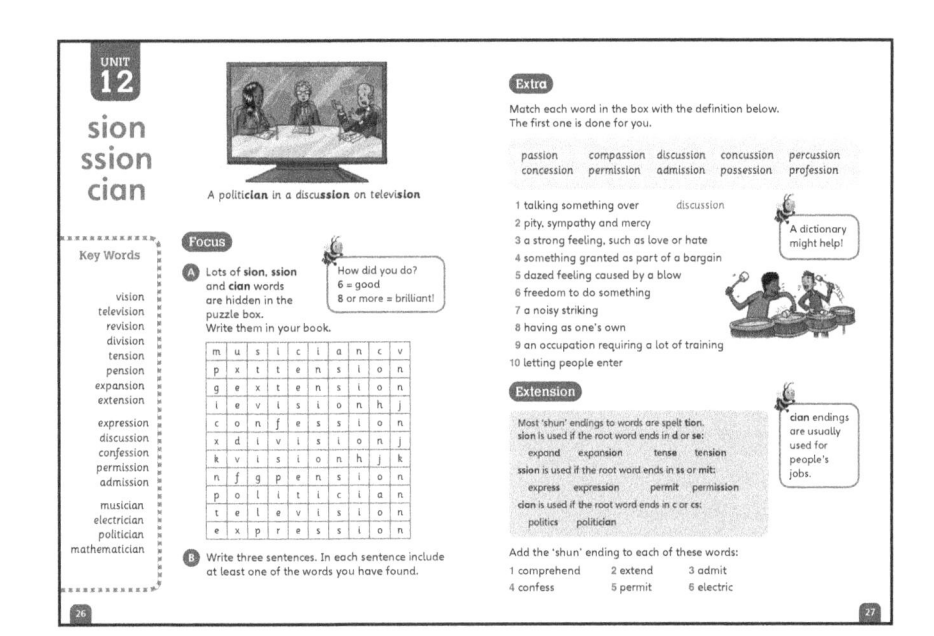

BACKGROUND NOTES AND SUGGESTIONS

As with the **tion** pattern words in the previous unit, many of these words can prove difficult to learn for some children. However working on the words in groups as shown in the *Supporting word lists* can ease some difficulties.

Note that **tion** words (see Book 3 Unit 12) tend to be more common than **sion** words, which are often formed from verbs ending in **d** or **de**, e.g. *collide/collision, divide/division*

Pupil Book answers

Focus

A musician confession politician vision extension division expression tension pension vision

B Teacher to check individual answers

Extra

1 discussion   2 compassion
3 passion   4 concession
5 concussion   6 permission
7 percussion   8 possession
9 profession   10 admission

Extension

1 comprehension 2 extension
3 admission   4 confession
5 permission   6 electrician

Resource sheet answers

Focus

A vision   confusion   pension
    television exclusion   extension
    division   illusion   suspension

B 1 pension
    2 television
    3 division

C vision television revision invasion occasion version diversion excursion pension extension

Extension

A 1 depression   2 possession
    3 impression   4 expression
    5 profession   6 concussion
    All the words end in **ss** and so only require **ion** to form the abstract noun

B 1 explosion   2 invasion
    3 division   4 persuasion
    5 extension   6 expansion
    7 erosion   8 corrosion

C express expression
    decide decision
    discuss discussion
    propel propulsion
    include inclusion
    provide provision
    collide collision
    revise revision

Supporting word lists

usion
fusion transfusion confusion
conclusion exclusion inclusion
delusion illusion disillusion

ision
vision television provision
supervision revision division
decision incision precision collision

asion
invasion occasion persuasion

osion
explosion erosion corrosion

ersion
version conversion
diversion immersion

ension
pension suspension tension
extension dimension
comprehension

ansion
mansion expansion

ession
session aggression compression
depression impression progression
expression oppression suppression
obsession possession
recession concession succession
procession profession confession

ission
mission admission commission
omission permission submission
transmission intermission

ussion
concussion discussion percussion

assion
passion compassion

BOOK 4 — UNIT 13

LEARNING TARGETS

Pupil Book: Focus
to match the target suffix words to pictures

Pupil Book: Extra
to use deduction to discover the meanings of the target prefixes

Pupil Book: Extension
to use phrases based around the target words

Resource sheet: Focus
to trace and copy letter patterns and complete word fans

Resource sheet: Extension
to define and use given phrases using prefixed words

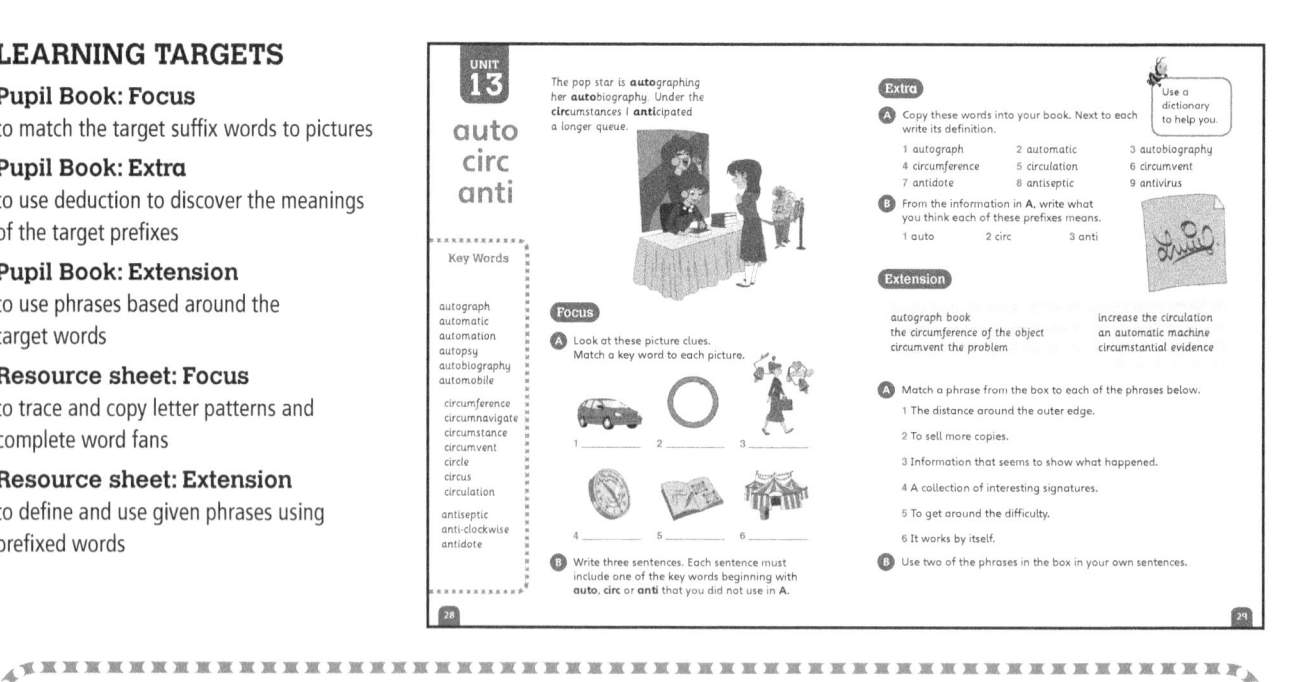

BACKGROUND NOTES AND SUGGESTIONS

The unit introduces three further, rather more sophisticated, prefixes – **auto** meaning *self* or *own*, **circum** meaning *round* or *about* and **anti**, meaning *against*. Use the opportunity to revisit some of the prefixes practised previously. The following unit develops the work on prefixes.

Pupil Book answers

Focus

A
1. automobile
2. circumference
3. automatic
4. anti-clockwise
5. autograph
6. circus

B Teacher to check individual answers

Extra

A/B Teacher to check individual answers

Extension

A
1. the circumference of the object
2. increase the circulation
3. circumstantial evidence
4. autograph book
5. circumvent the problem
6. an automatic machine

B Teacher to check individual answers

Resource sheet answers

Focus

A Children should copy the patterns

B automatic autobiography
automobile autograph

circumference circumstance
circumvent circumnavigate

antiseptic antidote
antifreeze antibiotic

Extension

A Teacher to check individual answers

B Teacher to check individual answers

Supporting word lists

autograph autopsy automation
autobiography automobile automatic

circumference circumnavigate
circumstance circumvent circulate
circulation circus circle circular

antiaircraft antiauthority antibiotic
antibodies anticlimax anticlockwise
antidepressant antidote antiglare
antihunting antiwar antipasti
antirust antiseptic antismoking

BOOK 4 — UNIT 14

LEARNING TARGETS

Pupil Book: Focus
to match key prefix words with pictures and associated activity

Pupil Book: Extra
to research definitions of target words;
to deduce the meanings of the target prefixes

Pupil Book: Extension
to introduce and practise using a range of other prefixes

Resource sheet: Focus
to copy letter patterns and make/use new words with the addition of the target prefixes

Resource sheet: Extension
to complete a table of prefixes

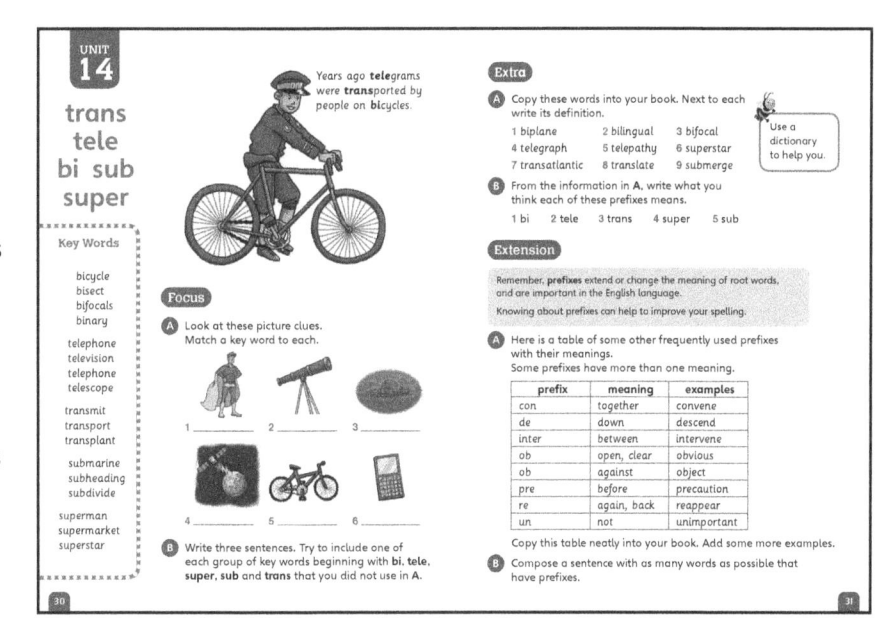

BACKGROUND NOTES AND SUGGESTIONS

As in the previous unit, this unit introduces a selection of rather more advanced prefixes – **trans** meaning *across*, **tele** meaning *distant*, **bi** meaning *two* or *twice*, **sub** meaning *under* or *beneath* and **super** meaning *above* or *beyond*.

As with the previous groupings, these prefixes encompass a range of words, some of which stand separate from their root (e.g. *transatlantic*) and others which leave an apparently meaningless stem if removed (e.g. *transmit*). This tends to occur in words 'borrowed' from other languages.

The Resource Extension section gives an opportunity to become familiar with and use a number of other prefixes, but also use the opportunity offered by the focus of this unit to revisit some of the prefixes practised previously.

Pupil Book answers

Focus

A
1 superman
2 telescope
3 submarine
4 transmit
5 bicycle
6 telephone

B Teacher to check individual answers

Extra

1 biplane – aircraft with two sets of wings
2 bilingual - speaking two languages
3 bifocal - having two focal points (as in spectacles)
4 telegraph - a means of sending messages a long distance along wires
5 telepathy - an apparent communication between people using only thoughts
6 superstar – a very famous performer or sports personality
7 transatlantic - across the Atlantic Ocean
8 translate - to express in another language
9 submerge – to cover with water

B
1 bi – two
2 tele - far off
3 trans - across, over
4 super - above
5 sub - under

Extension

A/B Teacher to check individual answers

Resource sheet answers

Focus

A Children should copy the patterns

B
1 telephone
2 telescope
3 transport
4 bifocals
5 television
6 telegraph
7 transplant
8 bicycle

C Teacher to check individual answers

Extension

bi	two
tele	ar off
trans	across
anti	against
pre	previous
im	not, without
post	after
sub	under
mis	wrong, wrongly
un	not
super	over
in	not, without
sus	below
pro	ahead, before
ir	not
il	not

Teacher to check individual word examples

Supporting word lists

transmit transmission transplant
transfer transport transparent
translucent translate
transatlantic transaction transcend
transcontinental transcribe transcript
transform transformer
transfuse transgression transistor
transpose transverse

telecommunications telegraph
telemarketing telepathy telephone
telephoto telescope telethon
television televise

bicentenary biceps bicycle
biennial bifocal bifurcate bigamy
bilateral bilingual bimonthly binary
binoculars biped biplane bisect

superb supercar supercharge
superconductor supercooled
superdeluxe superfast superfluous
superhuman superimpose
superintend superior superliner
supermarket supernatural
superman superwoman superstar

subdivide subheading submarine
submerge subdue subfreezing subway
substitiute
subvert subcommittee subsection

BOOK 4

Check-Up 1

Focus
1 bread
2 feather
3 mask
4 glass
5 nurse
6 puppy
7 kitten
8 choir
9 treasure
10 puncture
11 election
12 station
13 television
14 magician
15 circle
16 autograph
17 bicycle
18 telephone
19 submarine
20 superman

Extension

A 1 jumping
2 running
3 passing
4 throwing
5 hopping
6 shaving

B 1 unkind
2 impossible
3 disobey
4 illegal
5 unnecessary
6 misbehave
7 invisible
8 reorganise
9 immodest
10 irregular
11 disservice
12 decompose

C 1 crossly
2 cleverly
3 carefully
4 merrily
5 heavily
6 gently
7 tragically
8 truly

D 1 dangerous
2 famous
3 furious
4 victorious
5 glorious
6 various
7 ambitious
8 glamorous

E 1 attraction
2 election
3 education
4 operation
5 expansion
6 division
7 confession
8 extension

F Teacher to check individual answers

BOOK 4

UNIT 15

LEARNING TARGETS

Pupil Book: Focus
to add the target suffixes to a selection of words before sorting them

Pupil Book: Extra
to identify the target suffixes in a group of words

Pupil Book: Extension
to secure other suffixes from previous units in the course

Resource sheet: Focus
to match target words to pictures

Resource sheet: Extension
to secure the rules for adding the suffix ic

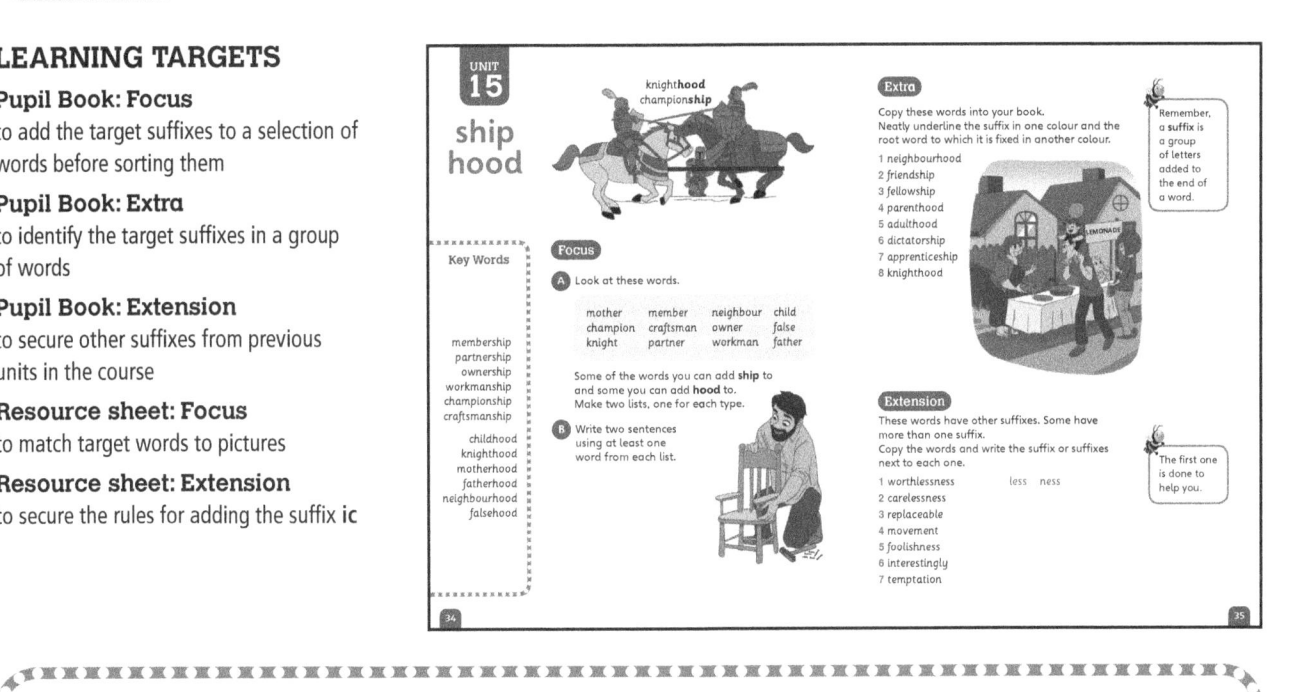

BACKGROUND NOTES AND SUGGESTIONS

This unit gives further focus on the all-important suffixes that form abstract nouns. In most cases these suffixes are simply added to the root word, and thus are not difficult to construct. However, some of the words formed by using these endings are quite difficult and might need some discussion and exemplification.

Pupil Book answers

Focus

A
motherhood membership
neighbourhood championship
childhood workmanship
falsehood ownership
knighthood partnership
fatherhood craftmanship

B Teacher to check individual answers

Extra

1 neighbour<u>hood</u>	2 friend<u>ship</u>
3 fellow<u>ship</u>	4 parent<u>hood</u>
5 adult<u>hood</u>	6 dictator<u>ship</u>
7 apprentice<u>ship</u>	8 knight<u>hood</u>

Extension

1 worthlessness	less	ness
2 carelessness	less	ness
3 replaceable	able	
4 movement	ment	
5 foolishness	ish	ness
6 interestingly	ing	ly
7 temptation	ation	

Resource sheet answers

Focus

championship   membership
authorship   friendship
craftsmanship   partnership

Teacher to check individual answers

Extension

A
1 photographic
2 geometric
3 majestic
4 economic
5 historic
6 specific
7 horrific
8 geographic

B Children should note that final **y** is dropped before **ic** is added

C Teacher to check individual answers

Supporting word lists

craftsmanship apprenticeship membership
ownership workmanship championship
partnership dictatorship fellowship

knighthood neighbourhood childhood
falsehood fatherhood motherhood

75

BOOK 4 — UNIT 16

LEARNING TARGETS

Pupil Book: Focus
to select **ch**, **que** or **gue** to complete key words and associated activity

Pupil Book: Extra
matching key words with definitions

Pupil Book: Extension
to find definitions of selected key **ch** (French derived) words

Resource sheet: Focus
to match words to pictures and use given words in sentences

Resource sheet: Extension
to complete exercises which highlight confusing words

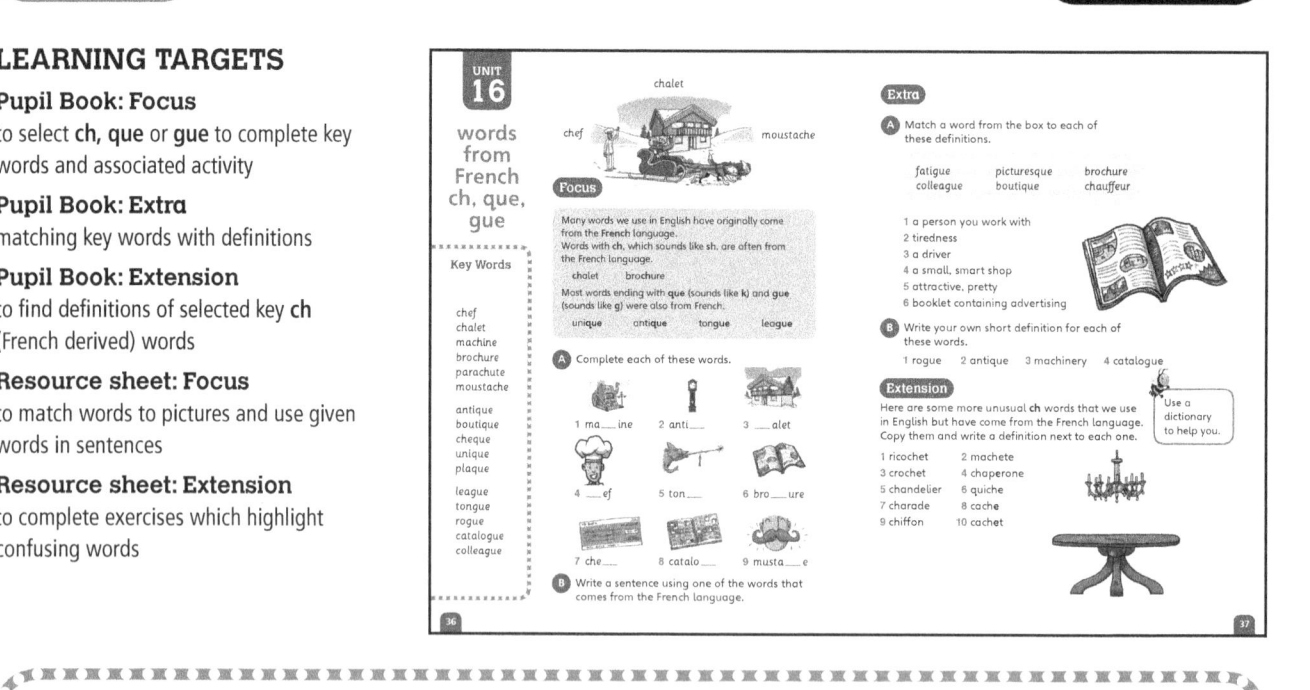

BACKGROUND NOTES AND SUGGESTIONS

Certain 'tricky' words defy grouping with others. However, within this unit, three letter pattern groups are identified – **que**, **gue** and **ch** grapheme being sounded **sh**. Like many of the words that apparently defy English logic, these have been borrowed from another language – in this case, French.

Pupil Book answers

Focus
A
1 machine 2 antique 3 chalet
4 chef   5 tongue   6 brochure
7 cheque   8 catalogue 9 mustache

B Teacher to check individual answers

Extra
A
1 colleague   2 fatigue
3 chauffeur   4 boutique
5 picturesque 6 catalogue

Teacher to check individual answers

Extension
Teacher to check individual answers

Resource sheet answers

Focus
A
1 parachute 2 tongue
3 chalet   4 catalogue
5 antique   6 machine

B Teacher to check individual answers

Extension
A
1 chef   2 brochure
3 chalet   4 machine
5 charades 6 chandelier

B Teacher to check individual answers

C Teacher to check individual answers

Supporting word lists

ei as in tree (cei words)
receive receipt deceive ceiling
perceive conceit

ei as in cape
rein veil vein feint
reign beige
neigh weigh eight weight
sleigh freight
eighty eighteen eightieth
neighbour

ei as in kite
height
either neither
eiderdown

other ei words
their leisure weird protein heir
sovereign foreign

ch as sh
brochure chandelier
chef chivalry chauffeur
crochet machete machine
moustache parachute ricochet

BOOK 4 — UNIT 17

LEARNING TARGETS

Pupil Book: Focus
to match key words to pictures and identify suffixes

Pupil Book: Extra
to build family groups of words related to the same root

Pupil Book: Extension
to use a dictionary to support word definitions

Resource sheet: Focus
to sort words by target digraphs and letter patterns;
to complete cloze activity

Resource sheet: Extension
to sort words by target digraphs and letter patterns and appreciate some related characteristics

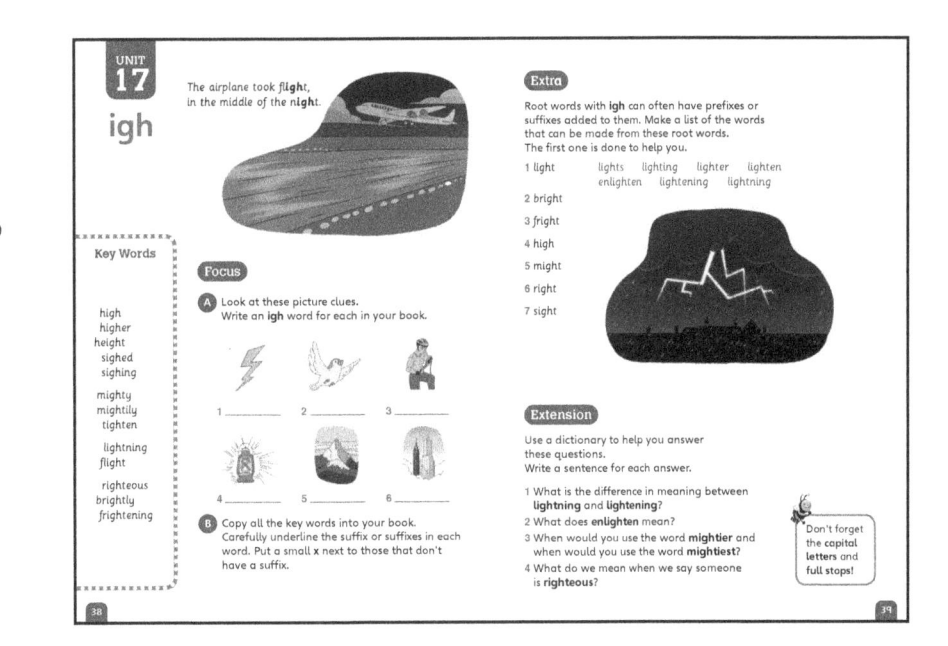

BACKGROUND NOTES AND SUGGESTIONS

igh is a 'classic' letter pattern, from which children can draw considerable satisfaction once learnt. Most words that end in the **ight** phoneme use **ight**. A few words use the digraph **i-e**, including common words such as *kite* and *white*. Some technical and scientific words end in **yte** (e.g. *byte*) and **ite** (e.g. *bauxite*).

Pupil Book answers

Focus

A
1 lightning 2 flight
3 tighten 4 brightly
5 height/mighty 6 higher/height

B high higher height sighed sighing mighty mightily tighten lightning flight righteous brightly frightening

Extra
1 light lights lighting lighter lighten enlighten lightening lightning
2 bright brighter brightest brighten brightening brightened
3 fright frighten frightening frightened
4 high higher highest height
5 might mighty mightier mightiest
6 right rightly righteous
7 sight sighted sighting unsightly

Extension
Teacher to check individual answers.

Resource sheet answers

Focus

A
hike	bright	shy
spike	night	sky
like	light	cry
bike	fright	dry

B Teacher to check individual answers

C
1 night 2 sky
3 like 4 fright
5 light 6 cry

Extension

A Teacher to check individual answers

B 1 Resource sheet asks for an entire sentence for each answer. Suggest: **c** most often comes before the **ial** ending.
2 **ough** can represent several different sounds
3 Teacher to check individual answers

Supporting word lists

high sigh thigh

fight light might night right sight

tight light blight flight slight

bright fright

brighten frighten lighten tighten

enlighten lightning

righteous

BOOK 4
UNIT 18

LEARNING TARGETS

Pupil Book: Focus
to add **al** as a prefix

Pupil Book: Extra
to consider the meaning of the target prefixes

Pupil Book: Extension
to write a short story using the target prefixes

Resource sheet: Focus
to secure the **al** prefix

Resource sheet: Extension
to secure the **a**, **af**, **ad** and **al** prefixes; to write a short story

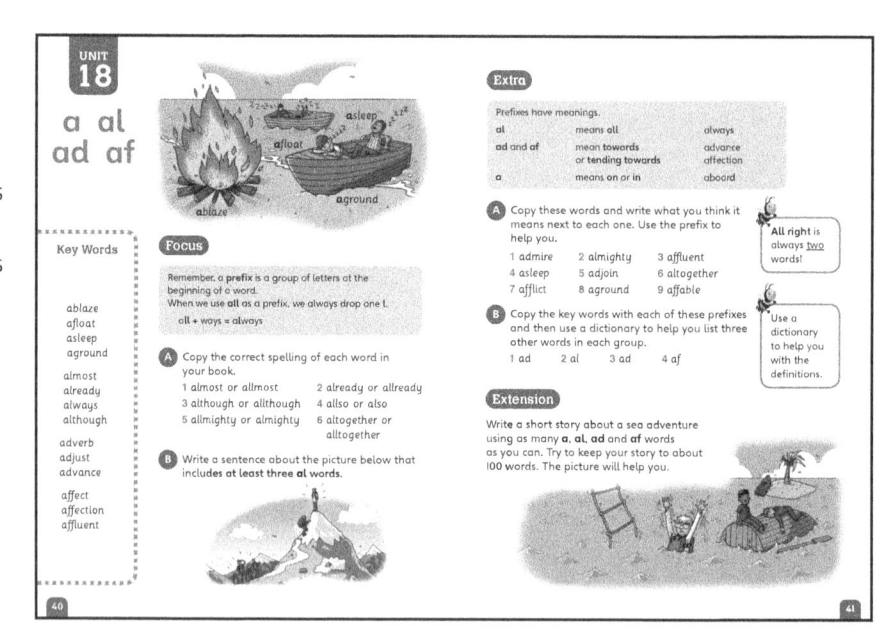

BACKGROUND NOTES AND SUGGESTIONS

As outlined earlier, the key rule to secure is that when adding any prefix to a root word, we just add it. In other words, the children should never be tempted to 'adjust' the spelling, for example to eliminate double letters.

As has been taught, prefixes modify the meaning of the root, sometimes radically by forming the antonym, though in the case of the prefixes covered in this unit, more subtly.

Another characteristic of some of the prefixes in this unit is that whilst forming the beginning of a word, they can't be detached to leave a recognisable root word. This is particularly true of the **af** prefix, which means *tending towards*; **ad** means **towards**; **al** means **all**; **a** means *in a state of*.

Pupil Book answers

Focus
A
1 almost
2 already
3 although
4 also
5 almighty
6 altogether

B Teacher to check individual answers

Extra
A/B Teacher to check individual answers

Extension
Teacher to check individual answers

Resource sheet answers

Focus
A Teacher to check individual answers

B Teacher to check individual answers

Extension
A Teacher to check individual answers

B Teacher to check individual answers

Supporting word lists

ad
addition adjoin adjacent adjust admire advance advise adjective adverb advent

af
affection affect affix affable affluent afflict affirm

al
already always altogether also although almighty almost

a
afield astride another abide aboard away afloat awake alive alert around asleep ablaze apart alone aloft aground

BOOK 4
UNIT 19

LEARNING TARGETS

Pupil Book: Focus
to match key word plurals to pictures

Pupil Book: Extra
to construct plural forms of target words

Pupil Book: Extension
to add suffixes to the target word types

Resource sheet: Focus
to secure the formation of **f** plurals

Resource sheet: Extension
to construct rules for making the **f** plural forms

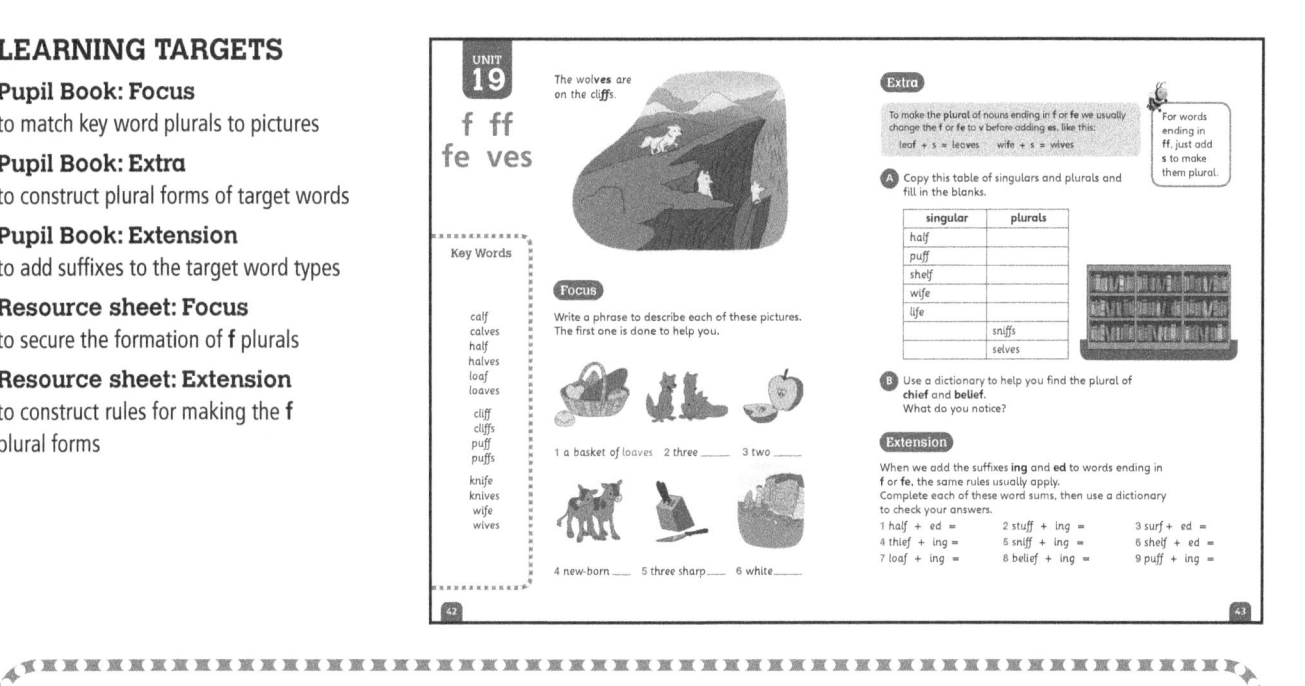

BACKGROUND NOTES AND SUGGESTIONS

The thrust of this unit is to teach the plural forms of words ending in **f**, **ff** and **fe**. Most words ending in **f** change to **ves** in the plural. Words ending in **ff** add **s** and words ending in **e** take **ves**.

It is important to note that sometimes, when a word is used in a different class, moving from noun to verb (e.g. *belief, grief*), **ves** is used. Hence *beliefs* (plural noun) and *believes* (verb).

Pupil Book answers

Focus

1 loaves	2 wolves	3 halves
4 calves	5 knives	6 cliffs

Extra

A
half	halves
puff	puffs
shelf	shelves
wife	wives
life	lives
sniff	sniffs
self	selves

B Children should note that both 'chief' and 'belief' take **s** to form their plural.

Extension
1 halved
2 stuffing
3 surfed
4 thieving
5 sniffing
6 shelved
7 loafing
8 believing
9 puffing

Resource sheet answers

Focus
wolves
shelves
scarves
loaves
leaves
calves
halves

Extension
Teacher to check individual answers

Supporting word lists

f/ves
scarf self shelf leaf loaf calf half self thief wolf

ff/s
sniff puff cuff staff stuff bluff cliff

fe/ves
life wife knife

ve/ves
believe swerve save glove curve

exceptions
chief/chiefs belief/beliefs safe/safes

BOOK 4 — UNIT 20

LEARNING TARGETS

Pupil Book: Focus
to identify the missing letters to complete target word endings;
to complete a cloze activity

Pupil Book: Extra
to find the answers to clues using words with the target endings

Pupil Book: Extension
to add **n**, **en** or **on** to complete words

Resource sheet: Focus
to complete words sums using the target word endings;
to complete cloze activity

Resource sheet: Extension
to complete various activities selecting the appropriate target word endings

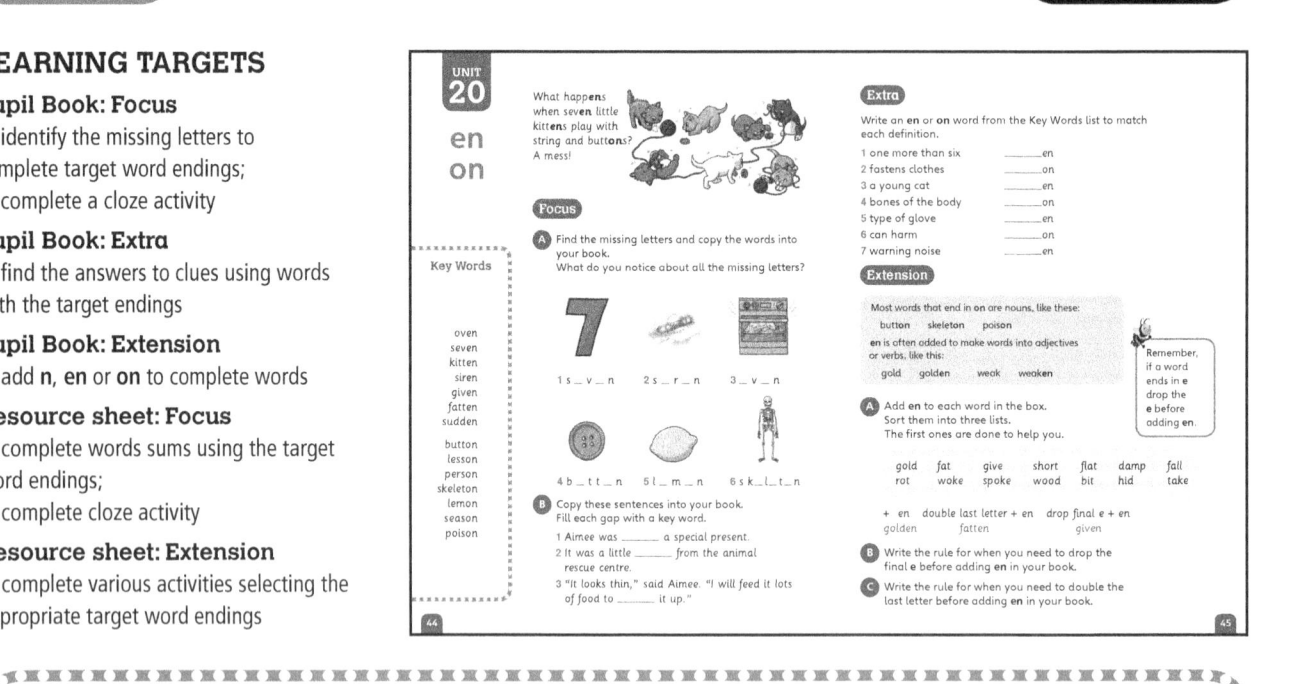

BACKGROUND NOTES AND SUGGESTIONS

It will be noted that, whilst not an infallible rule, most adjectives and verbs end in **en** rather than **on**. A few nouns end in **en** (e.g. *garden, kitten, heaven*), but more end in **on**.

Most **on** endings are part of the longer **tion** or **sion** suffix patterns (see Unit 11 and Unit 12).

Pupil Book answers

Focus
A 1 seven 2 siren 3 oven
   4 button 5 lemon 6 skeleton

B 1 given 2 kitten 3 fatten

Extra
1 seven 2 button 3 kitten
4 skeleton 5 mitten 6 poison
7 siren

Extension
A golden   fatten   given
   shorten   flatten   dampen
   fallen   rotten   woken
   spoken   wooden   bitten
   hidden   taken

B/C Children should note that the same rules apply (for doubling final consonant and adding to words ending in **e**) as they do for other vowel suffixes.

Resource sheet answers

Focus
A happen   cotton
   kitten   lesson
   sudden   season
   given   reason
   siren   prison

B kitten cotton

C Teacher to check individual answers

Extension
A 1 lesson listen
   2 fallen
   3 reason attention
   4 skeleton
   5 fallen
   6 taken
   7 position
   8 person

B 1 hasten   2 squadron
   3 citizen   4 falcon
   5 burden   6 oxygen
   7 matron   8 poison
   9 iron   10 hyphen

Teacher to check individual sentences

Supporting word lists

batten fatten flatten
bitten kitten mitten rotten
seven given siren
dampen happen
golden wooden soften heaven
sudden burden oxygen

cotton button mutton glutton
lesson reckon ribbon common
lemon matron pardon
skeleton squadron
piston prison person reason
season iron

BOOK 4 — UNIT 21

LEARNING TARGETS

Pupil Book: Focus
to form the singular possessive from a short phrase

Pupil Book: Extra
to form the plural possessive to describe pictures

Pupil Book: Extension
to learn where to place the apostrophe in irregular possessive noun forms

Resource sheet: Focus
to practise writing the singular possessive from a short phrase

Resource sheet: Extension
to practise writing the plural possessive from a short phrase

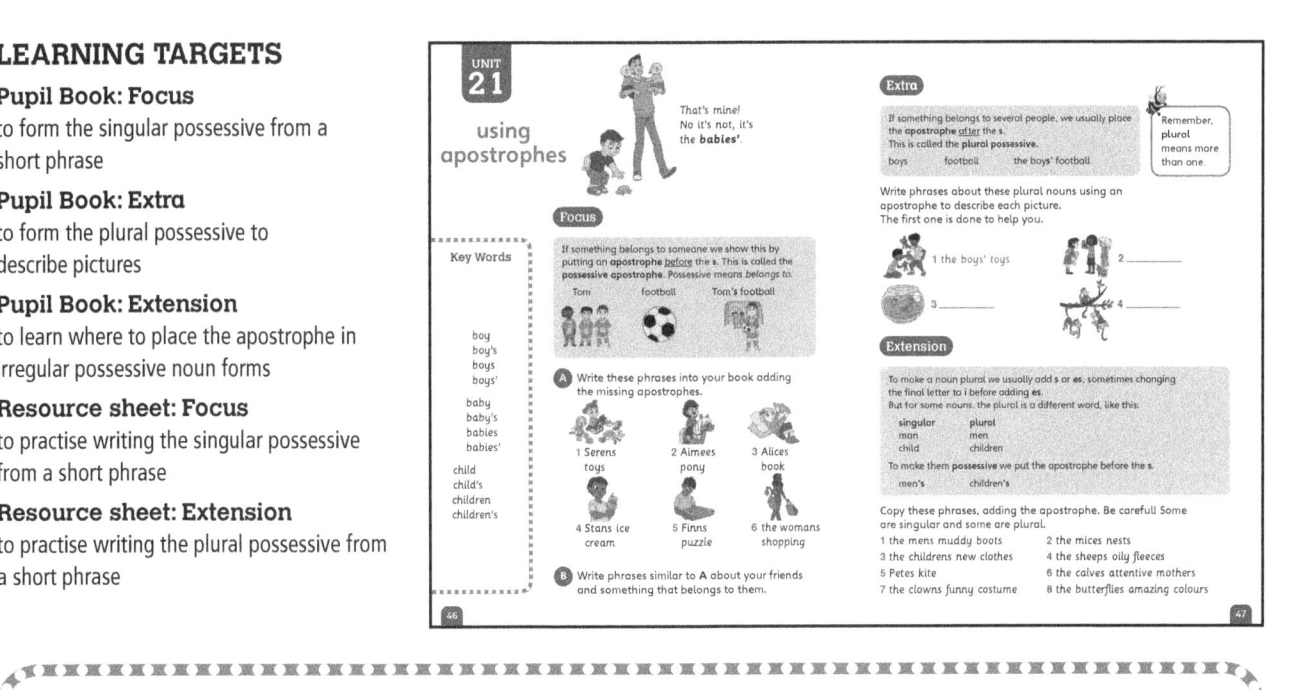

BACKGROUND NOTES AND SUGGESTIONS

The focus of this unit is on apostrophes when used to denote possession. Earlier in the course the apostrophe has been used to indicate a contraction and also possession – but only the singular possessive form.

This unit consolidates the singular possessive (*boy's*), moving on to the regular plural possessive (*boys'*) and the irregular form in which plural words are involved (*children's*).

Pupil Book answers

Focus

A 1 Seren's toys
   2 Aimee's pony
   3 Alice's book
   4 Stan's ice cream
   5 Finn's puzzle
   6 the woman's shopping

B Teacher to check individual answers

Extra

1 the boys' toys
2 the girls' pets
3 the fishes' bowl
4 the monkeys' bananas

Extension

1 the men's muddy boots
2 the mice's nests
3 the children's new clothes
4 the sheeps' oily fleeces
5 Pete's kite
6 the calves' attentive mothers
7 the clown's funny costume
8 the butterflies' amazing colours

Resource sheet answers

Focus

the dog's ball
Sam's bike
the hen's egg
Ellie's book
the bird's nest
Sarah's flute
the man's car

Extension

the dog's lead
the children's towels
Ben's pillow
the workmen's mugs
the cat's little kittens
the five policemen's helmets

Supporting word lists

children women men
people geese mice
barracks deer

BOOK 4 — UNIT 22

LEARNING TARGETS

Pupil Book: Focus
to match words which are homophones

Pupil Book: Extra
to recognise homophones and
near-homophones

Pupil Book: Extension
to use homophones correctly in sentences

Resource sheet: Focus
to match appropriate homophones
to pictures

Resource sheet: Extension
to select and use correct homophones

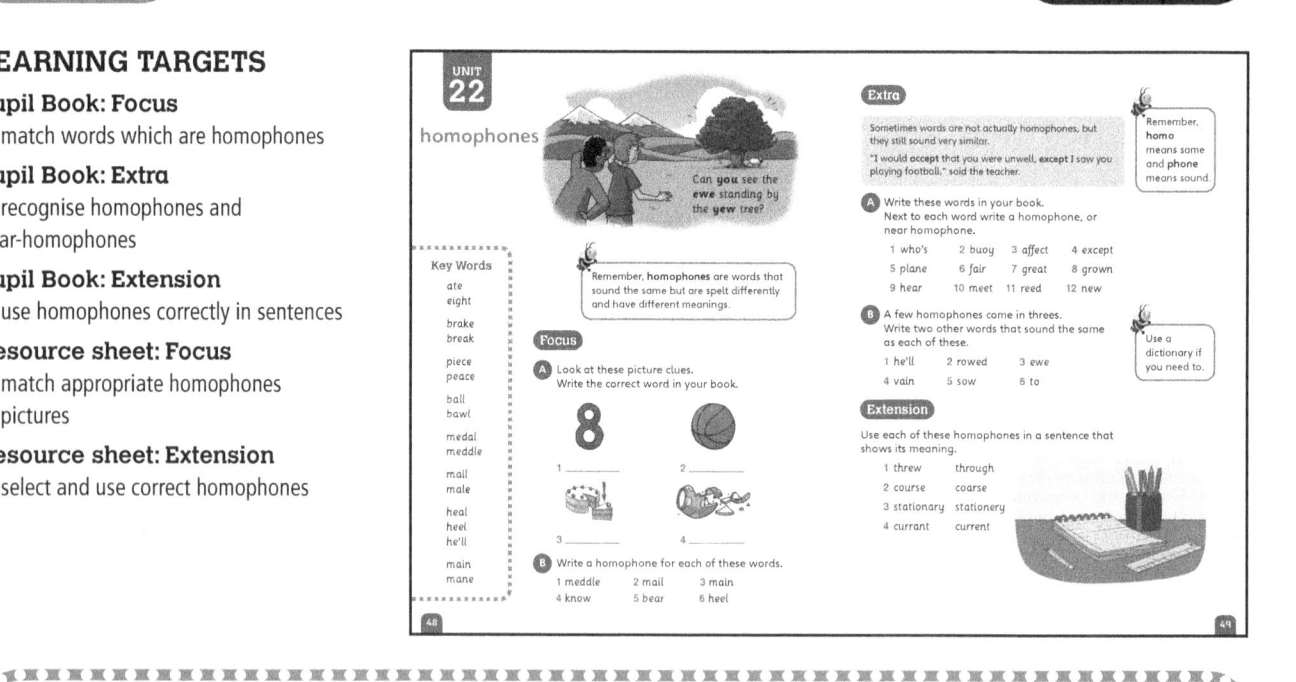

BACKGROUND NOTES AND SUGGESTIONS

As noted previously, homophones are words with the same (*homo*) sound (*phone*) but different spelling and meanings, whereas homonyms have the same sound and spelling but different meanings.

In this unit we develop and extend earlier work on the homophones, moving on from words which are high-frequency in children's writing to those which are less often used but still cause problems from time to time. Reports on children's performance have suggested that children should learn to spell words where there are different ways of representing vowel diagraphs, such as *brake* and *break*, which covers most homophones.

Pupil Book answers

Focus

A
1 eight 2 ball
3 piece 4 break

B
1 medal 2 male
3 mane   4 no
5 bare   6 heal

Extra

A
1 whose 2 boy   3 effect
4 accept 5 plain 6 fare
7 great 8 groan 9 here
10 meat 11 read 12 knew

B
1 heel heal   2 road rode
3 you yew   4 vane vein
5 so sew   6 too two

Extension
Teacher to check individual answers

Resource sheet answers

Focus

A
rain   deer
night sun
key   hare

B Teacher to check individual answers

C Teacher to check individual answers

Extension

A
1 weak
2 sales
3 hire
4 meet
5 flour
6 knot
7 knows
8 knew, would
9 steel
10 rain, through

B Teacher to check individual answers

Supporting word lists

Some of these are not strictly homophones, but are 'near homophones' and are being included because in some regions they can sound very similar and cause confusion.

were we're
where wear
there their they're
you yew ewe
to two too
be bee
new knew
right write
through threw
hole whole
are our
see sea
no know
morning mourning
great grate
I eye
in inn
heard herd
might mite
place plaice
eyes ice
for four
of off

BOOK 4 — UNIT 23

LEARNING TARGETS

Pupil Book: Focus
to identify syllables in the key words

Pupil Book: Extra
to identify syllables and vowels in given multi-syllabic words

Pupil Book: Extension
to write rhyming double-letter words and divide into syllables

Resource sheet: Focus
to identify syllables in the key words

Resource sheet: Extension
to identify and divide words into syllables

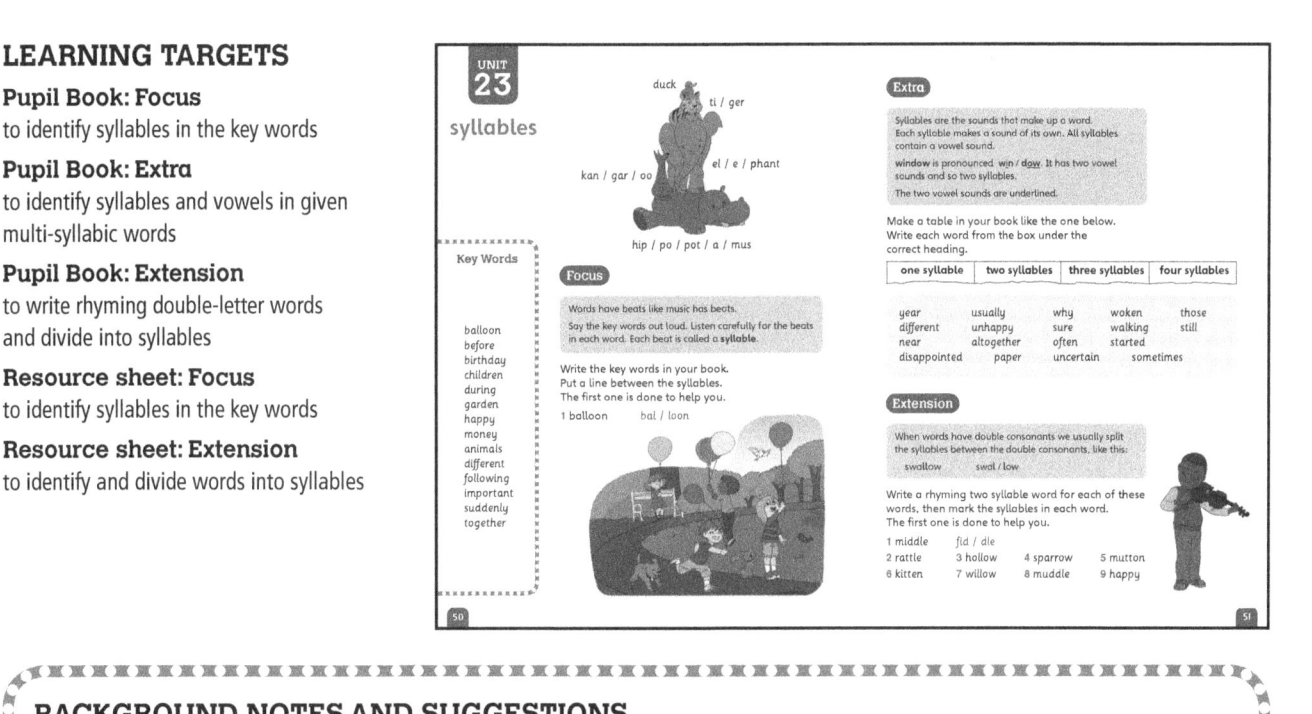

BACKGROUND NOTES AND SUGGESTIONS

Identifying syllabic patterns in multi-syllabic words is another prop that some children find helpful to the mastery of good spelling. In this unit, particular attention is given to words that include double-letter patterns as these can often confuse.

Pupil Book answers

Focus

bal/loon	be/fore	birth/day
child/ren	dur/ing	gar/den
hap/py	mo/ney	a/ni/mals
dif/fer/ent	fol/low/ing	im/port/ant
sud/den/ly	to/ge/ther	

Extra

one syllable	two syllables
year	started
why	woken
those	walking
sure	paper
still	sometimes
near	often

three syllables	four syllables
unhappy	usually
different	altogether
uncertain	disappointed

Extension
Teacher to check individual answers, though note that double-letter words should have their syllables split between the double letters.

Resource sheet answers

Focus

A
1 money 2
2 donkey 2
3 happen 2
4 fork 1
5 elephant 3
6 gorilla 3
7 rocket 2
8 ear 1
9 biscuit 2
10 airport 2

B
1 hap/py
2 sil/ly
3 birth/day
4 Sa/tur/day
5 twen/ty
6 yes/ter/day
7 hap/pi/ly
8 Fri/day
9 mea/dow
10 im/poss/i/ble
11 un/hap/pi/ly
12 gar/den/er

Extension

A apple 2; people 2; seventeen 3; unfair 2; antelope 3; unfortunately 5; impossibility 6; alligator 4; however 3; orange 2

B
August	sister
summer	nephew
July	uncle
weekday	grandson
forest	teacher
trousers	painting
badger	reading
squirrel	playful

C Teacher to check individual answers

BOOK 4 — UNIT 24

LEARNING TARGETS

Pupil Book: Focus
to match key words to pictures

Pupil Book: Extra
to relate **ive** words to other words from the same family

Pupil Book: Extension
to collect **ive** words that could be used to describe a person

Resource sheet: Focus
to complete a word fan using the target letter pattern;
to write sentences with target letter pattern

Resource sheet: Extension
to create words using a range of roots, prefixes and suffixes

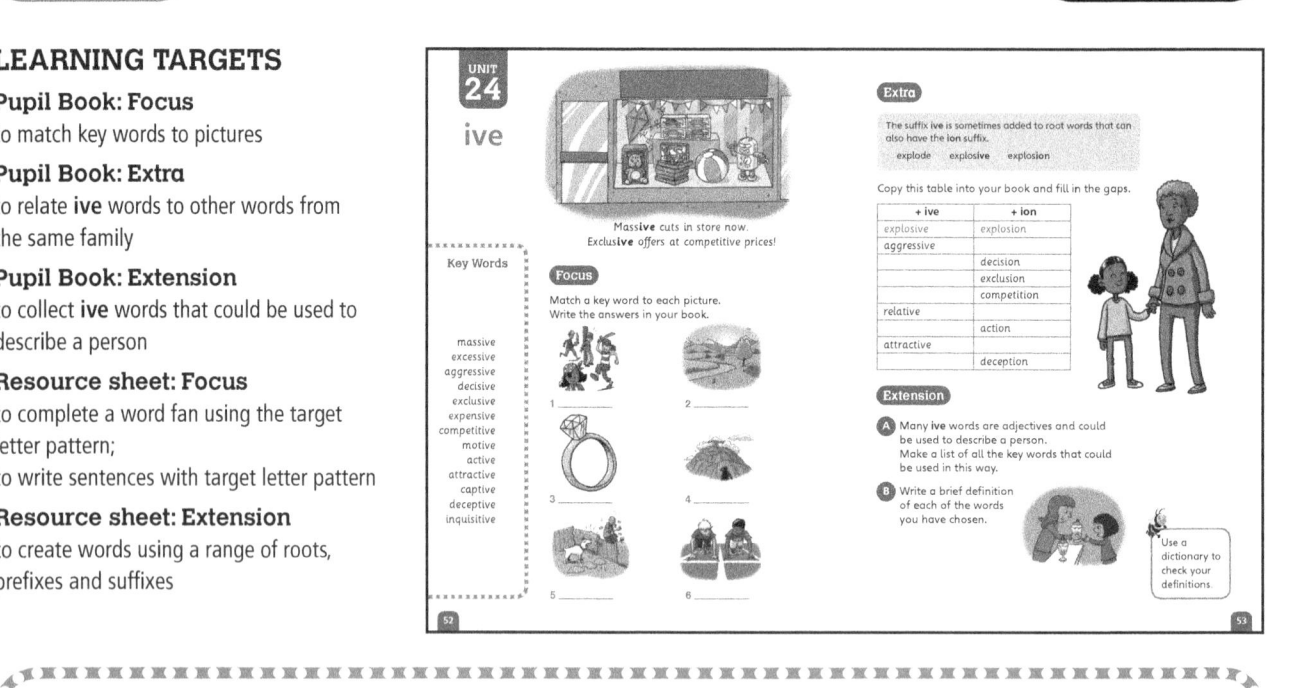

BACKGROUND NOTES AND SUGGESTIONS

The suffix **ive**, which generally forms the adjective in a word family, is usually preceded by an **s** or **t** as exemplified in the *Supporting word lists*.

Pupil Book answers

Focus
A
1 captive   2 attractive
3 expensive 4 massive
5 aggressive 6 competitive

Extra

+ive	+ion
explosive	explosion
aggressive	aggression
decisive	decision
exclusive	exclusion
competitive	competition
relative	relation
active	action
attractive	attraction
deceptive	deception

Extension
A Teacher to check individual answers
B Teacher to check individual answers

Resource sheet answers

Focus
A Children should copy the pattern

B massive
excessive
active
attractive
inventive

C Teacher to check individual answers

Extension
decide — deciding decided decidedly
         decisive decision
attract — attracting attracted attractive
          attraction
thank — thanking thanked thankful
        (thankfully)
construct — constructing constructed
            constructive construction
secret — secretly secretive
weak — weaker weakly
       weakness weaken
tidy — tidying tidied tidily tidiness
move — moving moved mover
       movement movable
false — falsely falsehood
revolt — revolting revolted revolution
         (revolutionary)
happy — happily happiness unhappy
        happier happiest

words in brackets require addition of two suffixes

Supporting word lists

sive
massive excessive aggressive decisive
explosive exclusive expensive

tive
native inquisitive competitive
motive relative active attractive
captive deceptive

others
forgive

BOOK 4 — UNIT 25

LEARNING TARGETS

Pupil Book: Focus
to complete a cloze activity

Pupil Book: Extra
to learn to distinguish the correct suffix form by considering the antonym

Pupil Book: Extension
to add the suffixes to words ending in e

Resource sheet: Focus
to copy target patterns and words and complete word sums

Resource sheet: Extension
to select required word endings and use selected words in sentences

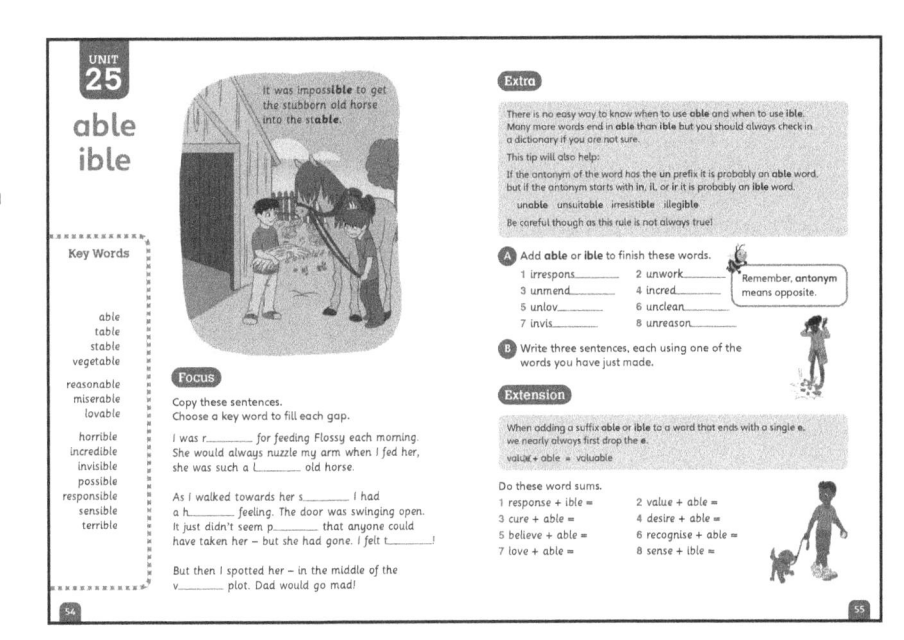

BACKGROUND NOTES AND SUGGESTIONS

As indicated in the pupil text, it is worth remembering that there are many more words ending in **able** than there are ending in **ible**, so if uncertain the safer option is to use **able**!

Note that if the antonym of the word starts with **un** it is an **able** word, but if the antonym starts with **in**, **il** or **ir** it is rather more likely to be an **ible** word, though it could be either, e.g. *unsuitable*, *irresistible*, *illegible*.

Another way to help distinguish between these endings is to appreciate that dropping **able** usually leaves a generally recognisable word (e.g. *valuable*, *agreeable*), whereas dropping **ible** is more likely to leave a 'stem' (e.g. *horrible*, *edible*).

Pupil Book answers

Focus
I was <u>responsible</u> for feeding Flossy each morning. She would always nuzzle my arm when I fed her, she was such a <u>lovable</u> old horse.

As I walked towards her <u>stable</u> I had a <u>horrible</u> feeling. The door was swinging open. It just didn't seem <u>possible</u> that anyone could have taken her - but she had gone. I felt <u>terrible</u>! But then I spotted her - in the middle of the <u>vegetable</u> plot. Dad would go mad!

Extra
A
1 irresponsible
2 unworkable
3 unmendable
4 incredible
5 unlovable
6 uncleanable
7 invisible
8 unreasonable

B Teacher to check individual answers

Extension
1 responsible
2 valuable
3 curable
4 desirable
5 believable
6 recognisable
7 lovable
8 sensible

Resource sheet answers

Focus
A Children should copy the patterns

B
table
stable
miserable
possible
terrible
invisible
horrible

Extension
A
suit	suitable	suitably
sense	sensible	sensibly
value	valuable	valuably
response	responsible	responsibly
notice	noticeable	noticeably
reason	reasonable	reasonably
recognise	recognisable	recognisably
disagree	disagreeable	disagreeably
horror	horrible	horribly
rely	reliable	reliably
access	accessible	accessibly

B Teacher to check individual answers

Supporting word lists

able
able disable table stable fable constable vegetable probable usable lovable suitable reliable miserable valuable agreeable advisable curable capable dependable perishable creditable noticeable reasonable believable disagreeable incurable unrecognisable [and many other antonyms]

ible
sensible responsible legible visible forcible horrible terrible possible incredible audible edible

BOOK 4 UNIT 26

LEARNING TARGETS

Pupil Book: Focus
to find target words in a wordsearch

Pupil Book: Extra
to identify potential problem letters in words which contain unstressed vowels

Pupil Book: Extension
to use an appreciation of syllables to help children to avoid dropping unstressed vowels

Resource sheet: Focus
to practise key words and identify unstressed vowels

Resource sheet: Extension
to practise key words and identify unstressed vowels and syllables

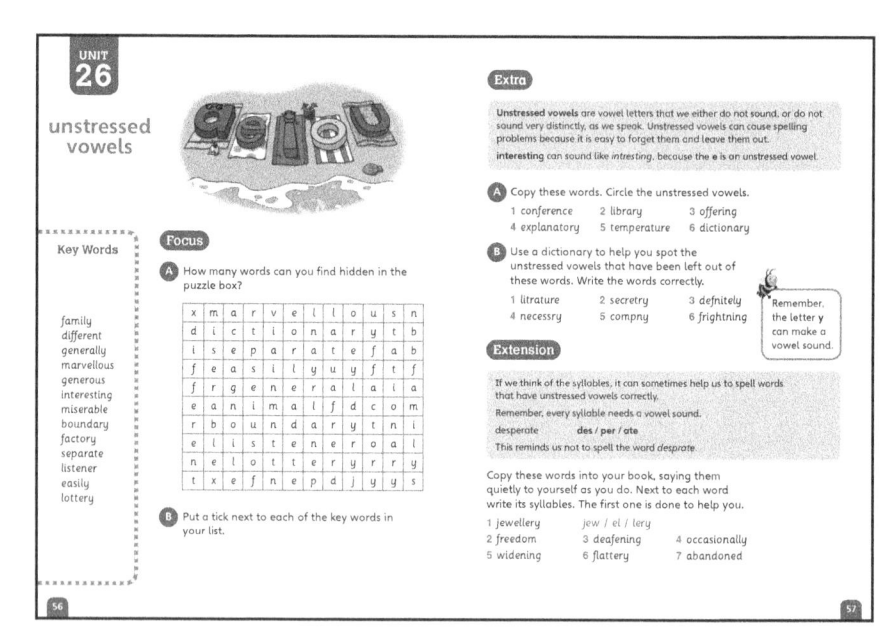

BACKGROUND NOTES AND SUGGESTIONS

Unstressed vowels in polysyllabic words are, according to a recent report on children's performance, among the most predictable causes of incorrect spelling.

Undoubtedly the key is to encourage the children to think carefully about word roots, but also to consider certain suffixes as well e.g. **ary**, **ery** and **ory** (see Book 6 Unit 19). Notice also the frequent occurrence of **er** and **en** in words in the *Supporting word lists*.

Pupil Book answers

Focus

A dictionary different miserable factory listener separate marvellous family stationary easily animal general boundary lottery

B *The following should be ticked:*
different miserable factory listener separate marvellous family easily boundary lottery

Extra

A
1 conference 2 library
3 offering 4 explanatory
5 temperature 6 dictionary

B
1 literature 2 secretary
3 definitely 4 necessary
5 company 6 frightening

Extension

1 jewellery jew/el/lery
2 freedom free/dom
3 deafening deaf/en/ing
4 occasionally o/cca/sion/al/ly
5 widening wid/en/ing
6 flattery flat/ter/y
7 abandoned a/ban/doned

Resource sheet answers

Focus

A
1 family
2 primary
3 nursery
4 general
5 lottery
6 vegetable
7 prisoner
8 library

B Teacher to check individual answers

Extension

1 difference difference dif/fer/ence
2 familiar familiar fam/i/li/ar
3 category category cat/e/gor/y
4 poisonous poisonous poi/son/ous
5 company company com/pa/ny
6 conference conference con/fe/rence
7 definitely definitely def/in/ite/ly
8 dictionary dictionary dic/tion/a/ry
9 prosperous prosperous pros/pe/rous
10 average average a/ver/age

Supporting word lists

deafening conference offering desperate definite definitely description boundary animal business stationary stationery marvellous memorable reference miserable messenger prepare freedom frightening flattery smuggler formal general different doctor dictionary difference prosperous easily factory family explanatory extra secretary primary library literate illiterate literacy literature lottery Wednesday generally generous heaven hospital separate widening interested interest disinterest jewellery voluntary poisonous category centre company compromise original carpet abandoned abominable familiar predict

BOOK 4 .... UNIT 27

LEARNING TARGETS

Pupil Book: Focus
to identify root words in words with prefixes and suffixes

Pupil Book: Extra
to construct words from roots, prefixes and suffixes

Pupil Book: Extension
to consider the origin of selected root words

Resource sheet: Focus
to create words by combining roots with prefixes and suffixes

Resource sheet: Extension
to complete word webs;
to introduce new prefixes and suffixes (diminutives)

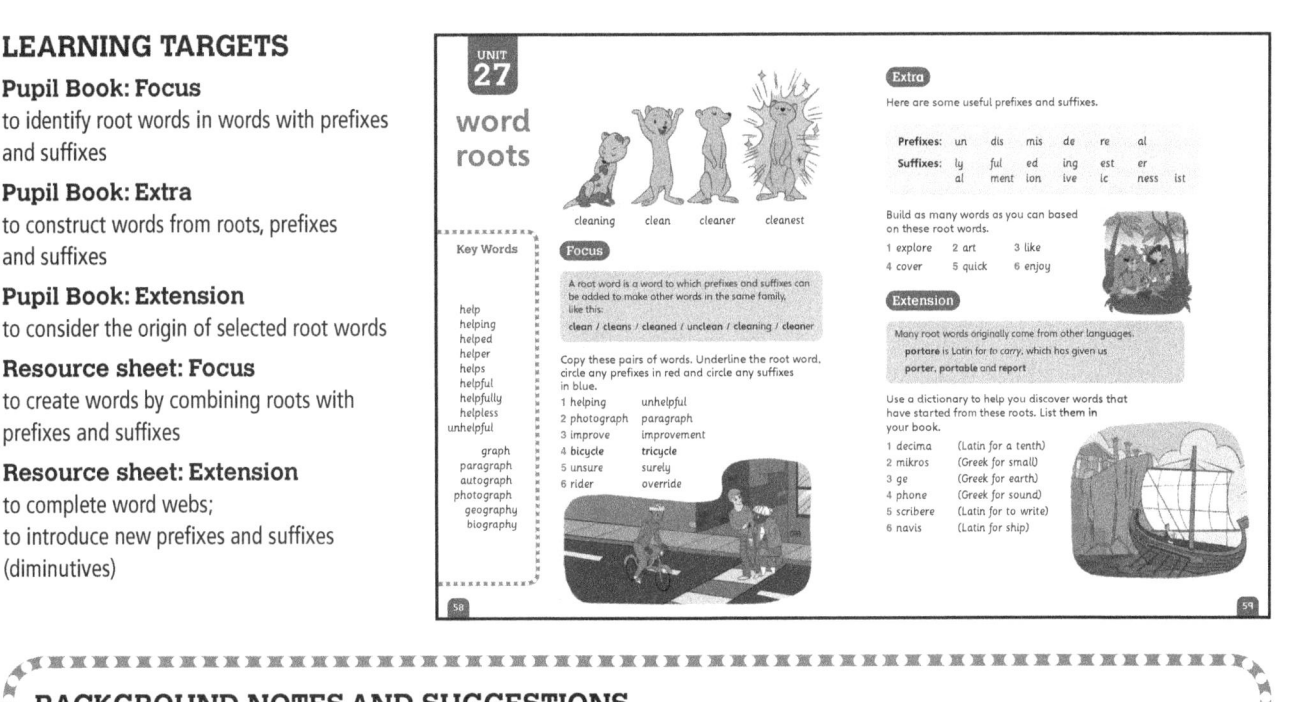

BACKGROUND NOTES AND SUGGESTIONS

Prefixes and suffixes have been recurring themes throughout the course to this point, but in this unit the relationship between affixes and roots is brought into sharp focus. Also, the concept is taught that root words often come from other languages and, in many cases, that these date back to early times.

It might well be helpful for some children for there to be a brainstorming session, collecting and comparing words with common roots and using the words collected to seek to determine the meaning of particular roots. Often, by beginning to understand and recognise the presence of roots, spelling can be made easier, e.g. knowing the root *graphein* (*write*) means that children will more easily remember that *autograph, photograph*, etc. have **ph** rather than **f** at the end.

Pupil Book answers

Focus
1 hel**p**ing   un**help**ful
2 photo**graph**   para**graph**
3 im**prove**   im**prove**ment
4 bi**cycle**   tri**cycle**
5 un**sure**   **sure**ly
6 **rid**er   over**ride**

Extra
1 explored exploring explorer exploration unexplored
2 artful artfully artist artistic arty
3 unlike dislike likable likely likeness liked liking disliked disliking
4 uncover discover discovery uncovered uncovering covering covered discovering discovered
5 quickly quicken quickened quicker quickest quickening
6 enjoyed enjoying

Extension
Teacher to check individual answers which may include:
1 decima: decimal, December, decade, decagon
2 mikros: microscope, microphone, micrometer
3 ge: geography, geology, geometry
4 phone: telephone, phoneme, phonics, microphone, phonograph

5 scribere: scribe, scribble, manuscript, describe, inscription
6 navis: navy, navigate, navigation

Resource sheet answers

Focus
A 1 quickly   2 normally
    3 hopeful   4 careful
    5 active   6 massive
    7 artist   8 balloonist
    9 acidic   10 heroic

B 1 secretively   2 instrumentalist
    3 unhelpfully   4 misinformation
    5 inactive

Extension
A Teacher to check individual answers
B Teacher to check individual answers

Supporting word lists

Root word	L=Latin Gr=Greek	Meaning	Examples
accidere	L	happen	accident decide incident
aequus	L	equal	equal equality equator
annus	L	a year	annual biennial annals
atmos	Gr	vapour	atmosphere atmospheric
biblion	Gr	book	bibliography
civis, civilis	L	citizen	civic civilised civilian
dictatum	L	to say or tell	dictate dictionary contradict
hydor	Gr	water	hydrant hydraulic hydrogen
manus	L	the hand	manufacture manual manacle
monos	Gr	alone, single	monologue monopoly monogram
pathos	Gr	feeling	pathetic sympathy apathy
prima	L	first	prime primary primitive
sentire	L	to feel, think	sense sensible scent sentence
sphaira	Gr	sphere	spherical hemisphere
venire	L	to come	convene intervene advent event

87

BOOK 4 — UNIT 28

LEARNING TARGETS

Pupil Book: Focus
to secure the terms vowel and consonant and practise ordering skills

Pupil Book: Extra
to revise and secure alphabetical ordering by second and third letter

Pupil Book: Extension
to use a dictionary for checking definitions

Resource sheet: Focus
to familiarise letter order in the alphabet

Resource sheet: Extension
to secure alphabetical ordering by second letter;
to practise using guide words

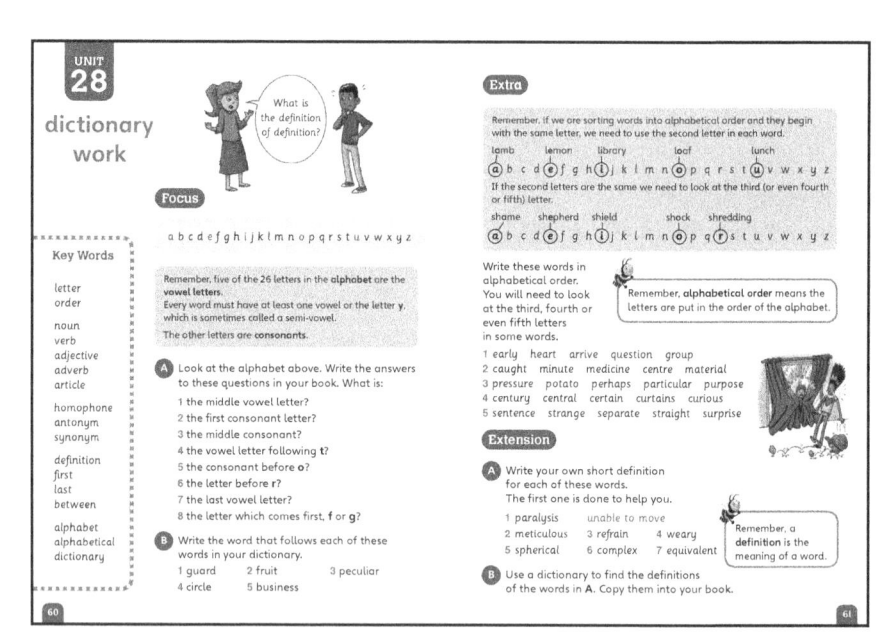

BACKGROUND NOTES AND SUGGESTIONS

This unit provides an opportunity to secure alphabetical ordering skills and for the children to begin to become comfortable with using a dictionary for checking the definitions of words.

Pupil Book answers

Focus

A 1 i 2 b 3 n 4 u 5 n 6 q
     7 u 8 f

B Teacher to check individual answers

Extra

A 1 arrive early group heart question
    2 caught centre material medicine minute
    3 particular perhaps potato pressure purpose
    4 central century certain curious curtains
    5 sentence separate straight strange surprise

Extension
Teacher to check individual answers

Resource sheet answers

Focus

A 1 row   2 sow   3 tow
    1 boat 2 float 3 goat

B 1 shop 2 slop   3 stop
    1 thin 2 tip   3 trip
    1 cap   2 cloud 3 crowd
    1 ant   2 apple 3 aunt

Extension

A Teacher to check individual answers

B 1 plane   2 jingle
    3 sheet   4 hat
    5 digger   6 stud
    7 dragonfly 8 panic
    9 wonder   10 berry

BOOK 4

Check-Up 2

Focus
1 chef 2 reins 3 lightning 4 night
5 asleep 6 aground/afloat 7 loaves 8 calves
9 oven 10 skeleton 11 stable 12 vegetable
13 library 14 secretary 15 dictionary 16 alphabet

Extra

A 1 membership 2 neighbourhood 3 workmanship 4 ownership
5 motherhood 6 childhood 7 championship 8 partnership

B 1 machine 2 moustache 3 brochure
4 cheep 5 chef 6 chalet

C Teacher to check individual answers

D Teacher to check individual answers

E 1 calves 2 shelves 3 leaves 4 knives

F 1 Tom's football 2 the boys' hats 3 Jess's homework 4 the children's party

G 1 hear 2 weight 3 knew 4 fare

H 1 birth/day 2 gar/den 3 dif/fer/ent 4 def/in/ite/ly

I 1 explosive 2 exclusive 3 active 4 attractive

J 1 irresponsible 2 unworkable 3 invisible 4 unreasonable

K 1 libr<u>a</u>ry 2 off<u>e</u>ring 3 temp<u>e</u>rature 4 veg<u>e</u>tables

Extension

A 1 dis ed 2 ir re able 3 un ing ly 4 less ness

B 1 halved 2 surfed 3 thieving 4 sniffing
5 shelved 6 believing

C 1 shorten 2 fatten 3 hidden 4 given

D 1 the women's party shoes 2 the mice's food
3 the children's school 4 the donkeys' stable

E Teacher to check individual answers

F 1 responsible 2 curable 3 sensible

Book 5 Scope and Sequence

Unit	Pupil Book Focus	Pupil Book Extra	Pupil Book Extension	Resource Book Focus	Resource Book Extension
1	**ar are** finding target words	identifying sound families	adding suffixes	letter patterns; word building	identifying root words
2	**word roots** arranging word families	word building	identifying Latin and Greek roots	sorting word families	identifying Latin and Greek word families
3	**ir ire** finding target words	identifying sound families	completing a wordsearch; writing definitions	letter patterns; identifying rhyming words	identifying word families
4	**y endings (nouns)** finding and using target words	target word quiz	using *ies* plurals	making *y* nouns	making *y* plurals; writing sentences
5	**adding s or es** identifying simple plurals	making *y* ending plurals	identifying singular/plural verb forms	making plurals; identifying pronouns	making plural nouns and singular verbs
6	**words ending a i o u** picture quiz	making *o* ending plurals	identifying word origins	picture matching	solving clues; completing a wordsearch
7	**silent letters** finding target words	identifying letter associations	alphabetical ordering	identifying silent letters; picture matching	writing sentences; correcting spellings
8	**unusual plurals** finding target words	making *f/fe* ending plurals	dictionary work; identifying irregular plurals	picture matching; writing plural nouns	working with tricky plurals
9	**able ible ably ibly** word building; word sums	identifying the *able/ible* rule	using *able/ible/ably/ibly* suffixes	letter patterns; word building; picture matching	using *able/ible/ably/ibly*; writing sentences
10	**mnemonics** identifying simple mnemonics	mnemonic quiz	identifying mnemonics; creating mnemonics	finding small words within words	creating mnemonics
11	**ow endings** letter patterns; target word quiz	sorting words by phoneme	working with syllables	using *llow/rrow*; completing a wordsearch	working with syllables
12	**et endings** writing missing vowel letters; target word quiz	recognising letter patterns	working with syllables	using *acket/icket/ocket*; completing crossword	working with syllables
13	**ull ul** finding target words	making adjectives	adding *ful* suffix; cloze activity	letter patterns; word building	solving clues; completing a wordsearch
14	**fer + suffixes** completing a wordsearch	doubling final *r*	alphabetical ordering	using suffixes	making word webs

The darker cells introduce statutory material for this year group in the National Curriculum for England.
The paler cells denote revision of a topic covered in previous years.

Unit	Pupil Book Focus	Pupil Book Extra	Pupil Book Extension	Resource Book Focus	Resource Book Extension
15	**hyphens and apostrophes** making contractions	making hyphenated prefixes	identifying hyphens and compound words	matching contractions; using hyphens	making contractions; writing sentences with compound /prefixed words
16	**ough** finding target words	identifying homophones	sorting by phoneme	using *ough/ought*; cloze activity; writing sentences	working with jumbled letters; writing definitions of homophones
17	**ost oll** finding target words and rhyming words	making *oll/oal/ole* words	adding *al/all*	using *ost/oll*; cloze activity; writing sentences	adding *l/ll*; writing sentences
18	**same letters, different sound** choosing rhyming words	sorting by phoneme	identifying *ear* pattern identifying; *ough* pattern	finding rhyming words using picture clues	sorting *ough* pattern; writing sentences
19	**homophones** finding target words; writing homophones	identifying near homophones	using homophones in sentences	writing and finding homophones	working with triple homophones
20	**ious eous cious tious** key word quiz	using *our/ous* rule; identifying root words	identifying *cious/tious* rule	letter patterns; finding *ous* words	checking spellings; writing sentences
21	**cal cial tial** completing a wordsearch	making adverbs; writing sentences	identifying *cial/tial* rule	word building; writing sentences	checking spellings; writing sentences
22	**ie** wordsearch; *ie* word quiz	using *f/fe* plurals	making word webs	word building; writing sentences	understanding the *ie* spelling rule
23	**ei** finding target words; completing a wordsearch	identifying *ie* rule	identifying *ei* homophones	word building	working with jumbled letters; cloze activity
24	**ey endings** letter patterns; target word quiz	making *y* ending plurals	identifying singular/plural verb forms	using *ey/ney/key*; completing a wordsearch	sorting *y* plurals
25	**ild, ind** cloze activity; letter patterns	identifying homonyms	adding prefixes and suffixes	word building; writing sentences	making word fans; cloze activity
26	**e or e̸** finding target words	word sums with *e + ing*	using *e* + vowel/consonant suffix	adding *ing*; cloze activity	building words with suffixes
27	**tricky words** completing a wordsearch	identifying double letters	frequent spelling problems	writing words from picture clues; cloze activity	using a dictionary to write definitions; correcting spellings
28	**using a thesaurus** finding synonyms	finding antonyms	writing sentences	verb/noun word quiz	finding synonyms; writing thesaurus entries

BOOK 5 — UNIT 1

LEARNING TARGETS

Pupil Book: Focus
to match target words to pictures based on target letter patterns

Pupil Book: Extra
to sort target words according to phonemes

Pupil Book: Extension
to build target words using suffixes provided

Resource sheet: Focus
to practise key letter patterns;
to practise word building

Resource sheet: Extension
to secure a range of suffixes in the context of target words

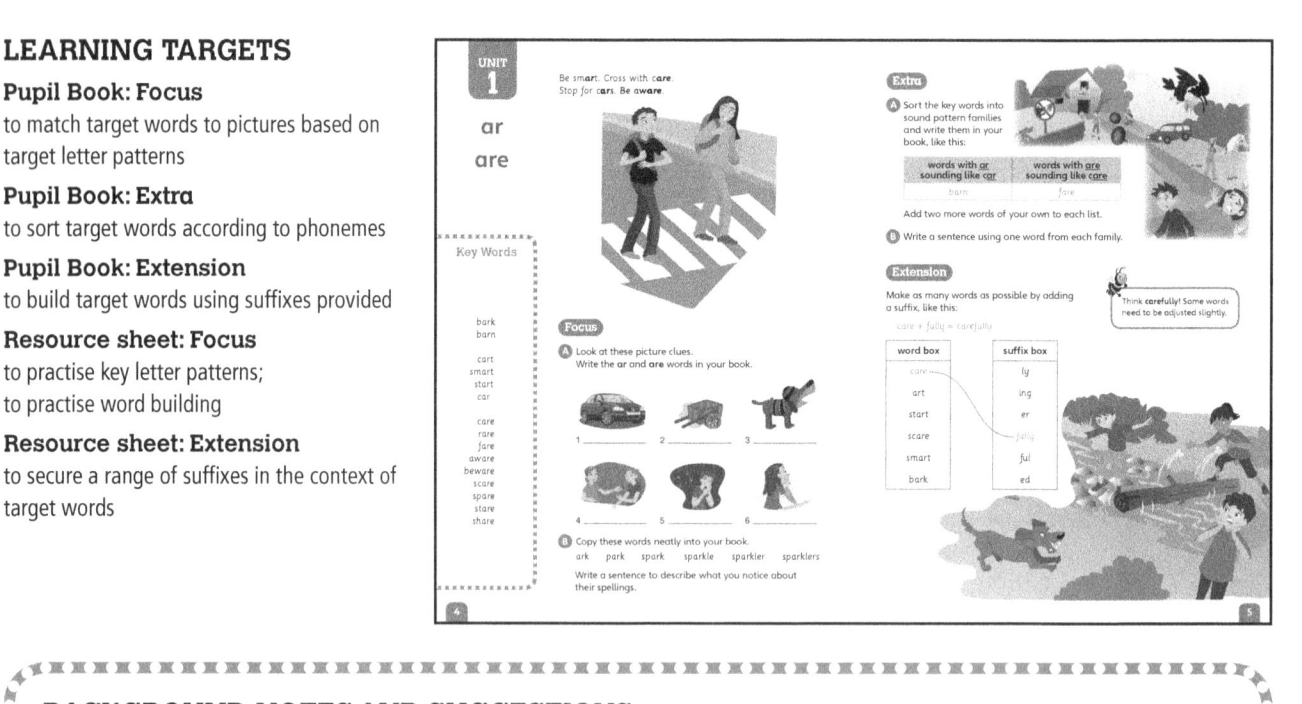

BACKGROUND NOTES AND SUGGESTIONS

The unit's main focus is teaching the **are** pattern, with its distinctive sound correspondence. In so doing it gives an opportunity to revisit the important **ar** patterns, especially with their suffixes.

Pupil Book answers

Focus
A 1 car 2 cart 3 bark
  4 share 5 scare 6 stare

B The children should notice that each word is developed by adding one or two letters to the previous word in the sequence.

Extra

ar	are
barn	fare
bark	care
cart	rare
smart	aware
start	beware
car	scare
	spare
	stare
	share

Extension
A carefully artful starter scared
  smartly barking

B Teacher to check individual answers

Resource sheet answers

Focus
A Children should copy the patterns

B 1 car   2 bar
  3 arm   4 art
  5 chart 6 spark
  7 care   8 share

C car arm art share

Extension
1 starting started starter
2 smartest smartly smarter
3 marching marched marcher
4 barking barker barked
5 sharing shared sharer
6 staring stared starer

Teacher to check individual answers

Supporting word lists

ark bark dark lark mark park shark spark
arm farm harm charm
art cart dart part tart start smart chart
barn darn yarn
card hard lard yard
harp scarp sharp
barge large charge
scarf
harsh marsh
arch march

bare care dare fare mare rare
glare spare stare scare snare share
aware beware

BOOK 5 — UNIT 2

LEARNING TARGETS

Pupil Book: Focus
to sort families of words by their roots

Pupil Book: Extra
to construct words from roots, prefixes and suffixes

Pupil Book: Extension
to consider the Latin and Greek origin of selected root words

Resource sheet: Focus
to sort words with target roots

Resource sheet: Extension
to identify ancient roots

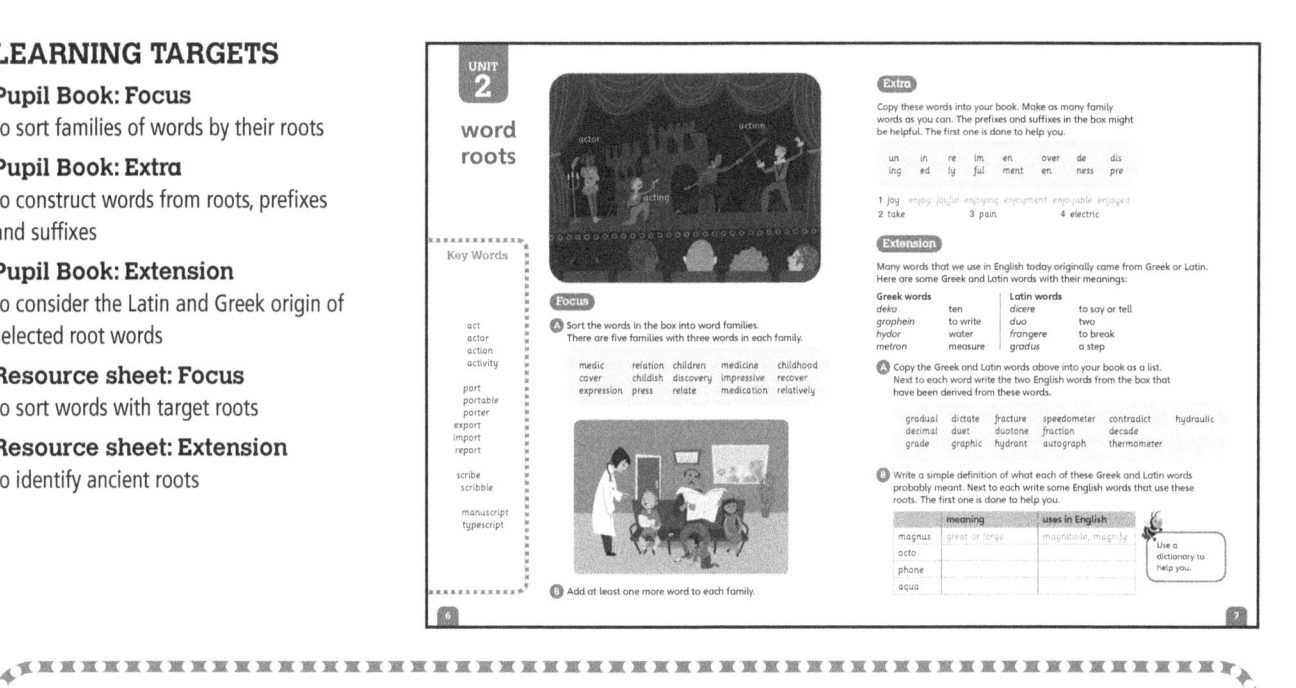

BACKGROUND NOTES AND SUGGESTIONS

Prefixes and suffixes have been taught and developed throughout *Nelson Spelling* to this point and in this unit much of this work is secured. Also, the concept is expanded upon that root words often come from other languages and that, often, these date back to early times.

Some children will find it helpful for there to be a brainstorming session, collecting and comparing words with common roots and using the words collected to seek to determine the meaning of particular roots. Often, by beginning to understand and recognise the presence of 'roots', spelling can be made easier, e.g. knowing the root *graphein* (write) means that children will more easily remember that *autograph*, *photograph*, etc. have **ph** rather than **f** at the end.

Also, the Pupil Book Extra section could provide an opportunity to remind children of the rule, that words ending with a single consonant preceded by a short vowel double the consonant before adding **ing**, which has been covered and practised previously throughout the course.

Pupil Book answers

Focus

A
medic	relation	children
medicine	relate	childhood
medication	relatively	childish
cover	impressive	
discovery	press	
recover	expression	

B Teacher to check individual answers.

Extra

1 joy: enjoy joyful enjoying enjoyed enjoyment enjoyable
2 take: taking taken mistaken retake intake painstaking mistaking mistakenly overtake
3 pain: pained painful painfully painkiller painless painstaking
4 electric: electricity electronic electrify electrocute electrician electrical electrochemical electrode electrically electrode electromagnetic (*and many others*)

Extension

A
deka:	decimal decade
graphein:	graphic autograph
hydor:	hydraulic hydrant
metron:	speedometer thermometer
dicere:	dictate contradict
duo:	duotone duet
frangere:	fracture fraction
gradus:	gradual grade

B Teacher to check individual answers

Resource sheet answers

Focus

scribe	decimal	prime
scribble	December	primary
describe	decade	primitive
telephone	tripod	geology
telegraph	triplets	geography
television	trio	geometry

Teacher to check additional words.

Extension

A
1 benefit: bene (well, good)
2 geology: ge (the Earth)
3 circle: circus (ring)
4 century: centum (a hundred)
5 factory: facere (to make)
6 monologue: monos (alone, single)
7 accident: accidere (to happen)
8 sympathy: pathos (feeling)
9 captain: caput (the head)
10 metropolis: polis (a city)

B Teacher to check individual answers

93

BOOK 5

Supporting word lists

Root word	L=Latin Gr=Greek	Meaning	Examples
accidere	L	happen	accident, decide
aequus	L	equal	equal, equality
annus	L	a year	annual, biennial
atmos	Gr	vapour	atmosphere, atmospheric
biblion	Gr	book	bibliography
civis, civilis	L	citizen	civic, civilised
dictatum	L	to say or tell	dictate, dictionary
hydor	Gr	water	hydrant, hydraulic
manus	L	the hand	manufacture, manual
monos	Gr	alone, single	monologue, monopoly
pathos	Gr	feeling	pathetic, sympathy
prima	L	first	prime, primary
sentire	L	to feel, think	sense, sensible
sphaira	Gr	sphere	spherical, hemisphere
venire	L	to come	convene, intervene

BOOK 5

UNIT 3

LEARNING TARGETS

Pupil Book: Focus
to match the target letter patterns to pictures

Pupil Book: Extra
to sort the key words according to phonemes

Pupil Book: Extension
to find and define target **ire** words in a wordsearch puzzle

Resource sheet: Focus
to copy target letter patterns and match words to pictures

Resource sheet: Extension
to create and use words by adding suffixes and prefixes to target root words

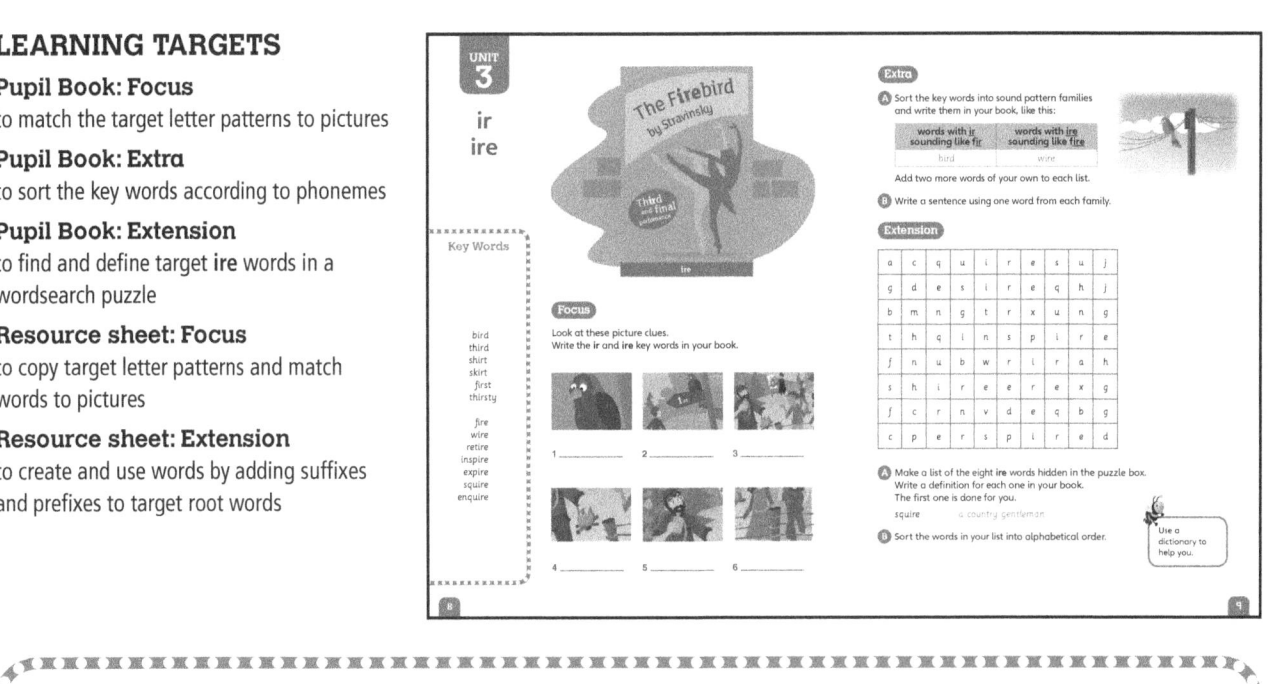

BACKGROUND NOTES AND SUGGESTIONS

Whilst it is not a vowel digraph which appears very frequently, several of the words in which **ir** does occur are frequently used by children.

Also, the **ire** letter pattern, whilst containing **ir**, has a separate and distinct phoneme.

Pupil Book answers

Focus

1 bird	2 first	3 enquire
4 fire	5 thirsty	6 wire

Extra

ir	ire
bird	fire
third	wire
shirt	retire
skirt	inspire
first	expire
thirsty	squire
	enquire

Extension

A squire – a country gentleman
acquire – to get or gain
desire – to want
inspire – to exert a good effect
shire – a county
perspire(d) – to sweat (sweated)
enquire – to ask
expire – to come to an end

B acquire desire enquire expire inspire
perspire shire squire

Resource sheet answers

Focus

A Children should copy the patterns

B thirsty bird shirt fire

C third wire first skirt

Extension

A Teacher to check individual answers

B Teacher to check individual answers

Supporting word lists

fir sir stir
bird third
dirt flirt skirt shirt
firm
swirl twirl
first thirst thirsty
chirp
birth mirth birthday

fire hire wire shire tired
retire retirement
inspire inspiration expire
enquire enquiry
squire
perspire perspiration
acquire acquisition

95

BOOK 5 — UNIT 4

LEARNING TARGETS

Pupil Book: Focus
to match key words to pictures and associated activities

Pupil Book: Extra
to complete a puzzle focusing on the target words

Pupil Book: Extension
to secure plural forms of words ending in **y**

Resource sheet: Focus
to complete a word fan and match words to pictures

Resource sheet: Extension
to form plurals of words ending in **y**;
to form adjectives from nouns by adding **y**

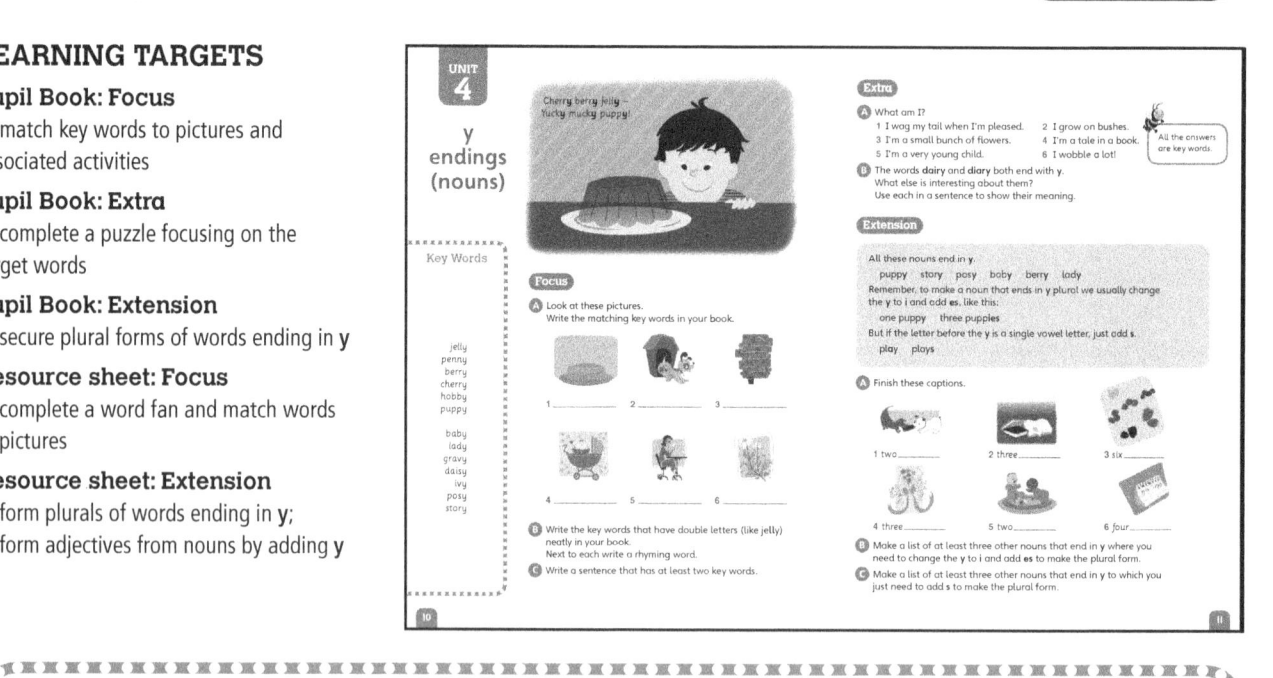

BACKGROUND NOTES AND SUGGESTIONS

The **y** (sounding **ee**) nouns (and adjectives) offer an opportunity to practise some of the other letter patterns learnt earlier in the course. The Supporting word lists are arranged in groups to help facilitate this possibility.

By selecting words from the Key Words list, the effect of double consonants 'shortening' the preceding vowel can be demonstrated (e.g. baby, hobby).

Pupil Book answers

Focus

A
| 1 jelly | 2 puppy | 3 ivy |
| 4 baby | 5 lady | 6 daisy |

B Teacher to check individual answers

C Teacher to check individual answers

Extra

A
| 1 puppy | 2 berry | 3 posy |
| 4 story | 5 baby | 6 jelly |

B Teacher to check individual answers

Extension
1 two puppies   2 three books
3 six berries   4 three posies
5 two babies   6 four days

B Teacher to check individual answers

C Teacher to check individual answers

Resource sheet answers

Focus

A Children should copy the patterns

B
jelly	penny
berry	puppy
baby	posy
lady	story

C jelly baby puppy penny

Extension

A
1 plays	2 trays
3 tries	4 flies
5 ladies	6 stories
7 valleys	8 babies
9 posies	10 puppies
11 alleys	12 curries
13 ponies	14 countries
15 berries	16 hobbies

B
1 rainy   2 misty
3 windy   4 cloudy
5 snowy

Children should write a sentence for each word

Supporting word lists

nouns

daddy nanny nappy tabby granny
jelly jetty penny teddy berry cherry
dolly holly hobby lorry poppy
buggy dummy gully mummy
puppy tummy
baby lady gravy
story

other word classes

flashy scratchy lazy crazy
messy smelly pretty
silly chilly
dotty bossy foggy rocky spotty
fussy muddy funny sunny
lucky mucky dusty rusty
rainy brainy
easy leafy creaky creamy
sleepy cheeky

BOOK 5 — UNIT 5

LEARNING TARGETS

Pupil Book: Focus
to match key words to pictures with related rhyming activities

Pupil Book: Extra
to secure the rule for when to add **es** to make plural nouns;
to secure the rule for when to change a final **y** to **i** before adding **es** to make plural nouns

Pupil Book: Extension
to consider the rules for spelling 'singular' verbs

Resource sheet: Focus
to add **es** to form plural nouns;
to use pronouns

Resource sheet: Extension
to secure the main pluralisation rules

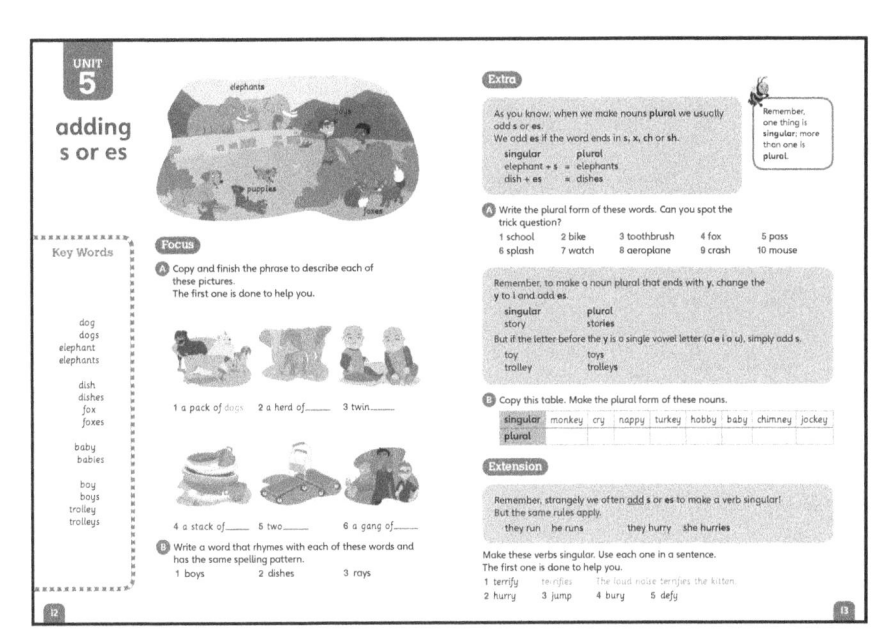

BACKGROUND NOTES AND SUGGESTIONS

The opportunity is provided in this unit to revisit, and, where necessary, secure the correct spelling of plural forms of nouns and certain 'singular' forms of verbs, where the basic requirement is the addition of **s** or **es**. This includes the rules concerning the changing of the final **y** to **i** in certain circumstances.

There is nothing taught in this unit that hasn't been covered previously, but many teachers have expressed their desire to see such crucial spelling rules repeated throughout the course.

Pupil Book answers

Focus
A
1 dogs 2 elephants 3 babies
4 dishes 5 trolleys 6 boys

B Teacher to check individual answers

Extra
A
1 schools 2 bikes
3 toothbrushes 4 foxes
5 passes 6 splashes
7 watches 8 aeroplanes
9 crashes 10 mice

B
singular	plural
monkey	monkeys
cry	cries
nappy	nappies
turkey	turkeys
hobby	hobbies
baby	babies
chimney	chimneys
jockey	jockeys

Extension
1 terrifies 2 hurries 3 jumps
4 buries 5 defies

Teacher to check individual sentences

Resource sheet answers

Focus
A Children should notice that all words end in *sh* or *ch*.

B
1 crashes 2 dishes
3 wishes 4 bushes
5 matches 6 catches
7 torches 8 brushes
9 radishes 10 arches

C
1 I brush <u>my</u> hair.
2 It's not your torch, it's <u>mine</u>.
3 We ate radishes for <u>our</u> lunch.

D Teacher to check individual answers

Extension
A
1 convoys 2 punches
3 crayons 4 flashes
5 cuckoos 6 crashes
7 feathers 8 brushes
9 hutches 10 passes
11 hurricanes 12 foxes
13 benches 14 knives
15 potatoes 16 photos
17 kites 18 wives

B
1 calls 2 teaches
3 sings 4 throws
5 buries 6 pays
7 defies 8 flies
9 snatches 10 catches
11 marries 12 tosses
13 copies 14 boxes

Supporting Word lists

Words that take s
There are a great number, including:
game table pen cup pond book school teacher

Some words that take es
ash bush glass inch watch brush dish kiss tax box grass pass bus gas sandwich fox class

Some words ending in consonant + y
army berry jelly party city penny baby fly puppy nappy cherry lorry baby daisy posy story

Some words ending in vowel + y
donkey monkey key day display toy delay ray boy valley trolley chimney turkey journey abbey alley jockey

97

BOOK 5 — UNIT 6

LEARNING TARGETS

Pupil Book: Focus
to complete a picture puzzle using animal names ending in vowel letters

Pupil Book: Extra
to practise the plural spellings of words ending in o

Pupil Book: Extension
to investigate words that end in vowel letters other than e

Resource sheet: Focus
to match target words to pictures

Resource sheet: Extension
to find words in a wordsearch that match definitions

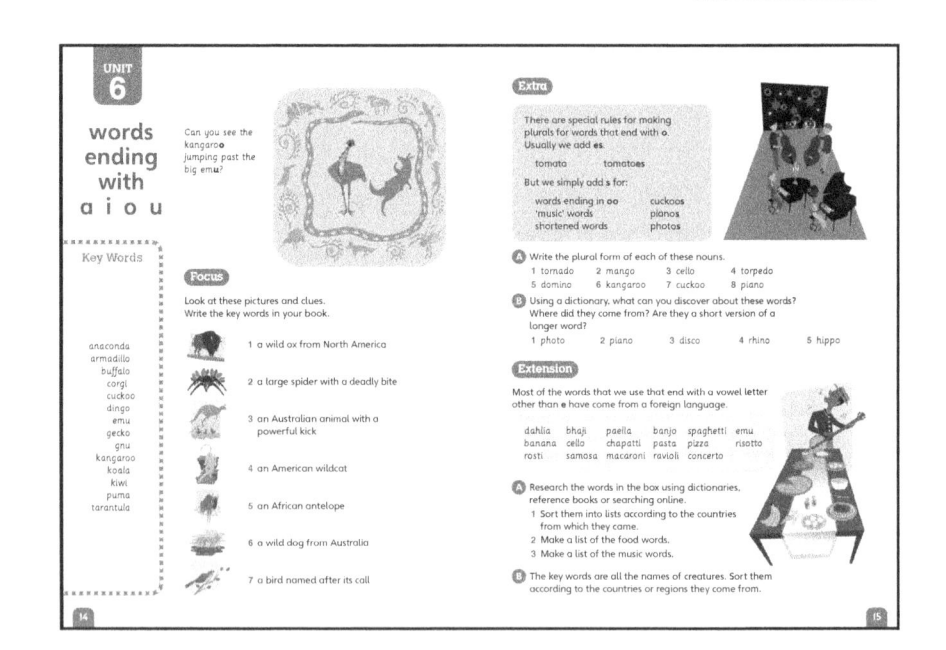

BACKGROUND NOTES AND SUGGESTIONS

As can be immediately seen from the *Supporting word lists*, the common feature of words with a vowel letter other than e is that they have been borrowed from another language – often relatively recently.

The majority of words ending in o take s for their plural, although the majority of such words that children will use frequently take es. It is suggested that children are made aware of this, using the s plural form for music-related words (e.g. *pianos*), for shortened forms (e.g. *photos*) and for the words ending in oo (e.g. *cuckoos*).

The *Supporting word lists* include some words that retain the plural spelling of their original language. It should be noted that this is true of many pasta words, some of which are usually used in the plural form e.g. *spaghetti*.

Pupil Book answers

Focus
1 buffalo 2 tarantula 3 kangaroo
4 puma 5 gnu 6 dingo
7 cuckoo

Extra
A 1 tornadoes 2 mangoes
3 cellos 4 torpedoes
5 dominoes 6 kangaroos
7 cuckoos 8 pianos

B 1 photo – shortened form of *photograph*
2 piano – shortened form of *pianoforte* (from Italian *piano e forte* meaning 'soft and loud')
3 disco – shortened form of *discotheque*
4 rhino – shortened form of *rhinoceros* (from Greek for 'nose' and 'horn')
5 hippo – shortened form of *hippopotamus* (from Latin and Greek for 'river horse')

Extension
A 1 India: bhaji chapatti samosa
Italy: spaghetti cello pasta pizza risotto macaroni ravioli concerto
Mexico: dahlia (named after Swedish botanist)
Spain: paella
Switzerland: rosti
USA: banjo
Australia: emu (from *ema*, Portugese for 'ostrich')
Africa: banana (from Spanish or Portugese)

2 bhaji paella spaghetti chapatti pasta pizza risotto rosti samosa macaroni ravioli banana
3 banjo cello concerto

B Americas: tarantula buffalo armadillo puma anaconda
Australasia: dingo emu kangaroo kiwi koala
Europe: corgi cuckoo
Africa: gnu
Asia: gecko

Resource sheet answers

Focus
Teacher to check individual answers

Extension
1 kangaroo 2 volcano 3 soprano
4 torpedo 5 mango 6 pasta
7 bhaji 8 macaroni 9 emu
10 chapatti 11 dahlia 12 cello
13 gecko 14 gnu 15 kiwi

Supporting Word lists

words ending in a
anaconda area banana dahlia siesta piazza sofa pizza puma sonata magnolia camera fiesta tarantula gala rota tombola paella samba umbrella pagoda samosa viola pasta sauna visa

words ending in i
ski corgi kiwi bhaji chapatti

words ending in o (which take s to make the plural)
armadillo piano patio yo-yo dingo jumbo piccolo sombrero banjo disco solo kimono bongo radio matzo risotto casino cello concerto gecko oratorio rhino hippo photo

words ending in oo (which take s to make the plural)
cuckoo igloo zoo kangaroo tattoo

words ending in o (which take es to make the plural)
buffaloes dominoes heroes torpedoes vetoes volcanoes cargoes echoes mangoes flamingos

words ending in u
Zulu haiku emu gnu guru

words ending in a, i, o or u (which keep the plural spelling of their original language) antennae bacteria criteria fungi phenomena macaroni ravioli spaghetti strata

BOOK 5

UNIT 7

LEARNING TARGETS

Pupil Book: Focus
to match key words to pictures

Pupil Book: Extra
to reinforce the awareness of letters associated with silent letters

Pupil Book: Extension
to practise alphabetical ordering by third and fourth letters

Resource sheet: Focus
to identify words with silent letters;
to match words to pictures

Resource sheet: Extension
to spell correctly words with silent letters

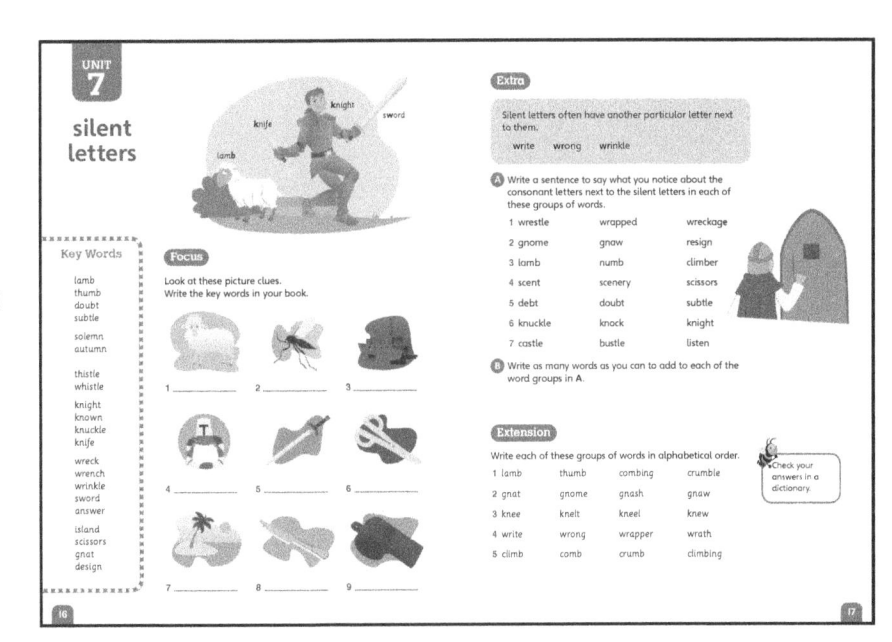

BACKGROUND NOTES AND SUGGESTIONS

As has been noted previously, many silent letters were originally pronounced but due to the general evolution of language they have become silent. Silent letters need to be returned to frequently as they can be a constant difficulty for some children learning to spell accurately.

A related theme is the various contexts in which certain vowel letters are not sounded individually. Some teachers choose to teach these as silent (e.g. **a** in *head*, **e** in *gone*), though the term is conventionally reserved for consonant letters.

Another complexity in our language that is similar to silent letters are the unstressed letters, especially vowels, and these are covered in depth as the course progresses.

The children will now be aware of the letter associations linked to silent letters and this is the main thrust of this unit. There are some specific patterns to consolidate in this unit, including **wr**, **gn**, **mb**, **sc**, **bt**, **kn** and **st**.

Pupil Book answers

Focus
1 lamb 2 gnat 3 wreck
4 knight 5 sword 6 scissors
7 island 8 knife 9 whistle

Extra
A/B Teacher to check individual answers

Extension
1 combing crumble lamb thumb
2 gnat gnash gnome gnaw
3 knee kneel knelt knew
4 wrapper wrath write wrong
5 climb climbing comb crumb

Resource sheet answers

Focus
A knight scissors doubt lamb
   wreckage whistle answer design

B / C scissors answer whistle
     wreckage knight lamb

Extension
A Teacher to check individual answers
B Teacher to check individual answers
C
1 gnat   2 thistle
3 whole   4 island
5 salmon   6 budget
7 scientific   8 thumb
9 ballet   10 sword
11 biscuit   12 Wednesday
13 dumbstruck   14 miniature
15 cupboard   16 guitar

Supporting word lists
b (after m)
lamb limb bomb comb tomb
dumb numb climb plumb crumb
thumb plumber

b (before t)
debt doubt subtle

initial k
knit knob knot
knelt knack knock
knee kneel knife knight
knew known knuckle

initial w
wrap wrapper wrapped wrapping
wriggle wriggled wriggler wriggling
whole wholemeal wholesome wholly
sword swordfish

medial w
answer answered answering
other silent letter words

h
wheel whether which whisker
whisper white
hour honest honour
rhyme rhythm rhubarb rheumatism

h (after c)
ache anchor architect
chaos character chemical
choir chord chorus
echo

g
reign resign design sign

n
autumn column condemn

t
thistle whistle castle listen

99

BOOK 5 — UNIT 8

LEARNING TARGETS

Pupil Book: Focus
to write a phrase to match key words to pictures

Pupil Book: Extra
to secure plurals associated with **f**, **ff** and **fe**

Pupil Book: Extension
to use a dictionary to check irregular plural forms

Resource sheet: Focus
to match plural forms to pictures

Resource sheet: Extension
to secure the main rules for pluralisation

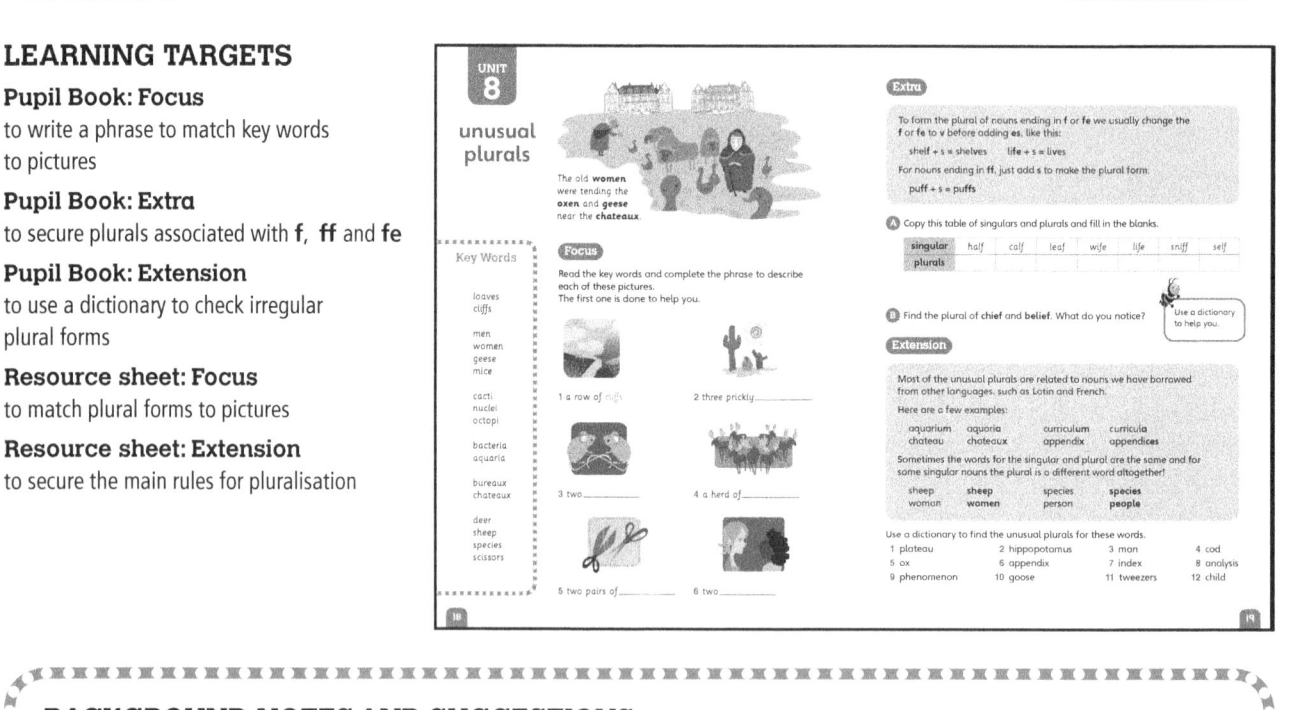

BACKGROUND NOTES AND SUGGESTIONS

Encourage the children not just to learn the unusual plurals but to seek out their derivations, either online or in a dictionary.

Pupil Book answers

Focus
1 a row of cliffs
2 three prickly cacti
3 two mice
4 a herd of moose
5 two pairs of scissors
6 two women

Extra

A

singular	plural
half	halves
calf	calves
leaf	leaves
wife	wives
life	lives
sniff	sniffs
self	selves

B chiefs   beliefs
Teacher to check individual answers

Extension
1 plateaux (or plateaus)
2 hippopotamuses
3 men   4 cod
5 oxen   6 appendices
7 indices   8 analyses
9 phenomena   10 geese
11 tweezers   12 children

Resource sheet answers

Focus

A
mice	men
sheep	children
geese	boxes
berries	deer

B 1 monkeys   2 halves
3 radios   4 circles
5 classes   6 engines

Extension
1 tradegies   2 cuffs
3 indexes   4 octopuses
5 kangaroos   6 scarves or scarfs
7 cacti   8 buffalo or buffaloes
9 binoculars   10 chateaus
11 pennies   12 jeans
13 radishes   14 daisies
15 torches   16 midwives
17 princesses   18 matchboxes
19 oxen   20 teeth
21 formulas or formulae
22 lay-bys
23 eyelashes
24 concertos or concerti

Supporting word lists

f/ves
scarf self shelf leaf loaf calf half self thief wolf

ff/s
sniff puff cuff staff stuff bluff cliff handcuffs

fe/ves
life wife knife

ve/ves
believe swerve save glove curve

exceptions
chief/chiefs belief/beliefs safe/safes handkerchiefs

words ending in o (which take s to make the plural)
kimono bongo radio matzo risotto casino cello concerto gecko oratorio rhino hippo photo

words ending in oo (which take s to make the plural)
cuckoo igloo zoo kangaroo tattoo

words ending in o (which take es to make the plural)
buffaloes dominoes heroes torpedoes mangoes flamingoes

words ending in us (which take i to make the plural)
cactus nucleus focus

words ending in is (which take es to make the plural)
analysis crisis thesis

words that change the vowel, the word, have a different ending or stay the same

man/men   foot/feet
child/children   person/people
tooth/teeth   mouse/mice

sheep deer fish *(sometimes)*

BOOK 5 — UNIT 9

LEARNING TARGETS

Pupil Book: Focus
to complete a phrase with a key word to match a picture;
to complete word sums using the target suffixes

Pupil Book: Extra
to learn ways to know when to use the target suffixes

Pupil Book: Extension
to consider the relationship between **able** and **ation**; to secure the rule for adding **able/ible** to words ending in **e**

Resource sheet: Focus
to create words by adding target suffixes

Resource sheet: Extension
to revise the rules when adding **able/ible** to words

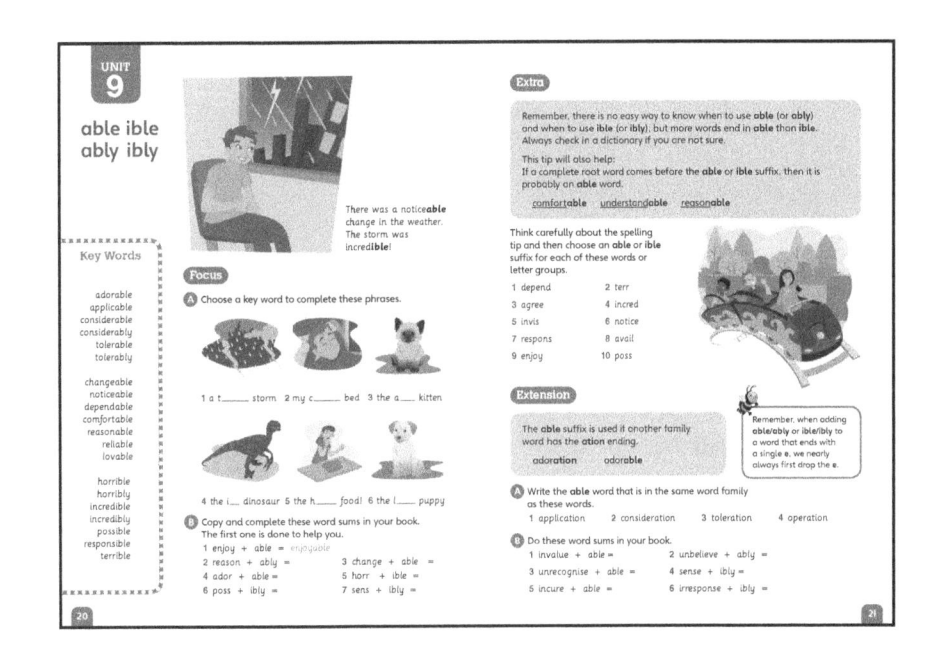

BACKGROUND NOTES AND SUGGESTIONS

As noted previously, there are many more words ending in **able** and **ably** than there are ending in **ible** and **ibly**, so if uncertain the safer option is to go for **able**!

Note that if the antonym of the word starts with **un** it is an **able** word, but if the antonym starts with **in**, **il** or **ir** it is rather more likely to be an **ible** word, though it could be either, e.g. *unsuitable, irresistible, illegible*.

Another way to help distinguish between these endings is to appreciate that dropping **able** usually leaves a recognisable word (e.g. *valuable, agreeable*), whereas dropping **ible** is more likely to leave a 'stem' (e.g. *horrible, edible*).

Whilst in most cases the final **e** is dropped before adding **able/ably** or **ible/ibly** to a root word, this is not invariably the case. Encourage the children to collect examples of exceptions e.g. *changeable, noticeable*.

Pupil Book answers

Focus
A
1. a terrible storm
2. my comfortable bed
3. the adorable kitten
4. the incredible dinosaur
5. the horrible food
6. the lovable puppy

B
1. enjoyable
2. reasonably
3. changeable
4. adorable
5. horrible
6. possibly
7. sensibly

Extra
1. dependable
2. terrible
3. agreeable
4. incredible
5. invisible
6. noticeable
7. responsible
8. available
9. enjoyable
10. possible

Extension
A
1. applicable
2. considerable
3. tolerable
4. operable

B
1. invaluable
2. unbelievably
3. unrecognisable
4. sensibly
5. incurable
6. irresponsibly

Resource sheet answers

Focus
A Children should copy the patterns

B adorable invisible
sensible reliable

C invisible sensible adorable

D sensibly enjoyably

Extension
A
1. The *able* suffix is more common.
2. The *able* suffix is usually added when a complete root word is used.
3. If a root word ends in *e* the *e* is nearly always dropped.
4. Yes.

B
1. dependable
2. adorable
3. considerable
4. responsible
5. enjoyable
6. sensible
7. comfortable
8. lovable
9. valuable
10. removable
11. horrible
12. reliable
13. miserable
14. understandable

C Teacher to check individual answers

Supporting word lists

able
able disable
table stable fable constable vegetable
probable usable lovable suitable reliable
miserable valuable agreeable advisable
curable capable dependable perishable
creditable noticeable reasonable
believable disagreeable incurable
unrecognisable

ible
sensible responsible legible visible
forcible horrible terrible possible
incredible audible edible

BOOK 5 UNIT 10

LEARNING TARGETS

Pupil Book: Focus
to learn how to devise visual cues in spelling

Pupil Book: Extra
to learn and practise ways to create mnemonics

Pupil Book: Extension
to use mnemonics to secure a number of difficult spellings

Resource sheet: Focus
to find smaller words in longer words

Resource sheet: Extension
to create mnemonics for some words with difficult spellings

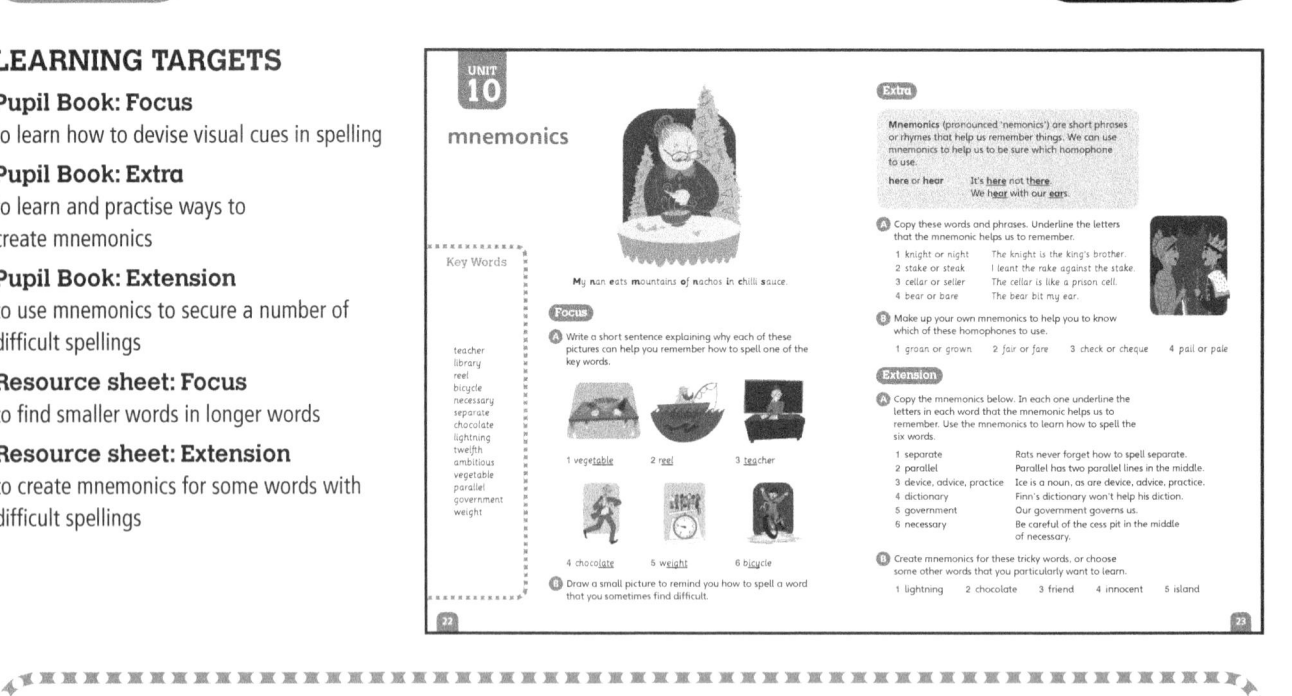

BACKGROUND NOTES AND SUGGESTIONS

Throughout the course, techniques and devices to aid children in learning to spell are employed. The use of mnemonics is one that will work for some children with a few of the more awkward words. It is certainly not a method to spend too much time working on, but in its limited way it can be helpful as an aid to memorising particularly confusing spellings. Once learnt, the mnemonics are likely to remain with the pupil into adulthood!

Pupil Book answers

Focus
A Teacher to check individual answers

B Teacher to check individual answers

Extra
A
1 <u>k</u>night <u>k</u>ing's
2 <u>stake</u> <u>rake</u>
3 <u>cell</u>ar <u>cell</u>
4 <u>bear</u> <u>ear</u>

B Teacher to check individual answers

Extension
A
1 <u>Rat</u>s never forget how to spell sepa<u>rat</u>e.
2 Para<u>ll</u>el has two para<u>ll</u>el lines in the middle.
3 <u>Ice</u> is a noun, as are dev<u>ice</u>, adv<u>ice</u>, pract<u>ice</u>.
4 Finn's <u>diction</u>ary won't help his <u>diction</u>.
5 Our <u>govern</u>ment <u>govern</u>s us.
6 Be careful of the <u>cess</u> pit in the middle of ne<u>cess</u>ary.

B Teacher to check individual answers

Resource sheet answers

Focus
Teacher to check individual answers

Extension
Teacher to check individual answers

BOOK 5 — UNIT 11

LEARNING TARGETS

Pupil Book: Focus
to identify related letter patterns associated with the final **ow** grapheme;
to complete sentences with picture clues

Pupil Book: Extra
to sort words with the target vowel digraph according to its phoneme

Pupil Book: Extension
to secure earlier work on syllabification

Resource sheet: Focus
to complete and find words with the target endings;
to complete wordsearch activity

Resource sheet: Extension
to practise identifying syllables

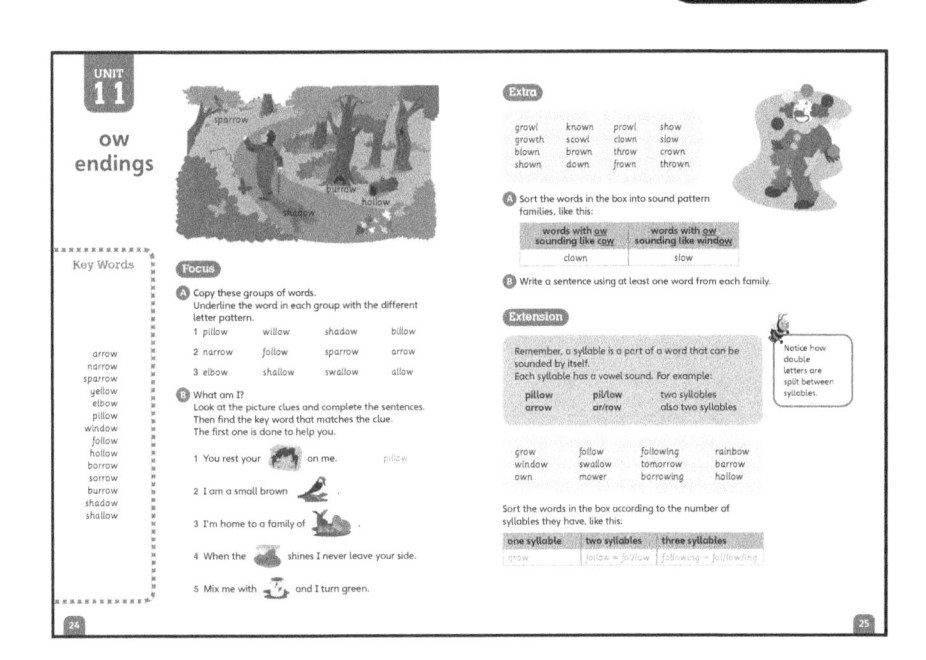

BACKGROUND NOTES AND SUGGESTIONS

The key feature of most words which have the ending **ow** is that it represents the long **o** phoneme (as in *rose*), rather than the regular **ow** sound (as in *cow*). Some children will also recognise that the bottom group of words in the *Supporting word lists* have a long **o** sound as most of them are past tense and their root words have a final **ow**.

Pupil Book answers

Focus

A
1 pillow willow <u>shadow</u> billow
2 narrow <u>follow</u> sparrow arrow
3 <u>elbow</u> shallow swallow allow

B
1 pillow   2 sparrow   3 burrow
4 shadow   5 yellow

Extra

ow (like cow)	ow (like window)
clown	slow
growl	known
prowl	show
scowl	growth
brown	blown
crown	throw
drown	shown
frown	thrown

B Teacher to check individual answers.

Extension

one syllable	two syllables	three syllables
grow	fol/low	fol/low/ing
own	rain/bow	to/mor/row
	win/dow	bor/row/ing
	swal/low	
	bar/ow	
	mow/er	
	hol/low	

Resource sheet answers

Focus

A
yellow   burrow   hollow
pillow   borrow   shallow
follow   sorrow   swallow

B
1 I have a new, soft, yel<u>low</u> pil<u>low.</u>
2 The rabbit lives in a bu<u>rrow.</u>
3 It was difficult to swal<u>low</u> the medicine.

C swallow shallow arrow burrow
borrow follow hollow pillow
wallow allow

Extension

A
1 con<u>ti</u>nent   2 unfor<u>tu</u>nate
3 b<u>o</u>rrowing   4 s<u>o</u>rrowful
5 all<u>o</u>wing   6 grump<u>i</u>ly
7 swall<u>o</u>wing   8 useful<u>ly</u>

B
1 dis/ap/pear   2 ex/er/cise
3 fac/to/ry   4 hos/pi/tal
5 ba/na/na   6 an/y/thing
7 mar/vel/lous   8 de/ter/mine
9 hope/ful/ly   10 ag/ri/cul/ture
11 a/lu/mi/ni/um   12 in/de/pen/dent
13 ske/le/ton   14 py/ja/mas
15 e/le/phant   16 re/cog/nise
17 to/mor/row   18 de/tec/tive

(Note: In 1 the vowel grapheme is formally *ear*, but *ea* is an acceptable answer)

Supporting Word lists

bow low mow row sow tow know
blow flow glow slow crow grow stow snow show throw
arrow barrow harrow marrow narrow
bellow fellow yellow elbow
billow pillow willow widow window minnow
follow hollow
burrow furrow tomorrow sorrow sparrow
shadow shallow swallow
rainbow crossbow hedgerow
own sown blown flown grown shown thrown known
bow cow how now row sow brow
owl fowl howl growl prowl scowl
down gown town brown crown
drown frown crowd

BOOK 5 — UNIT 12

LEARNING TARGETS

Pupil Book: Focus
to match key words to pictures and find rhyming words with the target letter patterns

Pupil Book: Extra
to identify common letter patterns in words

Pupil Book: Extension
to secure earlier work on syllabification

Resource sheet: Focus
to complete and find words with the target endings;
to complete wordsearch activity

Resource sheet: Extension
to practise identifying syllables

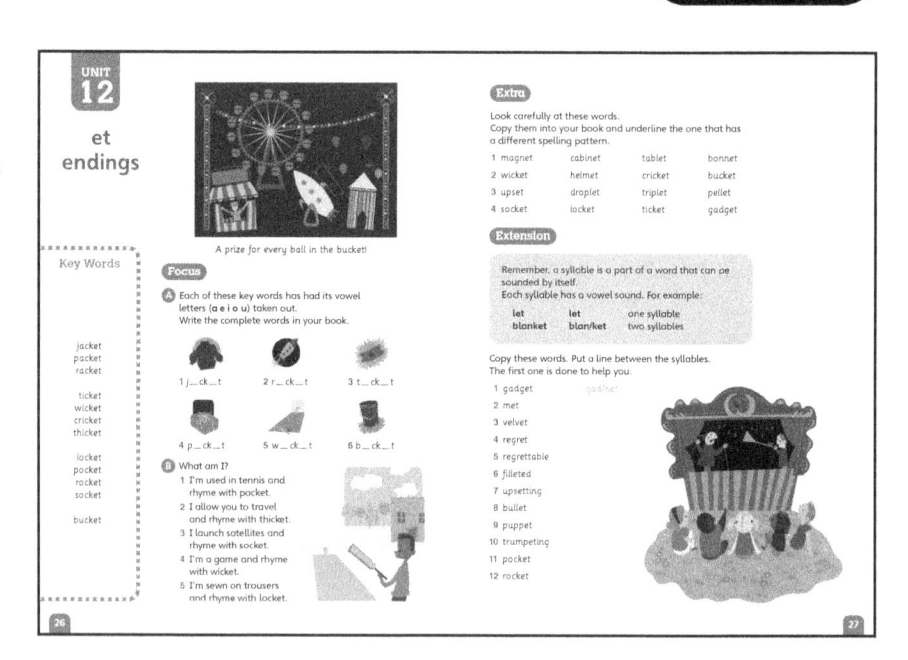

BACKGROUND NOTES AND SUGGESTIONS

This word ending can frequently cause difficulties and raise questions in the young writer's mind – especially as the **e** is not normally stressed, leading to confusion over whether to spell it with an **e** or an **i**.

Another opportunity is afforded for thinking about syllables. The only sure thing about syllabification is that each syllable should include a vowel sound, though this need not be a vowel letter. Also, some syllables can comprise a single letter (e.g. *happ/y*) though the normal convention would be to split between the double consonants (*hap/py*).

Pupil Book answers

Focus

A
1 jacket   2 rocket   3 ticket
4 packet   5 wicket   6 bucket

B
1 racket   2 ticket   3 rocket
4 cricket   5 pocket

Extra
1 magnet cabinet <u>tablet</u> bonnet
2 wicket <u>helmet</u> cricket bucket
3 <u>upset</u> droplet triplet pellet
4 socket locket ticket <u>gadget</u>

Extension
1 gad/get   2 met
3 vel/vet   4 re/gret
5 re/gret/ta/ble 6 fil/let/ed
7 up/set/ting   8 bul/let
9 pup/pet   10 trum/pet/ing
11 poc/ket   12 roc/ket

Resource sheet answers

Focus

A
jacket	ticket	locket
packet	wicket	pocket
racket	cricket	rocket

B We need a <u>wicket</u> to play <u>cricket</u>.
Have you bought a <u>ticket</u>?
There's a secret <u>pocket</u> in my <u>jacket</u>.

C bucket ticket cricket wicket socket
packet racket jacket rocket pocket

Extension

A
1 magnet   2 bonnet
3 rocket   4 packet
5 triplet   6 puppet
7 grumpy   8 useful
9 helpful   10 wriggle
11 artful   12 rocking

B
1 wic/ket   2 buc/ket
3 soc/ket   4 slow/ly
5 par/rot   6 jum/ping
7 but/ton   8 pri/son
9 pain/ful   10 hope/ful
11 e/scape   12 an/swer
13 be/cause 14 hel/ping
15 use/ful/ly 16 ad/ven/ture

Supporting Word lists

magnet tablet jacket packet racket
gadget blanket cabinet
helmet velvet pellet
fillet ticket wicket cricket triplet thicket
bonnet locket pocket rocket socket
upset bullet puppet bucket trumpet

BOOK 5 — UNIT 13

LEARNING TARGETS

Pupil Book: Focus
to match key words to pictures and use words that incorporate the **fully** letter pattern

Pupil Book: Extra
to add the **ful** suffix

Pupil Book: Extension
to secure the rule for adding the **ful** suffix to words ending in **y**

Resource sheet: Focus
to copy letter patterns and words and complete word sums

Resource sheet: Extension
to use target words found in wordsearch activity

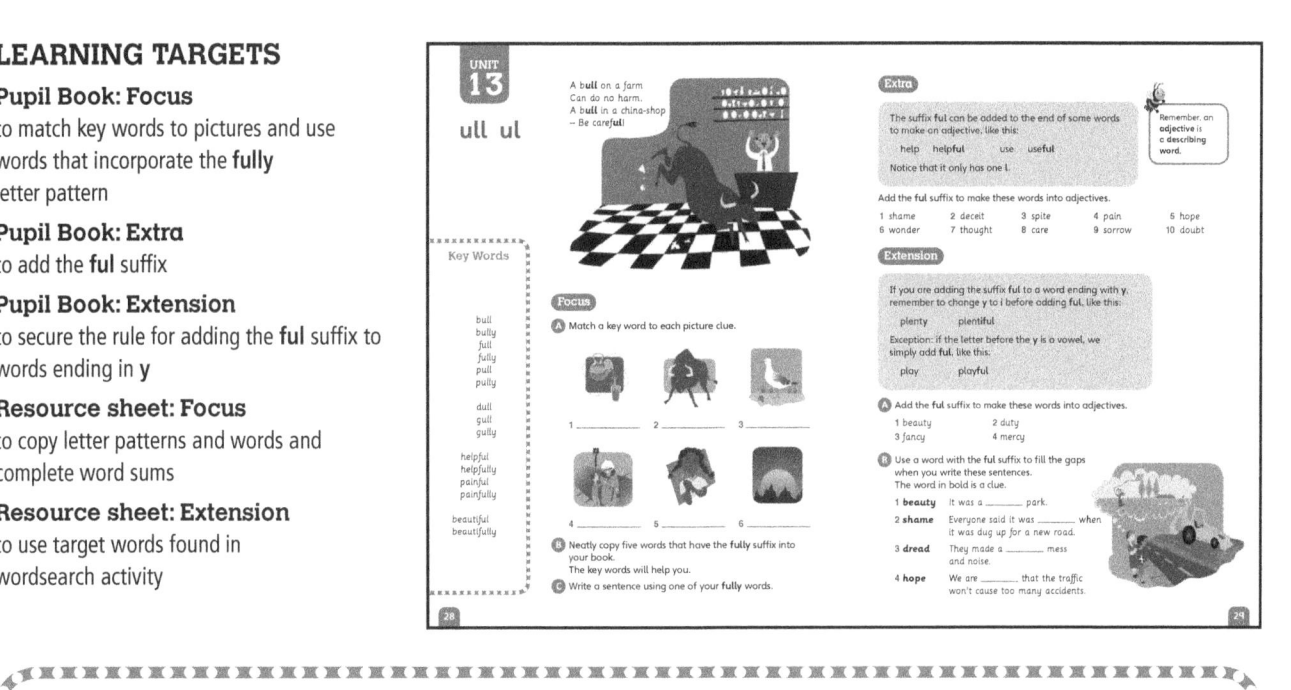

BACKGROUND NOTES AND SUGGESTIONS

Although several frequently used words also feature it, the most significant occurrence of this pattern is in the suffixes **ful** and **fully**. As such it presents a further opportunity to practise and secure the rule:

to add a suffix when a word ends with **y** (that sounds **ee**);
change the **y** to an **i** before adding the suffix (*plenty plentiful; beauty beautifully*).

Pupil Book answers

Focus
A
1 full 2 bull 3 gull
4 helpful 5 painful 6 beautiful

B Teacher to check individual answers

C Teacher to check individual answers

Extra
1 shameful 2 deceitful
3 spiteful 4 painful
5 hopeful 6 wonderful
7 thoughtful 8 careful
9 sorrowful 10 doubtful

Extension
A
1 beautiful 2 dutiful
3 fanciful 4 merciful

B
1 beautiful 2 shameful
3 dreadful 4 hopeful

Resource sheet answers

Focus
A Children should copy the patterns

B
gully
fully
bully
helpfully
usefully
painfully

Extension
A
1 useful
2 helpful
3 full
4 deceitful
5 bull
6 painfully
7 beautifully
8 bully
9 gull
10 dull
11 shameful
12 pull

B Teacher to check individual answers

Supporting word lists

bull full pull
bully fully pulley
gull dull
useful usefully
careful carefully
faithful faithfully
graceful gracefully
dreadful dreadfully
thoughtful thoughtfully
sorrowful sorrowfully
wonderful wonderfully
plenty plentiful plentifully
beauty beautiful beautifully
duty dutiful dutifully
mercy merciful mercifully

BOOK 5 UNIT 14

LEARNING TARGETS

Pupil Book: Focus
to find target words in a wordsearch;
to identify target words with **rr**

Pupil Book: Extra
to learn the rule and exceptions for doubling
r before a suffix

Pupil Book: Extension
to practise alphabetical ordering of
similar words

Resource sheet: Focus
to complete word sums and match
word definitions

Resource sheet: Extension
to build word families by creating word webs

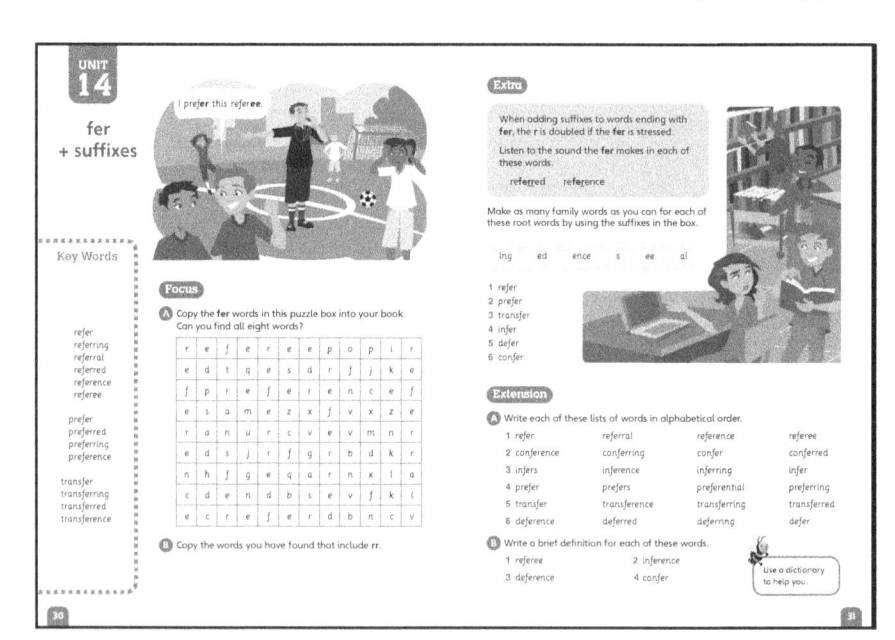

BACKGROUND NOTES AND SUGGESTIONS

This is one of the more subtle spelling 'rules' that, for some children, will need considerable practice. When adding suffixes to words ending with **fer**, the **r** is doubled if the **fer** is stressed.

As will be seen in Pupil Book Extra, the rule does not apply when adding **s**.

Pupil Book answers

Focus

A refer referee reference referred
preference referral transfer

B referred preferred referral

Extra

1 referring referred refers reference
referee referral
2 preferring preferred preference prefers
3 transferring transferred
transference transfers
4 inferring inferred inference infers
5 deferring deferred deference
defers deferral
6 conferring conferred
conference confers

Extension

1 refer referee reference referral
2 confer conference
conferred conferring
3 infer inference inferring infers
4 prefer preferential preferring prefers
5 transfer transference
transferred tranferring
6 defer deference deferred deferring

B Teacher to check individual answers

Resource sheet answers

Focus

A 1 reference
2 preference
3 inference
4 deferring
5 transferring
6 conferring
7 referring
8 conferred
9 referred
10 preferred

B 1 refer
2 infer
3 defer
4 prefer

Extension

A, **B** and **C**
Teacher to check individual answers

Supporting word lists

refer referring referral
referred reference referee
prefer preferred preferring
preference preferential
infer inferring inferred
inference
transfer tranferring
transferred transference
defer deferring deferred
deferral deference
confer conferring
conferred conference

BOOK 5

Check-Up 1

Focus
1 card
2 scare
3 actor
4 autograph
5 bird
6 spire
7 puppy
8 baby
9 babies
10 foxes
11 kangaroo
12 lamb
13 scissors
14 mice
15 teacher
16 shadow
17 rocket
18 comfortable
19 bull
20 referee

Extension

A Teacher to check individual answers

B 1 babies 2 trolleys 3 dishes 4 plays 5 potatoes
  6 cellos 7 women 8 cacti 9 aquaria 10 deer

C 1 gn 2 mb 3 kn 4 st

D 1 enjoyable 2 possible 3 incredible 4 reasonable 5 sensible

E 1 swal/low 2 to/mor/row 3 rain/bow 4 up/set/ting 5 re/gret/ta/ble

F 1 shameful 2 careful 3 hopeful 4 plentiful 5 beautiful

G 1 transferred 2 inferred 3 referred 4 preferred 5 deferred

BOOK 5 — UNIT 15

LEARNING TARGETS

Pupil Book: Focus
to practise writing simple contractions;
to reconstruct contracted forms

Pupil Book: Extra
to use hyphens when adding prefixes

Pupil Book: Extension
to use hyphens in the context of compound words

Resource sheet: Focus
to match contractions with their words;
to organise hyphenated words into compound and prefixed words

Resource sheet: Extension
to recognise contractions that relate to specific words;
to use hyphens in the context of compound and prefixed words

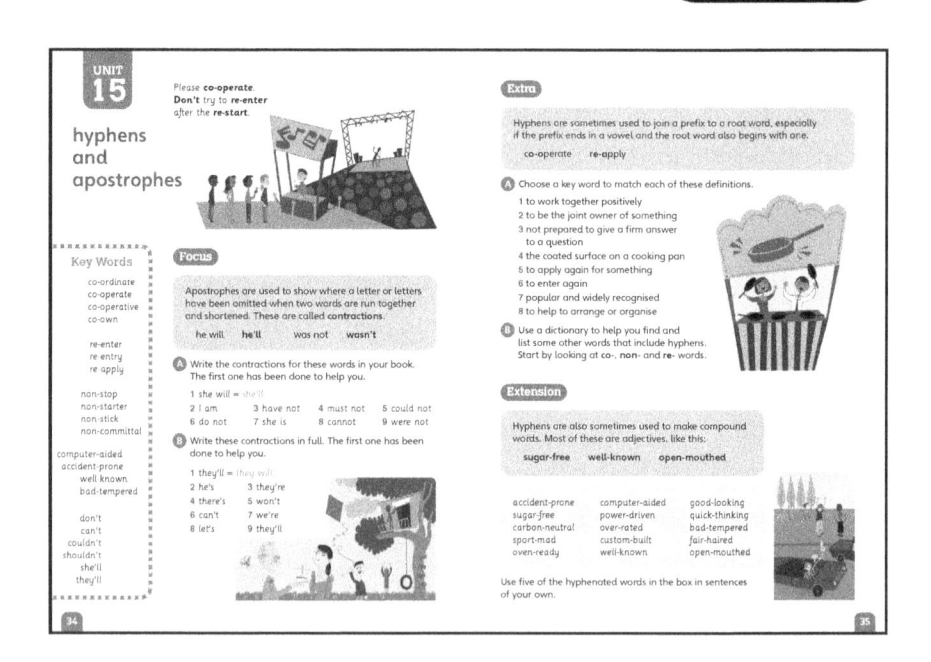

BACKGROUND NOTES AND SUGGESTIONS

Hyphens most commonly impinge on spelling when certain prefixes are employed, such as **co** and **non**. However, the use of the hyphen is sometimes a matter of preference.

Hyphens are also used to compound some adjectives, such as in *well-known*, *accident-prone*. Apostrophes, however, are not optional in contractions and the possessive case, where they can cause some pupils considerable problems. In the former, the apostrophe should be placed as close to the omitted letter(s) as possible – not in the former space between the contracted words.

Won't, *shan't* and *can't* warrant special attention, as does *its* and *it's*. It is confusing that the possessive form of *it* does <u>not</u> have an apostrophe – *it's* is the contraction of *it is*. Apostrophes in the context of the possessive case are practised elsewhere (e.g. Book 4, Unit 21).

Pupil Book answers

Focus
A
1 she'll   2 I'm   3 haven't
4 mustn't   5 couldn't   6 don't
7 she's   8 can't   9 weren't

B
1 they will   2 he is   3 they are
4 there is   5 will not   6 cannot
7 we are   8 let us   9 they will

Extra
A
1 co-operate   2 co-own
3 non-committal   4 non-stick
5 re-apply   6 re-enter
7 well-known   8 co-ordinate

B Teacher to check individual answers

Extension
Teacher to check individual answers

Resource sheet answers

Focus
A
he's – he is
they'll – they will
weren't – were not
would've – would have
she'll – she will
don't – do not

B compound words:
sugar-free   quick-thinking
well-known   fair-haired
oven-ready   accident-prone

prefixed words:
co-operate   non-stop
re-emerge   co-author
de-ice   co-own

Extension
A Teacher to check individual answers

B
1 compound word
2 prefixed word
3 compound word
4 compound word
5 prefixed word
6 prefixed word

Teacher to check individual sentences.

Supporting word lists

I'm I'll I've I'd (I had/I would)
he's she's it's there's that's
you're we're they're
you've we've they've
you'd he'd she'd we'd they'd
don't can't isn't doesn't won't
aren't shan't
haven't couldn't wouldn't shouldn't
wasn't weren't
o'clock pick 'n' mix ma'am

co-ordinate co-operate
co-operative co-own

re-enter re-entry re-apply
re-usable re-apply

non-stop non-starter
non-stick non-committal

accident-prone
computer-aided good-looking
sugar-free power-driven
quick-thinking carbon-neutral over-rated
under-performing

BOOK 5 — UNIT 16

LEARNING TARGETS

Pupil Book: Focus
to match key words to pictures

Pupil Book: Extra
to select appropriate homophones to complete an activity

Pupil Book: Extension
to select **ough** and **augh** words according to sounds represented

Resource sheet: Focus
to complete and find words with the target endings

Resource sheet: Extension
to unscramble **ough** words;
to use **ough** related homophones

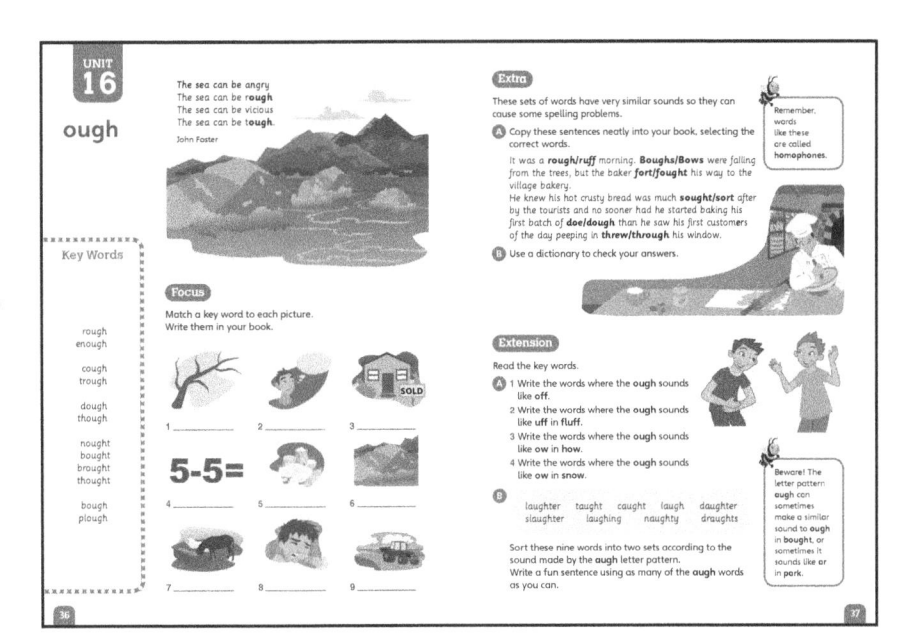

BACKGROUND NOTES AND SUGGESTIONS

The grapheme/phoneme relationship of the words in this unit is unusually variable, and worthy of class or group work. It is also susceptible to regional variations, which may require specific teacher input.

Work might usefully be done on the homophonic words within the group, of which there are several (e.g. *dough/doe*). Also, discuss the difference between *bought* and *brought*.

Pupil Book answers

Focus

1 bough	2 thought	3 bought
4 nought	5 dough	6 rough
7 trough	8 cough	9 plough

Extra

A It was a <u>rough</u> morning. <u>Boughs</u> were falling from the trees, but the baker <u>fought</u> his way to the village bakery. He knew his hot, crusty bread was much <u>sought</u> after by the tourists and no sooner had he started baking his first batch of <u>dough</u> than he saw his first customers of the day peeping in <u>through</u> his window.

B Children to check answers in a dictionary

Extension

A
1 cough trough
2 rough enough
3 bough plough
4 dough though

B
laughter	taught
laugh	caught
laughing	daughter
draughts	slaughter
	naughty

Teacher to check individual answers

Resource sheet answers

Focus

A
rough	brought
tough	nought
enough	thought
though	fought
plough	drought

B The ground was too r<u>ough</u> to pl<u>ough</u>. A long dr<u>ough</u>t had left the stream dry. The was hardly en<u>ough</u> water left in the stream.
It all had to be br<u>ough</u>t in buckets from the well.

C Teacher to check individual answers

Extension

A
1 rough	2 enough
3 cough	4 trough
5 dough	6 bought
7 brought	8 plough
9 drought	10 bough

B
1 dough	2 through
3 bough	4 fought
5 rough	

Teacher to check individual answers

Supporting word lists

as in off
cough trough

as in puff
rough tough enough

as in no
dough though

as in moo
through throughout

as in port
ought bought fought nought sought
brought thought wrought

as in how
bough plough slough drought

as in kookaburra
borough thorough

BOOK 5　　UNIT 17

LEARNING TARGETS

Pupil Book: Focus
to match key words to pictures and to find related rhyming words

Pupil Book: Extra
to find the answers to clues, the answers of which carry the target spelling patterns

Pupil Book: Extension
to secure the earlier work on using **al** as a prefix

Resource sheet: Focus
to complete word sums;
to complete cloze activity with target letter patterns.

Resource sheet: Extension
to select **l** or **ll** to complete words

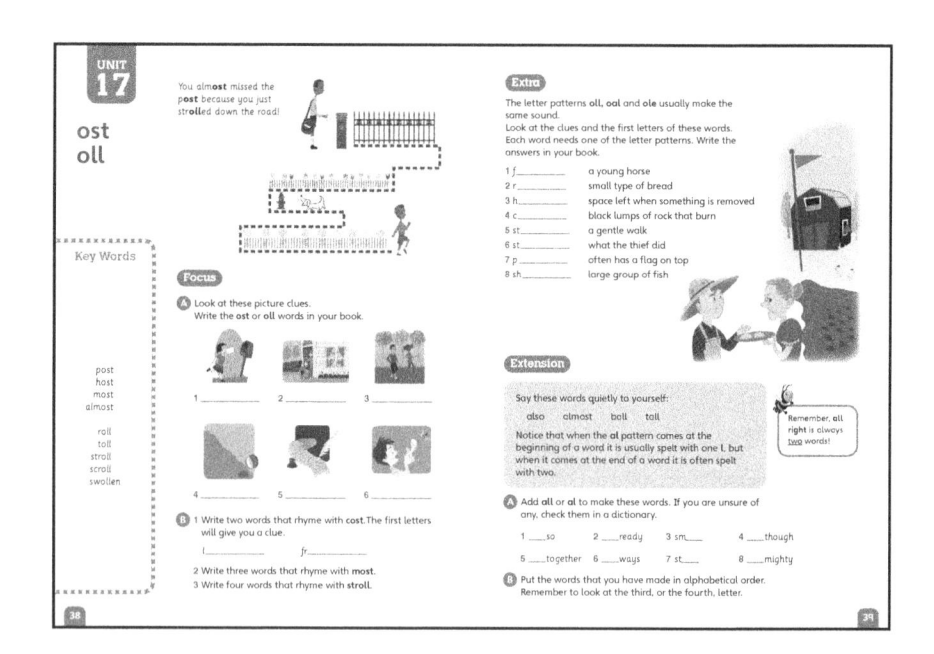

BACKGROUND NOTES AND SUGGESTIONS

Children enjoy collecting 'odd-ones out': perhaps groups can be challenged to find words in which the letters are masquerading as other letters – such as the **o** in *honey*.

This unit also offers an opportunity for class or group work on a single or double **l**, nearly always a spelling problem.

Pupil Book answers

Focus

A 1 post　2 host　3 stroll
　　4 roll　5 scroll　6 swollen

B 1 lost frost
　　2 Teacher to check individual answers
　　3 Teacher to check individual answers

Extra
1 foal　2 roll　3 hole
4 coal　5 stroll　6 stole
7 pole　8 shoal

Extension

A 1 also　2 already　3 small
　　4 although　5 altogether　6 always
　　7 stall　8 almighty

B almighty already also although altogether always small stall

Resource sheet answers

Focus

A most　toll
　　post　roll
　　host　stroll
　　almost　scroll

B We went for a st**roll** to p**ost** a sc**roll** and alm**ost** had to pay a t**oll**!

C Teacher to check individual answers

Extension

A 1 almost　2 bull
　　3 full　4 already
　　5 beautiful　6 painful
　　7 always　8 altogether

B 1 also　2 helpfully
　　3 almost　4 bully
　　5 useful　6 successful
　　7 thoughtfully　8 dreadful
　　9 although　10 alligator

Teacher to check individual answers

Supporting word lists

As well as ost and oll letter patterns, the list below includes other irregular o words which are worth practising

ost	most post host almost
oll	toll poll roll scroll stroll swollen
old	old bold cold fold gold hold sold told scold
olk	folk yolk
olt	bolt colt jolt
on	monkey money honey front
oth	both sloth other brother smother

BOOK 5 — UNIT 18

LEARNING TARGETS

Pupil Book: Focus
to write rhyming target words using picture clues

Pupil Book: Extra
to sort words according to the phonemes represented by **ea**

Pupil Book: Extension
to sort words according to the phonemes represented by **ear**;
to sort words according to the phonemes represented by **ough**

Resource sheet: Focus
to write target 'rhyme' words

Resource sheet: Extension
to sort words according to the phonemes represented by **ough**

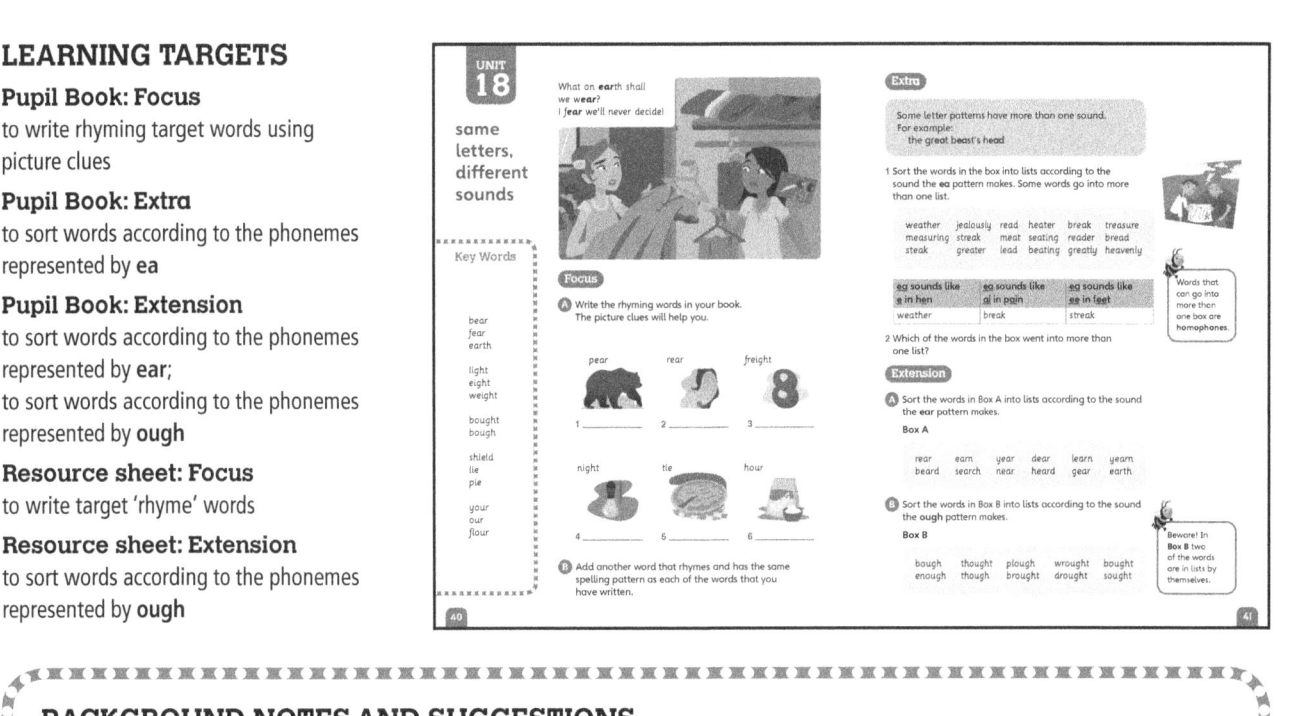

BACKGROUND NOTES AND SUGGESTIONS

This unit develops nicely from Book 3 Unit 17 where different letter patterns with the same sound were taught. In this unit the focus is on the more well-known variations of phoneme associated with certain vowel digraphs. Many such variations can be related to preceding letters e.g. **e** before **igh** usually gives the long **a** sound. Also, although the *Supporting word lists* have been organised into sub-sections, it should be recognised that these might vary according to dialect.

Pupil Book answers

Focus
A 1 bear 2 ear 3 eight
4 light 5 pie 6 flour

B Teacher to check individual answers

Extra
A
ea (like hen)	ea (like pain)	ea (like feet)
weather	break	streak
jealousy	steak	heater
read	greater	meat
bread	greatly	seating
treasure		reader
lead		lead
measuring		beating
heavenly		read

B 1 Teacher to check individual answers
2 Teacher to check individual answers

Extension
A beard year near dear rear gear
learn earn yearn search heard earth

B bough drought plough
thought wrought sought bought
brought
enough
through

Resource sheet answers

Focus
tie   shield
night   weight
hour   pour
plough   bought

Extension
A
as in 'off'   cough trough
as in 'cuff'   rough tough enough
as in 'no'   dough though
as in 'too'   through throughout
as in 'fort'   ought brought
                   bought thought
as in 'how'   drought bough plough
as in 'kookaburra' borough thorough

B Teacher to check individual answers

Supporting word lists

ight
right fight light night
eight freight weight
tight height

ear
pear wear bear
hear rear fear clear beard
year dear tear near gear ear
search earn yearn learn heard
earth heart hearth

oo
boot food hoot loot mood pool root
soot took book cook foot look nook
good hood hook rook

ough
bough plough drought
enough cough
though dough
bought brought sought thought wrought

ie
lie pie tie fried lied tried
grief piece niece field shield

our
armour favour colour honour rumour
neighbour
pour your
flour hour

BOOK 5 — UNIT 19

LEARNING TARGETS

Pupil Book: Focus
to match key words to pictures;
to write selected homophones

Pupil Book: Extra
to match homophones and define their meanings

Pupil Book: Extension
to put homophones in a sentence to show their meaning

Resource sheet: Focus
to write selected homophones;
to use homophones in sentences

Resource sheet: Extension
to use homophones in context;
to write selected homophones

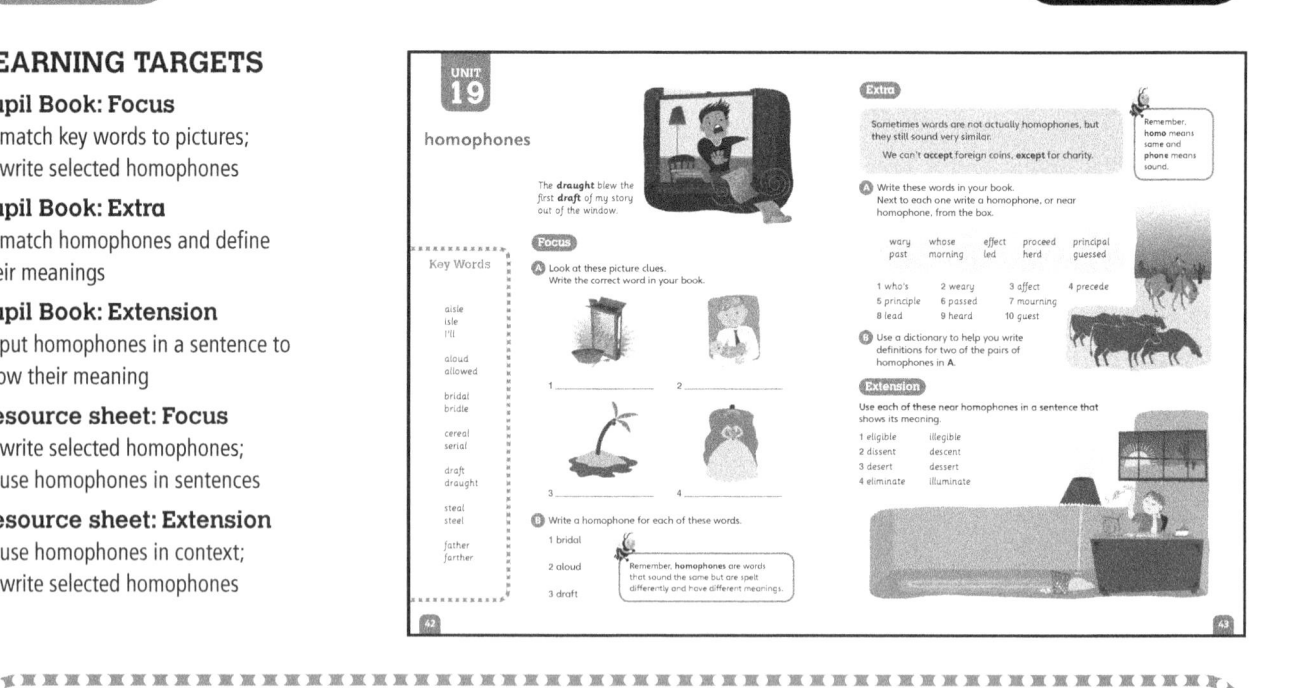

BACKGROUND NOTES AND SUGGESTIONS

As noted previously, homophones are words with the same (*homo*) sound (*phone*) but different spelling and meanings, whereas homonyms have the same sound and spelling but different meanings. In this unit we develop and extend earlier work on the homophones, moving on from words which are high-frequency in children's writing to those which are less often used but still cause problems from time to time.

Reports on children's performance have suggested that children should learn to spell words where there are different ways of representing vowel digraphs, such as *brake* and *break*, which covers most homophones.

Pupil Book answers

Focus
A 1 cereal 2 father
   3 isle 4 bridal

B 1 bridle 2 allowed 3 draught

Extra
A 1 whose 2 wary 3 effect
   4 proceed 5 principal 6 past
   7 morning 8 led 9 herd
   10 guessed

B Teacher to check individual answers

Extension
Teacher to check individual answers

Resource sheet answers

Focus
A 1 creek 2 their/they're
   3 heal/he'll 4 to/too
   5 dear 6 hour
   7 fought 8 dryer
   9 sell 10 board
   11 ate 12 stare
   13 weight 14 main

B Teacher to check individual answers

Extension
A / **B** Teacher to check individual answers

C 1 vein vain
   2 for fore
   3 sees seize
   4 rode rowed
   5 soar sore
   6 wear where
   7 knead need
   8 heel he'll

Supporting word lists

air, heir
altar, alter
bare, bear
blew, blue
bough, bow
buy, by, bye
allowed, aloud
ascent, assent
beach, beech
board, bored
boy, buoy
ceiling, sealing
cellar, seller
check, cheque
draft, draught
feat, feet
flour, flower
groan, grown
hair, hare
hear, here
knight, night
know, no
loan, lone
mail, male
missed, mist
pail, pale
peak, peek
peer, pier
practice, practise
rain, reign, rein
road, rode, rowed
rose, rows
sail, sale
sea, see
sew, so, sow
soar, sore
son, sun
stake, steak
tail, tale
their, there
tide, tied
vain, vane, vein
wait, weight
won, one
you, yew, ewe
cereal, serial
coarse, course
fair, fare
flour, flower
hail, hale
hall, haul
heard, herd
knot, not
leak, leek
maid, made
meat, meet
more, moor
pain, pane
peal, peel
plain, plane
principal, principle
read, reed
scene, seen
seam, seem
sight, site
sole, soul
stair, stare
stationary, stationery
team, teem
threw, through
too, to, two
waist, waste
week, weak
wood, would

BOOK 5 — UNIT 20

LEARNING TARGETS

Pupil Book: Focus
to match key words to definitions

Pupil Book: Extra
to learn the rules for adding the target suffix to **ous** endings

Pupil Book: Extension
to learn the rules for adding the target suffix to **ce** and **tion** endings

Resource sheet: Focus
to copy letter patterns and complete target words

Resource sheet: Extension
to find and use target words

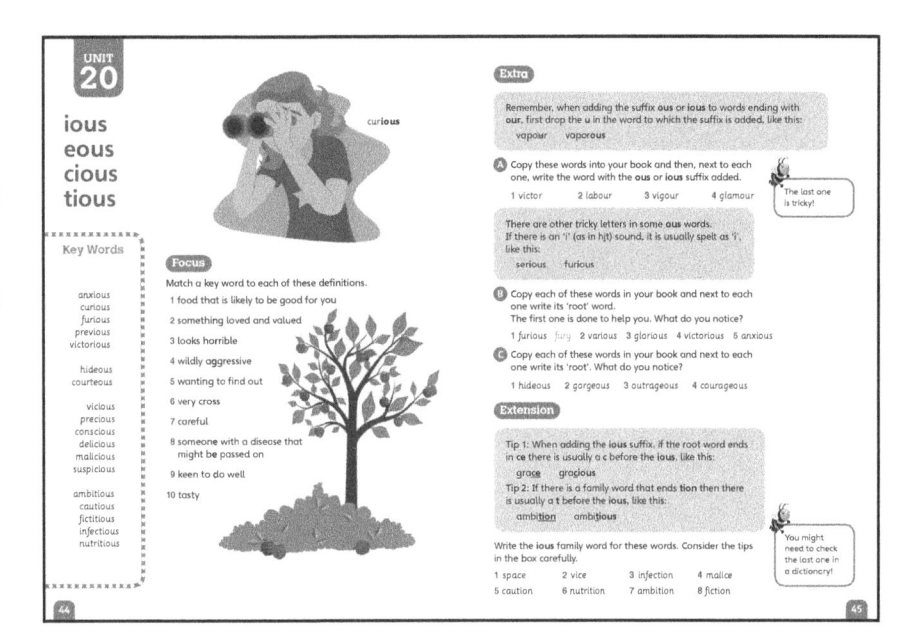

BACKGROUND NOTES AND SUGGESTIONS

The key to this spelling pattern is knowing when to include the **i** and when to omit it. The grouping in the Supporting word lists may help. Sometimes it is sounded – if so include it (e.g. *various*); but there are other important words where it is silent and these need to be learnt, though in some cases it helps to think whether related words would have an **i** (e.g. *anxious – anxiety*), and it should always be used between a **c** and **ous** (e.g. *gracious, precious*).

Remember also that the medial **e** in *outrageous* and *courageous* is necessary for the central **age** phoneme.

Pupil Book answers

Focus
1 nutritious   2 precious
3 hideous   4 vicious
5 curious   6 furious
7 cautious   8 infectious
9 ambitious   10 delicious

Extra

Ⓐ 1 victorious   2 laborious
   3 vigorous   4 glamorous

Ⓑ 1 fury   2 vary   3 glory
   4 victory   5 anxiety

Pupil to note that all the words end with **y**

Ⓒ 1 hide   2 gorge
   3 outrage   4 courage

Pupil to note that all the roots end with **e**

Extension
1 spacious   2 vicious
3 infectious 4 malicious
5 cautious   6 nutritious
7 ambitious   8 fictitious

Resource sheet answers

Focus

Ⓐ Children should copy the pattern

Ⓑ / Ⓒ
furious infectious delicious
ambitious courteous anxious
hideous suspicious nutritious

Extension

Ⓐ 1 mutinous   2 nervous
   3 vigorous   4 cautious
   5 outrageous   6 glamorous
   7 courageous   8 mysterious
   9 humorous   10 beauteous
   11 furious   12 gaseous
   13 nutritious 14 melodious
   15 famous   16 victorious

Ⓑ Teacher to check individual answers

Ⓒ Teacher to check individual answers

Supporting word lists

famous nervous jealous enormous
generous dangerous prosperous
marvellous ridiculous glamorous
numerous tremendous hideous
outrageous courageous
spontaneous gorgeous

various curious furious previous serious
victorious glorious suspicious

anxious cautious
gracious malicious precious

BOOK 5 — UNIT 21

LEARNING TARGETS

Pupil Book: Focus
to find words with the target endings in a wordsearch;
to identify those ending with **cial** and **tial**

Pupil Book: Extra
to add **ly** to words ending with **al**

Pupil Book: Extension
to apply the rule that **cial** usually comes after a vowel letter whereas **tial** comes after a consonant

Resource sheet: Focus
to copy letter patterns and words and complete word sums

Resource sheet: Extension
to recognise misspelt words

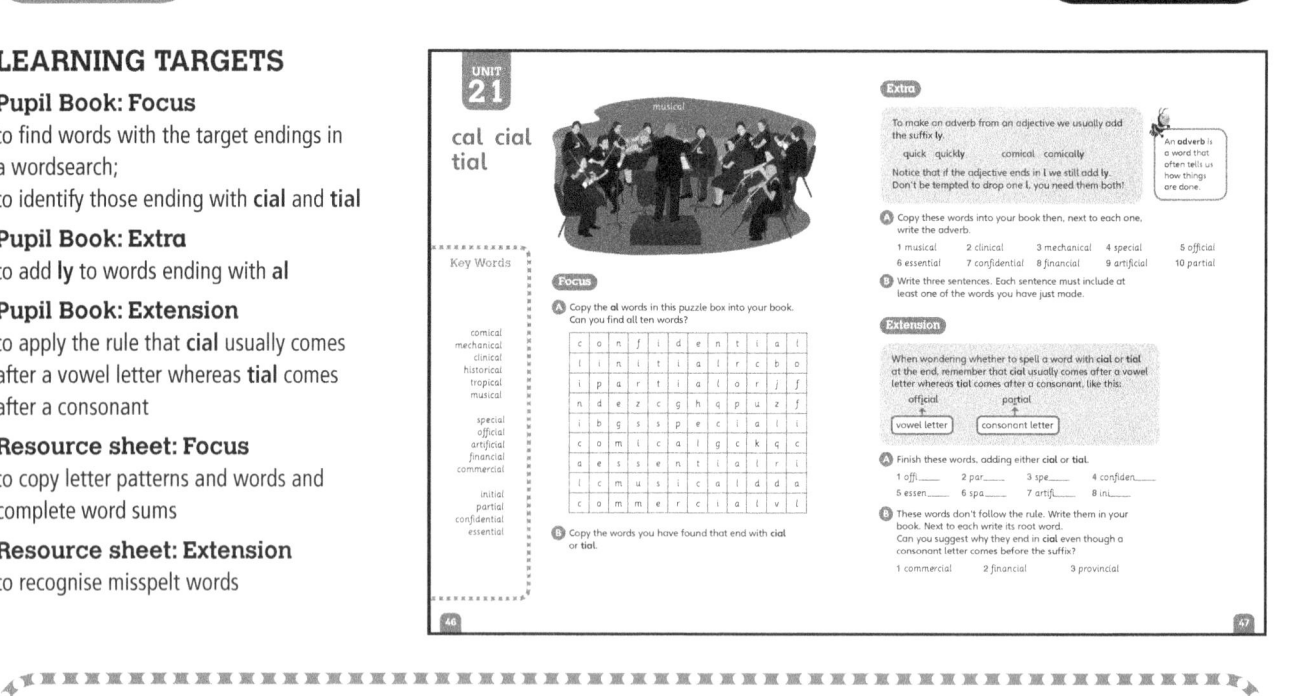

BACKGROUND NOTES AND SUGGESTIONS

These endings are notoriously awkward. It's worth trying to teach that **cial** is common after a vowel letter, whereas **tial** usually follows a consonant letter. However, there are the inevitable exceptions, e.g. *commercial, financial* and *provincial* (relating to their root words *commerce, finance and province*) and *initial*.

Pupil Book answers

Focus

A confidential clinical comical tropical partial special initial commercial essential musical

B confidential partial special initial commercial essential

Extra

A
1 musically
2 clinically
3 mechanically
4 specially
5 officially
6 essentially
7 confidentially
8 financially
9 artificially
10 partially

B Teacher to check individual answers

Extension

A
1 official
2 partial
3 special
4 confidential
5 essential
6 spatial
7 artificial
8 initial

B
1 commerce
2 finance
3 province

Pupil should note that the root word has a soft **c** and thus suffix is **cial** rather that **tial**

Resource sheet answers

Focus

A Children should trace and copy the patterns and words

B
financial   initial
special   partial
official   essential

C Teacher to check individual answers

Extension

A
1 special ✓
2 muscial ✗
3 initial ✓
4 confidencial ✗
5 finanical ✗
6 partial ✓
7 historical ✓
8 mechanitial ✗
9 commercial ✓
10 essenital ✗
11 tropcial ✗
12 artificial ✓

B musical confidential financial mechanical essential tropical

C Teacher to check individual answers

Supporting word lists

beneficial commercial crucial
facial financial glacial judicial
official prejudicial provincial
sacrificial special
social superficial

circumstantial confidential
consequential credential deferential
differential essential impartial influential
initial martial nuptial palatial partial
potential preferential residential
sequential spatial substantial

BOOK 5

UNIT 22

LEARNING TARGETS

Pupil Book: Focus
to find target words in a wordsearch;
to complete **ie** word quiz

Pupil Book: Extra
to revise the formation of plurals of nouns that end in **f** and **fe**

Pupil Book: Extension
to create a word web for words with target word pattern

Resource sheet: Focus
to complete a word fan and match target words to pictures

Resource sheet: Extension
to secure the **ie/ei** spelling rule

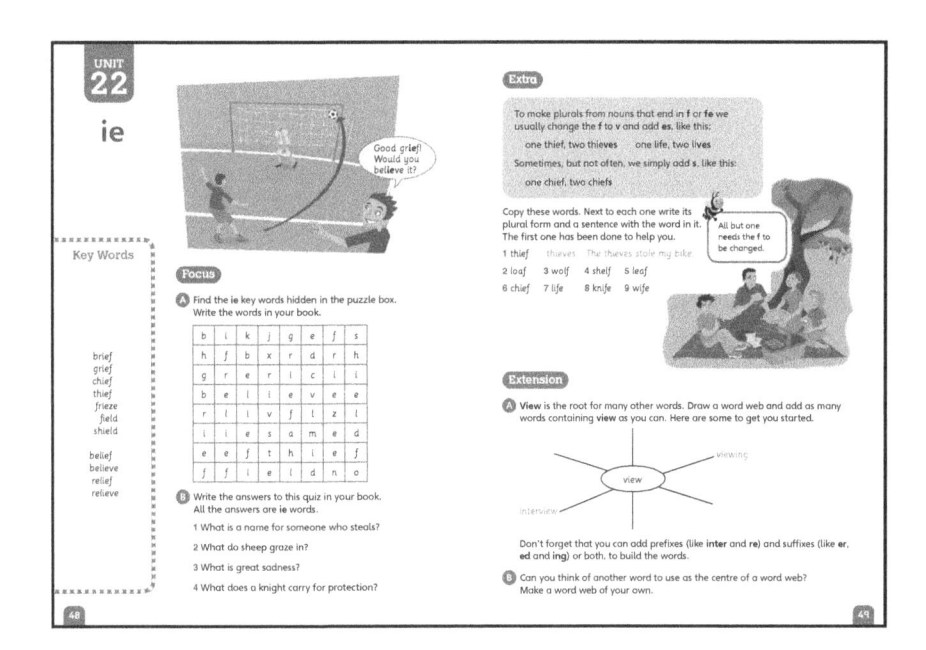

BACKGROUND NOTES AND SUGGESTIONS

This unit (and Unit 23 that follows) can usefully be taken together to teach and secure the rules relating to letter patterns in which **i** and **e** are adjacent. And following from some of the preceding units (e.g. Book 3 Unit 17), these provide further examples of digraphs that can make different sounds.

When a number of the target words are collected and listed it will become apparent that **ie** is more frequent than **ei**, and that **c** is usually followed by **ei** (the **i** before **e** rule), though beware of *science, ancient* and *glacier*. Several of the **ie** words end in **f**, giving an opportunity to practise, as class and group work, plurals of words that end in **f** and **fe**. Although included in the pattern, the last set of words in the *Supporting words lists* (ending in **iew**) might more properly be taken with other **ew** words, with the **i** as a silent letter.

Pupil Book answers

Focus
A believe brief relief belief field grief frieze thief shield

B 1 thief 2 field 3 grief 4 shield

Extra
1 thief thieves   2 loaf loaves
3 wolf wolves   4 shelf shelves
5 leaf leaves   6 chief chiefs
7 life lives   8 knife knives
9 wife wives

Teacher to check individual sentences

Extension
A Teacher to check individual answers that might include:
view review interview reviewed interviewed viewing reviewing interviewing viewer interviewer reviewer overview

B Teacher to check individual answers

Resource sheet answers

Focus
A Children should copy the pattern

B brief
grief
chief
relief
belief

C handkerchief grief briefcase

D Teacher to check individual answers

Extension
A 1 chief   2 shield
    3 receive   4 shriek
    5 achieve   6 yield
    7 piece   8 deceit
    9 conceit   10 niece
   11 medieval   12 perceive
   13 obedient   14 receipt

B 1 niece   2 shriek
    3 patient   4 shield
    5 field

Supporting word lists

as in bee
niece piece siege
brief grief frieze
shield chief thief shriek
belief believe relief relieve shriek
yield handkerchief mischief medieval
obedient glacier

as in hen
friend patient ancient

as in high
lie die pie tie
fiery quiet science

as in ear
pierce fierce pier

as in few
view review interview

BOOK 5 — UNIT 23

LEARNING TARGETS

Pupil Book: Focus
to match key words to pictures;
to find target words in a wordsearch

Pupil Book: Extra
to revise the **i** before **e** rule

Pupil Book: Extension
to review the homophones associated with **ei** words

Resource sheet: Focus
to complete word sums and match words to pictures

Resource sheet: Extension
to unscramble target words;
to use target homophones in a cloze activity

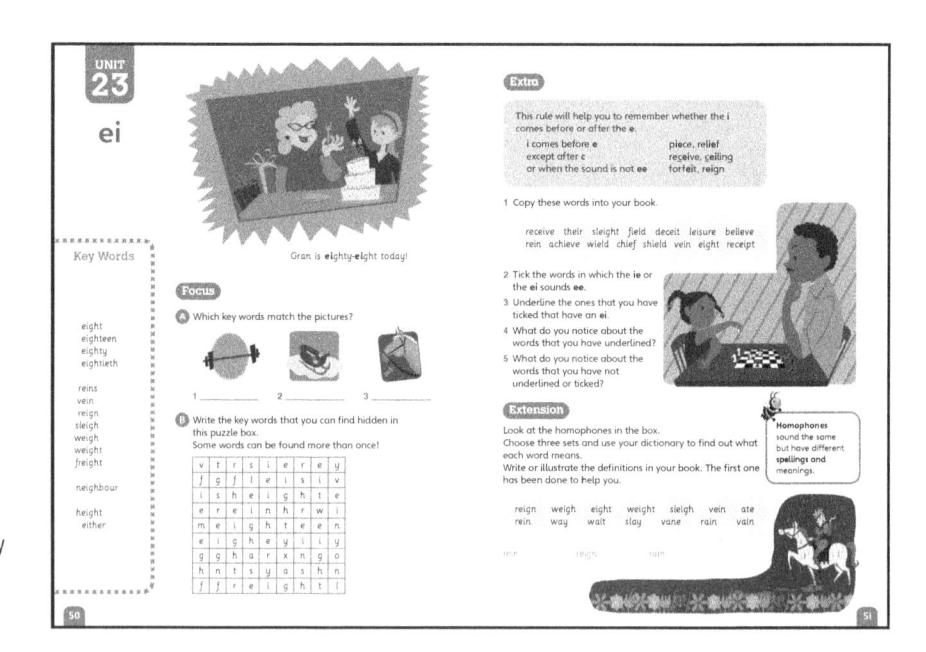

BACKGROUND NOTES AND SUGGESTIONS

Having covered **ie** in Unit 22, this unit introduces the most famous spelling rule of them all:

- **i** comes before **e** (when the sound is **ee**) (*piece, achieve*)
- except after **c** (*receive, ceiling, receipt*)
- or when the sound is not **ee** (*eight, reign, heir*)

It is said by some that there are so many exceptions that this rule is hardly worth teaching, but many of the words that children confuse when spelling do follow this rule and so it does have its place. The pattern **ei** is another example of a digraph that can make different sounds (see Supporting word lists). As noted previously, and as can be seen from the respective lists, **ei** is less frequent than **ie**.

Pupil Book answers

Focus
A 1 weight 2 sleigh 3 reins

B eight eighteen eighty reins
vein reign sleigh weigh weight
freight height

Extra
1 Teacher to check individual answers
2 receive field deceit believe achieve
wield chief shield receipt
3 receive deceit receipt
4 All have *c* before *ei*
5 None of them sound the *ei* as *ee*

Extension
Teacher to check individual answers

Resource sheet answers

Focus
A Children should trace and copy the pattern

B eight
eighteen
eighty
weigh
weight
freight
sleigh
height

C eight sleigh weight eighteen

Extension
A 1 vein
2 freight
3 reign
4 reins
5 sleigh
6 neighbour
7 protein
8 weird

B 1 The hungry boy <u>ate</u> too many biscuits.
My sister is <u>eight</u> today.
2 I just knew it would <u>rain</u> today.
Don't hold the horse's <u>rein</u> too tightly.
3 Feel the <u>weight</u> of this pumpkin!
You <u>wait</u> here while I get the shopping bags.

Supporting word lists

as in tree (cei words)
receive receipt deceive ceiling
perceive conceit

as in cape
rein veil vein feint
reign beige
neigh weigh eight weight
sleigh freight
eighty eighteen eightieth
neighbour

as in kite
height
either neither
eiderdown

others
their leisure weird protein heir
sovereign foreign

BOOK 5

UNIT 24

LEARNING TARGETS

Pupil Book: Focus
to find words that don't fit a given letter pattern and to use target words as answers to clues

Pupil Book: Extra
to secure the rule of making plural forms of nouns that end in **y**

Pupil Book: Extension
to make and use the singular form of verbs that end in **y**

Resource sheet: Focus
to complete words using selected word endings and find target words in a wordsearch

Resource sheet: Extension
to secure the rules for adding **s** to words ending with **y**

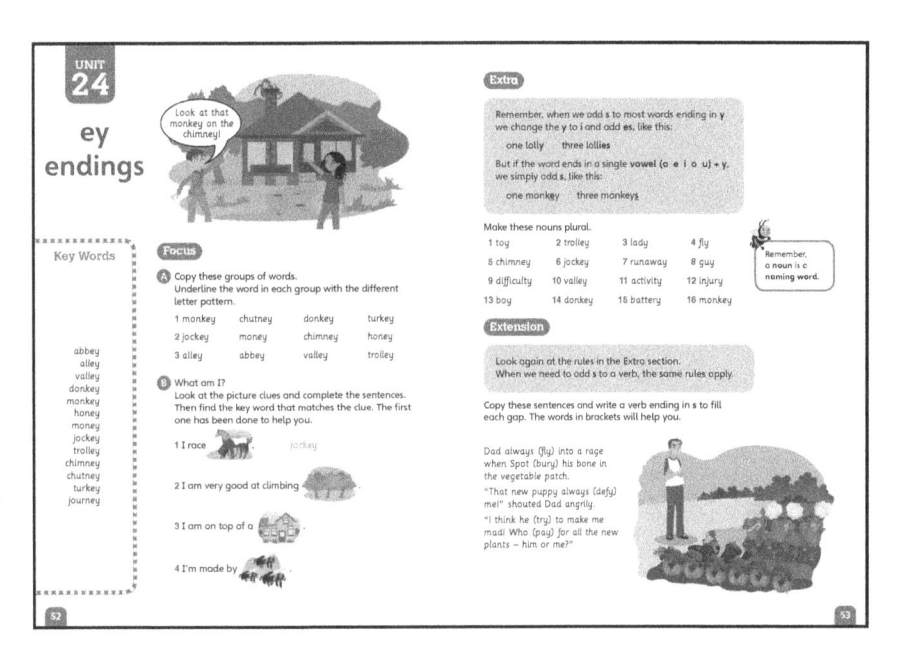

BACKGROUND NOTES AND SUGGESTIONS

This is a small group of words, but words which can cause problems, especially as they do not follow the normal plural rule for words ending in **y**.

To make the plural of a noun that ends in a consonant + **y**, we change **y** to **i** and add **es** *(baby, babies)*. To make the plural of a noun that ends in a vowel + **y**, we just add **s** *(monkey, monkeys)*.

Pupil Book answers

Focus

A
1 monkey <u>chutney</u> donkey turkey
2 <u>jockey</u> money chimney honey
3 alley <u>abbey</u> valley trolley

B
1 jockey   2 monkey
3 chimney 4 honey

Extra
1 toys   2 trolleys
3 ladies   4 flies
5 chimneys   6 jockeys
7 runaways   8 guys
9 difficulties 10 valleys
11 activities 12 injuries
13 boys   14 donkeys
15 batteries   16 monkeys

Extension
Dad always <u>flies</u> into a rage when Spot <u>buries</u> his bone in the vegetable patch.
"That new puppy always <u>defies</u> me!" shouted Dad angrily.
"I think he <u>tries</u> to make me mad! Who <u>pays</u> for all the new plants – him or me?"

Resource sheet answers

Focus

A valley   honey   monkey
    trolley   chimney jockey
    alley   journey turkey

B Teacher to check individual answers

C abbey alley monkey key chimney
    honey donkey turkey dopey jockey

Extension

<u>words ending in consonant + y</u>

balcony	balconies
butterfly	butterflies
country	countries
deputy	deputies
bakery	bakeries
defy	defies
lady	ladies
difficulty	difficulties
battery	batteries
injury	injuries
activity	activities

<u>words ending in vowel + y</u>

valley	valleys
chimney	chimneys
play	plays
destroy	destroys
guy	guys
jockey	jockeys
toy	toys
turkey	turkeys
volley	volleys
donkey	donkeys
journey	journeys

Supporting word lists

key donkey monkey hockey jockey
turkey alley valley volley trolley
barley honey chimney chutney
journey abbey dopey

BOOK 5 — UNIT 25

LEARNING TARGETS

Pupil Book: Focus
to complete a cloze passage using target words

Pupil Book: Extra
to revise and use homonyms in sentences

Pupil Book: Extension
to identify prefixes and suffixes related to target words

Resource sheet: Focus
to copy words and complete word sums

Resource sheet: Extension
to develop words from roots;
to complete cloze activity

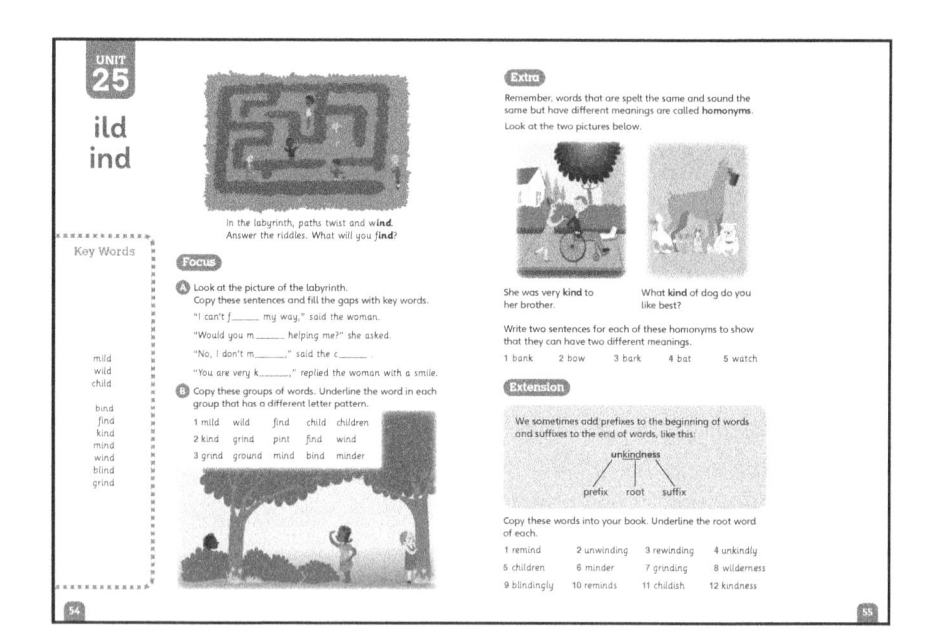

BACKGROUND NOTES AND SUGGESTIONS

The 'irregular' long **i** in the **ild** letter patterns is interesting to consider with the class, for often, whilst the root word has the long **i** phoneme, when part of an extended word the **i** reverts to its regular short form (e.g. *child/children, wild/wilderness, mild/mildew*).

Pupil Book answers

Focus

A "I can't fi<u>nd</u> my way," said the woman.
"Would you m<u>ind</u> helping me?" She asked.
"No, I don't m<u>ind</u>," said the ch<u>ild</u>.
"You are very k<u>ind</u>," replied the woman with a smile.

B 1 mild wild <u>find</u> child children
2 kind grind <u>pint</u> find wind
3 grind <u>ground</u> mind bind minder

Extra
Teacher to check individual answers

Extension
1 re<u>mind</u>
2 un<u>wind</u>ing
3 re<u>wind</u>ing
4 un<u>kind</u>ly
5 <u>child</u>ren
6 <u>mind</u>er
7 <u>grind</u>ing
8 <u>wild</u>erness
9 <u>blind</u>ingly
10 re<u>mind</u>s
11 <u>child</u>ish
12 <u>kind</u>ness

Resource sheet answers

Focus

A Children should copy the patterns and words

B find
mind
kind
blind
mild
child
grind

C Teacher to check individual answers

Extension

A Teacher to check individual answers

B Teacher to check individual answers

C 1 kindly
2 mindlessly
3 unkind
4 reminds

Supporting Word lists

mild wild child

blind find kind mind wind

blind grind pint remind rewind

unwind unkind behind

wilderness children mildew

BOOK 5 — UNIT 26

LEARNING TARGETS

Pupil Book: Focus
to match key verbs to pictures and related activities

Pupil Book: Extra
to practise adding **ing** to a range of modifier **e** words

Pupil Book: Extension
to add both vowel and consonant suffixes to a range of words

Resource sheet: Focus
to secure the rule for adding **ing** to verbs ending in **e**

Resource sheet: Extension
to secure the rules for adding various suffixes to words ending with **e**

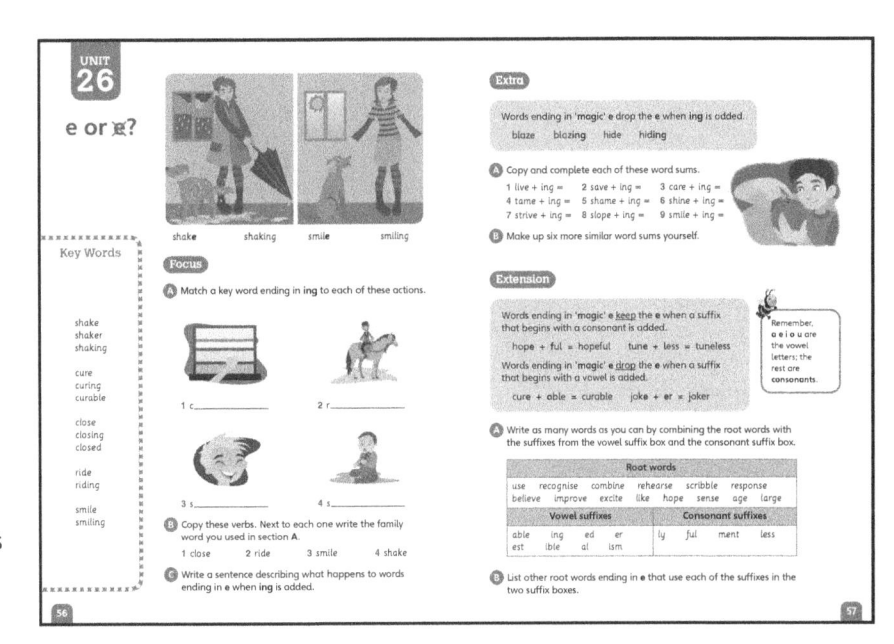

BACKGROUND NOTES AND SUGGESTIONS

This final unit returns to revise the significant spelling rule, which relates to some of the most frequently used words. Although already covered in several units, time spent securing this rule will be worthwhile.

To add a suffix when a word ends with **e**:
- drop the **e** if the suffix begins with a vowel or is **y** (*ice/icing/icy*)
- keep the **e** if the suffix begins with a consonant (*wake/wakeful*)

Unfortunately there are a few exceptions: *true/truly, argue/argument*.

Related to this is another rule worth noting with the children:
To add a suffix *able* or *ous* to a word that ends in **ce** or **ge**
- retain the **e** to keep the **c** or the **g** soft (*notice/noticeable, manage/manageable*)

Note: Suffixes that begin with a vowel are sometimes called 'vowel suffixes' and those that begin with a consonant can be called, 'consonant suffixes'.

Pupil Book answers

Focus

A
1 closing
2 riding
3 smiling
4 shaking

B
1 close closing
2 ride riding
3 smile smiling
4 shake shaking

C Pupils should realise that the **e** is dropped before the **ing** is added

Extra

A
1 living 2 saving 3 caring
4 taming 5 shaming 6 shining
7 striving 8 sloping 9 smiling

B Teacher to check individual answers

Extension

A
- usable using used user useful useless
- recognisable recognising recognised
- combining combined
- rehearsing rehearsed
- scribbling scribbled scribbler
- responsible
- believable believing believed believer
- improving improved improvement
- excitable exciting excited excitement
- likeable liking liked
- hoping hoped hopeful hopeless
- sensing sensed sensible senseless
- aged aging agism ageless
- larger largest largely

B Teacher to check individual answers

Resource sheet answers

Focus

A
1 making 2 raking
3 blaming 4 flaming
5 draping 6 scraping
7 gliding 8 sliding
9 liking 10 striking
11 skating

B Kamil is <u>baking</u> a cake.
Alice is <u>wiping</u> her eyes.
Hayden is <u>closing</u> the door.

Extension

1 useful using useful
2 believed believing believable
3 hopeful hoping hopeless
4 sensation sensing sensed
5 largely larger largest
6 ageless ageism ageing
7 shameful shameless shamed
8 carefree caring careless
9 excitable exciting excitement
10 rehearsal rehearsing rehearsed

Supporting word lists

There are very many words with a modifying e
Here is a small selection:
face race place grace trace space
spike strike spite sprite smile shine
glide slide bride
crime grime prime slime drive
slope broke smoke choke close prose
chose those
drove globe probe froze
conclude continue create imagine
improvise issue prepare queue
receive organise separate

BOOK 5
UNIT 27

LEARNING TARGETS

Pupil Book: Focus
to identify tricky soft **c** and soft **g** words in a wordsearch

Pupil Book: Extra
to give particular attention to tricky words with double letters

Pupil Book: Extension
to practise words where the grapheme/phoneme relationships are different from that that might have been expected

Resource sheet: Focus
to find and write tricky words from picture clues;
to complete cloze activity

Resource sheet: Extension
to find definitions for target words;
to recognise misspelt words

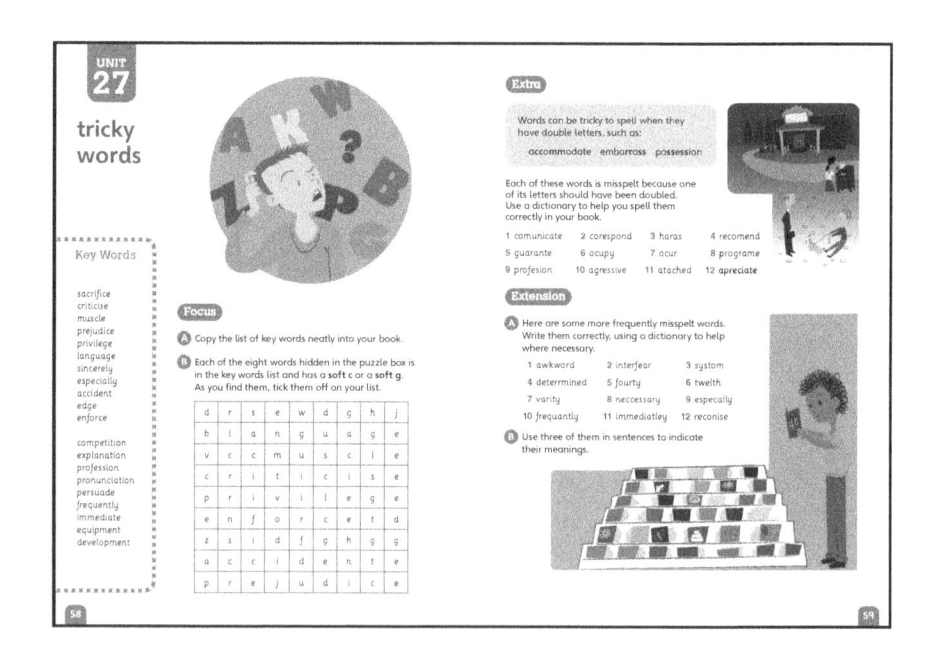

BACKGROUND NOTES AND SUGGESTIONS

The 'tricky' words in this unit have been selected to focus on problems that arise from the occurrence of soft **c** and soft **g**, from double letters and where grapheme/phoneme relationships are different from what might have been expected.

Pupil Book answers

Focus
A Pupils should copy all key words

B accident muscle prejudice privilege language edge enforce criticise

Extra
1 communicate
2 correspond
3 harass
4 recommend
5 guarantee
6 occupy
7 occur
8 programme
9 profession
10 aggressive
11 attached
12 appreciate

Extension
A
1 awkward
2 interfere
3 system
4 determined
5 forty
6 twelfth
7 variety
8 necessary
9 especially
10 frequently
11 immediately
12 recognise

B Teacher to check individual answers

Resource sheet answers

Focus
A accident edge muscle language

B edge language accident muscle

C
1 I had to <u>persuade</u> my sister to get in the water.
2 We checked we had all the <u>equipment</u> we needed before setting off.
3 Finn won the mountain bike <u>competition</u>.
4 My dad belongs to the teaching <u>profession</u>.
5 I didn't understand the <u>explanation</u> my gran gave me.

Extension
A Teacher to check individual answers

B
1 definate ✗
2 identity ✓
3 perswade ✗
4 suficient ✗
5 avaliable ✗
6 communicate ✓
7 existance ✗
8 accommodate ✓
9 oppertunity ✗
10 restaurant ✓

Incorrect words spelt correctly:

definite persuade sufficient available existence opportunity

BOOK 5 UNIT 28

LEARNING TARGETS

Pupil Book: Focus
to find synonyms in a page from a thesaurus

Pupil Book: Extra
to find antonyms from a thesaurus

Pupil Book: Extension
to improve sentences by referring to a thesaurus

Resource sheet: Focus
to answer questions from an example page in a thesaurus

Resource sheet: Extension
to write thesaurus entries for chosen words

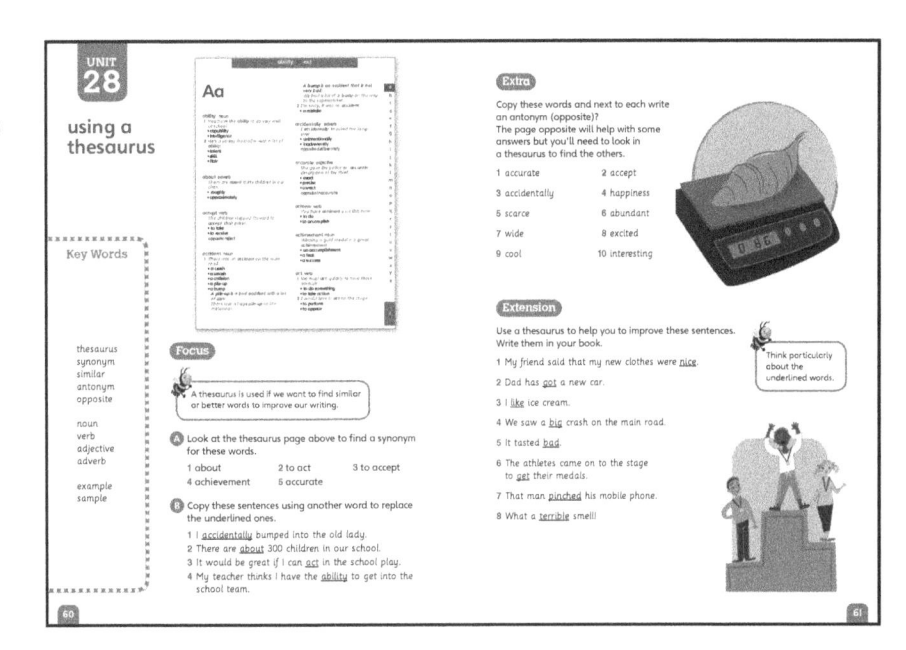

BACKGROUND NOTES AND SUGGESTIONS

It will be necessary for each child to have a suitable thesaurus available to undertake this unit. *The Oxford Junior Thesaurus* is such a volume for children at this stage. The ability, not only to understand the workings and organisation of a thesaurus, but to turn to it without hesitation, is important if a pupil's word selection during writing activities is to broaden and generally improve.

Before the work begins, remind children of the technical language required e.g. synonym, antonym etc.

Pupil Book answers

Focus

A
1 roughly approximately
2 to do something to take action to perform to appear
3 to take to receive
4 an accomplishment a feat a success
5 exact precise correct

B Teacher to check individual answers

Extra
Teacher to check individual answers

Extension
Teacher to check individual answers

Resource sheet answers

Focus
1 three
2 verb
3 retreat
4 Teacher to check individual answers
5 'reserve' is listed twice as one meaning is a noun and the other a verb
6 return

Extension
A / B
Teacher to check individual answers

BOOK 5

Check-Up 2

Focus
1 nought   2 plough   3 post   4 shoal
5 rein/s   6 light   7 eight   8 pie
9 shield   10 knife   11 scroll   12 weight
13 donkey   14 child   15 blind   16 automobile

Extra
A 1 haven't   2 she's   3 couldn't   4 don't   5 I'll
B 1 foal   2 roll   3 pole   4 shoal
C 1 bridle   2 morning   3 guessed   4 allowed   5 draught
D 1 victorious 2 laborious   3 vigorous   4 glamorous   5 furious
E 1 musically 2 officially   3 essentially 4 partially   5 clinically
F 1 wolves   2 shelves   3 leaves   4 chiefs   5 knives
   6 difficulties 7 valleys   8 activities   9 injuries   10 boys
G 1 weigh   2 eight   3 vein   4 reign/rein   5 sleigh
H 1 saving   2 careful   3 excitement   4 largest
I 1 recommend 2 guarantee   3 occupy   4 profession   5 attached

Extension
A 1 oven-ready   2 quick-thinking   3 over-rated   4 accident-prone
B 1 altogether   2 already   3 small   4 although   5 always
C Teacher to check individual answers
D 1 spacious   2 infectious   3 cautious   4 nutritious   5 ambitious
E 1 special   2 confidential   3 spatial   4 artificial   5 essential
F 1 definitely   2 interesting   3 immediately   4 necessary   5 forty

Book 6 Scope and Sequence

Unit	Pupil Book Focus	Pupil Book Extra	Pupil Book Extension	Resource Book Focus	Resource Book Extension
1	**simple plurals** finding target words	identifying *s/es/ies* endings	understanding irregular plural forms	picture matching; writing plurals	understanding spelling rules; writing plurals
2	**tricky plurals** finding target words	creating *f/fe* plurals	understanding *o* endings; identifying plural forms	picture matching; writing plurals	understanding spelling rules; writing plurals
3	**using prefixes** adding prefixes rule	understanding English origin prefixes	alphabetical ordering	adding prefixes	identifying antonyms; writing sentences
4	**using suffixes** finding target words; word sums	identifying *e* + suffix rules	using *e* ending + able/ible	using *e* + *ing*; cloze activity	understanding suffix rules
5	**using suffixes** finding target words; adding *ed*	identifying *y* ending + suffix	identifying single or double; dictionary work	using *y* + *ed*; cloze activity	using *y* + other suffixes
6	**maths and science words** finding target words	correcting common errors	matching definitions; dictionary work	adding missing letters	completing and making a crossword
7	**ph** completing a wordsearch; sentence writing	choosing *ph* or *f*	identifying Greek origins; dictionary words	word building; picture matching	adding missing letters; sorting words by silent letter; writing sentences
8	**tricky words 1** identifying common errors	identifying key letter omissions	correcting double-letter common errors	adding missing letters; sorting words by silent letter	editing activity
9	**word roots** identifying word roots	writing definitions of selected roots	identifying roots and Latin and Greek roots	identifying Latin and Greek roots	using a dictionary to write definitions
10	**word origins** identifying recent word imports	identifying word sources	sorting Italian roots	picture matching	identifying French word origins
11	**unstressed letters** completing a crossword	identifying unstressed vowels and consonants	working with syllables and unstressed vowels	finding unstressed letters	identifying syllables
12	**tricky words 2** completing a wordsearch	completing double letter quiz	correcting common errors	identifying *double letters* and *ough* words	writing definitions; marking a spelling test
13	**geography and history words** finding target words	correcting common history errors	matching words with definitions; dictionary work	adding missing letters	completing and making a crossword

The darker cells introduce statutory material for this year group in the National Curriculum for England.
The paler cells denote revision of a topic covered in previous years.

Unit	Pupil Book Focus	Pupil Book Extra	Pupil Book Extension	Resource Book Focus	Resource Book Extension
14	**ent ence ant ance** cloze activity	matching adjectives and nouns	making adverbs; writing phrases	completing a crossword; writing sentences	cloze activity; using a dictionary to write definitions
15	**silent letters** letter associations	completing a crossword	identifying syllables; sentence writing	sorting silent letter words; picture matching	writing sentences; correcting common errors
16	**useful connectives** completing a wordsearch	identifying common connectives	connectives cloze activity; writing sentences	completing a wordsearch	writing sentences with compound connectives
17	**homophones and near homophones** finding target homophones	identifying near homophones	identifying noun and verb homophones	writing sentences with homophones	writing definitions
18	**er ar or endings** finding target words; sentence writing	cloze activity	alphabetical ordering	matching words and pictures with clues	cloze activity; using a dictionary to write definitions
19	**ery ary ory endings** completing a wordsearch	adding endings; identifying word roots	understanding plural forms of target word patterns	matching words and pictures; sorting words	word puzzle; writing definitions and word roots
20	**tricky words 3** vowel letter puzzle	finding root words	correcting common errors	letter patterns; adding suffixes	adding suffixes; writing sentences
21	**British English or American English?** identifying American and English spellings	identifying problem suffixes	correction activity	sorting words; writing sentences	identifying equivalent words; writing a letter
22	**a + double letters** finding target words	completing a wordsearch	identifying syllables	letter patterns; picture matching	checking spellings
23	**ie ei** identifying the 'i before e' rule	completing a *ie/ei* table	identifying different *ie/ei* sounds	picture matching; writing sentences	word quiz; completing words
24	**more unstressed vowels** target word quiz; sentence writing	identifying unstressed vowels	identifying syllables and unstressed vowels	finding unstressed vowels	identifying syllables and unstressed letters
25	**tricky words 4** picture quiz cloze activity	correcting common errors	correcting common errors with unstressed letters	picture matching	completing a table; writing sentences
26	**ICT words** finding target words	correcting common errors	understanding internet language	writing labels	writing definitions
27	**tricky words 5** matching words and contractions	correcting common errors with double letters	correcting common errors with omitted letters	word matching	completing and making crosswords
28	**using a dictionary** alphabetical ordering	finding information using a dictionary	using guide words	alphabetical order	using guide words

BOOK 6

UNIT 1

LEARNING TARGETS

Pupil Book: Focus
to match key words to pictures

Pupil Book: Extra
to secure the rules when **es** is added to make a plural noun

Pupil Book: Extension
to practise using irregular plural nouns

Resource sheet: Focus
to write simple plurals

Resource sheet: Extension
to secure the main rules for pluralisation

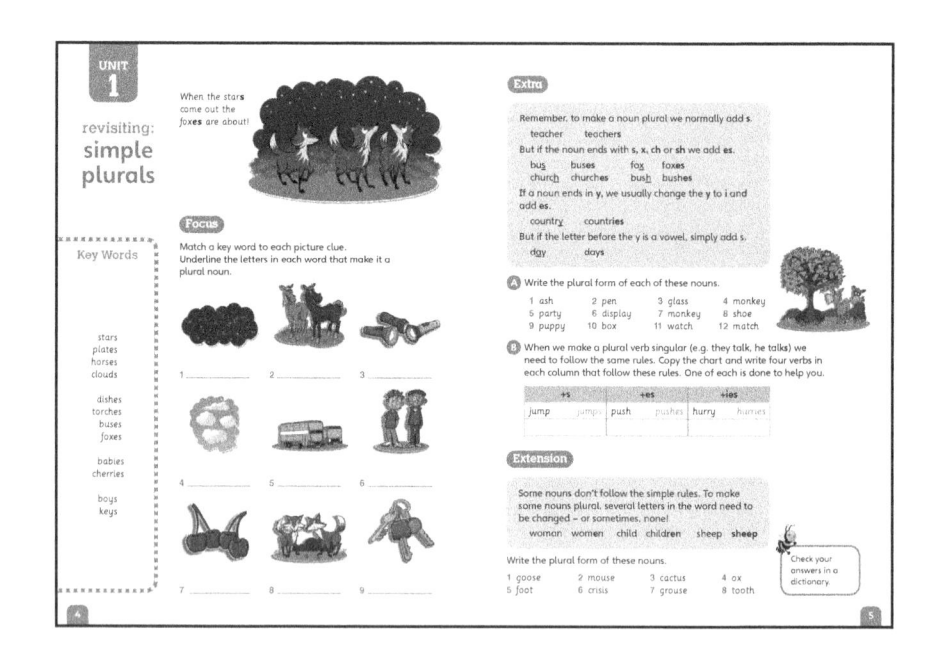

BACKGROUND NOTES AND SUGGESTIONS

This unit gives the opportunity to secure the main spelling rules relating to plural nouns.

For details of all the main spelling rules, see Teacher's Book page 25.

Pupil Book answers

Focus

1 stars	2 horses	3 torches
4 clouds	5 buses	6 boys
7 cherries	8 foxes	9 keys

Extra

A
1 ashes	2 pens	3 glasses
4 monkeys	5 parties	6 displays
7 donkeys	8 shoes	9 puppies
10 boxes	11 watches	12 matches

B Teacher to check individual answers

Extension

1 geese	2 mice
3 cacti	4 oxen
5 feet	6 crises
7 grouse	8 teeth

Resource sheet answers

Focus

A
torches	pens
shoes	foxes
rings	puppies
babies	boys

B
1 pencils	2 glasses
3 boxes	4 jellies
5 donkeys	6 berries
7 clouds	8 flies

Extension

A 1 By adding *s*
   2 When the noun ends with *s*, *x*, *sh* or *ch*
   3 If the noun has a vowel before the *y*, just add *s*, otherwise change the *y* to *i* before adding *es*

B
1 gardens	2 flowers
3 ducks	4 ants
5 patches	6 sheep
7 flies	8 circles
9 dishes	10 fish
11 radii	12 princesses
13 cities	14 days
15 mice	16 hutches
17 families	18 cacti
19 women	20 children
21 trays	

Supporting word lists

Words that take 's'
There are a great number, including:
game table pen cup pond book school teacher

Some words that take 'es'
ash bush glass inch watch brush dish kiss tax box grass pass bus gas sandwich fox class

Some words ending in 'consonant + y'
army berry jelly party city penny baby fly puppy nappy cherry lorry baby daisy posy story

Some words ending in 'vowel + y'
donkey monkey key day display toy delay ray boy valley trolley chimney turkey journey abbey alley jockey

126

BOOK 6

UNIT 2

LEARNING TARGETS

Pupil Book: Focus
to match key words to pictures

Pupil Book: Extra
to secure the rules for making plurals of words ending in **f** or **fe**

Pupil Book: Extension
to secure the rules for making plurals of words ending in **o**

Resource sheet: Focus
to write tricky plurals

Resource sheet: Extension
to secure the rules for making plurals of words ending in **o**

BACKGROUND NOTES AND SUGGESTIONS

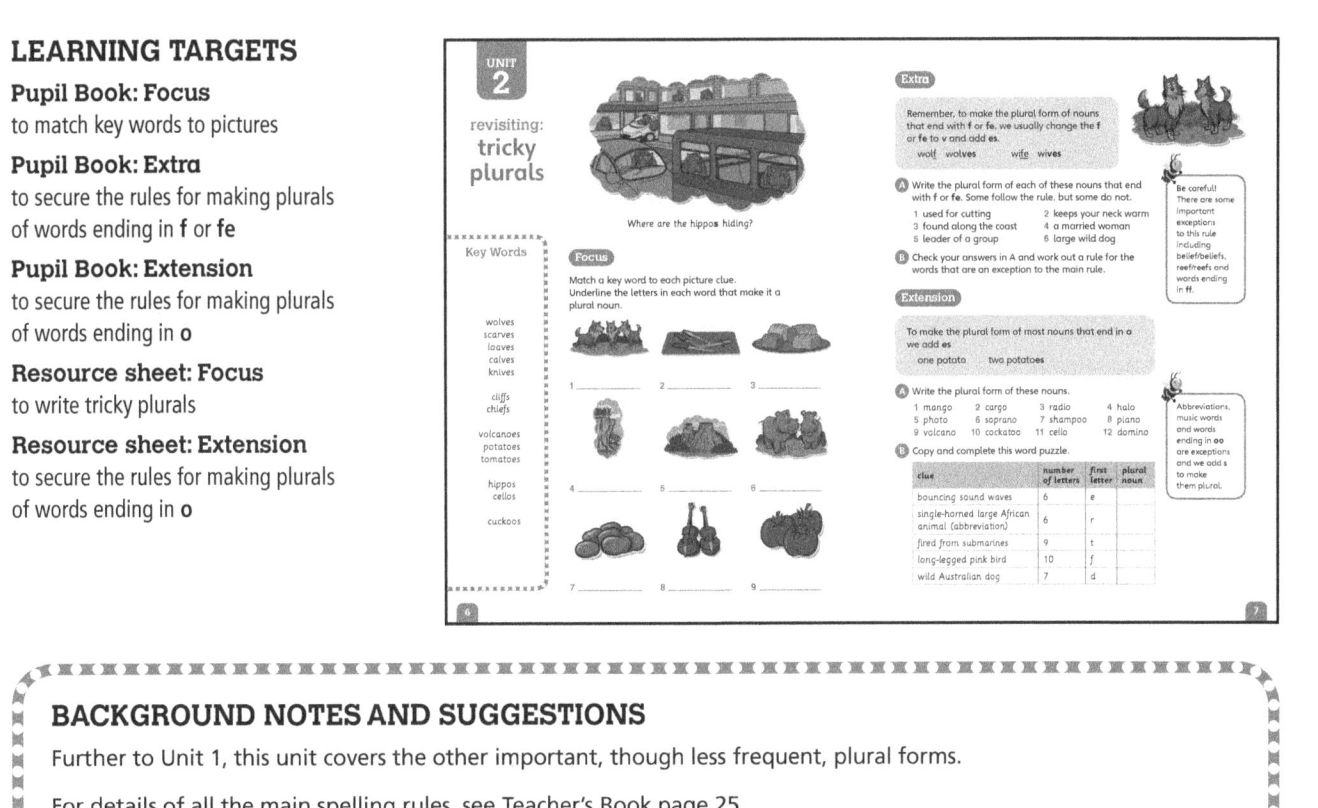

Further to Unit 1, this unit covers the other important, though less frequent, plural forms.

For details of all the main spelling rules, see Teacher's Book page 25.

Pupil Book answers

Focus
1 wolves   2 knives
3 loaves   4 cliffs
5 volcanoes   6 hippos
7 potatoes   8 cellos
9 tomatoes

Extra
A 1 knives   2 scarves
3 cliffs   4 wives
5 chiefs   6 wolves

B Teacher to check individual answers

Extension
A 1 mangoes   2 cargoes
3 radios   4 logos
5 photos   6 sopranos
7 shampoos   8 pianos
9 volcanoes   10 cockatoos
11 cellos   12 dominoes

B echoes
rhinos
potatoes
torpedoes
flamingoes
dingoes

Resource sheet answers

Focus
A knives   dominoes
tomatoes   loaves
pianos   cliffs
scarves   leaves

B 1 cuckoos   2 potatoes
3 hippos   4 chiefs
5 calves   6 photos
7 wives   8 halves

Extension
A 1 We change the *f* or *fe* to *v* and add *es*
2 Yes, just add *s*
3 By adding *es*
4 If the word is a musical word, an abbreviation or ends in *oo*, just add *s*

B 1 wolves   2 cliffs
3 volcanoes   4 wives
5 hippos   6 tomatoes
7 loaves   8 pianos
9 cuckoos   10 dominoes
11 shampoos   12 chiefs
13 scarves   14 reefs
15 rhinos   16 cockatoos
17 mangoes   18 roofs
19 beliefs   20 cellos
21 potatoes

Supporting word lists

f/ves
scarf self shelf leaf loaf calf half
self wolf

ff/s
sniff puff cuff staff stuff bluff
cliff handcuffs

fe/ves
life wife knife

ve/ves
believe swerve save glove curve

exceptions
chief/chiefs belief/beliefs safe/safes
handkerchief/handkerchiefs

words ending in o (which take s to make the plural)
armadillo piano patio yoyo dingo
jumbo piccolo sombrero banjo disco
solo kimono bongo radio matzo
risotto casino cello concerto gecko
oratorio rhino hippo photo

words ending in oo (which take s to make the plural)
cuckoo igloo zoo kangaroo tattoo

words ending in o (which take es to make the plural)
buffaloes dominoes heroes torpedoes
vetoes volcanoes cargoes echoes
mangoes flamingoes

127

BOOK 6 — UNIT 3

LEARNING TARGETS

Pupil Book: Focus
to secure the basic rule for adding prefixes

Pupil Book: Extra
to use 'English prefixes';
to research the meaning of selected prefixes

Pupil Book: Extension
to secure alphabetical ordering in words with the same prefixes

Resource sheet: Focus
to secure the basic rule for adding prefixes

Resource sheet: Extension
to form antonyms by changing prefixes

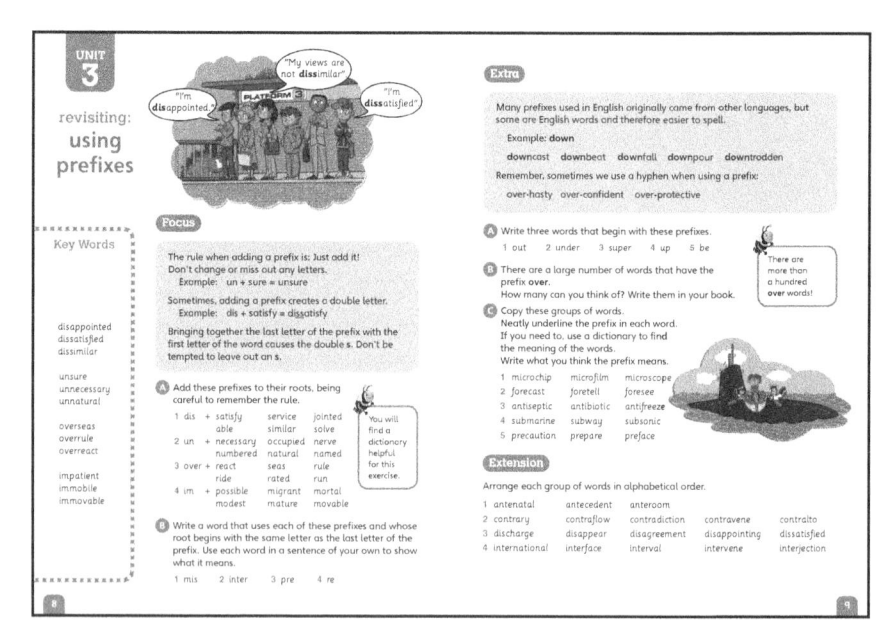

BACKGROUND NOTES AND SUGGESTIONS

There are many prefixes (see *Supporting word lists*), but the key rule never varies – Just add it! Too often children are tempted to adjust the spelling of a root word when adding a prefix – especially when the resulting new word has a double letter created at the interface of prefix and root word (e.g. *immodest*).

Pupil Book answers

Focus

A
1 dissatisfy disservice disjointed disable dissimilar dissolve
2 unnecessary unoccupied unnerve unnumbered unnatural unnamed
3 overreact overseas overrule override overrated overrun
4 impossible immigrate immortal immodest immature immovable

B Teacher to check individual answers

Extra

A Teacher to check individual answers

B Teacher to check individual answers

C
1 micro<u>c</u>hip micro<u>f</u>ilm micro<u>s</u>cope
2 fore<u>c</u>ast fore<u>t</u>ell fore<u>s</u>ee
3 anti<u>s</u>eptic anti<u>b</u>iotic anti<u>f</u>reeze
4 sub<u>m</u>arine sub<u>w</u>ay sub<u>s</u>onic
5 pre<u>c</u>aution pre<u>p</u>are pre<u>f</u>ace
(See Supporting words list for meanings of prefixes)

Extension

1 antecedent antenatal anteroom
2 contradiction contraflow contralto contrary contravene
3 disagreement disappear disappointing discharge dissatisfied
4 interface interjection international interval intervene

Resource sheet answers

Focus

1 unkind   2 disloyal
3 disapprove   4 dishonest

5 disagree   6 untrue
7 distrust   8 disappear
9 unhappy   10 inactive
11 impure   12 impossible
13 inaccurate   14 unclean
15 incorrect   16 impolite
17 invisible   18 imperfect
19 unseen   20 untidy

Extension

A
1 ascend   descend
2 encourage   discourage
3 export   import
4 exterior   interior
5 internal   external
6 decrease   increase
7 outside   inside
8 subsonic   supersonic
9 implode   explode
10 understate   overstate

B Teacher to check individual answers

Supporting word lists

Prefix	Meaning	Example
a	on	aboard afloat
a, ab, abs	away, from	avert abdicated
ac	to	accept
ante	before	antecedent
anti	opposite, against	antibiotic antidote
bi, bis	two, twice	bicycle
circum	round	circumference
con, com	together	connect compete
contra	against	contradict contrary
de	down	descend depress
dis	away, not	discharge disappear
ex	a) out of b) before	extract ex-Prime Minister
fore	previous	forecast foretell
im, in	a) in, into b) not	import incision incorrect
inter	between	international interval
mis	wrong	misconduct mischief
ob	a) open, b) against	obvious observe object
post	after	postpone postscript
pre	before	precaution preface
pro	a) in front of b) in favour of	proceed progress profess
re	a) again b) back	reappear retake return
sub	under	subway subsonic
super	over, beyond	superior superhuman
trans	across	transfer transport
un	not	unimportant
vice	acting for	vice-captain

BOOK 6

UNIT 4

LEARNING TARGETS

Pupil Book: Focus
to match key words to pictures;
to secure the rule for adding an inflectional ending to words ending in **e**

Pupil Book: Extra
to secure the rule for adding vowel and consonant suffixes to words ending in **e**

Pupil Book: Extension
to secure the rule for adding the suffixes **able** or **ible** to words ending in **e**

Resource sheet: Focus
to secure the rule for adding an inflectional ending to words ending in **e**

Resource sheet: Extension
to secure the rules for adding vowel and consonant suffixes

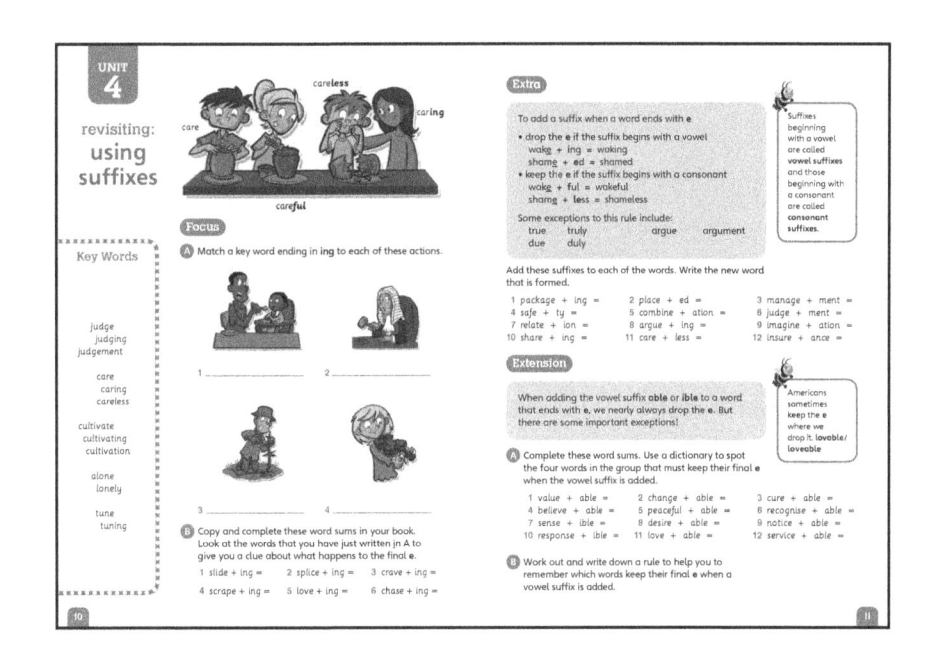

BACKGROUND NOTES AND SUGGESTIONS

This unit and the following unit seek to secure the key rules associated with adding vowel and consonant suffixes, i.e. suffixes which begin with a vowel or consonant respectively. It particularly considers the situation with regard to words ending in **e**.

Pupil Book answers

Focus

A
1. caring
2. judging
3. cultivating
4. tuning

B
1. sliding
2. splicing
3. craving
4. scraping
5. loving
6. chasing

Extra
1. packaging
2. placed
3. management
4. safety
5. combination
6. judgement
7. relation
8. arguing
9. imagination
10. sharing
11. careless
12. insurance

Extension

A
1. valuable
2. changeable
3. cureable
4. believable
5. peaceable
6. recognisable
7. sensible
8. desirable
9. noticeable
10. responsible
11. lovable
12. serviceable

B The final **e** is retained where it supports/is preceded by a soft **c** or **g**.

Resource sheet answers

Focus

A
1. driving
2. smiling
3. hiding
4. chiming
5. shaping
6. scraping
7. saving
8. tracing
9. raving
10. facing

B
1. chasing
2. grazing
3. shaving
4. riding
5. slicing

Extension

1	manage	managing managed manageable manager management
2	agree	agreeing agreed agreeable agreement
3	insure	insuring insured insurance insurable insurer
4	change	changing changed changeable changeless
5	sense	sensing sensed sensible senseless
6	love	loving loved lovable lover lovely loveless
7	relate	relating related relation
8	improve	improving improved improvable improver improvement
9	argue	arguing argued arguable arguer argument
10	care	caring cared carer careless careful
11	believe	believing believed believable believer
12	imagine	imagination imagining imagined imaginable

Supporting word lists

ly
nicely wisely likely completely
angrily prettily happily merrily heavily

ful
careful grateful

less
hopeless senseless useless careless
homeless lifeless

ness
likeness soreness

ment
improvement statement basement
pavement involvement excitement
encouragement advertisement judgement
arrangement replacement argument

able
usable lovable valuable advisable curable
noticeable believable
incurable unrecognisable
(and many other antonyms)

ible
sensible responsible forcible

BOOK 6 — UNIT 5

LEARNING TARGETS

Pupil Book: Focus
to add inflectional endings to words ending in **y**

Pupil Book: Extra
to add suffixes to words ending in **y**

Pupil Book: Extension
to become aware of where single letters are used where double letters might reasonably be expected

Resource sheet: Focus
to add inflectional endings to words ending in **y**

Resource sheet: Extension
to add a range of suffixes to words ending in **y**

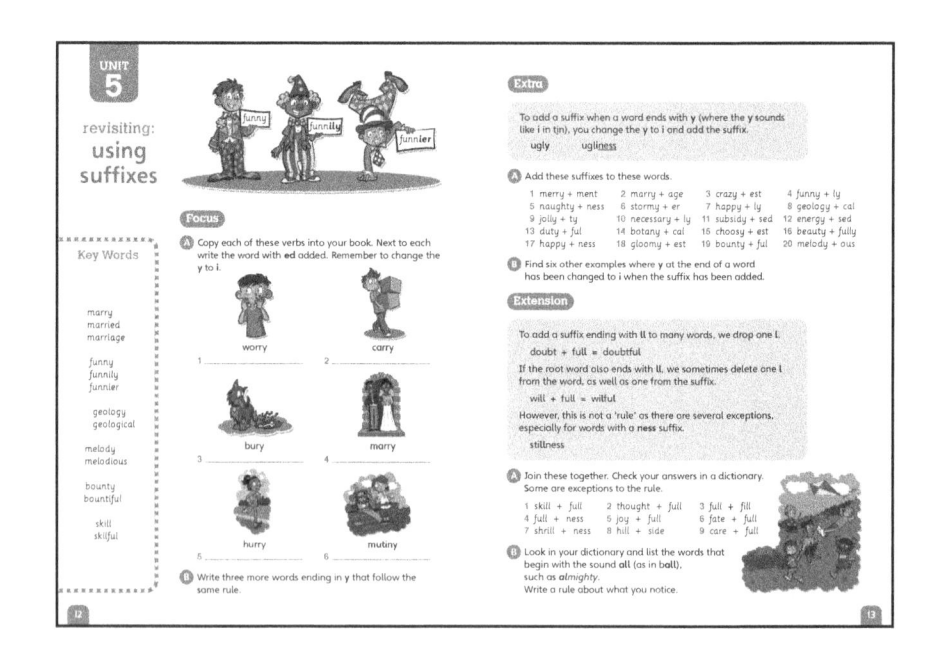

BACKGROUND NOTES AND SUGGESTIONS

This unit and the preceding unit seek to secure the key rules associated with adding vowel and consonant suffixes, i.e. suffixes which begin with a vowel or consonant respectively.

This unit focuses particularly on what to do when adding a prefix to a word ending in **y**, and the need to remain alert to single letters at the ends of words when a double letter might reasonably be expected.

Pupil Book answers

Focus
A
1 worried
2 carried
3 buried
4 married
5 hurried
6 mutinied

B Teacher to check individual answers

Extra
A
1 merriment
2 marriage
3 craziest
4 funnily
5 naughtiness
6 stormier
7 happily
8 geological
9 jollity
10 necessarily
11 subsidised
12 energised
13 dutiful
14 botanical
15 choosiest
16 beautifully
17 happiness
18 gloomiest
19 bountiful
20 melodious

B Teacher to check individual answers

Extension
A
1 skilful
2 thoughtful
3 fulfil
4 fullness
5 joyful
6 fateful
7 shrillness
8 hillside
9 careful

B Teacher to check individual answers

Resource sheet answers

Focus
A
1 carried
2 studied
3 identified
4 copied
5 qualified
6 married
7 defied
8 varied
9 worried
10 hurried

B
1 horrified
2 terrified
3 scurried
4 hurried
5 worried

Extension
A To add a suffix to a word that ends in *y* (where the *y* sounds like the *i* in 'tin'), change the *y* to an *i* and add the suffix

B
1 merriment
2 nastiness
3 furious
4 crazily
5 ugliness
6 hurried
7 victorious
8 buried
9 easier
10 beautiful
11 various
12 prettiest

C Teacher to check individual answers

Supporting word lists

+ed
qualify tarry scurry study defy copy worry carry bury marry hurry mutiny ferry vary quarry

ly
angrily prettily happily merrily heavily

ful
plentiful beautiful dutiful fanciful merciful

less
merciless

ness
laziness ugliness nastiness happiness emptiness heaviness business dryness

ment
enjoyment

BOOK 6 — UNIT 6

LEARNING TARGETS

Pupil Book: Focus
to match key words to pictures

Pupil Book: Extra
to correct common spelling errors

Pupil Book: Extension
to match target words to definitions

Resource sheet: Focus
to identify missing letters in target words

Resource sheet: Extension
to complete a simple crossword puzzle;
to make a crossword puzzle

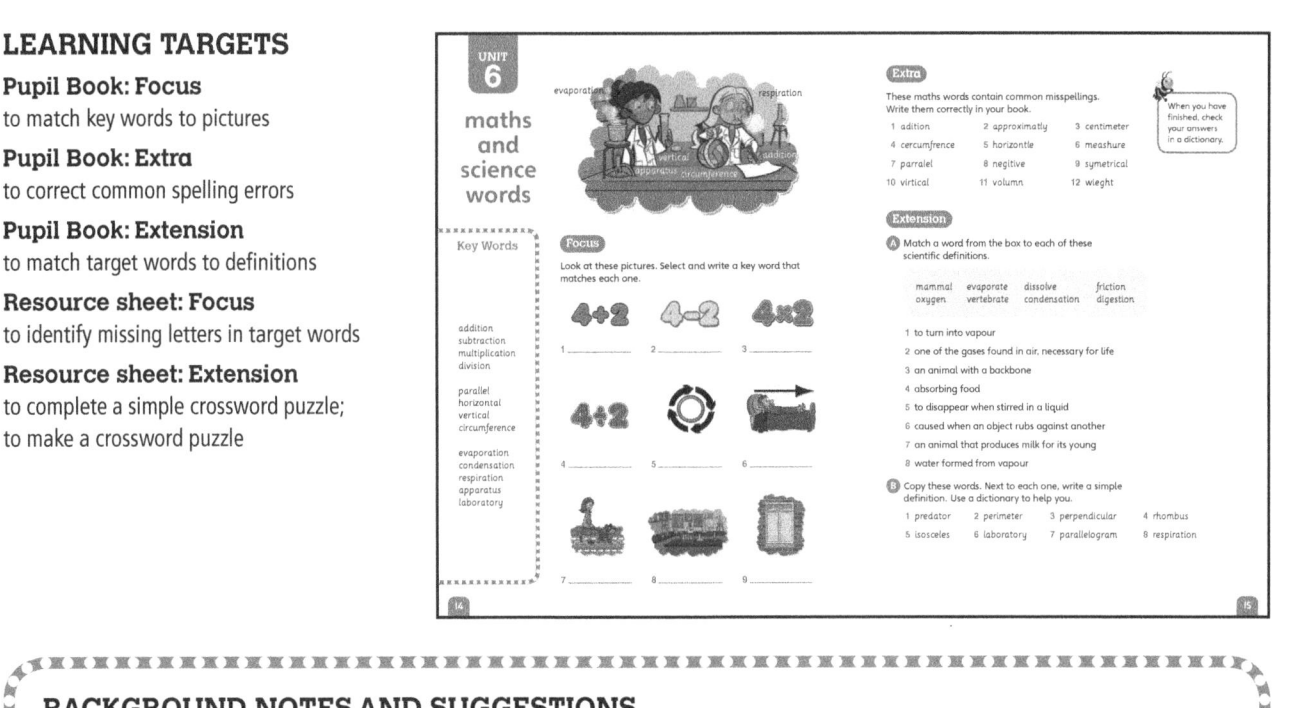

BACKGROUND NOTES AND SUGGESTIONS

The words taught in this unit have been identified as words Secondary School entrants at Year 7 often have difficulty with. It is acknowledged, however, that by no means all children entering secondary education fail to spell these words. The full list is supplied in the *Supporting word lists* (see also Book 6 Units 13 and 26).

Pupil Book answers

Focus
1 division
2 multiplication
3 subtraction
4 addition
5 circumference
6 horizontal
7 parallel
8 laboratory
9 condensation

Extra
1 addition
2 approximately
3 centimetre
4 circumference
5 horizontal
6 measure
7 parallel
8 negative
9 symmetrical
10 vertical
11 volume
12 weight

Extension
A
1 evaporate
2 oxygen
3 vertebrate
4 digestion
5 dissolve
6 friction
7 mammal
8 condensation

B Teacher to check individual answers

Resource sheet answers

Focus
1 addition
2 measure
3 angle
4 minus
5 calculate
6 perimeter
7 centimetre
8 square
9 decimal
10 subtraction
11 diameter
12 symmetry
13 division
14 triangle
15 estimate
16 vertical
17 horizontal
18 weight

Extension
A Across
2 estimate
3 diameter

Down
1 perimeter
4 metre
5 triple
6 radius

B Teacher to check individual answers

Supporting word lists

Science
absorb acid alkaline amphibian apparatus chemical circulate/circulation combustion condensation cycle digest/digestion disperse/dispersal dissolve distil/distillation element evaporation exchange freeze frequency friction function growth hazard insect laboratory liquid mammal method nutrient organism oxygen particles predator reproduce respire/respiration solution temperature thermometer vertebrate vessel

Maths
addition angle amount approximately average axis calculate centimetre circumference co-ordinate decimal degree diameter digit divide/division enough equilateral estimate fraction graph guess horizontal isosceles kilogram litre measure metre minus multiply/multiplication negative parallel/parallelogram perimeter perpendicular positive quadrilateral radius regular rhombus rotate/rotation square subtraction symmetry/symmetrical triangle/triangular vertical volume weight

BOOK 6

UNIT 7

LEARNING TARGETS

Pupil Book: Focus
to identify and copy target words from a wordsearch puzzle

Pupil Book: Extra
to determine whether selected words should be spelt with **f** or **ph**

Pupil Book: Extension
to sort words according to their Greek root

Resource sheet: Focus
to complete word sums and match pictures to words

Resource sheet: Extension
to complete words using either **ph** or **g**;
to identify words with silent **p** or silent **h**

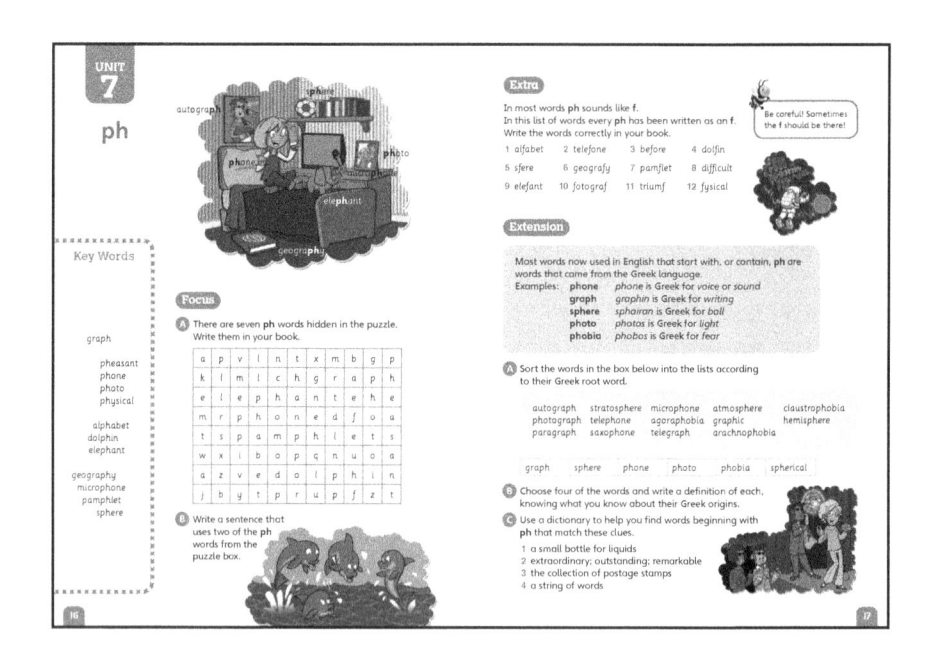

BACKGROUND NOTES AND SUGGESTIONS

This unit provides opportunities to consider English as a living, evolving language, borrowing words from other languages – and passing words to other languages (e.g. *le weekend*). Research can be undertaken using some dictionaries and, of course, online sources.

Pupil Book answers

Focus

A pheasant elephant phone pamphlets dolphin photo graph

B Teacher to check individual answers

Extra

1	alphabet	2	telephone
3	before	4	dolphin
5	sphere	6	geography
7	pamphlet	8	difficult
9	elephant	10	photograph
11	triumph	12	physical

Extension

A
graph	sphere	phone
autograph	stratosphere	microphone
graphic	atmosphere	telephone
paragraph	hemisphere	saxophone
telegraph		

photo	phobia
photograph	claustrophobia
	agoraphobia
	arachnophobia

B Teacher to check individual answers

C 1 phial 2 phenomenal
  3 philately 4 phrase

Resource sheet answers

Focus

A Children should copy the pattern

B phone
  pheasant
  photo
  physical
  elephant
  dolphin
  telephone
  microphone
  saxophone

C pheasant dolphin elephant photo

Extension

A 1 wei<u>gh</u>t 2 gra<u>ph</u>
  3 tele<u>ph</u>one 4 ne<u>ph</u>ew
  5 tou<u>gh</u> 6 hi<u>gh</u>
  7 ele<u>ph</u>ant 8 <u>ph</u>otogra<u>ph</u>
  9 lau<u>gh</u>ter 10 ni<u>gh</u>t
  11 al<u>ph</u>abet 12 <u>ph</u>ysical

B receipt rhinoceros
  pneumatic rhododendron
  pterodactyl rhubarb
  psychology rhymes
  pneumonia rhythm

C Teacher to check individual answers

Supporting word lists

initial ph
phone phase phrase phonic photo
physics pheasant photograph physical
physicist pharmacy philosophy
physiotherapy

medial ph
dolphin orphan hyphen pamphlet
graphic alphabet elephant telephone
saxophone microphone symphony
biography geography sphinx sphere
atmosphere hemisphere

final ph
graph autograph paragraph telegraph

BOOK 6

UNIT 8

LEARNING TARGETS

Pupil Book: Focus
to secure key silent letters

Pupil Book: Extra
to practise some awkward spellings

Pupil Book: Extension
to secure the spelling of significant words with double-letter patterns

Resource sheet: Focus
to practise common words with silent letters; to complete silent word table

Resource sheet: Extension
to edit a passage which focuses on misspelt words with silent letters

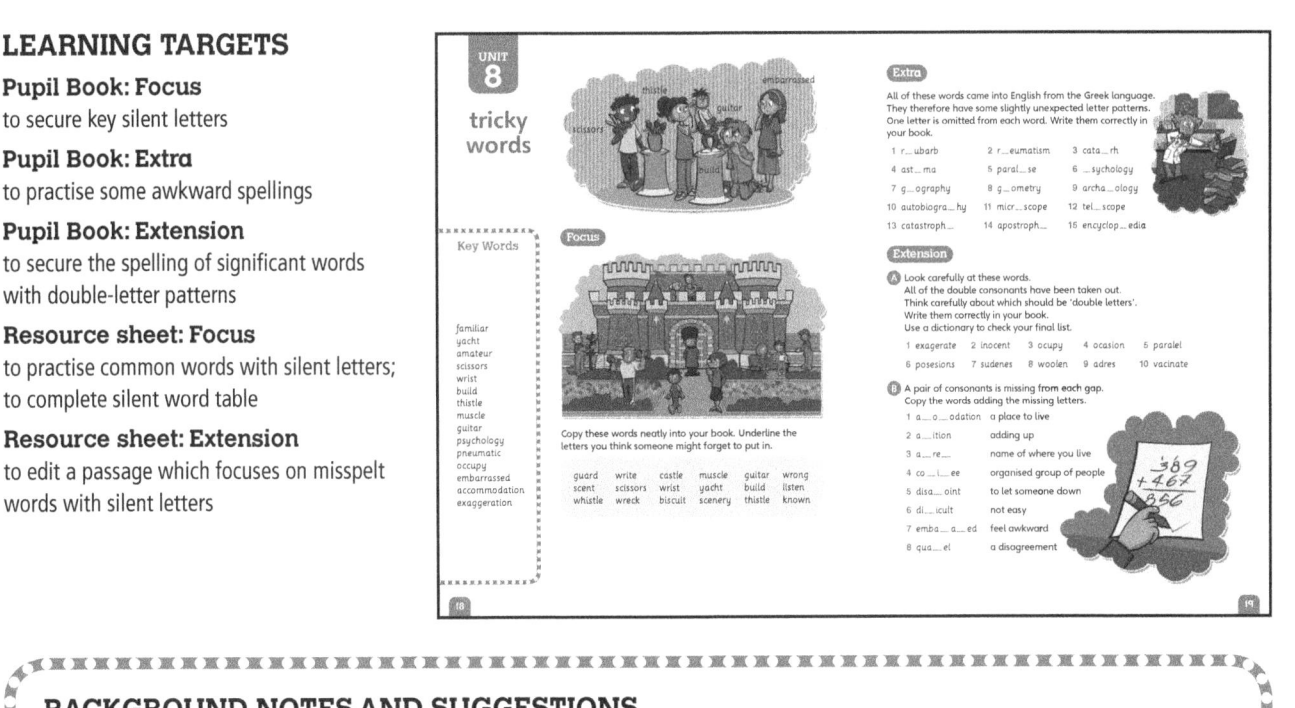

BACKGROUND NOTES AND SUGGESTIONS

It is important for the children to recognise the importance of editing, and to this end they can devise exercises for each other similar to the Extension Resource.

Pupil Book answers

Focus

<u>g</u>uard <u>w</u>rite cas<u>t</u>le mus<u>c</u>le g<u>u</u>itar <u>w</u>rong s<u>c</u>ent s<u>c</u>issors <u>w</u>rist ya<u>c</u>ht bui<u>l</u>d lis<u>t</u>en <u>wh</u>istle (*in Scotland*, whis<u>t</u>le) <u>w</u>reck bisc<u>u</u>it s<u>c</u>enery <u>th</u>istle <u>k</u>nown

Extra

1. rhubarb
2. rheumatism
3. catarrh
4. asthma
5. paralyse
6. psychology
7. geography
8. geometry
9. archaeology
10. autobiography
11. microscope
12. telescope
13. catastrophe
14. apostrophe
15. encyclopedia

Extension

A
1. exaggerate
2. innocent
3. occupy
4. occasion
5. parallel
6. possessions
7. suddenness
8. woollen
9. address
10. vaccinate

B
1. accommodation
2. addition
3. address
4. committee
5. disappoint
6. difficult
7. embarrassed
8. quarrel

Resource sheet answers

Focus

A
1. guinea pig
2. biscuit
3. build
4. wrong
5. guard
6. wreck
7. write
8. guitar

B
w	h	b	k
sword	hour	comb	knew
writing	honest	thumb	knock
wreckage	exhausted	climb	knee
wrap	shepherd	plumber	knife
answer			knuckle

Extension

The children should mark/correct as follows:

Sean and Josie stood <u>still</u>. Just a <u>moment</u> earlier a fox had <u>crossed</u> the <u>path</u>, <u>stopped</u> and <u>shaken</u> itself. Then it <u>slipped</u> <u>quietly</u> away. They waited in <u>silence</u> <u>hoping</u> to <u>see</u> it <u>again</u>, but <u>eventually</u> <u>realised</u> it must have <u>heard</u> them.

<u>When</u> they <u>returned</u> to the car park they <u>saw</u> a <u>notice</u> <u>asking</u> <u>visitors</u> not to <u>disturb</u> the <u>creatures</u> who might be <u>breeding</u> at this time of year.

"I hope we didn't <u>worry</u> that <u>beautiful</u> fox," said Josie.

"I'm <u>sure</u> we <u>didn't</u>," <u>replied</u> her <u>friend</u>, "but we'll go now and leave all the <u>animals</u> in <u>peace</u>."

Supporting word lists

silent letters

lamb limb combed numb
climbing plumber crumb thumbnail
debt doubt subtle
knitting knotted knocker knife knight
knew know known knowledge
wrapper wriggled wrinkle written wrote
wreckage wrist wholemeal
sword swordfish answer
whether whisper honest honour
rhyme rhythm rhubarb rheumatism
reign resign design sign
autumn column condemn
thistle whistle castle listen
badger gadget ledge midget porridge

double letters

abbreviation accommodate accompany
according aggressive apparent appreciate
assassinate attached commemorate
communicate community correspond
committee
difficulty disappointment embarrass
equipped especially exaggerate excellent
guarantee harass immediate innocent
interrupt marvellous necessary occasion
occupy
occur opponent opportunity parallel
possessions profession programme quarrel
recommend suddenness sufficient suggest
woollen vaccination

BOOK 6 UNIT 9

LEARNING TARGETS

Pupil Book: Focus
to sort families of words by their roots

Pupil Book: Extra
to match words to their Greek or Latin root

Pupil Book: Extension
to identify the Latin and Greek origin of selected words

Resource sheet: Focus
to identify the roots of selected words

Resource sheet: Extension
to identify the roots of selected words

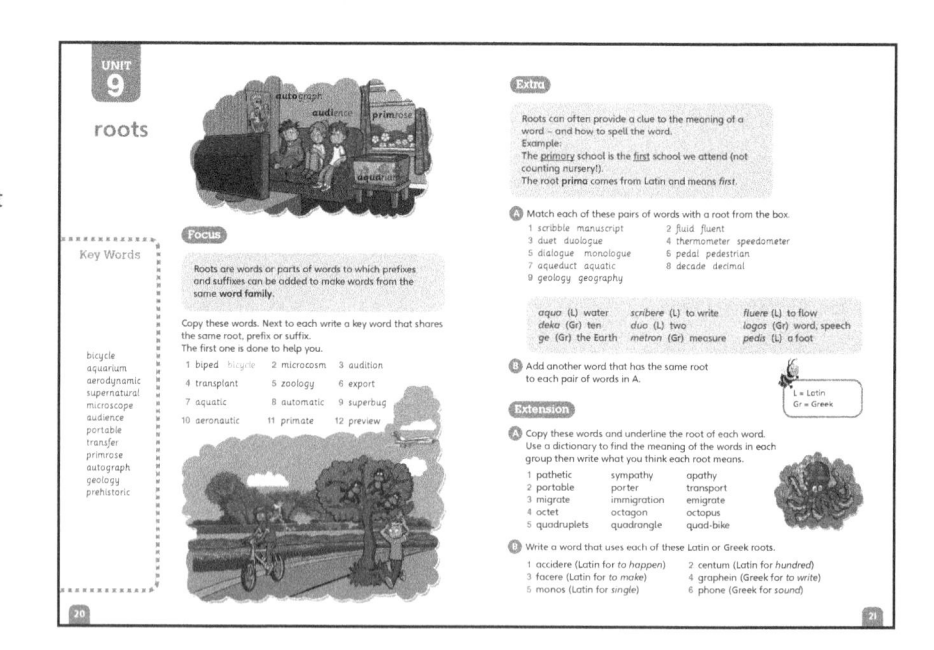

BACKGROUND NOTES AND SUGGESTIONS

Prefixes and suffixes have been taught and developed throughout *Nelson Spelling*, and in this unit the concept that root words often come from other languages and how these often date back to early times, is developed further.

For some children it will help for there to be an initial brainstorming session, collecting and comparing words with common roots and using the words collected to seek to determine the meaning of particular roots. Often, by beginning to understand and recognise the presence of 'roots', spelling can be made easier, e.g. knowing the root *bene* (*well, good*) means that children will more easily remember that *benefit, benefactor* etc. don't have an **i** where the second **e** is.

Pupil Book answers

Focus
1. biped bicycle
2. microcosm microscope
3. audition audience
4. transplant transfer
5. zoology geology
6. export portable
7. aquatic aquarium
8. automatic autograph
9. superbug supernatural
10. aeronautic aerodynamic
11. primate primrose
12. preview prehistoric

Extra
A
1. scribere (L) to write
2. fluere (L) to flow
3. duo (L) two
4. metron (Gr) measure
5. logos (Gr) word, speech
6. pedis (L) a foot
7. aqua (L) water
8. deka (Gr) ten
9. ge (Gr) the earth

B Teacher to check individual answers

Extension
A
1. (Gr) pathos feeling
2. (L) portare to carry, bear
3. (L) migrare to go
4. (L) octo, (Gr) okto eight
5. (L) quattuor four

B Teacher to check individual answers

Resource sheet answers

Focus
A Children should have drawn lines to join:
primus: primary, primrose
ge: geology, geography
pes, pedis: pedestrian, pedal
aer: aeroplane
deka: decade, decathalon

B Teacher to check individual answers

Extension
1. chrono logical (chronos, time; logos, study, speech)
2. astro naut (astron, star; nautes, sailor)
3. auto graph (autos, self; graphein, to write)
4. bio logy (bios, life; logos, study, speech)
5. micro scope (mikros, small; skopeein, to look at)
6. thermo meter (therme, heat; metron, measure)
7. audience (audire, to hear)
8. spectator (spectare, to look)
9. bene fit (bene, well; facere, to do)
10. aquarium (aqua, water)
11. anniversary (annus, year; vertere, to turn)
12. fracture (frangere, to break)

Supporting word lists
See Book 3 Unit 2 Supporting word lists

BOOK 6

UNIT 10

LEARNING TARGETS

Pupil Book: Focus
to sort words according to their languages of origin

Pupil Book: Extra
to sort words according to their sources

Pupil Book: Extension
to become aware of the characteristics of words now common in English that have been borrowed from Italian

Resource sheet: Focus
to match words to pictures of regions of origin

Resource sheet: Extension
to appreciate the connections between English and French words

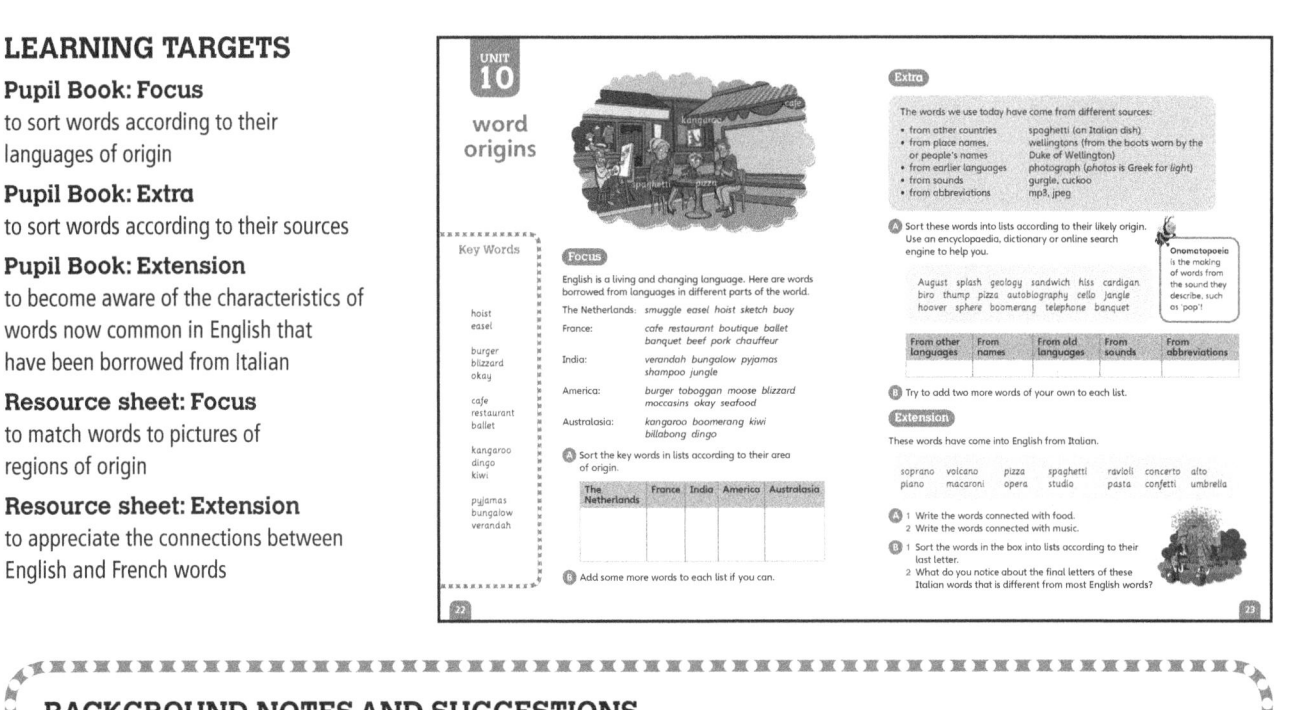

BACKGROUND NOTES AND SUGGESTIONS

This unit is a natural development from earlier units on roots and affixes, and in particular the activities related to words borrowed from Latin and Greek. Equally, it can be linked to the work on new words entering our language now.

The underlying objective of this material is to establish the notion that English is a growing, dynamic, living language.

Pupil Book answers

Focus

A *The Netherlands*: easel hoist
France: cafe restaurant ballet
India: verandah bungalow pyjamas
America: burger blizzard okay
Australasia: kangaroo kiwi dingo

B Teacher to check individual answers

Extra

A *From other languages*:
pizza cello banquet boomerang
From names:
cardigan biro sandwich August hoover
From old languages:
telephone sphere autobiography geology
From sounds:
hiss jangle thump splash

B Teacher to check individual answers

Extension

A 1 pizza spaghetti ravioli macaroni pasta

2 soprano concerto alto studio piano opera

B 1 pizza opera pasta umbrella spaghetti ravioli macaroni confetti soprano volcano concerto alto piano studio

2 Many Italian words end in a vowel letter other than *e*; this rarely occurs in English

Resource sheet answers

Focus

The Netherlands:	easel
France:	ballet
India:	pyjamas
Australasia:	kangaroo
Italy:	pizza
North America:	toboggan
Middle East:	zero caravan

Extension

Teacher to check individual answers

Supporting word lists

The Netherlands:
smuggle easel hoist
sketch buoy

France:
cafe restaurant boutique
ballet banquet

India:
verandah bungalow pyjamas
shampoo jungle

America:
burger toboggan moose
moccasins blizzard

Australia:
kangaroo boomerang

Middle East:
shawl cotton zero
caravan algebra

Italy:
pizza pasta cello piano volcano
concerto umbrella opera

BOOK 6 .... UNIT 11

LEARNING TARGETS

Pupil Book: Focus
to insert target words in a puzzle

Pupil Book: Extra
to identify potential problem letters in words which contain unstressed vowels and to introduce unstressed consonants

Pupil Book: Extension
to use an appreciation of syllables to help children to avoid dropping unstressed vowels

Resource sheet: Focus
to practise words with unstressed letters

Resource sheet: Extension
to identify unstressed letters and to divide target words into syllables

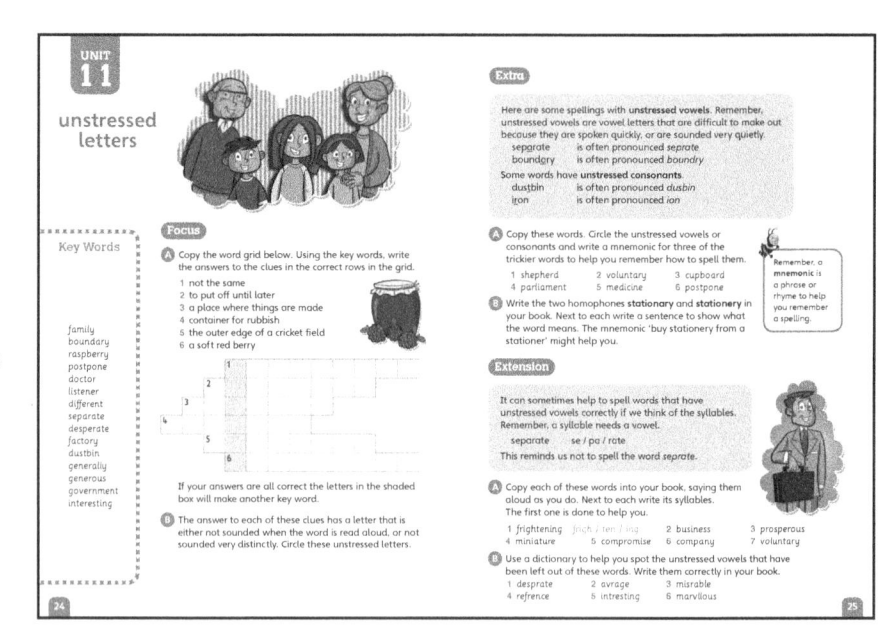

BACKGROUND NOTES AND SUGGESTIONS

As noted previously, unstressed vowels in polysyllabic words are, according to a recent report on children's performance in end of primary schooling tests, among the most predictable causes of incorrect spelling.

As is exemplified in this unit, whilst most unstressed letters are vowels, there are a number of significant words that have unstressed consonants (e.g. *dustbin*). Undoubtedly the key is to encourage the children to think carefully about word roots (e.g. *cupboard*) but also to consider certain suffixes as well e.g. **ary**, **ery** and **ory** (see Book 6 Unit 19). Also notice the frequent occurrence of **er** and **en** in words in the *Supporting word lists*.

Pupil Book answers

Focus
1 diff**e**rent 2 postp**o**ne
3 fact**o**ry 4 dus**t**bin
5 bound**a**ry 6 ras**p**berry

Letters in the shaded boxes spell the word 'doctor'

Extra
A 1 shep**h**erd 2 volunt**a**ry
3 cu**p**board 4 parl**i**ament
5 medi**c**ine 6 postp**o**ne

B Teacher to check individual answers

Extension
A 1 frightening frigh/ten/ing
2 business bus/i/ness
3 prosperous pro/sper/ous
4 miniature mi/nia/ture
5 compromise com/pro/mise
6 company com/pa/ny
7 voluntary vo/lun/ta/ry

B 1 desperate 2 average
3 miserable 4 reference
5 interesting 6 marvellous

Resource sheet answers

Focus
A Children should copy the words

B 1 fact**o**ry
2 diff**e**rent
3 dus**t**bin
4 cu**p**board
5 listen**i**ng
6 bound**a**ry
7 ras**p**berry
8 jewell**e**ry

Extension
A 1 laboratory lab/or/a/tory
2 evaporation e/vap/or/a/tion
3 apparatus ap/par/a/tus
4 organisation or/gan/is/a/tion
5 respiration res/pir/a/tion
6 temperature tem/per/at/ure
7 approximately ap/prox/im/ate/ly
8 average av/er/age
9 circumference cir/cum/fer/ence
10 isosceles i/sos/cel/es
11 positive pos/i/tive
12 government gov/ern/ment
13 independence in/de/pend/ence
14 parliament par/lia/ment
15 international in/ter/na/tion/al
16 important im/por/tant
17 marvellous mar/vel/lous
18 marriage mar/riage

Where two stressed letters are underlined, the child may recognise one or both

Supporting word lists

deafening conference offering desperate
definite definitely
description boundary animal business
stationary stationery
marvellous memorable reference miserable
freedom frightening flattery formal general
different doctor dictionary difference
factory family explanatory extra secretary
library literate illiterate literacy literature
Wednesday generally generous heaven
hospital separate
widening interested interest disinterest
poisonous category centre
company compromise original carpet
familiar predict

BOOK 6
UNIT 12

LEARNING TARGETS

Pupil Book: Focus
to find **ough** words in a wordsearch puzzle and associated activity

Pupil Book: Extra
to match double-letter key words to answer a puzzle

Pupil Book: Extension
to identify letters omitted from words with double letter patterns

Resource sheet: Focus
to practise selected doubled letter and **ough** target words

Resource sheet: Extension
to write word definitions and recognise misspelt double letter words

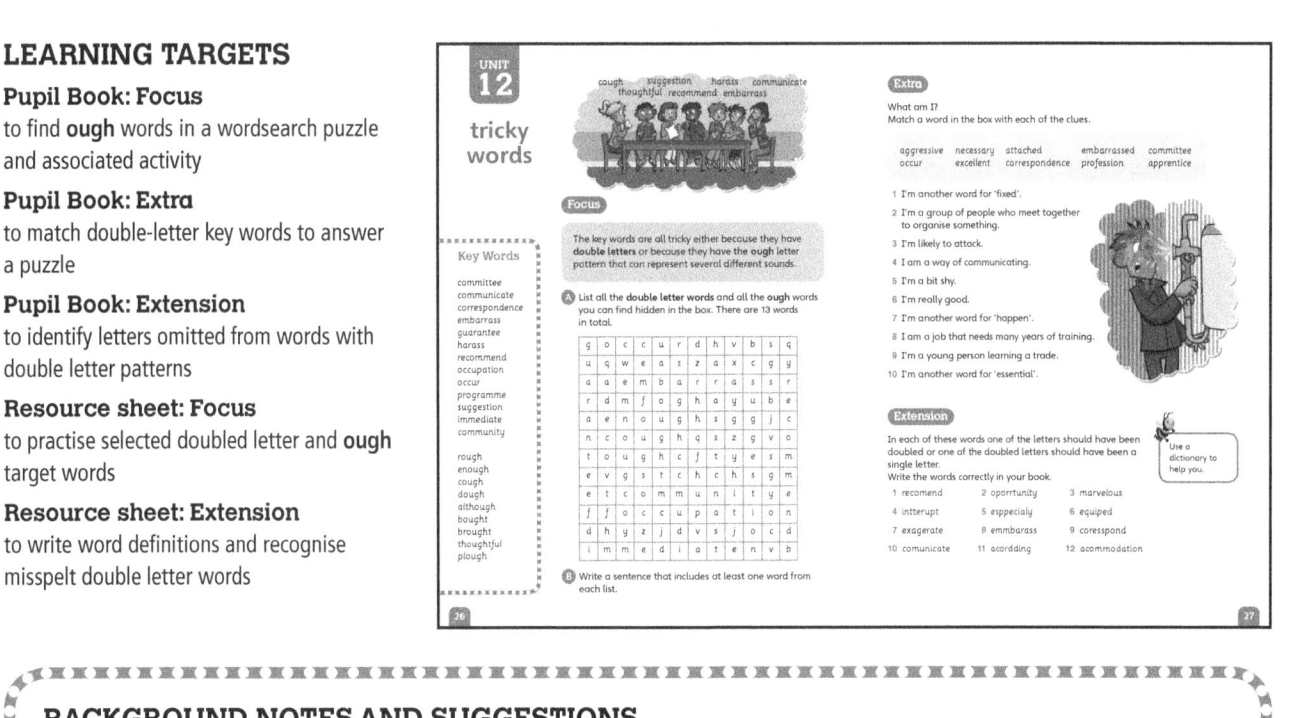

BACKGROUND NOTES AND SUGGESTIONS

There are two components to this unit. Firstly, there are those words that are known to cause problems – and not only to children – because of their double letters. The second category covered are words with the grapheme/phoneme relationship of **ough**. This is unusually variable and worthy of class or group work. Also, it is susceptible to regional variations, which may require specific teacher input. Work might usefully be done on the homophonic words within the group, of which there are several (e.g. *dough/doe*) and the near-homophones *bought* and *brought*.

Pupil Book answers

Focus

A bought cough tough enough embarrass harass suggestion guarantee occupation recommend occur community immediate

B Teacher to check individual answers

Extra

1 attached
2 committee
3 aggressive
4 correspondence
5 embarrassed
6 excellent
7 occur
8 profession
9 apprentice
10 necessary

Extension

1 recommend
2 opportunity
3 marvellous
4 interrupt
5 especially
6 equipped
7 exaggerate
8 embarrass
9 correspond
10 communicate
11 according
12 accommodation

Resource sheet answers

Focus

A Children should copy the words

B 1 I stayed up to watch the movie <u>although</u> I was tired.
2 We <u>bought</u> tickets to the football match.
3 Stan had a really bad <u>cough</u> which kept him awake.
4 The <u>plough</u> broke as the farmer started working in the field.
5 Alesha is a <u>thoughtful</u> girl.

Extension

A Teacher to check individual answers

B
sufficient	✓
aparent	✗
excelent	✗
occupy	✓
neccessary	✗
marvellous	✓
exagerrate	✗
guarrantee	✗
appreciate	✓
proffesion	✗

incorrect words spelt correctly:
apparent   excellent
necessary   exaggerate
guarantee   profession

Supporting word lists

as in off
cough trough
as in puff
rough tough enough
as in no
dough though
as in moo
through throughout
as in port
ought bought fought nought sought brought thought wrought
as in how
bough plough slough drought
as in kookaburra
borough thorough

BOOK 6   UNIT 13

LEARNING TARGETS

Pupil Book: Focus
to match key words to pictures

Pupil Book: Extra
to correct common spelling errors

Pupil Book: Extension
to match target words to definitions

Resource sheet: Focus
to write missing letters in selected target words

Resource sheet: Extension
to complete a crossword using target words; to make a target word crossword

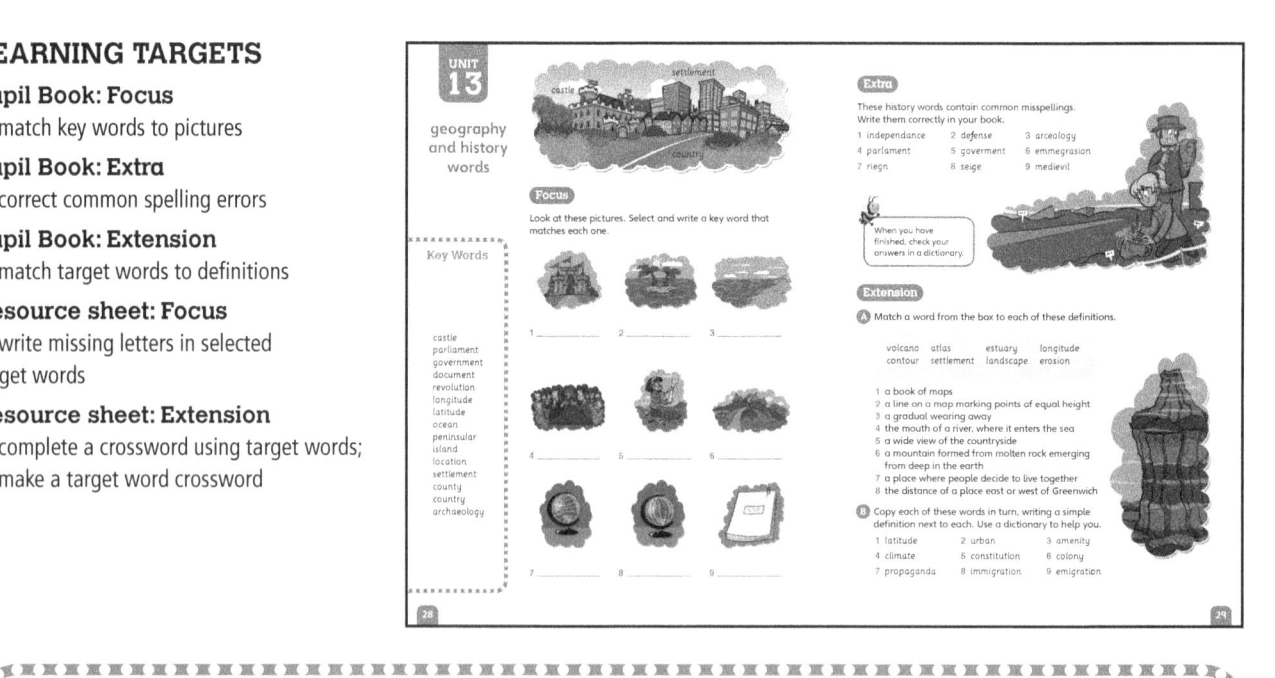

BACKGROUND NOTES AND SUGGESTIONS

The words taught in this unit are from *Appendix 2 of the Key Stage 3 Framework for Teaching English* document. The list was compiled by a number of secondary schools who were invited to identify words with which their new entrants at Year 7 often have difficulty. It is acknowledged that by no means all children entering secondary education fail to spell these words, but enough do for the KS3 teachers to need to give support. The full list is supplied in the *Supporting word lists* (see also Book 6 Units 6 and 26).

Pupil Book answers

Focus
1 castle   2 island
3 ocean   4 parliament
5 archaeology   6 settlement
7 latitude   8 longitude
9 document

Extra
1 independence   2 defence
3 archaeology   4 parliament
5 government   6 emigration
7 reign   8 seige
9 medieval

Extension
A
1 atlas   2 contour
3 erosion   4 estuary
5 landscape   6 volcano
7 settlement   8 longitude

B Teacher to check individual answers

Resource sheet answers

Focus
1 castle   2 weather
3 government   4 ocean
5 battle   6 desert
7 invasion   8 environment
9 erosion   10 atlas
11 soldiers   12 pollution
13 siege   14 longitude
15 parliament   16 estuary
17 reign   18 climate

Extension
Across
2 longitude
5 stream
6 valley

Down
1 atlas
2 latitude
3 globe
4 desert

Supporting word lists

History
agriculture/agricultural bias castle
chronology/chronological citizen
civilisation colony/colonisation conflict
constitution/constitutional
contradict/contradiction current defence
disease document dynasty
economy/economical emigration
government immigrant
imperial/imperialism
independence invasion motive parliament
politics/political
rebel/rebellion reign
republic revolt/revolution siege source
trade traitor

Geography
abroad amenity atlas authority climate
contour country county desert
employment erosion estuary function
globe habitat infrastructure international
landscape latitude location longitude
nation/national physical pollution poverty
provision region/regional rural settlement
situation tourist/tourism
transport/transportation urban
wealth weather

138

BOOK 6 UNIT 14

LEARNING TARGETS

Pupil Book: Focus
to complete a cloze activity using target words

Pupil Book: Extra
to match adjectives and nouns with the target letter patterns

Pupil Book: Extension
to create related adjectives and adverbs

Resource sheet: Focus
to solve target word puzzle

Resource sheet: Extension
to complete cloze activity

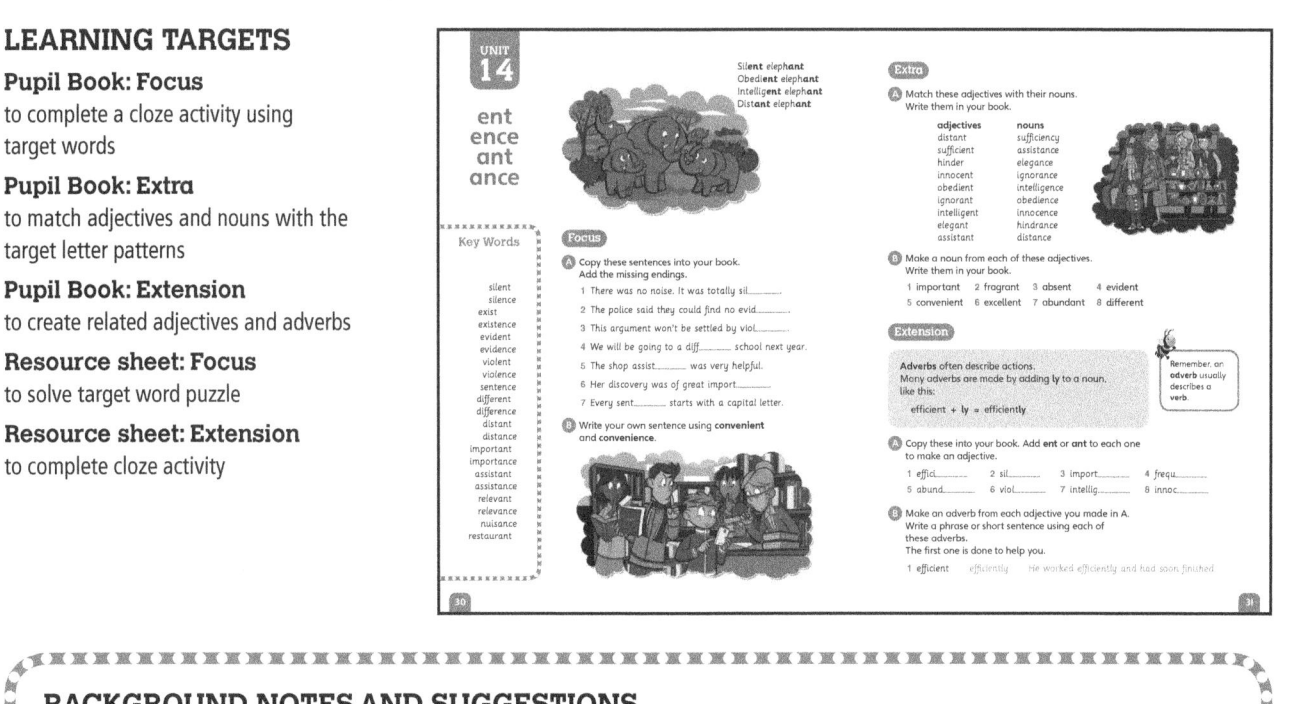

BACKGROUND NOTES AND SUGGESTIONS

One of the key teaching points in this unit is the inter-relationship of **ent/ence** and **ant/ance** endings. Remembering this can often help a child who, for example, has no problem spelling *distant*, to spell *distance*.

Pupil Book answers

Focus
A
1 silent   2 evidence
3 violence 4 different
5 assistant 6 importance
7 sentence

B Teacher to check individual answers

Extra
A
distant/distance
sufficient/sufficiency
hinder/hindrance
innocent/innocence
obedient/obedience
ignorant/ignorance
intelligent/intelligence
elegant/elegance
assistant/assistance

B
1 importance 2 fragrance
3 absence   4 evidence
5 convenience 6 excellence
7 abundance   8 difference

Extension
A
1 efficient / efficiently
2 silent / silently
3 important / importantly
4 frequent / frequently
5 abundant / abundantly
6 violent / violently
7 intelligent / intelligently
8 innocent / innocently

B Teacher to check individual answers

Resource sheet answers

Focus
A
1 distant   2 silent
3 infant   4 vacant
5 absent   6 violent

B Teacher to check individual answers

Extension
A There was a dist**ant** explosion, then complete sil**ence**. It was evid**ent** that the poachers were still in the area. The intelli**gence** reports had shown the need for urg**ent** action.
The government was concerned that, as a consequ**ence** of so much illegal hunting, some of the magnifi**cent** animals would soon become extinct. Other governments had offered assist**ance** to stop the defi**ance** of the illegal poaching gangs.
Some people said the poachers were simply ignor**ant** about the consequ**ences** of their actions. Others said this was just a conveni**ent** excuse! Whatever the reason, it was import**ant** that the rangers continued their frequ**ent** patrols, collecting evid**ence** to prosecute the poachers.

B
1 decent   2 arrogant
3 tenant   4 abundant
5 transparent 6 blatant

Teacher to check individual answers

Supporting word lists

silent / silence   consequent / consequence
innocent / innocence   violent / violence
different / difference   absent / absence
intelligent / intelligence
obedient / obedience
evident / evidence
convenient / convenience
distant / distance   important / importance
assistant / assistance   ignorant / ignorance
elegant / elegance   fragrant / fragrance
extravagant / extravagance

139

BOOK 6

Check-Up 1

Focus

1 torches 2 dishes 3 cherries 4 keys
5 wolves 6 knives 7 tomatoes 8 parallel
9 horizontal 10 laboratory 11 elephant 12 dolphin
13 guitar 14 yacht 15 caravan 16 volcano
17 doctor 18 dustbin 19 island 20 plough

Extension

A 1 shoes 2 berries 3 knives 4 kisses 5 donkeys
   6 cacti 7 sheep 8 cellos 9 women 10 phenomena

B 1 impossible 2 immigrate 3 immortal 4 immature 5 immovable

C 1 sensible 2 changeable 3 lovable 4 responsible 5 curable

D 1 marriage 2 funnily 3 stormier 4 happily
   5 necessarily 6 dutiful 7 joyful 8 thoughtful

E 1 alphabet 2 dolphin 3 geography 4 pamphlet 5 elephant

F 1 definitely 2 cupboard 3 parliament 4 medicine 5 miniature

G 1 exaggerate 2 interruption 3 embarass 4 accommodation 5 equipped

H 1 innocence 2 assistance 3 obedience 4 absence 5 ignorance

BOOK 6 — UNIT 15

LEARNING TARGETS

Pupil Book: Focus
to deduce which letters are associated with certain silent letters

Pupil Book: Extra
to complete a simple silent-letter crossword puzzle

Pupil Book: Extension
to secure syllabification in the context of silent letter words

Resource sheet: Focus
to identify words with a silent letter

Resource sheet: Extension
to spell correctly words with silent letters and use target words in sentences

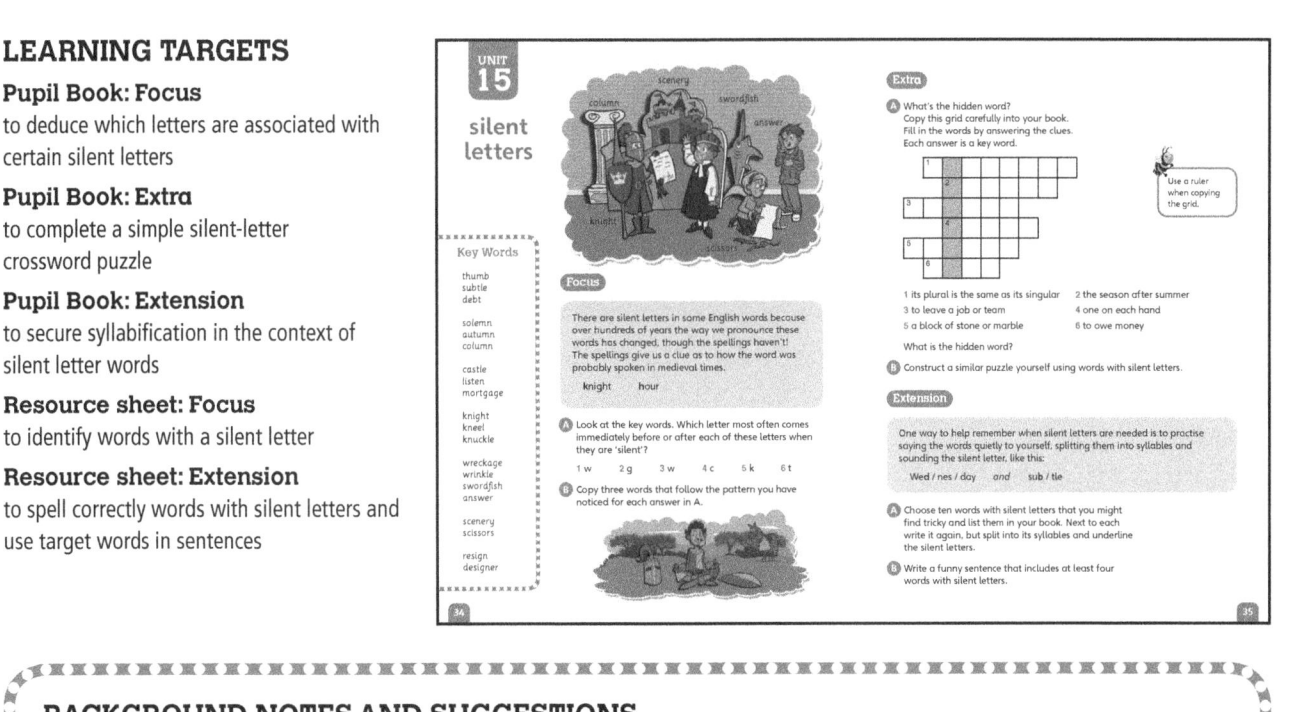

BACKGROUND NOTES AND SUGGESTIONS

In earlier units we have dealt with the most significant silent letters, which are important to teach as, unsurprisingly, they produce a disproportionate number of spelling errors in children's writing.

This unit gives the opportunity to secure the earlier learning and to build upon it.

Pupil Book answers

Focus

A 1 r 2 n 3 s 4 s 5 n 6 s

B Teacher to check individual answers

Extra

A 1 scissors 2 autumn 3 resign 4 thumb 5 column 6 debt
Hidden word: castle

B Teacher to check individual answers

Extension

A/**B** Teacher to check individual answers

Resource sheet answers

Focus

A knuckle scenery resign listen wrinkle scent comb answer column

B/**C** knuckle column answer wrinkle listen comb

Extension

A Teacher to check individual answers

B Teacher to check individual answers

C
1 rhubarb 2 design
3 scissors 4 whole
5 handsome 6 heirloom
7 written 8 scenario
9 chestnut 10 raspberry
11 autumn 12 guardian
13 swordfish 14 limb
15 yolk 16 pigeon

Supporting word lists

b (after m)
lamb limb bomb comb tomb dumb numb climb plumb crumb thumb plumber

b (before t)
debt doubt subtle

initial k
knit knob knot
knelt knack knock
knee kneel knife knight knew known

initial w
wrap wrapper wrapped wrapping
wriggle wriggled wriggler wriggling
wrinkle wrinkled wrinkly
write written wrote
wreck wrecker wrecked wreckage
wringer wretched wrangle wrist
whole wholemeal wholesome wholly
sword swordfish

medial w
answer answered answering

h
wheel whether which whisker whisper
hour honest honour
rhyme rhythm rhubarb rheumatism

g
reign resign design sign

n
hymn autumn column condemn

t
thistle whistle castle listen

BOOK 6 — UNIT 16

LEARNING TARGETS

Pupil Book: Focus
to find and copy familiar connectives from a wordsearch

Pupil Book: Extra
to find and analyse familiar compound connectives

Pupil Book: Extension
to select connectives for use in sentences

Resource sheet: Focus
to find and copy familiar connectives from a wordsearch

Resource sheet: Extension
to analyse and use familiar compound connectives

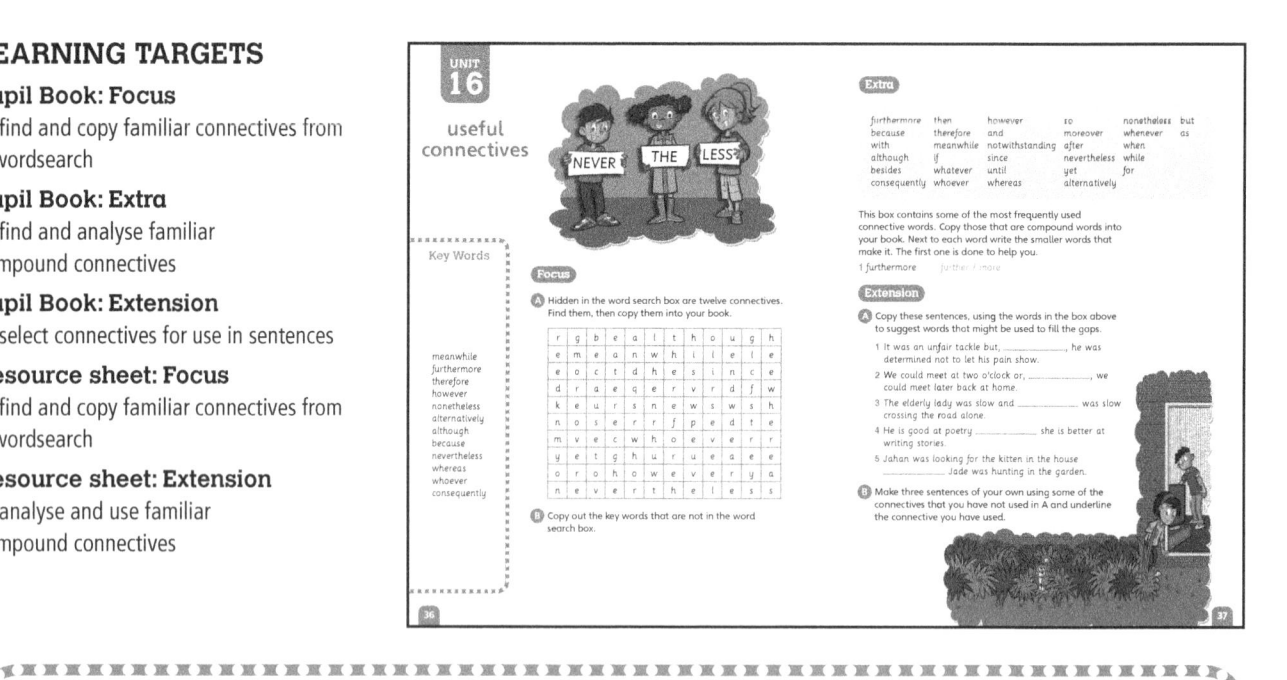

BACKGROUND NOTES AND SUGGESTIONS

Connectives are words and phrases that are used to link sentences or to extend sentences. They are commonly, and most readily, understood as conjunctions, but can also be adverbs or adverbial phrases.

Some connectives have, over time, become compound words. Note that they are similar to any other compound words in that the 'constituent' words don't change their spelling just because they have been compounded.

Pupil Book answers

Focus

A meanwhile and yet therefore however when since although because nevertheless whereas moreover whoever

B furthermore nonetheless alternatively consequently

Extra

1	furthermore	further/more
2	however	how/ever
3	nonetheless	none/the/less
4	therefore	there/fore
5	moreover	more/over
6	whenever	when/ever
7	meanwhile	mean/while
8	notwithstanding	not/with/standing
9	nevertheless	never/the/less
10	whatever	what/ever
11	whoever	who/ever
12	whereas	where/as

Extension

A Teacher to check individual answers which might include:
1. nevertheless
2. alternatively
3. consequently/therefore
4. whereas/but/yet/and
5. while/when/as/because/but/and

B Teacher to check individual answers

Resource answers

Focus

A Teacher to check individual answers

B therefore however whereas meanwhile whoever so until and or because whenever since

Extension

1. when/ever
2. mean/while
3. never/the/less
4. not/with/standing
5. how/ever
6. where/as
7. further/more
8. more/over
9. none/the/less

Teacher to check individual answers

Supporting word lists

furthermore then however so nonetheless but because therefore and moreover henceforward whenever as with meanwhile notwithstanding after when although if since nevertheless while besides whatever until yet for consequently whoever whereas alternatively

BOOK 6 — UNIT 17

LEARNING TARGETS

Pupil Book: Focus
to match key word homophones to pictures

Pupil Book: Extra
to consider words which cause confusion even though they are not strictly homophones

Pupil Book: Extension
to introduce some differences in verb and noun spelling

Resource sheet: Focus
to use pairs of homophones in sentences

Resource sheet: Extension
to differentiate between often confused homophones

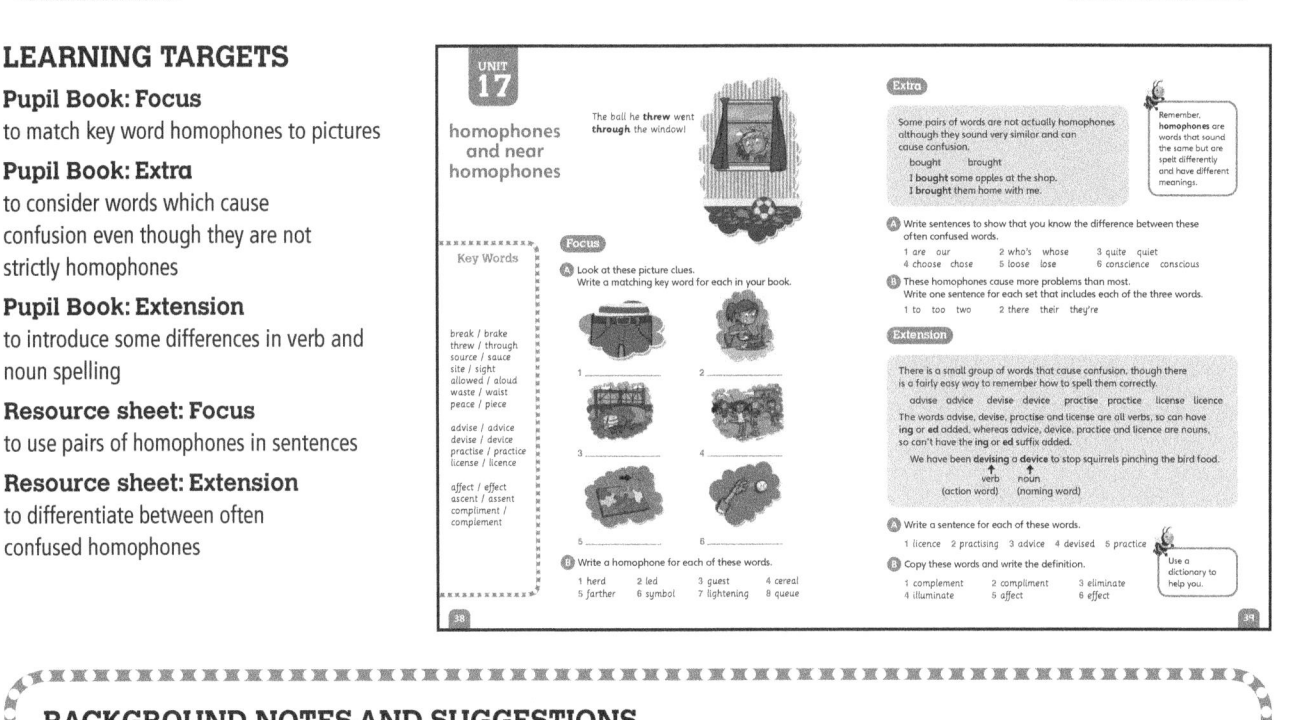

BACKGROUND NOTES AND SUGGESTIONS

In a recent report on children's performance, when asked to list words which children entering secondary education found difficult, teachers listed a number of homophones and 'confusions'. The particular examples cited are listed in the *Supporting word lists*.

Such reports have suggested that children should learn to spell words where there are different ways of representing vowel digraphs, such as *brake* and *break*, which covers most homophones.

As noted previously, homophones are words with the same (*homo*) sound (*phone*) but a different spelling and meaning, whereas homonyms have the same spelling and sound but different meanings. Please note homophones will vary depending on regional accents.

Pupil Book answers

Focus
A
1 waste 2 source 3 sight
4 brake 5 peace 6 through

B
1 heard 2 lead 3 guessed
4 serial 5 father 6 cymbal
7 lightning 8 cue

Extra
A / B Teacher to check individual answers

Extension
A / B Teacher to check individual answers

Resource sheet answers

Focus
Teacher to check individual answers

Extension
Teacher to check individual answers

Supporting word lists

foul, fowl
groan, grown   hail, hale
hair, hare   hall, haul
hear, here   heard, herd
hole, whole   hour, our
key, quay   knew, new
knight, night   knot, not
know, no   leak, leek
loan, lone   maid, made
mail, male   meat, meet
medal, meddle   mews, muse
missed, mist   more, moor
pail, pale   pain, pane
pause, paws   peace, piece
peak, peek   peal, peel
peer, pier   plain, plane
practice, practise   principal, principle
rain, reign, rein   read, reed
right, write   ring, wring
road, rode, rowed   rose, rows
sail, sale   scene, seen
sea, see   seam, seem
sew, so, sow   sight, site
soar, sore   sole, soul
son, sun   stair, stare
stake, steak   stationary, stationery
tail, tale   team, teem
their, there   threw, through
tide, tied   vain, vane, vein
waist, waste   wait, weight
week, weak   won, one
wood, would   you, yew, ewe

BOOK 6 — UNIT 18

LEARNING TARGETS

Pupil Book: Focus
to match key words to pictures;
to sort words into groups according to last two letters

Pupil Book: Extra
to complete a cloze activity using target words

Pupil Book: Extension
to order words alphabetically by later letters

Resource sheet: Focus
to match target words to clues and pictures

Resource sheet: Extension
to complete cloze activity;
to add correct endings to target words

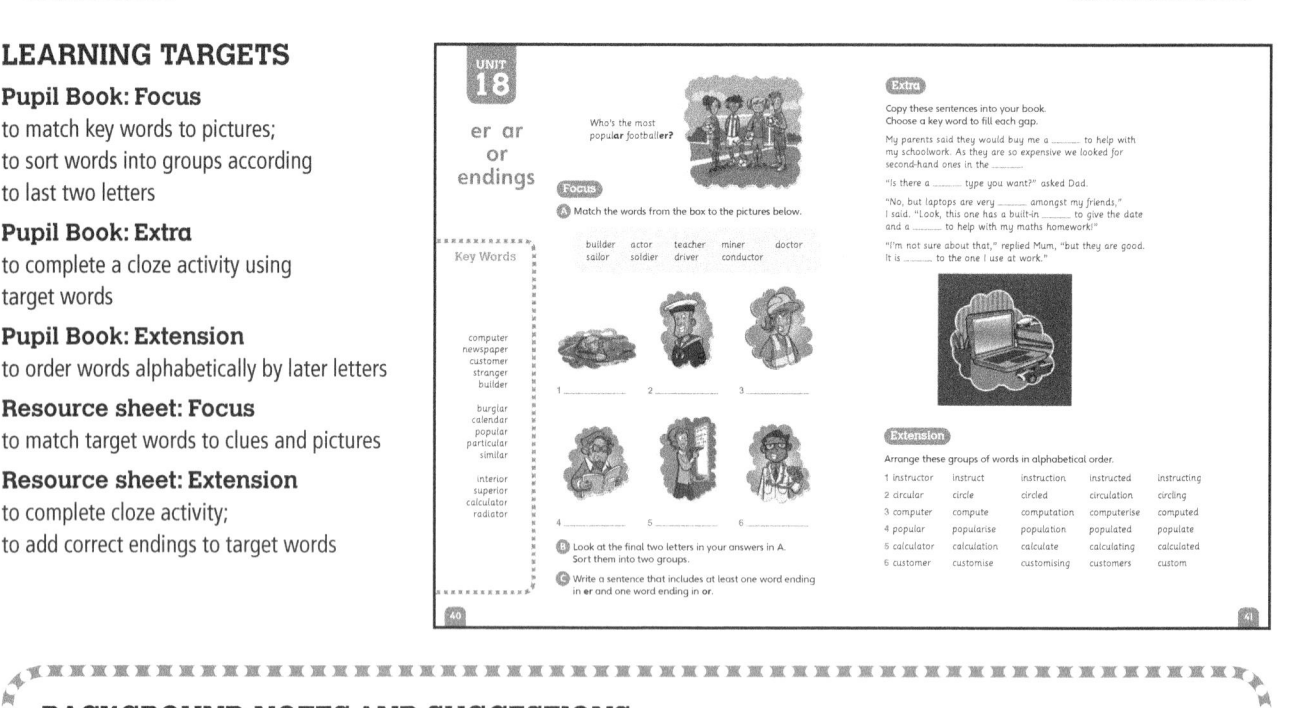

BACKGROUND NOTES AND SUGGESTIONS

Of **er**, **or**, **ar**, by far the most common ending is **er**. Otherwise there are few rules to help remember which ending to use, other than that few people/job words end in **ar**.

Pupil Book answers

Focus

A 1 driver   2 sailor   3 builder
       4 actor   5 teacher 6 doctor

B *er ending*: driver builder teacher
    or ending: sailor actor doctor

C Teacher to check individual answers

Extra
computer newspaper particular popular calendar calculator similar

Extension

A 1 instruct instructed instructing instruction instructor
    2 circle circled circling circular circulation
    3 computation compute computed computer computerise
    4 popular popularise populate populated population
    5 calculate calculated calculating calculation calculator
    6 custom customer customers customise customising

B/**C** Teacher to check individual answers

Resource sheet answers

Focus

A 1 customer   2 calendar
    3 escalator   4 circular
    5 similar   6 popular
    7 computer   8 radiator

B escalator computer calendar customer

Extension

A 1 regular customer computer
    2 popular
    3 burglar
    4 stranger
    5 similar particular earlier
    6 senior officer
    7 manager computer
    8 newspaper

B 1 circular   2 superior
    3 monster   4 calendar
    5 imposter/impostor   6 doctor
    7 spectacular   8 escalator

Teacher to check individual answers

Supporting word lists

people/job words
passenger customer robber prisoner
officer writer stranger teacher farmer
gardener plumber plasterer waiter
commuter explorer
doctor sailor author conductor emperor
solicitor visitor mayor inventor actor
burglar beggar

selection of other words
conquer deliver discover upper other
altogether whether weather shoulder
computer laughter surrender
motor radiator indicator anchor corridor
terror exterior reactor
altar calendar grammar vinegar cellar
regular popular singular peculiar similar

BOOK 6 — UNIT 19

LEARNING TARGETS

Pupil Book: Focus
to find and copy target words from a wordsearch puzzle

Pupil Book: Extra
to complete words with the appropriate target ending;
to determine the root word of selected target words

Pupil Book: Extension
to make plural forms of words ending with the target endings

Resource sheet: Focus
to match words to pictures and find words with target endings

Resource sheet: Extension
to complete puzzles related to the target letter patterns

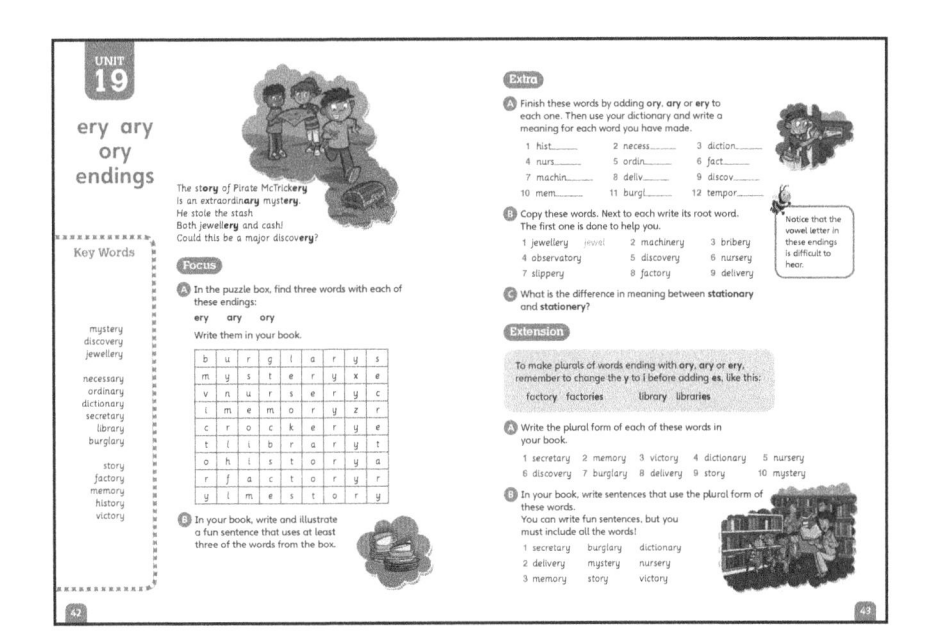

BACKGROUND NOTES AND SUGGESTIONS

Of the **ry** endings, **ary** is the most frequent, but **ery** is also quite often found in words children need to write. One way to check which is which, though not always easy to apply in practice, is to notice that in most **ery** words there's a smaller word with an **e** waiting to get out (e.g. *machine/machinery*).

Pupil Book answers

Focus
A burglary library secretary/mystery nursery crockery/ story factory victory memory history

B Teacher to check individual answers

Extra
A
1 history	2 necessary
3 dictionary	4 nursery
5 ordinary	6 factory
7 machinery	8 delivery
9 discovery	10 memory
11 burglary	12 temporary

Teacher to check definitions

B
1. jewellery — jewel
2. machinery — machine
3. bribery — bribe
4. observatory — observe
5. discovery — discover
6. nursery — nurse
7. slippery — slip
8. factory — factor
9. delivery — deliver

C stationary means not in motion; stationery is paper and other writing materials
The children should work out their own mnemonics

Extension
A
1. secretaries 2. memories
3. victories 4. dictionaries
5. nurseries 6. discoveries
7. burglaries 8. deliveries
9. stories 10. mysteries

B Teacher to check individual answers

Resource sheet answers

Focus
A library slippery factory
victory dictionary crockery

B Teacher to check individual answers

Extension
A THUNDERY
SILVERY
HISTORY
FACTORY
STATIONARY/STATIONERY
DELIVERY
MEMORY
SECRETARY
DYSENTERY

B DISCOVERY
Teacher to check individual sentences

C stationary - fixed, standing still
stationery - writing materials

D
1. thunder 2. silver
3. deliver 4. compliment
5. discover 6. jewel

Supporting word lists

ory
factory memory history victory story glory

ary
necessary primary library
boundary burglary salary January
February ordinary auxiliary dictionary

ery
bravery mystery machinery crockery
bribery grocery discovery nursery
jewellery slippery delivery

other ry words
century injury treasury jury fury
cavalry rivalry industry chemistry registry
laundry poultry country poetry tapestry

BOOK 6 — UNIT 20

LEARNING TARGETS

Pupil Book: Focus
to select key words to complete a puzzle

Pupil Book: Extra
to identify root words within 'tricky' words

Pupil Book: Extension
to correct the spelling of several frequently misspelt words

Resource sheet: Focus
to copy letter patterns and complete words with given suffixes

Resource sheet: Extension
to add suffixes to complete 'tricky' words; to use tricky words in sentences

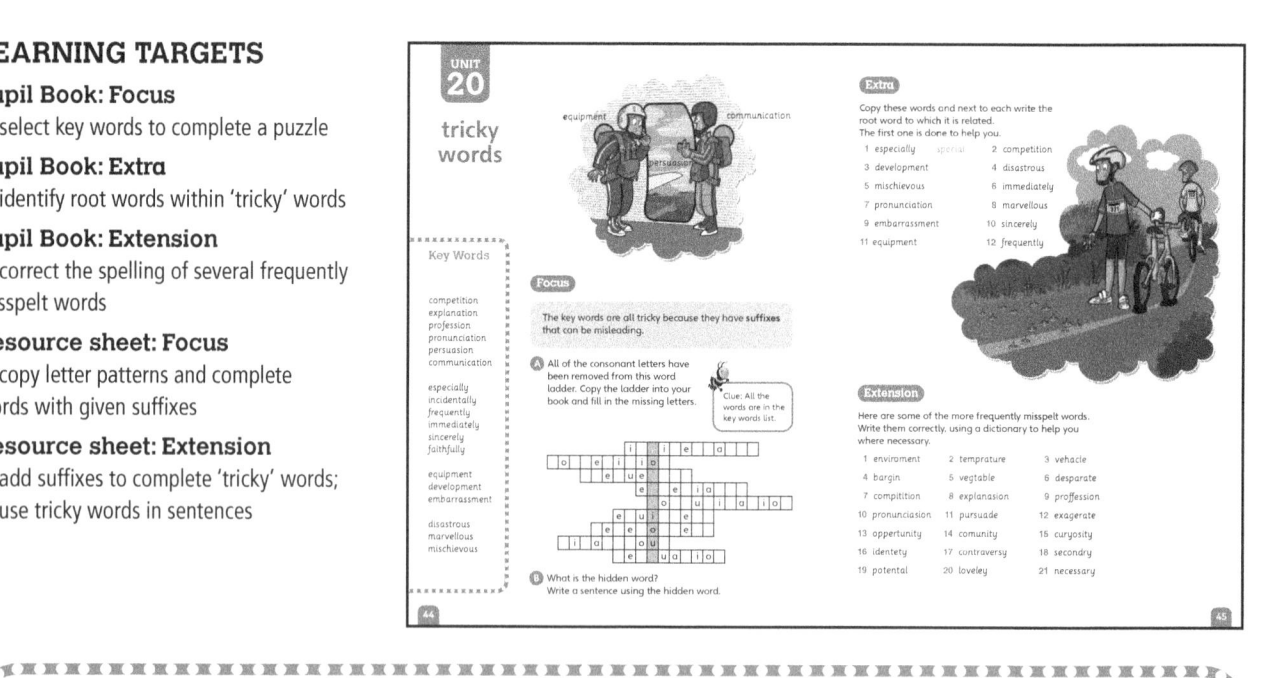

BACKGROUND NOTES AND SUGGESTIONS

The words in this unit have been selected as they have suffixes that can be misleading. This is usually because they have double letters or single letters that pupils are tempted to double.

Pupil Book answers

Focus

A incidentally competition frequently especially communication equipment development disastrous persuasion

B *Hidden word:* conscious
Teacher to check individual answers

Extra

A
1	especially	special
2	competition	compete
3	development	develop
4	disastrous	disaster
5	mischievous	mischief
6	immediately	immediate
7	pronunciation	pronounce
8	marvellous	marvel
9	embarrassment	embarrass
10	sincerely	sincere
11	equipment	equip
12	frequently	frequent

Extension

1 environment
2 temperature
3 vehicle
4 bargain
5 vegetable
6 desperate
7 competition
8 explanation
9 profession
10 pronunciation
11 persuade
12 exaggerate
13 opportunity
14 community
15 curiosity
16 identity
17 controversy
18 secondary
19 potential
20 lovely
21 necessary

Resource sheet answers

Focus

A Children should copy the patterns

B / C competition equipment procession faithfully dangerous embarrassment mischievous infectious similarly

Extension

A
1 incidentally
2 pronouncement
3 competition
4 marvellous
5 sincerely
6 equipment
7 communication
8 disastrous
9 rigorous
10 development
11 completely
12 accommodation
13 procession
14 definitely

B Teacher to check individual answers

C Teacher to check individual answers

BOOK 6   UNIT 21

LEARNING TARGETS

Pupil Book: Focus
to match a selection of American and British English spellings and comment on the differences

Pupil Book: Extra
to consider how words borrowed from other languages have been adapted in different ways in American and British English spellings

Pupil Book: Extension
to 'correct' a passage that uses American spelling

Resource sheet: Focus
to match and identify the key differences between certain British and American English spellings

Resource sheet: Extension
to find equivalent British spellings for American words; to use American spellings in a letter

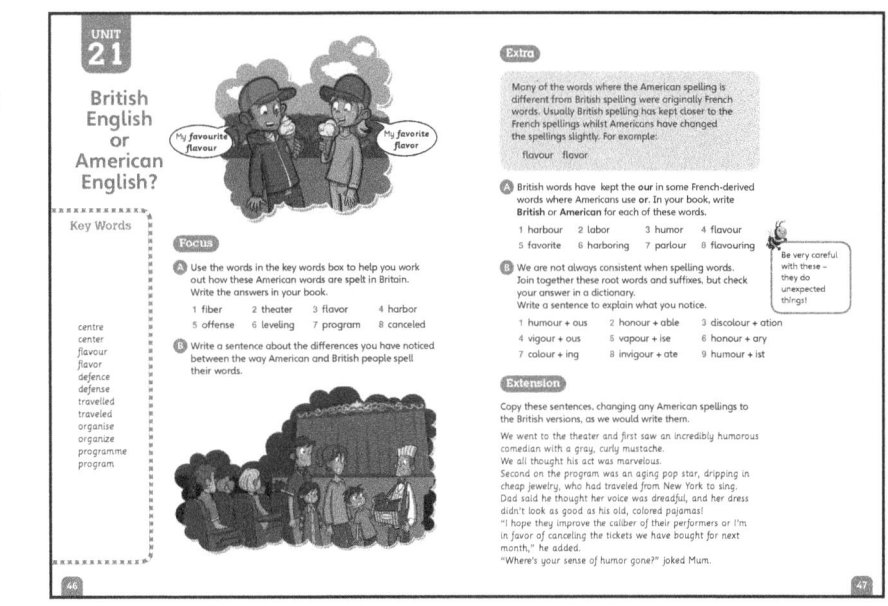

BACKGROUND NOTES AND SUGGESTIONS

This unit is intended to convey the important concept that spelling is constantly changing, as is all language. When these words were used in America when English-speaking migrants crossed the Atlantic, the spellings would have been the same – although it is also worth making the point that it was not until print became common that spelling began to be standardised.

The children might notice that American English spellings are often more straightforward than British English spellings.

Pupil Book answers

Focus

A
1. fibre
2. theatre
3. flavour
4. harbour
5. offence
6. levelling
7. colour
8. cancelled

B Teacher to check individual answers

Extra

A
1. British
2. American
3. American
4. British
5. American
6. American
7. British
8. British

B
1. humorous
2. honourable
3. colouring
4. vigorous
5. vaporise
6. honorary
7. discolouration
8. invigorate
9. humorist

Children notice that sometimes the *u* is dropped when the suffix is added and sometimes it is retained

Extension

We went to the <u>theatre</u> and first saw an incredibly humorous comedian with a <u>grey</u>, curly moustache.
We all thought his act was <u>marvellous</u>.
Second on the <u>programme</u> was an ageing pop star, dripping in cheap <u>jewellery</u>, who had <u>travelled</u> from New York to sing.
Dad said he thought her voice was dreadful, and her dress didn't look as good as his old, <u>coloured</u> <u>pyjamas</u>!
"I hope they improve the <u>calibre</u> of their performers or I'm in <u>favour</u> of <u>cancelling</u> the tickets we have bought for next month," he added.
"Where's your sense of <u>humour</u> gone?" joked Mum.

Resource sheet answers

Focus

A British: harbour humour colour honour theatre centre fibre flavour
American: harbor humor color honor theater center fiber flavor

B Teacher to check individual answers

Extension

A
1. grey
2. programme
3. defence
4. flavouring
5. centre
6. levelling
7. cancelled
8. labour
9. favourite
10. humour
11. pyjamas
12. jewellery

B Teacher to check individual answers

Supporting word lists

American English Spellings

our/or flavor harbor labor humor favor favorite

parlor honor color vigor vapor

re/er center theater fiber caliber

ll/l canceled traveled marvelous

other mustache program defense gray jail offense aging jewelry pajamas

147

BOOK 6

UNIT 22

LEARNING TARGETS

Pupil Book: Focus
to match key words to pictures

Pupil Book: Extra
to answer riddles with target words from the wordsearch box

Pupil Book: Extension
to secure syllabification

Resource sheet: Focus
to copy target letter patterns and match words to pictures

Resource sheet: Extension
to identify and copy 'correct' spellings

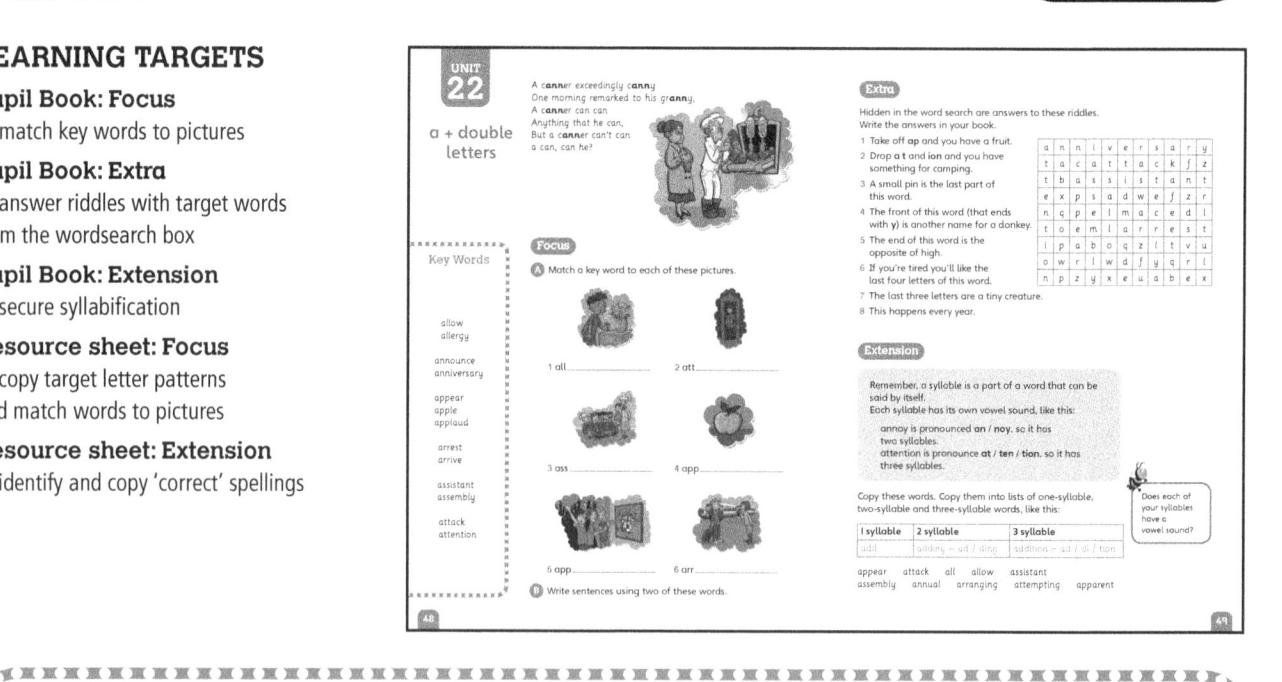

BACKGROUND NOTES AND SUGGESTIONS

Double consonant letters are a perennial problem for many young writers. This unit focuses on *a + double letters*, probably the most frequent association.

The Extension Resource practises some other tricky double letter combinations.

Pupil Book answers

Focus

A
1 allergy	2 attention
3 assembly	4 apple
5 applaud	6 arrive

B Teacher to check individual answers

Extra
1 appear	2 attention
3 attack	4 assembly
5 allow	6 arrest
7 assistant	8 anniversary

Extension

1 syllable	2 syllables	3 syllables
all	ap/pear	as/sis/tant
	at/tack	as/sem/bly
	al/low	an/nu/al
		ar/rang/ing
		at/tempt/ing
		ap/par/ent

Resource sheet answers

Focus

A Children should copy the patterns

B assist annoy apple
attract arrow accurate

Extension

1 addition	2 address
3 committee	4 disappoint
5 embarrass	6 exaggerate
7 innocence	8 occasion
9 opponent	10 parallel
11 possession	12 quarrel
13 stubbornness	14 suddenness
15 woollen	16 vaccination
17 accidentally	18 difficulty
19 accommodate	20 necessary

Supporting word lists

initial position
accurate accuse
allow allergy allude allusion
annoy annual announce anniversary
approach apply applaud appear appeal
arrest arrange arrive
assist assistant assembly
attack attract attention attempt attitude

medial position
dabble rabble scrabble
paddle saddle straddle
baffle raffle
gaggle haggle waggle straggle
apple dapple grapple
battle cattle rattle prattle

148

BOOK 6 — UNIT 23

LEARNING TARGETS

Pupil Book: Focus
to revise the basic 'i before e' rule

Pupil Book: Extra
to sort ie and ei words according to phoneme

Pupil Book: Extension
to select ie/ei letter patterns where the two letters represent separate phonemes

Resource sheet: Focus
to sort words with both target graphemes

Resource sheet: Extension
to practise and apply the 'i before e' rule; to secure some important words with ance, ence and ince endings

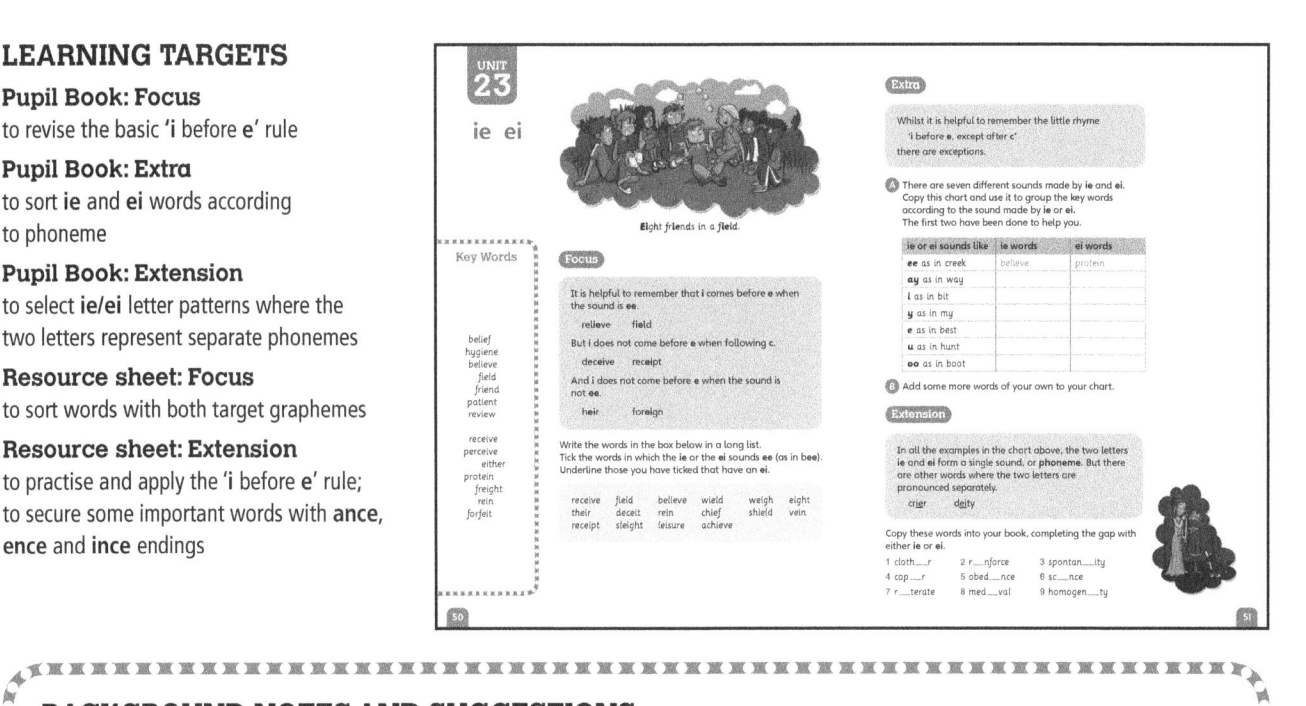

BACKGROUND NOTES AND SUGGESTIONS

This is perhaps the most often-quoted spelling rule, but one fraught with potential problems and exceptions. Indeed, some say it's hardly worth bothering with. However, once the various categories of target words have been secured it alleviates certain spelling problems.

Pupil Book answers

Focus
receive ✓   field ✓   believe ✓
wield ✓   weigh   eight
their   deceit ✓   rein
chief ✓   shield ✓   vein
receipt ✓   sleight   leisure
achieve ✓

Extra

A Teacher to check individual answers, which may include the following:

ie or ei sounds like:	ie words	ei words
ee as in 'creek'	diesel believe field hygiene belief	seize protein perceive receive
ay as in 'way'		freight rein
i as in 'bit'	sieve	foreign forfeit
y as in 'my'	hieroglyphics	height either
e as in 'best'	lieutenant friend	leisure
u as in 'hunt'	ancient patient	
oo as in 'boot'	view review	

B Teacher to check individual answers

Extension
1 clothier   2 reinforce
3 spontaneity   4 copier
5 obedience   6 science
7 reiterate   8 medieval
9 homogeneity

Resource sheet answers

Focus
A shield freight sleigh field eight reins

B Teacher to check individual answers

Extension
A 1 police   2 certain
  3 entrance   4 centre

B The c before the e is soft.

C 1 receive   2 receipt
  3 deceive   4 believe
  5 achieve   6 field

D 1 chance   2 fence
  3 since   4 mince
  5 pence   6 prince/prance
  7 advance   8 commence
  9 entrance   10 sentence
  11 offence   12 distance
  13 nuisance   14 experience

Supporting word lists

ie

as in *bee:* niece piece siege brief grief frieze shield chief thief shriek belief believe relief relieve yield handkerchief mischief medieval obedient glacier

as in *hen:* friend patient ancient

as in *high:* lie die pie tie fiery quiet science

as in *ear:* pierce fierce pier

as in *few:* view review interview

ei as in tree (cei words):
receive receipt deceive ceiling perceive conceit

as in *cape:*
rein veil vein feint reign beige neigh weigh eight weight sleigh freight eighty eighteen eighteenth neighbour sovereign foreign

as in *kite:* height either neither eiderdown

others: their leisure weird protein heir sovereign foreign

149

BOOK 6 · UNIT 24

LEARNING TARGETS

Pupil Book: Focus
to use target words to solve clues in a puzzle

Pupil Book: Extra
to identify potential problem letters in words which contain unstressed vowels

Pupil Book: Extension
to use an appreciation of syllables to help children to avoid dropping unstressed vowels

Resource sheet: Focus
to copy target words and identify unstressed vowels

Resource sheet: Extension
to demonstrate how an awareness of syllables can assist the spelling of words with unstressed vowels

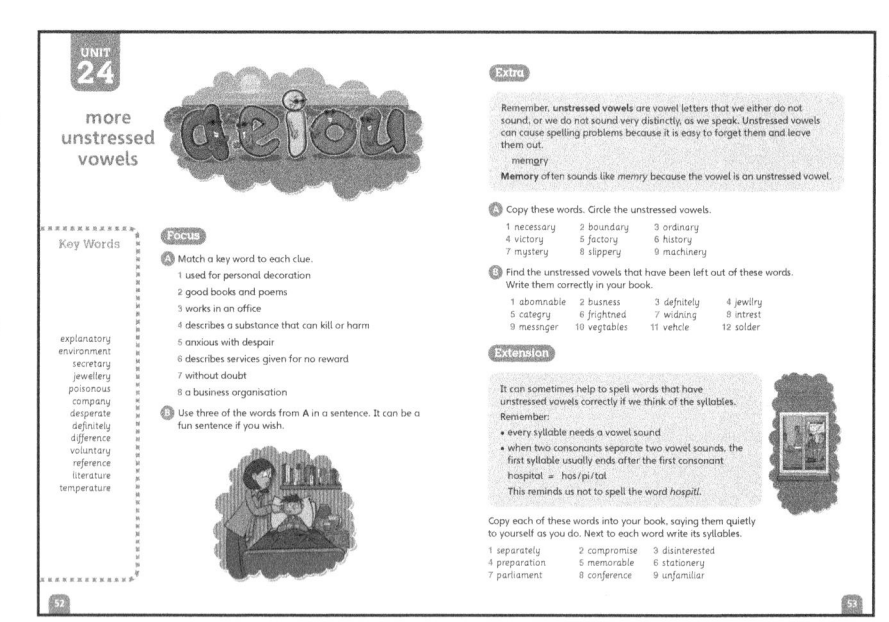

BACKGROUND NOTES AND SUGGESTIONS

As noted in a previous unit, unstressed vowels in polysyllabic words are, according to a report on children's performance, among the most predictable problem areas for spelling.

Whilst the key is to encourage the children to think carefully about word roots, it is also important for them to consider certain suffixes, in particular **ary**, **ery** and **ory**. As suggested elsewhere, notice the frequent occurrence of **er** and **en** in words in the *Supporting word lists*.

Pupil Book answers

Focus

A
1 jewellery   2 literature
3 secretary   4 poisonous
5 desperate   6 voluntary
7 definitely 8 company

B Teacher to check individual answers

Extra

A
1 necessary 2 boundary
3 ordinary   4 victory
5 factory   6 history
7 mystery   8 slippery
9 machinery

B
1 abominable 2 business
3 definitely 4 jewellery
5 category   6 frightened
7 widening   8 interest
9 messenger   10 vegetables
11 vehicle   12 soldier

Extension
1 separately   sep/ar/ate/ly
2 compromise   com/pro/mise
3 disinterested dis/in/ter/est/ed
4 preparation   pre/par/a/tion
5 memorable   mem/or/ab/le
6 stationery   sta/tion/e/ry
7 parliament   par/lia/ment
8 conference   con/fer/ence
9 unfamiliar   un/fa/mil/iar

Resource sheet answers

Focus

A / B
different   hospital
definitely   easily
interesting dictionary
frighten   secretary

Extension

A
reference   reference   ref/er/ence
actually   actually   act/u/al/ly
business   business   bus/i/ness
chocolate   chocolate   cho/co/late
conscience   conscience   cons/cience
conscious   conscious   cons/cious
definitely   definitely   def/in/ite/ly
happened   happened   hap/pened
imaginary   imaginary   i/ma/gin/a/ry
interesting interesting in/ter/es/ting
jealous   jealous   jea/lous
listening   listening   list/en/ing
marriage   marriage   mar/riage
outrageous   outrageous   out/rage/ous
potential   potential   po/ten/tial

B Wednesday February   environment
government   handbag   cupboard

Supporting word lists

deafening conference offering desperate definite definitely description boundary animal business stationary stationery marvellous memorable reference miserable messenger prepare freedom frightening flattery smuggler formal general different doctor dictionary difference prosperous easily factory family explanatory extra secretary primary library literate illiterate literacy literature Wednesday generally generous heaven hospital separate widening interested interest disinterest jewellery voluntary poisonous category centre company compromise original carpet abandoned abominable familiar predict

BOOK 6

UNIT 25

LEARNING TARGETS

Pupil Book: Focus
to match a key word to each word and picture clue

Pupil Book: Extra
to use a dictionary to check and correct misspelt tricky soft **c** and soft **g** words

Pupil Book: Extension
to use a dictionary to check and correct misspelt tricky words with unstressed letters

Resource sheet: Focus
to match a key word to each picture clue

Resource sheet: Extension
to match key words with their definitions

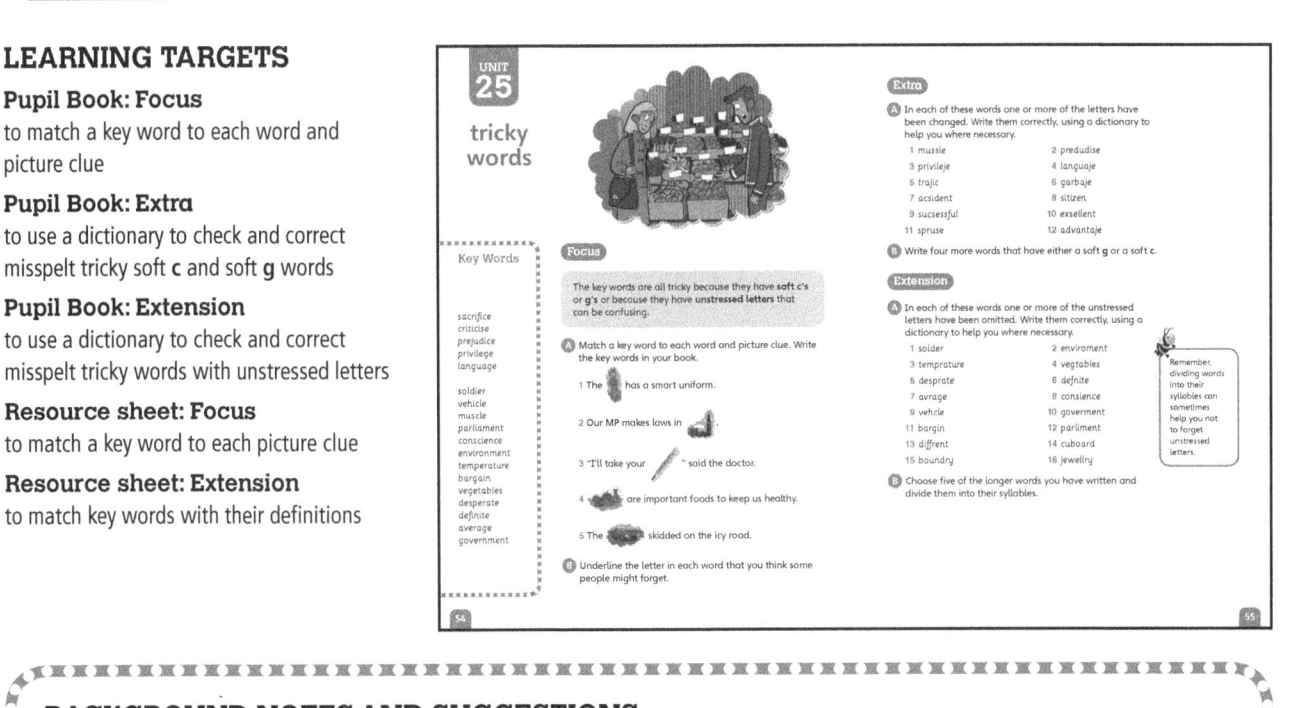

BACKGROUND NOTES AND SUGGESTIONS

The tricky words identified in this unit are those which have a soft **c** or **g** or because they have unstressed letters that can be confusing.

Pupil Book answers

Focus

A / B
1 soldier
2 parliament
3 temperature
4 Vegetables
5 vehicle

Extra

A
1 muscle
2 prejudice
3 privilege
4 language
5 tragic
6 garbage
7 accident
8 citizen
9 successful
10 excellent
11 spruce
12 advantage

B Teacher to check individual answers

Extension

A
1 soldier
2 environment
3 temperature
4 vegetables
5 desperate
6 definite
7 average
8 conscience
9 vehicle
10 government
11 bargain
12 parliament
13 different
14 cupboard
15 boundary
16 jewellery

Resource sheet answers

Focus

percentage temperature courage
vehicle privilege muscle
parliament margarine language
soldier vegetables bargain

Extension

A temperature
language
desperate
vegetables
privilege
definite
citizen
environment
vehicle
prejudice
parliament
successful

B Teacher to check individual answers

BOOK 6 — UNIT 26

LEARNING TARGETS

Pupil Book: Focus
to match key words to pictures

Pupil Book: Extra
to correct common spelling errors

Pupil Book: Extension
to write definitions of target words

Resource sheet: Focus
to label ICT equipment

Resource sheet: Extension
to use 'original' and 'new' meanings of some common ICT words

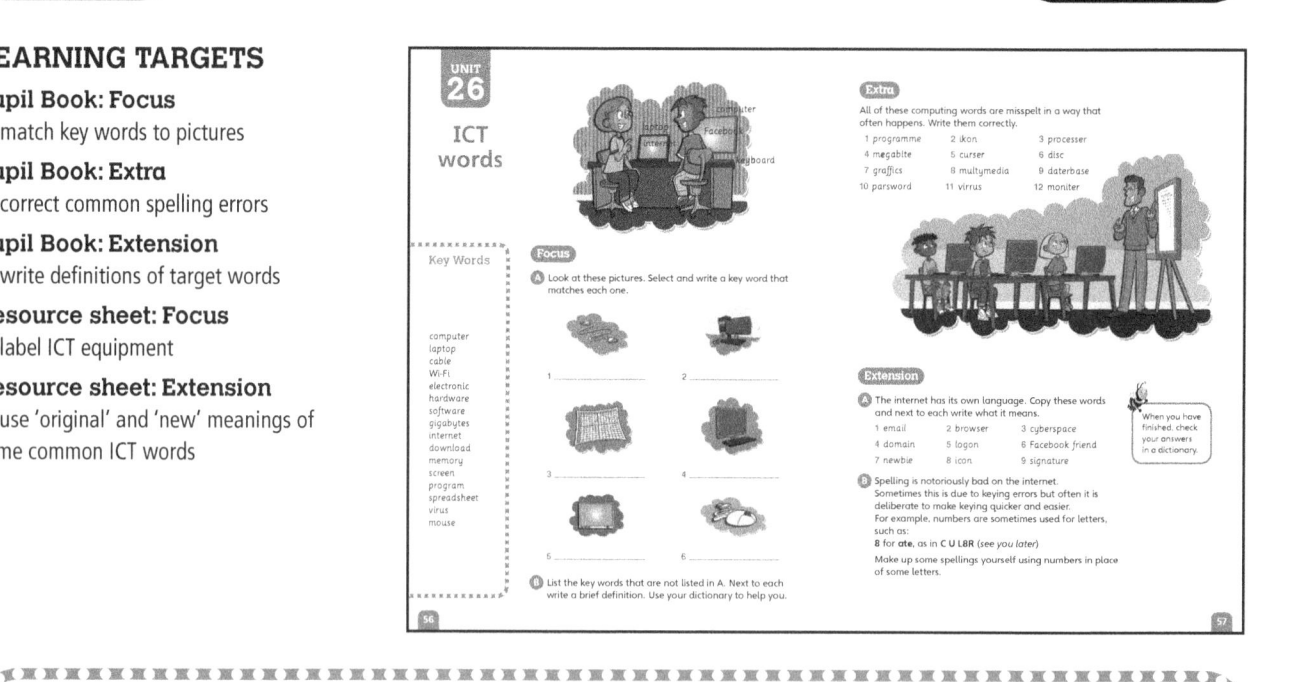

BACKGROUND NOTES AND SUGGESTIONS

The words taught in this unit, compiled by teachers in a number of secondary schools, are words with which their new entrants at Year 7 often have difficulty. It is acknowledged that by no means all children entering secondary education fail to spell these words, but enough do for teachers to need to give support.

The words *program* and *programme* can cause confusion, and can provide a useful focus for class or group discussion. (See also Book 6 Units 6 and 13)

Pupil Book answers

Focus

A
1. cable
2. computer
3. spreadsheet
4. internet
5. screen
6. mouse

B
laptop, Wi-fi, electronic, hardware, software, gigabytes, download, memory, program, virus

Teacher to check individual definitions

Extra

1. program
2. icon
3. processor
4. megabyte
5. cursor
6. disk
7. graphics
8. multimedia
9. database
10. password
11. virus
12. monitor

Extension

A
1. email: electronic mail
2. browser: a program for navigating the World Wide Web
3. cyberspace: the virtual world of the Internet
4. domain: an address on the Internet
5. logon: connecting to your service provider and going online
6. Facebook friend: someone given access to your Facebook site
7. newbie: someone who is new to the Internet
8. icon: image that represents a programme or file, which will run when the icon is pressed
9. signature: your personal way of signing off at the end of postings and email

B Teacher to check individual answers

Resource answers

Focus
Teacher to check individual answers

Extension
Teacher to check individual answers

Supporting word lists

binary hardware network
byte icon output
cable input password
cartridge interactive preview
CD-ROM interface processor
computer Internet program
connect/connection justify scanner
cursor keyboard sensor
data/database megabyte server
delete memory software
disk modem spreadsheet
document module virus
electronic monitor
graphic multimedia

BOOK 6 — UNIT 27

LEARNING TARGETS

Pupil Book: Focus
to secure contractions

Pupil Book: Extra
to practise words which have confusing double letters

Pupil Book: Extension
to practise a range of frequently misspelt words

Resource sheet: Focus
to match words to contractions

Resource sheet: Extension
to resolve double letter puzzles

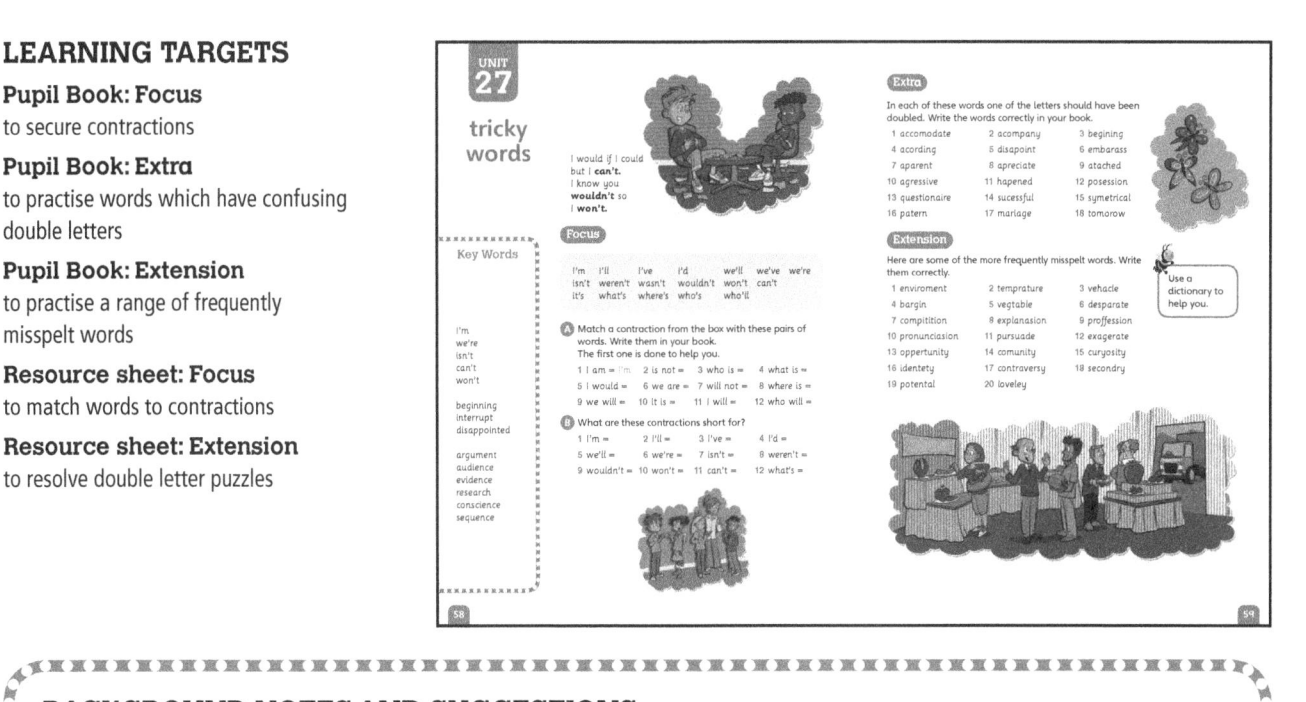

BACKGROUND NOTES AND SUGGESTIONS

Every device should be employed to help children learn the particularly confusing words, from which great satisfaction can be derived. The key is 'little and often', with 'Words of the Week', spelling competitions, etc. being employed whenever the opportunity lends itself.

Pupil Book answers

Focus

A
1. I am = I'm
2. is not = isn't
3. who is = who's
4. what is = what's
5. I would = I'd
6. we are = we're
7. will not = won't
8. where is = where's
9. we will = we'll
10. it is = it's
11. I will = I'll
12. who will = who'll

B
1. I am
2. I shall/I will
3. I have
4. I would/I had
5. we will/we shall
6. we are
7. is not
8. were not

Extra

1. accommodate
2. accompany
3. beginning
4. according
5. disappoint
6. embarrass
7. apparent
8. appreciate
9. attached
10. aggressive
11. happened
12. possession
13. questionnaire
14. successful
15. symmetrical
16. pattern
17. marriage
18. tomorrow

Extension

1. environment
2. temperature
3. vehicle
4. bargain
5. vegetable
6. desperate
7. competition
8. explanation
9. profession
10. pronunciation
11. persuade
12. exaggerate
13. opportunity
14. community
15. curiosity
16. identity
17. controversy
18. secondary
19. potential
20. lovely

Resource answers

Focus

we're	=	we are
will not	=	won't
who is	=	who's
should not	=	shouldn't
cannot	=	can't
I will	=	I'll
I'm	=	I am
what is	=	what's
do not	=	don't

Extension

A
1. beginning/questionnaire
2. marriage/embarrass
3. apparatus/disappear
4. assessment/necessary
5. accommodation/mammal

B Teacher to check individual answers

Supporting word lists

contractions
I'm I'd I've I'll;
you're you'd you've you'll;
he's he'd he'll;
she's she'd she'll;
it's;
we're we'd we've we'll;
they're they'd they've they'll;
that's there's;
who's who'd;
aren't isn't hasn't hadn't haven't;
didn't doesn't don't won't shan't can't
couldn't wouldn't shouldn't

tricky suffixes
beginning lovable noticeable valuable
changeable greenness meanness
nastiness happiness dryness truly

other tricky words
prejudice exercise magnificent incident
fascinate accident schedule ancient
anxious conscious disastrous
courageous carriage substantial guarantee
persuade restaurant behaviour laboratory
incredible responsible psychology
television catastrophe apostrophe
encyclopedia

BOOK 6 — UNIT 28

LEARNING TARGETS

Pupil Book: Focus
to revise alphabetical ordering of words

Pupil Book: Extra
to revise the functions of a dictionary and the information it contains

Pupil Book: Extension
to practise using guide words

Resource sheet: Focus
to practise alphabetical ordering of words by second and third letter

Resource sheet: Extension
to secure the use of guide words

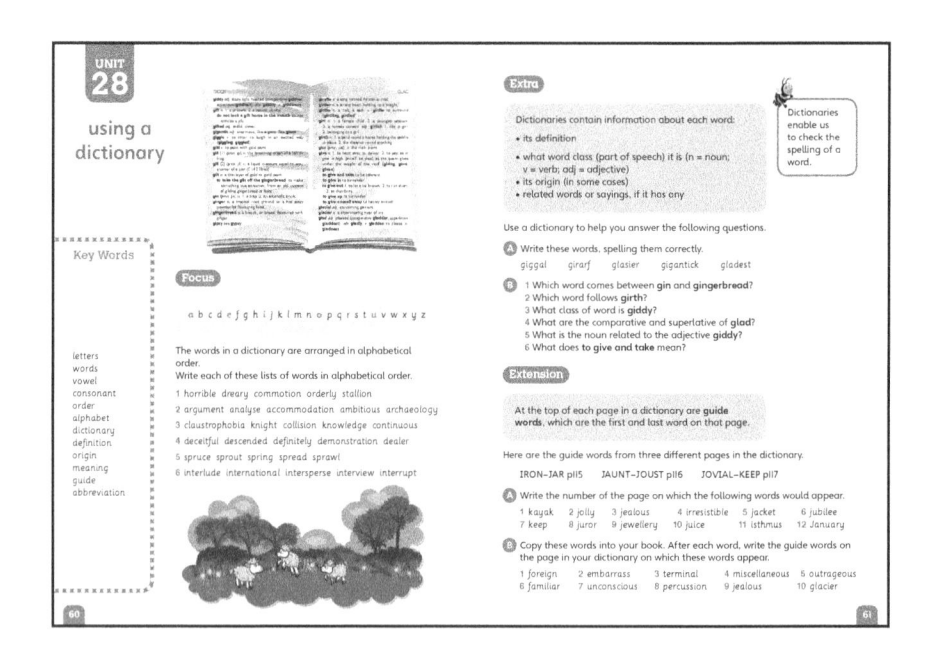

BACKGROUND NOTES AND SUGGESTIONS

As noted previously, the ability and motivation to use a dictionary as a matter of course is central to the development and continuing acquisition of a good standard in spelling. Further, it is one of those important study skills every student needs. This unit revises and extends some of the skills introduced previously.

Additional practice, whenever the opportunity lends itself, is strongly recommended, especially for children of this age. Please note that children may find it easier to use their own dictionary for the Pupil Book Extra section.

Pupil Book answers

Focus
1 commotion dreary horrible orderly stallion
2 accommodation ambitious analyse archaeology argument
3 claustrophobia collision continuous knight knowledge
4 dealer deceitful definitely demonstration descended
5 sprawl spread spring sprout spruce
6 interlude international interrupt intersperse interview

Extra
A giggle giraffe glacier gigantic gladdest

B
1 ginger
2 gist
3 adjective
4 gladder gladdest
5 giddiness
6 to be tolerant

Extension
A
1 117   2 116
3 116   4 115
5 115   6 117
7 117   8 117
9 116   10 117
11 115   12 115

B Teacher to check individual answers

Resource sheet answers

Focus
A
2 forty | 6 material | 6 research
1 fierce | 2 listening | 5 remember
4 guard | 5 marriage | 1 reaction
6 health | 1 knowledge | 3 reference
3 fulfil | 3 lonely | 4 relief
5 happened | 4 lovely | 2 receive

B
1 fierce | 1 knowledge | 1 reaction
2 forty | 2 listening | 2 receive
3 fulfil | 3 lonely | 3 reference
4 guard | 4 lovely | 4 relief
5 happened | 5 marriage | 5 remember
6 health | 6 material | 6 research

Extension
A
Children should have ticked the following:
interesting   audience   constant
improvise   autumn   construction
incapable   average   consistent
independent   award   consist
incense   audible
inclusive   auction
impulse   authority
imprison   axe

B Teacher to check individual answers

154

BOOK 6

Check-Up 2

Focus
1 thumb   2 column   3 castle   4 knight
5 scissors   6 cereal   7 lightning   8 calculator
9 computer   10 newspaper   11 apple   12 assembly
13 soldier   14 vegetables   15 mouse   16 alphabet

Extra

A 1 further/more 2 none/the/less 3 how/ever   4 where/as   5 what/ever

B 1 cymbal   2 guest   3 peace   4 led   5 lightening

C Teacher to check individual answers

D 1 necessary   2 dictionary   3 ordinary   4 machinery   5 memory

E 1 special   2 disaster   3 marvel   4 compete   5 equip

F 1 centre   2 flavour   3 defence   4 travelled   5 organise
      6 theatre   7 harbour   8 labouring   9 favourite   10 cancelled

G 1 ap/pear/ance 2 ar/rang/ing   3 ap/par/ent   4 an/nual   5 as/sem/bly

H 1 belief   2 perceive   3 friend   4 receive   5 forfeit

I 1 necess*a*ry   2 ordin*a*ry   3 temp*e*rature 4 bus*i*ness   5 int*e*resting

J 1 accommodate   2 beginning   3 disappointment 4 apparently 5 symmetrical
      6 marriage   7 successful   8 attached   9 necessarily 10 aggressive

Extension

A Teacher to check individual answers

B 1 instruct instructed instructing instruction instructor
      2 computation compute computer computing computerise

C 1 dictionaries 2 victories   3 memories   4 secretaries   5 nurseries

D 1 environment   2 temperature 3 desperate   4 competition   5 profession
      6 persuade   7 opportunity 8 secondary   9 potential   10 lovely

E 1 medieval   2 reinforce   3 science   4 reiterate   5 obedience

F 1 responsible   2 curable   3 sensible

G 1 language   2 tragic   3 accident   4 successful   5 excellent
      6 megabyte   7 curser   8 virus   9 graphics   10 multimedia

Revision Book answers

word roots

A <u>port</u>able, <u>aqua</u>rium, trans<u>fer</u>, aero<u>dynamic</u>, <u>aud</u>ience, pre<u>historic</u>

B Teacher to check individual answers

C Teacher to check individual answers

D Suggested answers: portable, porter, aquarium, aquamarine, geology, geography, inscribe, scribble

prefixes 1

A <u>dis</u>agree, <u>mis</u>behave, <u>im</u>patient, <u>ir</u>regular, <u>pre</u>occupied, <u>non</u>-effective

B
1 illogical 2 disagree
3 unaided 4 defrost
5 prediction 6 unexpected
7 immature 8 invisible
9 irresponsible 10 preview

C Teacher to check individual answers

D
prefix	meaning
un	not
dis	away, apart
de	opposite, remove
pre	before
re	again

prefixes 2

A <u>bi</u>sect, <u>sub</u>heading, <u>trans</u>plant, <u>circ</u>umnavigate, <u>anti</u>-clockwise, <u>ex</u>change

B
1 overrule 2 automatic
3 circumstance 4 antidote
5 automation 6 bifocals
7 transmit 8 overreact
9 supersonic 10 subdivide
11 antibody 12 subscribe
13 exclaim 14 telescope

C auto = self, circ = around, anti = against, over = above/beyond, tele = distance/from afar, bi = twice/two, trans = across, sub = under/below, super = above/beyond, ex = far/away/out of

D Teacher to check individual answers

ion cian

A Teacher to check individual answers

B
1 extension 2 situation
3 explosion 4 attraction
5 occasion 6 protection
7 subtraction 8 excursion
9 description 10 station
11 revision 12 eruption

C
1 evaporation 2 opposition
3 separation 4 circulation
5 calculation 6 imitation
7 inspiration 8 discussion
9 frustration 10 action

D
1 electrician/electric 2 politician/politics
3 musician/music 4 mathematician/mathematics

sure ture

A Teacher to check individual answers

B
1 sign 2 fix
3 sculpt 4 depart
5 compose 6 press
7 architect 8 expose
9 moist 10 close

C
departure	going away
manufacture	to make or produce on a large scale
enclosure	an enclosed area
structure	a supporting framework
displeasure	a displeased feeling
denture	a set of artificial teeth
pressure	a continuous force applied to something
agriculture	the process of working the land and rearing animals

D
1 closure 2 composure
3 nature 4 pleasure

able ible ably ibly

A ador<u>able</u>, avail<u>able</u>, incred<u>ible</u>, invis<u>ible</u>, responsi<u>bly</u>, noticea<u>bly</u>

B
1 accessible 2 irritable
3 adaptable 4 irresponsibly
5 collapsible 6 indigestible
7 reasonably 8 preferably

C Incorrect answers spelt correctly: advisable, adaptable, irresistibly, extendable, legible, excusable

D consideration/considerable, translation/translatable, navigation/navigable, conservation/conservable, operation/operable, adaptation, adaptable

ous

A Teacher to check individual answers

B
1 bumptious 2 cautious
3 contentious 4 delicious
5 atrocious 6 ferocious
7 malicious 8 nutritious
9 precious 10 scrumptious
11 spacious 12 suspicious

C Teacher to check individual answers

D
1 furious 2 victorious
3 outrageous 4 anxious
5 glamorous 6 glorious
7 vigorous 8 various
9 fictitious 10 infectious

ive

A mass<u>ive</u>, decis<u>ive</u>, talkat<u>ive</u>, competit<u>ive</u>, decept<u>ive</u>, protect<u>ive</u>

B
1 talkative 2 deceptive
3 competitive 4 protective

C
1 disrupt 2 attract
3 compete 4 detect
5 expense 6 intense
7 talk 8 argue

D
1 relative 2 active
3 explosive 4 deceptive
5 decisive 6 exclusive

y ey ly
A Teacher to check individual answers

B
1 slimy 2 grainy
3 muddy 4 dusty
5 brainy 6 creamy
7 bony 8 smoky

C Teacher to check individual answers

D
1 urgently 2 musically
3 prettily 4 simply
5 truly 6 heavily
7 humbly 8 frantically
9 electrically 10 wholly

le el al il (cial tial cal)
A Teacher to check individual answers

B
1 musical 2 accidental
3 tonsil 4 crumble
5 camel 6 metal
7 fossil 8 individual
9 paddle 10 hospital
11 sandal 12 nostril

C
1 confidentially 2 musically
3 commercially 4 essentially
5 mechanically 6 specially
7 partially 8 clinically

D
1 essential 2 historical
3 tropical 4 initial
5 commercial 6 financial
7 artificial 8 torrential
9 comical 10 official

ar or er ary ory ery; ant ent ance ence
A Teacher to check individual answers

B
1 1 calculate 2 strange
3 compute 4 instruct
5 custom 6 circle

2 Possible answers: composer/compose; builder/build; writer/write; dancer/dance; banker/bank; cleaner/clean; footballer/football

C
1 burglary/burglaries 2 dictionary/dictionaries
3 discovery/discoveries 4 cemetery/cemeteries
5 nursery/nurseries 6 memory/memories

D

adjectives	nouns
obedient	obedience
elegant	elegance
existent	existence
ignorant	ignorance
assistant	assistance
excellent	excellence
distant	distance

other endings: a i o u
A Teacher to check individual answers

B Teacher to check individual answers

C India – samosa, bhaji, chapatti
Switzerland – rosti
Italy – pizza, pasta, macaroni, spaghetti, ravioli, risotto
Spain – paella

D
1 cellos 2 kangaroos
3 pianos 4 radios
5 igloos 6 volcanoes
7 discos 8 hippos
9 concertos 10 cargoes
11 sombreros 12 piccolos
13 kimonos 14 zoos
15 cockatoos 16 mangoes

other endings: ow et en on
A Teacher to check individual answers

B racket, rac/ket; burrow, bur/row; shadow, sha/dow; rainbow, rain/bow; cricket, cric/ket; sorrow, sor/row; window, win/dow.

C Teacher to check individual answers

D
1 seven 2 siren
3 squadron 4 lesson
5 happen 6 common
7 lemon 8 season
9 oxygen 10 golden
11 burden 12 cotton

important letter patterns: ough igh ph
A Teacher to check individual answers

B enough – sounds like 'uff', trough – sounds like 'off', dough – sounds like 'ow' in snow, plough – sounds like 'ow' in how.
Teacher to check individual answers.

C Possible answers: enlighten/lightning/lightening; frightened/frightening/frighten; highly/highest/higher; brightly/brightest/brighter; unsightly; sightless; oversight

D Incorrect words spelt correctly: geography, photo, philosophy, physical

silent letters 1
A wreck, wrinkle, knight, thumb, whistle, ballet

B

silent b	silent w	silent t	silent k
debt	wreckage	fasten	knowledge
doubt	wrestle	thistle	knitwear
thumb	write	castle	knuckle
climber	wheel	rustle	knead
numbness	wrapped		

Teacher to check individual answers

C 1 r 2 n 3 t 4 s

D
1 knock 2 wrong
3 doubt 4 whole
5 wristwatch 6 listen
7 whistle 8 wriggle
9 plumber 10 knelt

silent letters 2: o h c n g

A c_ountry, r_hythm, s_cenery, autum_n, colum_n, _gnat

B
1. The man stole a sign and hid it in his garden behind the rhubarb.
2. Autumn came early this year making beautiful scenes across the country.
3. Our dog gnawed on a bone then buried it under the rhododendron bush.
4. The problem with the school choir is that they have no rhythm!

C Teacher to check individual answers

D Incorrect words spelt correctly: rhyme, chronic, solemn, scissors, heirloom

unstressed letters: vowels and consonants

A av_erage, sold_ier, envir_onment, veg_etable, desp_erate, diff_erence

B
1. factory
2. temperature
3. jewellery
4. literature
5. company
6. voluntary
7. easily
8. generous
9. separate
10. interesting
11. widening
12. literacy

C
1. boun/da/ry
2. dust/bin
3. shep/herd
4. fac/tory
5. pois/on/ous
6. par/lia/ment
7. post/pone
8. fright/en/ing

D Teacher to check individual answers

same letters different sounds

A b_ear/_earth, c_uriosity/_century, av_erage/lan_guage.
'Language' illustrates two sounds for the same letter in the same word.

B

words with c as in *cat*	words with c as in *mice*	words with g as in *goat*	words with g as in *cage*
category	prejudice	aggressive	language
coat	pronunciation	guarantee	lodger
occupy	necessary	language	average
controversy	cemetery		vegetable
community			

Teacher to check individual answers

C Teacher to check individual answers

D though (like 'o' in go), through (like 'oo' in too), cough (like 'off' in offer), rough (like 'uff' in suffer), plough (like 'ow' in flower), nought (like 'aw' in saw)

spelling rules: making simple plurals

A Teacher to check individual answers

B
1. bushes
2. schools
3. torches
4. cherries
5. chimneys
6. computers
7. daisies
8. journeys
9. gases
10. cities
11. toys
12. trolleys
13. brushes
14. parties

C

plural verb	plural noun
we walk	he walks
they push	she pushes
we run	he runs
they whisper	she whispers
we march	he marches
they jump	she jumps
we fix	he fixes
they scream	she screams

D Teacher to check individual answers

spelling rules: making tricky plurals

A Teacher to check individual answers

B
1. oxen
2. teeth
3. lives
4. gloves
5. cellos
6. children
7. data
8. kangaroos
9. flamingos
10. ellipses

C
1. a herd of oxen
2. a pair of gloves
3. a mouthful of teeth
4. a playground of children
5. a folder of data
6. an ensemble of cellos

D
1. possible answers: cacti, octopi, fungi, hippopotami
2. buzzes
3. scarfs, scarves
4. possible answers: deer, sheep, fish, aircraft, buffalo, scissors, series
5. plateaux, gateaux
6. possible answers: child, mouse, person, goose, man, woman, tooth
7. possible answers: scissors, clothes, goggles, glasses, shoes, jeans

homophones 1

A Teacher to check individual answers

B
1. sale
2. won
3. plane
4. real
5. past
6. key
7. our
8. choose

C

noun	verb
advice	advise
device	devise
practice	practise
licence	license

Teacher to check individual answers

D Teacher to check individual answers

homophone 2

A Teacher to check individual answers

B
1. rein, reign
2. heal, he'll
3. I'll, isle
4. their, they're
5. sees, seize
6. raise, raze
7. need, kneed
8. flu, flue

C	dairy	where milk is produced
	diary	a daily account
	emigrant	one who leaves a country to live elsewhere
	immigrant	one who comes to live in a country
	ensure	to make sure
	insure	to take out insurance
	lightening	to make lighter
	lightning	a flash of light in a storm

D Teacher to check individual answers

apostrophes and hyphens

A Teacher to check individual answers

B
1 should've   2 they're
3 you'll   4 I'd
5 mustn't   6 he'll
7 there's   8 couldn't
9 she's   10 I'll
11 must've   12 won't

C
1 the three teachers' whistles   2 Ellie's birthday party
3 the three dogs' bones   4 the five women's bags
5 Tuhil's football   6 the sheep's lambs
7 the child's scarf   8 the four donkeys' reins

D
prefixed words	compound words
de-ice	fair-haired
in-patient	well-mannered
non-negotiable	quick-thinking
re-elect	sport-mad
ex-captain	custom-build
anti-aircraft	power-driven
bi-weekly	oven-ready

more spelling rules: ie ei

A Teacher to check individual answers

B Possible answers:

words in which ie sounds ee	words in which ei sounds ee
achieve	ceiling
belief	receive
field	receipt
shield	deceive
relief	conceit

The 'ei' in the ei words is usually preceded by 'c'

C
1 eight   2 vein
3 reign   4 their
5 heir   6 ceiling
7 die   8 drier
9 feint   10 pier
11 frieze   12 tied

D
1 freight   2 eighty
3 believe   4 chief
5 receive   6 height
7 sleigh   8 crier
9 reinforce   10 obedience
11 protein   12 hygiene
13 belief   14 heir
15 interview

compound words

A Teacher to check individual answers

B
1 some + where   2 print + out
3 school + teacher   4 utter + most
5 mind + blowing   6 thumb + nail
7 land + mark   8 voice + over

C Possible answers:
1 weekday, weekend   2 nobody, no-one
3 tablecloth, tablespoon   4 football, footprint
5 custom-build, custom-made   6 sunshine, sunlight
7 rainbow, raindrop   8 self-respect, self-service

D Possible answers: nevertheless, meanwhile, afterwards, straightaway, otherwise, moreover

tricky words 1

A Teacher to check individual answers

B
1 interrupt   2 correspond
3 committee   4 programme
5 occupy   6 accompany
7 exaggerate   8 community

C Teacher to check individual answers

D
1 occupy   2 successful
3 aggressive   4 immediately
5 guarantee   6 accommodate
7 appreciate   8 sufficient
9 suggest   10 occasion
11 communicate   12 addition

tricky words 2

A Teacher to check individual answers

B
1 marvellous   2 desperate
3 achieve   4 embarrass
5 symbol   6 privilege
7 leisure   8 awkward
9 temperature   10 muscle
11 category   12 sufficient

C Teacher to check individual answers

D
1 accommodate, amateur, ancient, antique
2 nuisance, occupy, occur, opportunity
3 category, cemetery, conscious, convenience
4 relevant, restaurant, rhyme, rhythm

tricky words 3

A Teacher to check individual answers

B
1 available   2 variety
3 explanation   4 relevant
5 conscience   6 hindrance
7 mischievous   8 excellent
9 definite   10 language
11 environment   12 parliament

C persuade, develop, ancient, desperate, amateur, controversy, curiosity, equip, achieve, recognise

D Teacher to check individual answers

Glossary

affixes
prefixes and suffixes which are added to word roots, such as **un**cover**ed**

auditory memory
short-term memory of sound-letter relationships

blending
smooth running together of individual sounds, usually referring to consonant blends, such as **bl**ot, **cl**ap, sa**nd**, **str**ap

consonants
the letters and letter sounds that are not vowels

cvc
abbreviation for *consonant/vowel/consonant* as in h-a-t

cue
the clues used to help identify a word. These can be 'phonic' (predictable from sound), 'grammatical' (predictable from word ordering) or 'semantic' (predictable from meaning).

decoding
translating print into spoken words

digraph
a pair of letters that operate together to represent a single sound, such as c**l**own, **ch**in
   consonant digraph
   pair of consonant letters that operate together to represent a single consonant sound, such as **ch th sh**
   vowel digraph
   pair of vowel letters that operate together to represent a single vowel sound, such as **ow ee oo**

etymology
word origins and roots

grapheme
the written form of the smallest sound segment of a word, such as individual letters or digraphs

homographs
words that are spelt the same but sound different and have different meanings, such as *row* (argument) *row* (with an oar)

homonyms
words that sound the same, are spelt the same but have different meanings, such as *saw* (cutting tool) *saw* (past tense of 'see')

homophones
words that sound the same but have different spellings and meanings, such as *there, their*

inflections
the endings of verbs to indicate tense or singular/plural, such as jump**ed** jump**ing**; jump jump**s**
or the endings of nouns to indicate plurals, such as
   dog**s**, box**es**

kinaesthetic
physical sense of awareness

mnemonics
memory joggers, such as, 'When you are emba**rr**a**ss**ed, you turn **r**eally **r**ed and **s**tart to **s**tutter.'

morphology
the study of the elements of words that carry the meaning

orthographic
concerned with spelling

phoneme
the spoken form of the smallest sound unit of a word, such as individual letter sounds or digraph sounds

phonemic
the approach to spelling based on sound-symbol relationships

phonics
the relationship between the spoken and written forms of words; often used to mean the method of teaching reading using the phonetic values of letters or groups of letters

position
in a word, position is often defined as
   initial (**sh**eep)
   medial (sh**ee**p)
   final (shee**p**)

prefix
element added to the beginning of word to change or modify meaning, such as **un**necessary

rhyme
identity of sound, though not necessarily of letter pattern, between words or the endings of words

segmentation
process of identifying constituent parts of words

stem
core part of a verb, to which inflections may be added as required

suffix
element added to the end of a word to change or modify meaning, such as care**ful**

syllable
a part of a word including a vowel and its attached consonant sounds

tactile
concerning the sense of touch

vowels
the sounds at the heart of every syllable, that are represented by **a e i o u** and sometimes **y**

whole-word approaches
memorising of individual words by rote